1

Self-Confrontation Bible Study

Student Workbook

using the *Self-Confrontation* manual as a reference

BCF

STUDENT WORKBOOK

FOR THE

SELF-CONFRONTATION BIBLE STUDY

This *Student Workbook* is published by the Biblical Counseling Foundation, Inc., a non-profit, non-stock corporation founded in 1974 and incorporated in the Commonwealth of Virginia, USA, in 1977.

Copyright: The contents of this workbook are copyrighted © 2005, 2006, and 2007 by the Biblical Counseling Foundation, Inc. All rights reserved. Reproduction in any manner in whole or in part, in English and/or other languages, or storage in a retrieval system, or transmission in any form or by any means — electronic, mechanical, visual, audio, or any other — except for brief quotations in printed reviews is prohibited without written permission of the Biblical Counseling Foundation (BCF).

Scripture taken from the New American Standard Bible, © 1960, 1962, 1963, 1968, 1971, 1972, 1973, 1975, 1977 by The Lockman Foundation. Used by permission.

ISBN 978-1-60536-014-0

First-Third printings, 2005
Fourth printing, January, 2007
Fifth printing, June 2008
Sixth printing, February 2009

Biblical Counseling Foundation
42-600 Cook Street, Suite 100
Palm Desert, CA 92211-5143 USA

760.773.2667 telephone
760.340.3778 fax
orders@bcfministries.org e-mail for orders
admin@bcfministries.org e-mail for other
877.933.9333 (in USA) telephone for orders only
http://www.bcfministries.org webpage for orders and information

Table of Contents

A Personal Message W5

Acknowledgements W6

Overview of the Self-Confrontation Bible Study W7

Lesson 1:
You Can Change Biblically (Part One) W13

Lesson 2:
You Can Change Biblically (Part Two) W23

Lesson 3:
Man's Way and God's Way (Part One) W33

Lesson 4:
Man's Way and God's Way (Part Two) W41

Lesson 5:
Biblical Dynamics of Change W51

Lesson 6:
Biblical Basis for Change W65

Lesson 7:
Biblical Structure for Change W83

Lesson 8:
Biblical Practice Achieves Lasting Change W95

Lesson 9:
Dealing with Self (Part One) W101

Lesson 10:
Dealing with Self (Part Two) W115

Lesson 11:
Anger and Bitterness W123

Lesson 12:
Interpersonal Problems (Part One) (Learning How to Love Your Neighbor) W135

Lesson 13:
Interpersonal Problems (Part Two) (Learning How to Love Your Neighbor) W147

Lesson 14:
The Marriage Relationship (Part One) W159

Lesson 15:
The Marriage Relationship (Part Two) W167

Student Workbook for the Self-Confrontation Bible Study
© Biblical Counseling Foundation

Lesson 16:
Parent-Child Relationships (Part One) W175

Lesson 17:
Parent-Child Relationships (Part Two) W183

Lesson 18:
Depression W189

Lesson 19:
Fear and Worry W195

Lesson 20:
Life Dominating Practices of Sin (Part One) W201

Lesson 21:
Life-Dominating Practices of Sin (Part Two) W207

Lesson 22:
God's Standards for Life W215

Lesson 23:
Testimony of How God Has Used This Study in Your Life W221

Lesson 24:
Introduction to Biblical Discipleship/Counseling Training W223

Supplements

Supplement 1:
Answers to Questions in the *Student Workbook* W235

Supplement 2:
Victory Over Failures Plan: Guidelines and Worksheets W261

Supplement 3:
Biblical Practices for Facing, Dealing with, and Enduring Problems W309

A Personal Message

You are embarking on a course of study and practice of God's Word that has the potential of being one of your most life-changing experiences. The Self-Confrontation Bible Study is designed to help you in a very practical way to live according to biblical principles in every aspect of your life. You will learn how to face, deal with, and endure even the most difficult trials you may encounter in your personal relationships and circumstances.

As you look at the pages of the *Self-Confrontation* manual, you may be tempted to assume quickly that the amount of material found in each lesson is too much to grasp in a single Bible Study. Your assumption is correct, because the *Self-Confrontation* manual was not developed only for teaching a Bible Study. Rather, it is a reference manual that you can use repeatedly, throughout your life, to find out how God's Word applies to specific situations at the time they occur.

This **Student Workbook** is designed to guide you through the *Self-Confrontation* manual to help you easily learn the biblical principles in each lesson. The length of each lesson in the Bible Study has been planned to help you develop a pattern of living biblically, not necessarily to cover all that is contained in the manual.

Look forward eagerly to seeing the Lord working mightily in your life as you study and practice His inerrant, sufficient Word in the power of the Holy Spirit.

The BCF writing team

Acknowledgements

The core team of writers used by the Lord to develop this workbook consists of Steve and Shashi Smith and Bob Schneider. The BCF teachers used by the Lord to edit and revise this volume consist of Gary and Linda Hays, Gerald Nygren, and Lee Weeder. All of these individuals have given sacrificially of their time, talents, and energies without financial remuneration of any kind.

In addition, BCF staff members, including Cindy Johnson, Kate O'Donnell, Spencer Smith, Stuart Smith, and Bobbie Van Sant have devoted time to editing, graphic design, and printing of these materials.

The team of writers and editors has devoted years of intensive study and writing in the preparation of this work. The Lord has used the gifts and talents of each team member to contribute in a unique way to insure biblical accuracy and internal integrity.

OVERVIEW
OF THE SELF-CONFRONTATION BIBLE STUDY

Welcome to the Self-Confrontation Bible Study. This Bible Study presents biblical principles that God will use to change your life, as you apply them to your personal situation. These principles are contained in the Bible, which is the authoritative source for how to live a victorious and contented life in the power of the Holy Spirit. These principles are applicable in all cultures and do not change. They apply to the young and the elderly, to the poor and the wealthy, to the healthy and the ill. Therefore, you can be confident that the biblical principles taught in this study are also applicable to you no matter what situation, test, or trial you may experience.

This *Student Workbook* is designed to lead you through a personal life-application study of God's Word using the *Self-Confrontation* manual as a reference. This life-application focuses on living according to the two greatest commandments stated by Jesus Christ: loving God and loving your neighbor *(Matthew 22:37-39)*. God also warns in His Word, that *"the one who does not love his brother whom he has seen, cannot love God whom he has not seen" (I John 4:20)*. Relationships on this earth are direct indicators of our relationship with God. This Bible Study focuses on having a right relationship with the Lord and with our neighbor. Our "neighbor" does not refer to just the person next door; it is all-inclusive. It includes those we find easy to get along with as well as those who seem to be difficult. It includes our family members, employers, employees, students, teachers, church family, acquaintances, and even those we would call our enemies. Many believers struggle with their relationships with others and become defeated in the way they handle the matters of life. This is usually because self gets in the way; there is a great battle between the flesh and the spirit *(Galatians 5:17)*. It is necessary to deal with this war within; hence the title "Self-Confrontation."

The "Love Test"

You may be wondering why you should be doing a Bible Study in self-confrontation at this point in your spiritual life, especially if you have been a Christian for many years, or if you are involved in discipling others. You may be thinking that you have matured beyond the need for continued self-confrontation. So let's conduct an exercise that will help you determine how much you may need to practice self-confrontation.

EXERCISE: THE LOVE TEST

Let's start by looking at God's standard for success in life. Please read *Matthew 22:37-40*. In *verse 40* Jesus summarized all the commandments in Scripture with just two. What are those two commandments? (fill in the blanks below)

1. *Love God w/ all your heart, soul & mind*
   Love your neighbor as yourself.

This passage clearly shows that God's standard for the believer's life is wholehearted love for God and others. This is quite a contrast from the way we evaluate success. Our human evaluation of a person's success is often based on how much Scripture a person knows, how many individuals he has led to the Lord, how well he can preach, how skilled or knowledgeable he is, how persuasive he is, etc. Since God says that loving Him and loving others are His criteria for evaluating us, we need to pay close attention to how to practice love.

In light of this standard of evaluation, rate yourself on how loving you think you are toward others on a scale of zero to ten. Rating yourself zero would mean you are not loving at all, and ten would represent that you have perfect love. You do not need to show your rating to anyone else. Now, on a separate piece of paper, write down your rating.

You had some kind of criterion for measuring how loving you think you are. You might have thought, "Well, I am not perfect, but I am more loving than this other (specific) person." So, you may have rated yourself above a five. In other words, when we evaluate ourselves, we tend to compare ourselves with other people. But, instead of relying on our own opinions of what constitutes love, let's look at what God has given us as the characteristics (actions) of love by which we are to examine ourselves. Please read *I Corinthians 13:4-8a* and rate yourself again as you compare yourself with each of the scriptural characteristics or actions of love. Ask yourself, "When was the last time I was impatient (or failed to be forbearing or longsuffering)? In what ways have I been unkind to my family? Have I been jealous about anyone or about my rights or my time?" and so on. Now, in light of these biblical criteria for evaluation, does your number go down significantly?

2. *Yes,*

In addition to God showing us the actions (characteristics) of biblical love, He also tells us *how* to love. Read *John 13:14-15, 34-35*. How did Jesus say we are to love?

3. *Love like Christ Jesus loved us.*

Now, read *John 13:4-5*. This passage gives us just one example of how Jesus demonstrated love. Since He is the perfect example we are to follow *(I Peter 2:21-22)*, we are to evaluate our love using His example as the comparison. How did Jesus demonstrate His love to His disciples?

4. *He committed no sin*

Jesus laid aside His right to be served by serving His disciples instead. He set aside the traditional authority and dignity of a teacher by taking off his garments and washing their feet. In fact, Jesus said He did not come to be served but to serve. Loving means being a servant to others. We are to serve in the same way as Jesus did *(John 13:12-15)*.

Now, seeing the standard of unselfish, sacrificial love demonstrated by Jesus, rate yourself again, not just based on *I Corinthians 13:4-8a*, but this time be more specific in its application to your life. Instead of saying the word "love," substitute your name (for example, "John is patient," "John is kind," etc.). After each descriptive phrase characterizing love, also bring the standard of Jesus Christ into the picture so that you will ask yourself, "Based on Jesus' example, am I as patient as Jesus was patient? Am I as kind as Jesus was kind?"

Is your number getting higher or lower?

5.

What have you learned from this exercise?

6. *I have learned how I am so undeserving & how I'm nothing like Christ Jesus.*

The purpose of this exercise is not to discourage or humiliate you; rather, it should give you an appreciation of God's mercy and grace. It should also help you see the need for changes in your life. God loves us in spite of our sin, but His plan is for us to change into Christlikeness. In light of the ongoing battle within between the flesh and the spirit, the need for change never ceases while we are on this earth.

By now, you may be saying to yourself, "What is the use? My score is so low, I will never be like Jesus." It is encouraging to remember how the Apostle Paul described himself. What does each of the following passages say about Paul?

In *I Corinthians 15:9*, toward the beginning of his ministry he described himself as

7. "unworthy to be called an apostle."

Later, in *Ephesians 3:8*, further into his ministry, Paul described himself as

8. "very least of all the saints"

And just before his death, in *I Timothy 1:15*, Paul described himself as

9. of the foremost sinners.

The more Paul matured in the Lord, the more he saw himself as a sinner. It was not that he was sinning more; rather, he was increasingly aware of (sensitive to) his sin. It increasingly troubled him when he sinned. It also helped him increasingly to appreciate the grace and mercy of the Lord. This is a sign of spiritual maturity.

Let's review what we have learned from this exercise.

First, this exercise reveals how we tend to measure ourselves by man's standards rather than by God's perfect standard.

Second, this exercise reveals how easily we tend to focus on self instead of focusing on God. That is why confronting ourselves biblically is so important for as long as we live on this earth. The need to examine and confront self never ends.

The "**Love Test**" also tells us something about people we teach or disciple. Much of discipleship today is focused on activities and intellectual knowledge rather than on development of love for God and neighbor. We teach people how to conduct Bible studies and memorize Scripture but fail to teach them how to apply God's Word in daily living. For example, how do you help a mother who has outbursts of anger when her child disobeys? How do you help a person who has been caught up in and is now dominated by various sinful practices? How do you help someone who thinks his childhood experiences (his past) or the way he was treated by others is his reason for not being an overcomer in the present?

In summary, this study will help you learn how to face, deal with, and endure any difficulty in life in light of God's perfect standard as revealed in Jesus Christ and God's Word, and overcome the trials of life in a complete and ongoing manner. In addition to helping you deal with your own life, this study will also teach you how to disciple others in biblical patterns for living victoriously in all circumstances.

God's Word versus our opinions

One of the most important things to remember in completing this Bible Study is not to rely on your own opinions or the opinions of others. You will frequently need to ask: "What does God say?" and "How does this Scripture passage apply to me?" You must resist the temptation to give others your personal experiences and make that a basis for teaching how to live. God has not promised to bless our own wisdom or our experiences; but He *has* promised to bless His Word *(Isaiah 55:11)*. Only God's Word is to be the source and basis for teaching us how to live — not man's wisdom. This is always the emphasis of the Self-Confrontation Bible Study. If you are just being introduced to this material, you will realize very early that complete reliance on the Scriptures, not worldly wisdom, is the key to living a godly, contented life in the power of the Holy Spirit.

Materials for this study

Now let's look at the materials you will be using for the study. You will need a Bible, the *Self-Confrontation* manual, and this *Student Workbook*.

The Bible

Since the Bible is the primary teaching source for God's commandments and precepts, it is important that you use a literal translation of the Bible. While a paraphrase of the Bible may be useful as an expansion or supplemental study tool, it is important to memorize and understand the Bible in its most literal form. Because paraphrases are not translations, but interpretations, they may focus on man's insights rather than God's truth at certain points. When you study for your own benefit or to minister to others, it is important that you remain as faithful as possible to God's Word.

The Bible is applicable to every culture. It goes against man's wisdom and tradition in dealing with life regardless of culture, just as Jesus went against men's traditions (even among the religious leaders) in His culture when He spoke about how to deal with the problems of life. On the other hand, the Bible speaks to every heart because it is God's Word to man.

The *Self-Confrontation* manual

The resource for this study is the ***Self-Confrontation*** manual, which you can think of as a manual for in-depth discipleship. It is not the source, as is the Bible, but is to be used as a reference to direct you back to God's Word. It is designed to guide you through biblical principles that are fundamental to living the kind of victorious, contented life God intended for His children, regardless of the circumstances. The manual will always direct you to God's Word, not to man's opinion. Sometimes we don't really want to heed God's Word, because it goes against our feelings, or it challenges us to change what we are doing. It might be easier to listen to man's opinions or to follow our feelings. But we know that following God's Word is *always* best for us, and He has given us the Holy Spirit to encourage us and to give us the power to follow in God's way.

The ***Self-Confrontation*** manual is not a book you can sit down and read like a novel. It is designed to be a reference book, and as such, it contains much more material than can be covered in the Self-Confrontation Bible Study. In a sense, it is like a topical concordance. It contains many biblical references that cover both the fundamentals of the Christian life as well as how to deal with specific problem areas. It is also useful when you are trying to find biblical principles that will help a family member or friend, but we must start by applying the principles to ourselves, hence the title ***Self-Confrontation***. The **Student Workbook** will lead you through the foundational Scriptures and the essential sections of the ***Self-Confrontation*** manual in a series of 24 lessons.

Before we proceed further in the **Student Workbook**, let's look at the ***Self-Confrontation*** manual **TABLE OF CONTENTS** (*Self-Confrontation*, Pages 6-10).

The lessons build on one another.

- Lessons 1-8 establish the basic foundation for living according to God's Word. Lessons 9-21 deal with specific problem areas. All the lessons are specifically placed in a sequence that is helpful for dealing with the typical problems of life.

- Lessons 9 and 10 deal with the problem of preoccupation with self. A biblical view of self is a necessary prerequisite to understanding how to deal with all other problems of life.

- The subjects anger and bitterness are next in Lesson 11 because they are involved to some degree in most problems.

- With this as a foundation, relationship problems can be addressed properly; thus the next six lessons deal with various interpersonal problems.

- After dealing with the subjects of depression, fear, and worry, the list ends with lessons on life-dominating practices of sin.

Also, on Page 10 of the manual, you will see a reference to the section at the end of the *Self-Confrontation* manual called **SUPPLEMENTS AND PRACTICAL HELPS**. The supplements include materials that are:

- Common to more than one lesson,
- Important application worksheets, and
- Detailed additional information for reference.

While the manual is copyrighted, in the footers of some of the supplements you are granted permission to reproduce the page for personal or ministry use.

Now let's look at the structure of each lesson in the manual using Lesson 1 as an example. Please turn to Page 17 in the *Self-Confrontation* manual.

- The title page of each lesson contains the memory passage for that lesson (Page 17).
- The first page of each lesson lists the purposes and the outline of the lesson (Page 18).
- Since the lessons are based upon biblical principles, the second page, and sometimes also the third, lists the relevant biblical principles (Page 19).
- The pages that follow are expansions of the biblical principles (Pages 20-24).
- Then, the last pages of each lesson contain homework and a study guide for daily devotions (Pages 25-27). You will not need to complete the homework as assigned in the *Self-Confrontation* manual since you will be answering questions that are interspersed throughout the lessons in this workbook.

In summary, it is important to keep in mind that the *Self-Confrontation* manual contains many Scripture references to direct you back to God's Word. The Bible is our primary source. The manual is merely the resource to direct us to the source — the Word of God.

The *Student Workbook*

This *Student Workbook* is designed to lead you through a personal life-application study of God's Word using the *Self-Confrontation* manual as a reference. Each lesson has blank portions to complete, based on passages from the Bible. This is part of what you might call your homework. But the most important part of the homework is your "doing the Word," applying the principles to your own life. That is where the meaningful, lasting change will come.

This *Workbook* leads you through the key points of each lesson in the *Self-Confrontation* manual. It covers only a portion of the material in the manual and provides additional illustrations and questions that will help you understand how the biblical principles apply to your life.

The *Student Workbook* is structured in the form of a Bible Study either for your own personal use (if you have no group leader) or with a small group. If you are completing this study with a group, usually you will first complete the study on our own in preparation for meeting as a group. Then, you will come together on a weekly basis to learn what God is teaching you through His Word. Your leader will provide biblical guidance, as you progress through the meeting.

NOTE: *The Self-Confrontation course can also be taken in a more formal teacher-student setting. If you are using the **Student Workbook** on your own, we would strongly recommend that you also take the course in a classroom or group setting when available. The Biblical Counseling Foundation has instructor's guides to allow the course to be taught in a once-a-week format or in a one-week concentrated course. Many people have taken the course multiple times, finding that God gives them additional insights and challenges them in different ways each time.*

How to complete this study

To study each lesson, follow the directions in this *Workbook*. It will direct you to the Scriptures and, where appropriate, to the associated portions of the *Self-Confrontation* manual. Typically, the *Workbook* will ask you to read a paragraph or section in the *Self-Confrontation* manual and look up the relevant scripture references in the Bible. When you see a reference to pages in the *Workbook*, the page number will have a "W" before it (for example, Page W1, Page W2, etc.). When you see a reference to a page in the *Self-Confrontation* manual, it will be without the "W" (for example, Page 1, Page 2, etc.).

Often, the *Workbook* will not go sequentially through the pages as they occur in each lesson of the *Self-Confrontation* manual. Rather, you may read a biblical principle, and then jump to a section that amplifies that principle. Just follow the directions in the *Workbook*, and you won't get lost. If you are taking the study as part of a small group, bring your completed *Workbook*, your Bible, and your *Self-Confrontation* manual to the group meeting each week. When doing your study at home, you will need a table where you can have the *Workbook*, *Self-Confrontation* manual, and Bible handy all at the same time.

You should set aside a time each day to study. You may want to work on your lesson during the study portion of your daily devotional time. Each lesson also has a Scripture verse or verses to memorize. We will cover the importance of Scripture memory in Lesson 2. Usually, you will be able to complete each lesson if you spend about 20 to 30 minutes per day. Normally, each lesson can be completed within two hours of study each week. Answers to the fill-in-the-blank questions may be found in Supplement 1 toward the end of this *Workbook* (Page 235).

There are 24 lessons in the Self-Confrontation Bible Study. Sometimes classes or groups taking the study together may decide that they will cover half the study in one series of classes. For example, they might cover Lessons 1 through 12 first, then 13 through 24 in a second study. This is a decision for your teacher or group leader and fellow students to make.

In either case, you will benefit most from this study if you keep up with the weekly study and the homework. That is one of the main objectives — to help you become immersed in God's Word and to apply the biblical principles to your life. You can be assured that if you do the homework, and if you put into practice what God says to you through His Word in this study, you will be a changed person.

LESSON 1
YOU CAN CHANGE BIBLICALLY (PART ONE)

OPENING PRAYER AND SCRIPTURE MEMORY

Before you begin this lesson, ask for God's help in understanding His Word and for wisdom and strength to apply what you learn in the power of the Holy Spirit.

Begin memorizing *Ephesians 2:8-9* from a literal translation of the Bible. Then, be prepared to recite these verses at the end of this lesson. To help you with this, write the verses on cards and carry them with you throughout each day so that you memorize them during your spare time. Be sure you tell the person to whom you recite what translation you are using.

Also, in your own words, please write out the meaning of the memory verses below:

We have been saved through God's grace not our works, we should not boast for it is His grace that saved us.

WHY IS THIS BIBLE STUDY IMPORTANT FOR YOU?

Before you start this study, let's see why this Bible Study is so important for you at this time. Take a look at the cover of your **Self-Confrontation** manual. Note that the subtitle is "*A Manual for In-Depth Biblical Discipleship.*" You may ask, "What does confronting yourself have to do with discipleship?" and "What is in-depth biblical discipleship, anyway?"

As you already recognized from the "**Love Test**," you always will need to confront yourself. But why do you really need this particular study?

In order to answer this question, you need to start by reviewing God's overall plan for reaching the world and how you and I fit into His plan. We know His plan from Jesus' words just before He went back to heaven. According to *Acts 1:8*, what is God's plan for reaching the world?

1. *Sharing the gospel, being witness of what God has done in our lives.*

We know from this passage that the Lord's eternal plan is to use believers as His witnesses in their own communities, in the nations, and even in the remotest part of the earth.

The Lord not only tells us what His plan is; He also tells us how to fulfill the great task of reaching the world. Read *Matthew 28:19-20*. This frequently quoted passage describes God's method of equipping and encouraging His children to make disciples of Jesus Christ. What two parts are described in these verses as God's methodology for making disciples?

2. *Go make disciples, baptizing them, teaching them to make disciples.*

This is often called the "Great Commission" because it is a command to every believer. Of course, only believers are to be baptized, so evangelism is implied as part of making disciples. Often, this is the part of the "Great Commission" that is greatly emphasized. But the second part is just as important. It involves helping the new disciple to live God's way.

The discipleship process we just examined must be so thorough that the disciple learns to teach others in the same scriptural pattern of living he is being taught. God's plan is that every one of His children is to be involved in making disciples. This multiplication process is to be continued until the whole world is reached with the Gospel.

Let's look at *II Timothy 2:2*. How many spiritual generations are referred to in this verse?

3. _4, him, witnesses, faithful men, others_

God's plan involves a multiplication process, in which we learn God's principles, and then teach others, so that they can, in turn, teach still others.

But, often, we hear, "I cannot disciple because no one discipled me." Well, God does not give us a command without also giving us the capability to carry it out. The marvelous truth is that at the same time that we as believers are carrying out our responsibilities to make disciples, God is doing a wonderful work in our own lives. Read *Romans 8:28-29*. According to *verse 28*, what does God do in our lives?

4. _Works everything out for our good._

In *verse 29*, what is God's goal for every believer? In other words, what is the good He intends to accomplish in our lives?

5. _Be more like Christ._

Why hasn't every person in the world been discipled?

Since God's plan is perfect, powerful, complete, and easily understood, the question now is: "Why hasn't every person in the world been reached?" Obviously, God is not to blame. He is perfect in all His ways and His plan is perfect. The failure is on the part of man.

While man has failed in many ways, we will only look at four of the hindrances to God's plan for reaching the world.

Hindrance 1: Many reject the Gospel even when it is presented perfectly and with great love.

Jesus said in *Matthew 7:14*, "… *the way is narrow that leads to life, and few are those who find it.*" But just because God's way is narrow does not mean that man cannot find it. God tells us in *Romans 1:20*, "*For since the creation of the world His invisible attributes, His eternal power and divine nature, have been clearly seen, being understood through what has been made, so that they are without excuse.*"

He shows us that God is incredible.

It is certainly true that those who reject the message of salvation are totally responsible for their rejection. However, this does not excuse God's children from their responsibility to be witnesses to those who are unsaved. The next three hindrances relate to the lives of believers.

Hindrance 2: Believers often are not committed to being a part of God's plan because of their failure in dealing with personal and interpersonal problems.

Think briefly about the spiritual history of many believers. After receiving Christ, they experience a great new zeal for the Lord. In this "first love" experience, they are excited about their new lives in Christ; they understand how the Scriptures apply to their lives for the first time; they desire to have fellowship with other believers; they repent of their old ways.

But how long does this fervor last? For many believers, it lasts only a short time; perhaps six months, a year, or maybe even two. Why does this initial enthusiasm go away? Usually, they become unenthusiastic about reaching out when they find themselves in difficult situations or relationships. It is not unusual in the midst of a serious trial for them to fall back into some of their former sinful practices. But, because they are now believers, they are convicted by the Holy Spirit. They repent and their enthusiasm returns — but how long does this last? Since they have not been taught how to deal victoriously in other similar situations, they soon fall again.

While struggling with these ups and downs, many believers are not seeking to minister to others as part of God's plan to make disciples. They are too preoccupied with their own lives, caught up in the midst of personal and interpersonal problems.

Problems in life are not unusual *(James 1:2-4; I Peter 1:6-9)*, but more and more, the church has been weakened because believers, even those who have known Christ for years, have never learned how to face and deal with the problems of life in a biblical way.

Satan understands very well the far-reaching potential of multiplication through discipleship, so he actively attempts to neutralize the effectiveness of believers through temptations to discouragement and defeat. He knows that when believers are preoccupied with their struggles they are not fully involved in making disciples and their part of the multiplication chain is broken.

Hindrance 3: There is a failure to look to the Scriptures as the all-sufficient source and to the body of Christ for guidance in dealing with the problems of life.

Though Scripture provides guidance for every personal and interpersonal problem of life, many church leaders have been wooed away from the crucial ministry of helping those who have fallen and are looking to the secular world for guidance. Instead of counseling from the Bible, these leaders refer their troubled sheep to counselors who approach life either totally or partially through humanistic psychology. In many Christian advanced education institutions, students are told that when they enter the ministry, they should expect to have people come to them with three kinds of problems: physical, so called "mental," and spiritual problems. These students are encouraged to refer those with physical and "mental" problems to outside experts, since they are only being trained to deal with spiritual problems in their institution. What the students do not realize is that most of the people who will be coming to them for help in the future will be dealing with what the world categorizes as "mental" problems, such as, depression, anxiety, interpersonal problems, fear, and drug abuse.

Although the world says there are three kinds of problems, the Bible only describes two. Jesus acknowledged two kinds of problems: the physically sick, who need a physician (addressing physical problems), and the sinners, who need the Savior (addressing spiritual problems) *(based on Matthew 9:11-13)*. While the Lord normally uses medical doctors to treat physical problems, He has provided the Scriptures for guidance on how to face, deal with, and endure every other problem of life. God makes no distinction between what the world calls "mental" and "spiritual" problems.

The claim that the Scriptures provide guidance for every problem of life may be new to you, and it may seem radical, but please do not dismiss it until you have had the opportunity to investigate it thoroughly. When you study Lessons 3 and 4, you will examine thoroughly the claims of the Scriptures. At that point, you can make an informed assessment of the Bible's applicability to the problems of life, even the most difficult ones.

Sadly, many people who should be helped by church leaders are referred to others who neglect the Bible as their source, either partially or completely. Is it any wonder that the church lacks spiritual vitality when the ideas and philosophies of the world are substituted for the truths of God's powerful Word? In contrast, church leaders should be concentrating on helping Christians overcome defeat and live victoriously.

Hindrance 4: The church has not emphasized discipleship the way that Jesus trained His disciples.

Often, when believers speak of fulfilling the "Great Commission" *(Matthew 28:19-20)*, they concentrate primarily on evangelism. Discipleship *does* involve evangelism as the first step, but biblical discipleship is much deeper than that. It concentrates further on teaching disciples how to live victorious lives in Christ. Jesus, our supreme example for how to disciple, spent most of His time training the twelve men He called to be His disciples. Yes, the Lord taught the masses; however, His primary objective in teaching was to train His disciples so that they would continue the process of making disciples after He returned to heaven. He trained them thoroughly to face, deal with, and endure all situations of life. As a result, they all (except for the one who betrayed Him) remained victorious in the power of the Holy Spirit.

To illustrate the wisdom of God's plan for reaching the world, let us compare the difference between increasing by multiplying and increasing by adding. Suppose that you were able to use radio, television, and the Internet to present the Gospel to very large groups of people on an ongoing basis. And suppose that as you preached the Gospel, you were able to lead 100,000 people to Christ every day. By the end of one year over 36 million people (365 days in a year x 100,000 per day) would be added to the kingdom of Christ. This result would be viewed by most as marvelous.

In contrast, suppose that you concentrated on discipleship in the same way that Jesus discipled. The Lord, while He was on this earth, concentrated His ministry on only a few disciples with the goal of training them in depth. He trained them so thoroughly that they were then able to repeat His example in reaching others. Now, suppose that you were privileged to lead someone to the Lord, and then, you concentrated primarily on discipling just that one person. And suppose that you spent an entire year discipling this new believer, so that by the end of the year, he was able, not only to lead another to the Lord, but was able to disciple the new convert in the same way he was discipled. This method of multiplying may seem to grow slowly in the beginning but it has great potential.

For the first few years, the "increase by multiplying" plan seems to achieve extremely low results in comparison to the "increase by adding" plan. But let's look at the outcome as the years go by. The following chart compares the results of the two methods.

COMPARISON OF ADDING VERSUS MULTIPLYING

Year	Adding 100,000 each day	Multiplying by 2 each year
1	36.5 million	2
2	73 million	4
3	109.5 million	8
⋮	⋮	⋮
32	1.168 billion	4.3 billion
33	1.204 billion	8.6 billion*
⋮	⋮	⋮
181	6.6 billion	3×10^{45}

* The world's population is approximately 6.6 billion

Theoretically, by doubling the number of disciples each year it would take less than 33 years to reach the world of approximately 6.6 billion people. In contrast, the method of adding to the church would reach only a little over a billion people in 33 years. Following this method would take a total of 181 years to reach the same number of people.

This comparison does not take into account the fact that some people choose to be uninvolved in discipleship, but it does illustrates dramatically the effectiveness of God's plan. The in-depth discipleship that Jesus taught, established, and practiced is the key to spreading the Gospel because it keeps the spiritual reproduction going from generation to generation.

As we have already seen in *Matthew 28:19-20,* biblical discipleship is God's plan. But biblical discipleship as described and demonstrated in the Scriptures is much broader and deeper than the "discipleship" that is often practiced today. Let's go back to *Matthew 28:20.* Jesus made it clear in this passage that making disciples includes teaching disciples to observe *all* that He taught. Notice the topics Jesus dealt with in the Sermon on the Mount (scan through Chapters 5-7 in the book of *Matthew*). What were the subjects he talked about?

Name at least five subjects.

6. *Christ came to fulfill the law, Anger, Divorce, Lust, Oaths, Retaliation, loving your enemies, giving, fasting, Don't be Anxious, Judging others.*

Jesus talked much about the difficulties of life, such as anger, persecution, reconciliation, lustful temptations, retaliation, divorce, hatred, and worry. He was preparing His disciples to deal with and endure the problems of life. So the word *"all"* in *verse* 20 indicates that discipleship is thorough. Biblical discipleship includes all of what is often categorized as counseling since it deals with every aspect of a person's life. It is in-depth discipleship.

* Be discipled & make disciples

Hopefully, now you are convinced that this Bible Study is important to you, and you recognize that the purposes of this study are: 1) to teach you how to face, deal with, and endure all difficulties of life; and 2) to prepare you to help others to overcome their difficulties of life.

INTRODUCTION TO LESSON 1

The **OVERVIEW OF THE SELF-CONFRONTATION BIBLE STUDY** and the first lesson in the *Self-Confrontation* manual establish a foundation for the entire Bible Study. They lay the basic foundation of salvation — the Lord Jesus Christ is the Rock upon Whom everything for living is built. Man cannot please God, overcome the problems of life, and have meaning or fruitfulness in life without a personal relationship with Jesus Christ.

BEGINNING OF CHANGE

A. Read the purposes of **LESSON 1: YOU CAN CHANGE BIBLICALLY (PART ONE)** *(Self-Confrontation,* Page 18). The first two purposes of Lesson 1 were taught in the overview session of this Bible Study. In this lesson you will concentrate on the third purpose.

B. As mentioned in the **OVERVIEW OF THE SELF-CONFRONTATION BIBLE STUDY,** the lessons are based on biblical principles. The reason for this is that biblical principles are applicable in all cultures and do not change. They are also applicable to all tests and trials of life. Therefore, you can be confident that the 105 principles listed in the *Self-Confrontation* manual will be applicable to your life no matter what your situation or place in life is. Remember, the second page of each lesson in the *Self-Confrontation* manual begins with the biblical principle or principles related to the lesson.

Start by reading the text in the box at the top of Page 19 of the *Self-Confrontation* manual. Notice that the box contains many Scripture references. Every statement in the manual is substantiated with the Scriptures. However, some lists of references, as in this box, are preceded by the words *"based on."* Take a moment to read the special note on Page 16 of the *Self-Confrontation* manual, which explains the use of the phrase *"based on."*

C. Read *Principle 1* on Page 19. You do not need to read all of the Scripture passages at this point. You will be directed to a few of these passages later.

Notice that *Principle 1* is a summary of the salvation message.

You may wonder why this study includes a detailed explanation of the salvation message. The reasons are twofold:

1. First, many churchgoers have not wholeheartedly committed themselves to Christ as Lord and Savior. Thinking that they are believers because they attend church or have made an emotional response to a gospel message, these individuals are trying to live God's way without His empowering grace.

2. Second, many believers lack assurance of salvation. Part of the reason for this is that they are not aware of the essential elements of the plan of salvation. Thus, they often live in a defeated manner.

D. Many people, even those who have attended church for years, are unaware of the essential elements of the salvation message. There is also much mis-teaching in the body of Christ about some of those elements. Since salvation is the basic foundation for spiritual growth and is the prerequisite for overcoming life's problems, it is vital that you understand and have responded to all the aspects of salvation in your life. For example, let's begin by looking at the primary word relating to the biblical meaning of the word *"belief."* Consider how you would distinguish between a believer and an unbeliever. List some of the things that believers do that people think indicate they are truly believers.

7. *They are assured, they don't lack self esteem. Confidant.*

But can unbelievers display outwardly all of the characteristics you wrote down? Read *Matthew 7:21-23* and *II Corinthians 11:13-15*. Will those who perform miraculous feats necessarily get to heaven? *Ephesians 2:8-9.*

8. *No, because their works won't get them to heaven*

To illustrate, let's consider the life of Judas — none of the other disciples seemed to detect his sin (read *John 13:21-25*). They could not distinguish whether he was a believer or an unbeliever based on what they saw of his life. Outwardly, he looked the same as the true disciples.

So how can you know whether or not you are a believer? To understand the characteristics of a true believer, it is necessary to know the essential truths regarding salvation.

E. To understand these truths better, please turn in the *Self-Confrontation* manual to Page 20.

1. Read the points under Sections **I.**, **II.**, and **III.** on Pages 20 and 21. **NOTE:** *You may not need to spend much time looking up the verses, since most churchgoers are very familiar with these sections. If you have not heard much teaching about the plan of salvation, please review these sections.*

2. We will spend more time on Section **IV. God empowers you to choose** …, since there are so many misunderstandings and unbiblical teachings about these points.

Under Section **IV.** (Page 21):

a. Read the topic sentence, then Paragraph A. and Subparagraph 1. under A. Highlight in your manual the reference to *Romans 10:8-13* (the second reference in **IV. A. 1.**).

NOTE: *Because there are hundreds of Scripture references in each lesson, it will be impossible to remember the foundational verses unless you highlight in your manual the ones taught. For this reason, you should highlight references to the verses you look up as you progress through this study. You may also want to highlight the verses in your Bible so you can find them easily.*

Read *Romans 10:8-10* in your Bible. What two things does God say result in salvation?

9. <u>truth in wisdom, everlasting life (heaven)</u>

Notice that salvation includes both believing in the heart and confessing with the mouth Jesus as Lord. This is a public declaration that Jesus is Lord of your life. The word "Lord" means master. You are to submit to Him as your master or head. This means that you are placing yourself under His management. As seen by this passage, if you do not consider Jesus Christ as your Lord, you cannot have confidence that He is your Savior.

b. Read **IV. A. 2.** Then, highlight in your manual and read *Mark 1:15* in your Bible. What two things did Jesus say for people to do for salvation?

10. <u>repent & confess your sins.</u>

Repentance is very important since it is an admission that you have been going against God's purposes, that you are sorry for opposing God, and you are turning around to go God's way. Also, notice that in *Luke 13:3**, Jesus says that unless a person repents, he will perish. Many groups teach that you should not tell someone that he needs to repent for salvation purposes. They claim that repentance is a "work." This is not so; repentance is not a work, but turning a around which carries with it the very important admission of having gone the *wrong* way. This does not mean a person has done any works yet. The righteous works that follow salvation are the fruit of repentance.

*NOTE: Luke 13:3 is not listed in **IV. A. 2.** in your manual, so please write the reference into your manual.*

c. Read Subparagraphs 3. and 4.

Then, highlight in your manual and read *John 1:12* in your Bible. Notice in *verse 12* that receiving and believing are synonyms. This verse leads us to a deeper understanding of the biblical truth about belief. In the sixth chapter of John's Gospel, Jesus says something rather startling to the people who have been following Him. He had just fed over 5,000 the day before and left them that night. So when they found Him on the other side of the Sea of Galilee the next day, He chided them in *verse 26* saying, "Truly, truly, I say to you, you seek Me, not because you saw signs, but because you ate of the loaves, and were filled." They were only interested in getting more food. In *verse 35*, He said, "I am the bread of life." Furthermore, Jesus said, "He who eats Me, he will also live because of Me" (*verse 57*). This was so strange that He even had to explain to His disciples that He was talking about a spiritual truth by relating believing in Him with feeding on Him. The Lord said that to become children of God, we must receive Jesus into our lives just as completely as we receive physical food into our bodies.

Highlight in your manual and read *John 17:3*. What is eternal life equated with? <u>Knowing he is the 1 & only.</u>

11. <u>Trusting & Believing the Lord. Greatest thing</u>

The word *know* in the Scriptures describes the most intimate of relationships when it refers to one person knowing another. For example, Adam knew Eve intimately as his wife. When a man and wife marry, they become one. Now read *verses 22 and 23 of John 17*. How are we to be related to Jesus Christ?

12. <u>We are to be related because when we are saved we become one w/ Christ.</u>

In fact, in *II Corinthians 11:2*, God says that Christians are what?

13. _Virgins to Christ._

So, the new believer begins a life of intimacy with the Lord of the universe. Clearly the Lord desires for us to have an intimate relationship with Him. This is truly amazing.

It is also important to understand that faith and works go together. Good works are a response to God's gift of salvation. When a person is born again, he will live differently. He becomes espoused to the Lord. It would seem strange for a prospective bride to suggest to her future husband that they continue to live as if they were still single after they are married (e.g., not telling others they are married, making decisions independently, having exclusively separate groups of friends, etc.).

It is the same way in making a commitment to Jesus Christ. How are we saved, according to *Ephesians 2:8-10*?

14. _Not through our works, but through grace_

Salvation is by grace through faith, not by works; but what does *verse 10* tell us is the result of our being saved?

15. _good works?_

When you receive the Lord Jesus Christ, you *will* do good works because you are a new creation. You will live differently, obeying and serving Christ out of your love for Him. So, God tells us we are not saved by good works, but as saved people, the way we show we are saved is by our good works.

3. Read the contents of Section **V. By faith, you can take the first step of biblical change** on Page 22 of the *Self-Confrontation* manual. Do you recognize the need to make this commitment? You can do so right now by:

    - Confessing to God that you are a sinner, that you have been in rebellion toward Him and need His forgiveness,

    - Telling God that you repent of your sin and intend to follow His way rather than your own,

    - Acknowledging to God that neither you nor anyone else but Jesus Christ can save you because He alone died to pay the penalty for sins and rose from the dead so that you might have a new life,

    - Inviting the Lord Jesus Christ to come into your life as your Savior and Lord, and

    - Thanking God for His grace and mercy toward you and adopting you as His child.

    If you have just made this commitment, put a check here (___) and tell another believer who can help you grow spiritually.

4. Read Section **VI. You must understand that man's way of solving problems falls short of God's solutions** on Pages 22-23. *NOTE: You do not need to spend much time looking up the referenced verses.*

5. Read Section **VII. You need to understand the difference between man's way and God's way** on Pages 23-24. *NOTE: You do not need to spend much time looking up the referenced verses.* Notice that man's way is a life oriented on self, while God's way is a life that is intimately related to Him and totally focused on living for Him.

SCRIPTURE RECITATION

Recite *Ephesians 2:8-9* to someone at home, in class, or elsewhere. Put a check here (___) when you have accurately recited the verses.

ADDITIONAL HOMEWORK

Here are some additional assignments. You will need to decide how much time you can spend on the additional homework.

A. In your own words, write the meaning of *Ephesians 2:8-9*.

16. *We are not saved by our works but through Christ's grace not by anything we do.*

B. Describe how a person can be saved. Write at least one Scripture reference for each point.

17. *Repentance:*

QUESTION AND CONCLUSION

A. What was the most significant truth you learned in completing this lesson?

18. *Christ loves us & died for us, we don't do anything to deserve his grace. We don't deserve salvation.*

B. This lesson establishes a foundation for the entire Bible Study. It lays the basic foundation of salvation which involves:

- Confessing to God that you are a sinner, that you have been in rebellion toward Him and need His forgiveness,
- Telling God that you repent of your sin and intend to follow His way rather than your own,
- Acknowledging to God that neither you nor anyone else but Jesus Christ can save you because He alone died to pay the penalty for sins and rose from the dead so that you might have a new life, and
- Inviting the Lord Jesus Christ to come into your life as your Savior and Lord.

Student Workbook for the Self-Confrontation Bible Study
- Lesson 1 -
© Biblical Counseling Foundation

C. If you have not already made this commitment, consider reading the Gospel of John and write down Jesus' explanation of how a person can be saved and have eternal life.

PREVIEW OF NEXT LESSON

When you receive Christ into your life, it does not mean that all of your present problems will disappear or that you won't have any more problems in the future. But it does mean that you can face, deal with, and endure any problem of living in a way that you never could have before you were saved. In fact, you can begin the process of biblical change immediately. The next lesson describes the wonderful changes that take place as a result of being born spiritually. These changes equip believers to grow spiritually and live victoriously.

LESSON 2
YOU CAN CHANGE BIBLICALLY (PART TWO)

OPENING PRAYER AND SCRIPTURE MEMORY

Before you begin this lesson, ask for God's help in understanding His Word and for wisdom and strength to apply what you learn in the power of the Holy Spirit.

Begin memorizing *Matthew 7:1, 5* and review *Ephesians 2:8-9*. Then, be prepared to recite them at the end of this lesson. Remember to write the verses on cards and carry them with you throughout each day so that you can memorize them during your spare time.

Also, in your own words, please write out the meaning of the new memory verses below:

Do not judge for one day God will judge us, make sure your heart is right before trying to tell someone else theres isn't.

INTRODUCTION TO THE LESSON

A. The first two lessons in the *Self-Confrontation* manual establish a foundation for the entire Bible Study. In this Bible Study, the overview session and Lesson 1 laid the basic foundation of salvation — the Lord Jesus Christ is the Rock upon Whom everything for living is built. Man cannot please God, overcome the problems of life, and have meaning or fruitfulness in life without a personal relationship with Jesus Christ. Lesson 2 explains changes that take place in a person's life as a result of the new birth.

B. The process of lasting biblical change begins when you receive the Lord Jesus Christ. As a result of the new birth, each believer has:

1. A new relationship with God,
2. Divine empowering now available to live the Christian life,
3. A new purpose for living, and
4. A new plan for spiritual growth.

C. It is particularly important for every believer to understand these truths as a vital part of his overcoming all hindrances to spiritual growth and living victoriously, even in the midst of difficult circumstances and relationships. There are a number of misconceptions among new believers that tend to invite defeat. We see some examples with a couple of exercises.

EXERCISE: LIVING BY FAITH

Let's conduct an exercise to stimulate your thinking about what is important in the life of a believer. Think back to when you first became a believer. What were some of the changes that took place in your life immediately after you received Christ? If you can, list at least three changes.

1. ① I was emmidiatley convicted of my sin // knew I wasn't innocent.
   ② Christ showed me his grace.
   ③ I had a horrible attitude.

If you are like many other believers, you probably listed things like: "I had a peace and joy that I never had before," "I became more interested in the Bible," "I felt happy," "I felt relief that my sins were forgiven," "I desired to be with other believers," etc.

Many of the changes people remember are related to their feelings. Now think back: What did you do when those feelings disappeared? Often, new believers depend on and tend to live by their feelings. Then, when the initial enthusiasm and euphoria of the first love experience with the Lord disappear, they become defeated very easily.

This is why believers need to learn how to live at a deeper level and have a better understanding of the resources God has provided for living according to His standards.

EXERCISE: WHAT IS SPIRITUAL?

Another misconception has to do with what activities we tend to consider as "spiritual." For the next exercise, list at least five types of activities in which a believer is involved on a daily basis.

2. 1. Daily Divotionals. (reading the gospel)
   2. Prayer
   3. Sharing the gospel
   4. accountability
   5. Fellowship

Now put a check by each of the above activities you would consider to be "spiritual."

Many people, in response to this question, put check marks by things that we tend to group into a certain category of spiritual activities, e.g., reading the Bible, praying, witnessing to others, going to church, etc. You may have also listed some of the other daily activities of life, such as going to work or school, fixing meals, washing dishes, going shopping, disciplining children, and so on. It is important to recognize that *all* these activities are spiritual.

Normally, only a very small portion of the time in a believer's day is spent in devotions and various church meetings which are the only activities many consider to be "spiritual." This is a wrong understanding of spirituality.

Most of a believer's typical week is spent in the spiritual battles of life which occur as he carries out his daily or routine responsibilities. It is relatively easy to live victoriously during daily devotions, or when involved in most church activities, because fewer trials or tests occur at these times. It is much more difficult to exhibit the fruit of the Spirit (*Galatians 5:22-23*), that is, love, joy, peace, patience, etc., when you must deal with people who do not act the way you would like! It is often in the daily routine of life that you are most challenged to live obediently and, thus, to grow spiritually.

In summary, the two exercises just conducted help us to see that our understanding of spiritual growth is often very different from the teaching of the Bible. Many Christians are defeated because they tend to live by their feelings and they are unprepared for the daily problems and responsibilities of life. There is great hope in learning *not* to live by our feelings, as we will see in subsequent lessons.

BEGINNING TO GROW

A. Read the purposes of **LESSON 2: YOU CAN CHANGE BIBLICALLY (PART TWO)** (*Self-Confrontation*, Page 30).

B. Read *Principle 2*, **BIBLICAL PRINCIPLES: YOU CAN CHANGE BIBLICALLY (PART TWO)** (*Self-Confrontation*, Page 31). Note that the first part of *Principle 2* is simply a paraphrase of *Colossians 2:7*. Highlight in your manual and read *Colossians 2:6-10*, then, answer the following questions:

What are believers warned against?

3. *The world, sin.*

What are believers exhorted to do instead?

4. *be built up in the Lord to face our sins*

Since you are to be established and growing in the Lord, He has graciously given you everything you need to continue in Him.

C. Before looking at *Principle 3*, let's expand the teaching on *Principle 2* by turning to **YOU CAN CHANGE BIBLICALLY (PART TWO)** on Pages 32-34 in the *Self-Confrontation* manual. We will come back to *Principle 3* later, after we have studied *Principle 2* in detail.

1. Four of the areas in a person's life that change significantly as a result of the new birth are described in Paragraphs A. through D.

   a. Read the first paragraph of A., starting with **"God's perspective and your assurance."** Highlight or underline the phrase, "a different relationship with God" (This phrase is at the beginning of the third line in the paragraph). This section describes the believer's new relationship with God. Highlight or underline the first sentence of each subparagraph. Pick out one of the nine points that gets your attention the most, and read at least one of the Scriptures listed under that point. Which point did you choose, and what do the referenced Scriptures tell you?

   5. ① *We are declared righteous through Christ,* ② *peace w/ God,* ③ *no longer seperated,* ④ *given eternal life,* ⑤ *confidence & assurance,* ⑥ *God's promised He will enable us to handle any problem* ⑦ *new creation,* ⑧ *Certainty that God's work in me will continue till His return.* ⑨ *Adopted into His family.*

   3 B(Romans 8:14-16) *we are His children, if children then heirs of God.*

   b. Read the first paragraph of **B. God's sufficiency and your resources** on Page 33 of the *Self-Confrontation* manual. Highlight or underline the phrase, "God's divine power."

This section describes the divine empowering available to all believers. Then read each subparagraph.

c. Read the first paragraph of **C. God's purpose and your focus.** Highlight or underline the phrase, "a different purpose." This section describes the believer's new purpose for living.

1) Read Subparagraph 1. Instead of pleasing self, Gods says we are to please

6. _____

2) Read Subparagraph 2. Instead of our focus being on

7. _____

our focus should be on

8. _____

d. Read the first paragraph of **D. God's plan and your obedience.** Highlight or underline the phrase, "God's plan." This section describes the new plan for the believer's spiritual growth. Read each of the subparagraphs. In Subparagraph 1., our obedience is to be in response to what?

9. _____

What is our obedience not to be dependent on (also in Subparagraph 1.)?

10. _____

We will study these in greater depth later on.

2. Read the title sentence of Section **II. The process of biblical change ends when ...** (*Self-Confrontation*, Page 34). What does this tell you about the rest of your life here on earth?

11. _____

Change is not pleasant at times. Yet we know that true peace, joy, and contentment, which are possible even in the greatest difficulties, can come only as we become more and more like Christ. This is where self-confrontation comes in — understanding where we are (or are not) in our walk with the Lord and putting His principles into action in the power of the Holy Spirit.

AN ESSENTIAL FOR DISCIPLESHIP

A. Not only is self-confrontation a part of our personal commitment to the Lord, it is essential for discipleship. So far, we have learned that as a result of the new birth, four significant changes take place in your life. You gain: 1) a new relationship with God, 2) divine empowering now available by which to live the Christian life, 3) a new purpose for living, and 4) a new plan for spiritual growth. Now let's see how self-confrontation relates to discipleship. Please turn to **BIBLICAL SELF-CONFRONTATION: AN ESSENTIAL FOR DISCIPLESHIP** (*Self-Confrontation*, Page 35).

B. Read the box at the top of Page 35. The biblical principles presented in this study are essential for living as an overcomer in Christ. Because this is an in-depth discipleship Bible Study, we will see how these principles apply to every area of life. All of the questions on this page are samples of what will be addressed in the remainder of this study. Pick two of the questions that are most challenging to you and look up at least one of the referenced Scriptures for each question. Paraphrase what each Scripture passage says about your walk with the Lord.

12. _____
_____
_____
_____

PREPARATION FOR DISCIPLING OTHERS

A. Not only has God given believers everything they need to be established in Him; He also tells them to prepare themselves to help others. This brings us to the truths found in *Principle 3*. Let's turn back to Page 31 of the *Self-Confrontation* manual.

1. Read the first sentence of *Principle 3*. *Principles* 2 and 3 correspond to the two purposes of this study: 1) to teach you how to face, deal with, and endure problems in your own life; and 2) to prepare you to help others.

2. Highlight in your manual, then read *Matthew 7:1-5*. In *verse 1*, the word "judge" means to pass sentence on someone. Jesus said that we are *not* to do this, but in *verse 5*, what are we to do first, before dealing with anyone else's problems?

    13. _____

    Only when we take the log out of our own eyes, will we see clearly to take the speck out of our brothers' eyes. Think of it this way. When a speck of dust gets into your eye, what happens? Even with the tiny speck, your eye begins to water and you cannot see clearly. Your vision becomes distorted and things may even seem to be magnified or abnormal. Imagine what it would be like if you had a log in your eye. It is obvious that you would need to remove the log before you could see clearly to help someone else.

    In some ways, this is a very dangerous Bible Study. You see, if you listen to the teaching from Scripture but do not apply it in your own life (i.e., you do not take the log out of your own eye), what does Jesus say about you?

    14. _____

    God's Word gives great hope by showing you that if you take the log out of your own eye, you *will* see clearly how to take the speck out of another's eye. This is important because, according to *verse 5*, you are responsible to do more than simply point out the speck in the eyes of others. Instead, you have an additional responsibility to get involved in their lives and serve them as you help them remove the speck from their eyes. We see this responsibility explained more fully in the next sentence of *Principle 3*.

3. Read the second sentence of *Principle 3*. In your manual, highlight the reference *Galatians 6:1-5*, and look it up in the Bible.

    In *verse 1*, who is responsible for restoring others?

    15. _____

Who are the ones that are spiritual?

16. _____

To determine what God calls spiritual, notice in *Galatians 5:25* that we are to walk in the Spirit; therefore, those who are walking in the Spirit are the ones who are spiritual. Being spiritual is not defined by how long you have been a Christian, how much Bible education you have, or whether you are a leader in your church. Even a very young Christian can be spiritual (that is, walk in the Spirit). Therefore, all of us, no matter how young or old in the Lord, are commanded to restore others as long as we are fervently following the Lord.

Note in *verse 2* of *Galatians 6* that you are to help others bear their burdens, but notice in *verse 5* that each one is to bear his own load. So, it is important that you do not carry any burden that the other is able to carry

Also, note in *verse 4* that you are responsible to examine your own life and are not to compare yourself to any standard other than God's. Also, notice that self-confrontation is to be ongoing even *while* helping others.

Note in *verse 5* that the goal is just the opposite of most counseling methods. In most worldly counseling, the counselee becomes more dependent on the counselor as time goes on, not less dependent. The biblical discipler/counselor should be encouraging the disciple to depend on the Lord completely, not to depend on the discipler/counselor.

B. *Principle 3* is expanded upon in the next subject, **BIBLICAL SELF-CONFRONTATION: A PREREQUISITE FOR HELPING OTHERS BIBLICALLY** on Page 36 of the *Self-Confrontation* manual.

Read the box at the top of Page 36. Highlight in your manual the reference to *Hebrews 5:14* at the bottom of the page and then read *Hebrews 5:12-14* to understand the verse in context. Even though only *verse 14* is quoted in the manual, the Scriptures are the authority, not the manual. Therefore, it is important to read the verse in your own Bible. In *verse 14*, what is the key to growth in spiritual discernment?

17. _____

Intellectually understanding all the biblical truths in this study will not produce maturity. It is the personal *practice* of the truths that brings maturity.

C. The Scriptures will be painting a picture of you during this Bible Study that you may not always like. You may be punctured by God's Word in many ways as you study, but you will gain immensely from the experience if you remain open to the Holy Spirit's conviction. Conviction, even if it does not feel good, is the loving, gracious work of the Holy Spirit in your life to show you that you need to change to develop Christlikeness.

The work of God's Word on our lives can be illustrated by considering what happens at a picnic when the sun comes out immediately after a rain. What effect does the energy from the sun have on muddy ground?

18. _____

What about butter sitting out in a dish on the picnic cloth — how does the sun affect it?

19. _____

Notice that it is the same sun and the same intensity, but with two different results. In the same way, we harden or soften ourselves depending upon our response to the Word of God.

You will not remain the same after studying God's Word in this Bible Study. You can choose to respond God's way and soften toward the Lord in loving obedience, or you can refuse to respond and delude yourself *(read Hebrews 3:12-13; James 1:22-25).* We'll cover these in greater depth later.

FOUNDATIONS FOR GROWTH

In order to learn how to live according to God's Word, it is important to learn God's Word as it applies to your life. Two daily disciplines that will help you immensely to learn how to live consistently as a doer of the Word are daily devotions and Scripture memory. Turn to Page 38 of the *Self-Confrontation* manual and read the box at the top of the page. Also turn to and read *Psalm 1:1-4*. Notice in *Psalm 1:2,* that a person is blessed if he does what?

20. _____

Meditation in the Scriptures is quite different from the meditation practiced by the secular world. The world encourages you to empty your mind and let it drift into areas that ignore life as it is. Biblical meditation is just the opposite. God tells us to take every thought captive *(II Corinthians 10:5)* and think only whatever is true, honorable, right, pure, lovely, and of good repute *(Philippians 4:8)* about the very situations you are facing. We are never to let our minds wander away from God's way.

    A. Under **DAILY DEVOTIONS** *(Self-Confrontation,* Page 38), Section **I. Developing a habit of daily devotions**, read Paragraphs B., E., F., and G. Then highlight the reference, *Psalm 19:7-11*, in Paragraph E. Now, turn to this passage in the Bible and list the words in the passage that describe what God's Word is like and what it does in us.

<u>What God's Word is like</u>	<u>What God's Word does in us</u>
21.	

Daily devotions should be times that help you learn to be *devoted* to the Lord. Sadly, many believers, knowing only that they should "have daily devotions," simply learn to read Scripture verses, passages, or devotional books, and often, these do not apply to their lives or the circumstances they are facing. It is important to recognize that devotional time spent in God's Word should directly relate to the very areas in your life where God has your attention. Most often trials, relationships, and responsibilities are where our attention is turned already.

To help you develop a plan to apply the Scriptures to your life, read Paragraph D. under Section II. on Page 39 of the *Self-Confrontation* manual and the note underneath the paragraph. Then, turn to the **BIBLE STUDY AND APPLICATION FORMAT** form on Page 437 of the *Self-Confrontation* manual. This form is a useful aid to studying the Word of God with a view toward application to our own lives. Notice the heading of each column on the first page of the supplement. The format is based on *II Timothy 3:16-17*. Using this format, you can apply a particular Scripture passage to your life by writing down the following:

- Teaching — What is the commandment or principle? (What is God's truth?)
- Reproof — How have I failed to live by it? (Where did I go astray from God's way?)
- Correction — What do I need to do? (What do I need to do to return to God's way?)

- Training in Righteousness — What is my specific plan? *(How* will I do what God commands me to do?)

Look at Pages 438 and 439 for examples. You can make copies of the blank form, or use a notebook or separate piece of paper to study God's Word in this way.

EXERCISE: BIBLE STUDY AND APPLICATION FORMAT FOR PSALM 1:2

As an exercise, complete a **BIBLE STUDY AND APPLICATION FORMAT** for *Psalm 1:2.* Use the following space to record your thoughts on these verses.

Teaching — What is the commandment or principle?

22. _____

Reproof — How have I failed to live by it?

23. _____

Correction — What do I need to do?

24. _____

Training in Righteousness — What is my specific plan? *(How* will I do what God commands me to do?)

25. _____

B. Now turn back to **SCRIPTURE MEMORY** on Page 39 in the *Self-Confrontation* manual. Read Paragraphs B., C., G., and J. of Section **I.**

In Paragraph B., highlight the reference, *Matthew 4:1-10,* and turn to this passage in your Bible. How did Jesus counter Satan's temptations?

26. _____

Note that, when Jesus was tempted by Satan, He focused on the Word, not on the temptation or Satan.

In Paragraph G., highlight the reference, *Psalm 119:9, 11* and turn to this passage in your Bible. What benefits are there to treasuring God's Word in your heart and obeying it completely?

27. _____

It is important for you to have a specific plan for memorizing God's Word, starting with the verses that apply directly to your life in your current trials, tests, and temptations. If you do not already have a plan for Scripture memory, choose one of the four plans listed on Pages 41-42 and begin your memory work immediately. These plans are designed as helps.

Read the topic sentence, Section **II. Memorizing Scripture can extend** ... on Page 40 of the *Self-Confrontation* manual. Develop a specific plan for devotions that is appropriate for you. For example, a devotional time in the morning helps you to start your day in the way the Lord wants you to go. It reminds you to live that day in the way that pleases the Lord. Then, Scripture memory and review help you keep your mind focused on God's Word throughout the day.

It is best to memorize at times other than during your devotional time. Take advantage of "free" moments during the day to review memory verses. You will be making wise use of the "empty" times when temptations often arise due to undisciplined thinking. What types of free moments can you think of that are possibilities for you?

28. _____

_____

_____

Then, a short devotional time in the evening helps you to review the day before the Lord, allowing you to judge yourself in light of God's standards and to make changes in your practices of life out of your commitment of loving obedience to Him.

SCRIPTURE RECITATION

Recite *Mathew 7:1* and *5* to someone at home, in class, or elsewhere. Also, recite *Ephesians 2:8-9*. Put a check here (___) when you have accurately recited the verses.

QUESTIONS AND CONCLUSION

A. Our focus is not to be on living for self, but instead is to be on:

29. _____

B. For how long in your life does the Bible say you can expect to see changes you will need to make?

30. _____

C. What are you to do before you take the speck out of someone else's eye?

31. _____

D. What two daily disciplines did you learn about in this lesson that will help you be a consistent doer of the Word?

32. _____

E. What was the most significant truth you learned in completing this lesson?

33. _____

_____

This lesson has described the changes that take place in one's life as a result of the new birth. The Lord has provided for every one of His children tremendous riches beyond compare. You learned that His children also have responsibilities. They are to please Him by confronting themselves on a daily basis and by helping others in their spiritual walk.

Two very important daily practices are daily devotions and Scripture memory. If you have not already established these daily practices, you should start immediately by setting a time to spend, perhaps 15 minutes each day to study the Bible and pray. In addition, write on a card the Scripture passage you should memorize this week and carry it with you. Take advantage of those spare moments during the day by taking out the card and reciting your passage.

PREVIEW OF NEXT LESSON

The next lesson expands on this lesson by describing, in detail, the authority, power, and provision that are available to the believer. During the lesson, you will answer the question, "Does God provide complete and adequate guidance through the Bible, the Holy Spirit, and prayer to face, deal with, and endure every difficulty of life?"

LESSON 3

MAN'S WAY AND GOD'S WAY (PART ONE)

OPENING PRAYER AND SCRIPTURE MEMORY

Before you begin this lesson, ask for God's help in understanding His Word and for wisdom and strength to apply what you learn in the power of the Holy Spirit.

Begin memorizing *II Timothy 3:16-17*. Also, review the Scripture memory passages assigned in the previous lessons. Then, be prepared to recite them at the end of this lesson. Remember to write the verses on cards and carry them with you throughout each day.

Also, in your own words, please write out the meaning of the new memory verses below:

_____

_____

_____

_____

INTRODUCTION TO THE LESSON

A. The first two lessons in the *Self-Confrontation* manual established a foundation for the entire Bible Study. Lesson 1 laid the basic foundation of salvation — the Lord Jesus Christ is the Rock upon Whom everything for living is built. Man cannot please God, overcome the problems of life, and have meaning or fruitfulness in life without a personal relationship with Jesus Christ. Lesson 2 explained what happens in a person's life as a result of the new birth. Lesson 3 expands on Lesson 2. Lesson 3 focuses on God's authority, empowering, and provision available to the believer.

In this and in the next lesson, you will see the stark contrast between living by faith and living according to man's wisdom.

Also, you will see that we will not cover some subjects or points in as much detail as others. You have probably already noticed that we have skipped over certain portions rather quickly. Even though we only touched on some subjects, that does not mean that we consider them to be less important. Since certain topics are already well taught in most Bible-believing churches, we will concentrate our time in this Bible study on what is sometimes misunderstood, neglected, or mis-taught.

B. Read the purposes of **LESSON 3: MAN'S WAY AND GOD'S WAY (PART ONE)** (*Self-Confrontation*, Page 48).

THE SUFFICIENCY OF THE SCRIPTURES

A. Turn to **BIBLICAL PRINCIPLES: MAN'S WAY AND GOD'S WAY (PART ONE)** (*Self-Confrontation*, Page 49). The three biblical principles on this page are very important and generally, these subjects are well taught in most Bible-believing churches. Therefore, we will concentrate only on what is sometimes neglected or mis-taught about God's Word, the Holy Spirit, and prayer. Let's start with *Principle 4*.

B. Read *Principle 4*. Note that the *only* authority we have for knowing God's way is the Bible. Here is an illustration to help you understand how important God's Word is.

> *ILLUSTRATION:* The designers and manufacturers of a machine or vehicle write a user's manual to help buyers know how to operate it. To keep the machine functioning properly, you must follow the instructions in the user's manual very carefully.
>
> Similarly, the Bible is our user's manual from God. He who created and formed us gives us His specific directions in His manual, the Word, for how we should live and for the changes we need to make to be fruitful in our lives. The Bible provides clear instructions to God's children for how to face, deal with, and endure every aspect of life before Him. To use any other book or teaching, even partially, is to invite confusion and defeat in a believer's life.
>
> Suppose you were using a machine and the user's manual said that it required a specific type of fuel. As you are using the machine, you recognize that you need more fuel. Contrary to the instructions in the user's manual, you decide that instead of filling the fuel tank with the appropriate fuel, you will put in water. What would happen to the machine? Of course, the machine would not operate properly and eventually not at all. The machine must have the proper fuel.
>
> In the same way, the faithful believers in years past understood the value of the Bible very well. Their standard was "faith only" and "Scripture only." They taught that the Scriptures were both without error *and* sufficient. This means that the Bible is not only without error, but it also has all the guidance needed. It is enough.
>
> Sadly, in recent years, even though many churches affirm that the Scriptures are without error, many of these same churches seem to have abandoned the truth that God's Word is sufficient, or complete, to deal with all the problems of life.

C. Let's look at what the Bible tells us about its work and purpose in our lives. Remember, the teaching parts of each lesson beyond the principles section serve as an expansion of each principle. So let's expand on *Principle 4* and then we will come back to the next principle. Let's turn to Page 50 in the *Self-Confrontation* manual, **SCRIPTURE IS YOUR AUTHORITY**. We are going to focus on Paragraphs B., G., and H., since they address major truths often mis-taught among believers. We will come back to *Principles 5* and *6* later.

1. Read the topic sentence of Paragraph B., and then, turn to *II Timothy 3:16-17*.

    a. Who is the author of the Scriptures?

    1. _____

    b. What four things are the Scriptures profitable for?

    2. _____

    c. Explain what each of the following words means:

    3. Teaching: _____

    Reproof: _____

    Correction: _____

    Training in Righteousness: _____

    d. In *verse 17* what is the resulting effect of God's Word in your life?

    4. _____

God says that the Scriptures will help us know how to deal with *every* situation of life in a victorious way. Notice that the word "every" signifies that nothing is left out.

Many believers say that the Bible is without error, but that it does not provide enough guidance to deal with the very serious problems of life. This statement is inconsistent. Since the Bible claims to provide guidance for *every* matter regarding how to live, it would be in error if it were not sufficient to deal with *every* problem of life. Therefore, to be consistent, if you say that the Bible is inerrant, you must also say that it is sufficient.

Some will counter by saying, "All truth is God's truth." They say, "Let's not rule out the possibility that some truths may be understood separately from the Bible." Certainly, believers should be willing to receive truth wherever it exists, and in many disciplines, such as mathematics or medicine, much truth is found outside the Bible. But the Bible was not written for the purpose of teaching us mathematics or medicine. (It is important to remember that where mathematics or medical issues are addressed in the Bible, the Scriptures are accurate.) The Bible was written for the purpose of teaching us how to live. In the case of how to live before God, before others, and deal with one's self, the Bible has all the truth necessary. It has all that is necessary to equip us for every good work.

The Scriptures were written for the express purpose of showing us how to face, deal with, and endure every problem of life. This includes even the very serious so-called "mental" problems of today. For example, even though a person may exhibit bizarre behavior and may appear not to comprehend reality, he is responsible for every moral deed (thought, speech, and actions). God tells us in His Word that He will judge every person for every deed *(based on Ecclesiastes 12:13-14; Romans 2:5-6)*. This subject will be explained in more detail in Lesson 4.

God's Word even shows us how to face, deal with, and endure difficult physical problems. While the Lord normally uses medical doctors to treat physical problems, He uses the Scriptures to provide guidance on how to act and have joy in the midst of each problem. For example, even though a broken arm needs to be treated medically, the Lord provides us guidance in His Word and strength through the Holy Spirit to act biblically in the midst of the pain. In the same way, when a person's mental capacity is altered due to an impaired brain, the Lord may use a medical doctor to treat the physical impairment, but He holds every person responsible for moral choices. Even though a person with defective thinking may understand little, he still can determine whether or not he will demonstrate love.

Note that the four items listed in *II Timothy 3:16-17* have been used as the basis for the **BIBLE STUDY AND APPLICATION FORMAT** *(Self-Confrontation,* Supplement 3) which was explained in Lesson 2.

2. Read Paragraph G. on Page 51. We will read several of the Scripture passages referenced in this paragraph.

   a. According to *II Peter 1:3*, what has God granted believers?

      5. _____

      In *II Peter 1:4*, what does God say His Word enables us to do?

      6. _____

   b. Read *Deuteronomy 4:2*. What caution does this passage give us regarding God's Word?

      7. _____

c. Read *Proverbs 30:6*. What does this passage say happens to those who add to God's Word?

8. _____

_____

3. Read Paragraph H. and *Isaiah 55:8-9, 11*. What do these verses tell you about the power of God's Word?

9. _____

While we cannot depend on man's reasoning, we can know God's way through the Word.

So far, we have been talking about our user's manual, the Bible. It provides us all the instructions we need to know how to face, deal with, and endure every aspect of life. To use any other book or teaching, even partially, is to invite confusion and defeat in a believer's life.

THE NECESSITY OF THE HOLY SPIRIT

A. Not only do we have God's Word, but the Holy Spirit empowers us. We see this in *Principle 5* (*Self-Confrontation*, Page 49). Read *Principle 5*.

B. To expand on *Principle 5*, let's turn to **THE HOLY SPIRIT EMPOWERS YOU TO SOLVE YOUR PROBLEMS** (*Self-Confrontation*, Pages 53-55). Read the contents of the box at the top of Page 53.

1. Read *John 16:7-13*. According to *verse 7*, why was it to the Apostle's advantage that Jesus go back to the Father?

10. _____

Suppose you were there, listening to Jesus teaching this truth, and He asked, "Whom would you rather have with you, Me or the Holy Spirit?" Whom would you choose? Why?

11. _____

_____

Many people would choose Jesus, thinking how marvelous it would be to sit under His teaching continuously. But think again. Jesus limited Himself as a human being to be in only one location at a time. When He restricted Himself to His earthly body, He could only go home with one person. On the other hand, the Holy Spirit is with every believer no matter where he goes.

According to *John 16:13*, what does the Holy Spirit guide us into?

12. _____

2. Read *I Corinthians 2:5-14*. What do *verses 12-14* tell you about what a believer can understand, as opposed to someone who is not a believer?

13. _____

Even though an unbeliever has many years of education and experience, he cannot understand the things given to us by God, because they are spiritually appraised. Yes, he may know *facts* about the Bible, but he cannot understand how God's Word applies to life. Understanding is much more than intellectual knowledge.

3. There is much teaching in the body of Christ about the Holy Spirit, and this is a very important subject. But we will only emphasize some aspects not commonly understood or practiced by believers since so much truth about the Holy Spirit is taught well.

4. Read the section entitled **I. The Holy Spirit is fully divine** ... (*Self-Confrontation*, Pages 53-54).

5. In Section **II. The Holy Spirit provides an overcoming** ..., read Paragraph B., on Page 54. When you reach Subparagraph 11., read *I John 2:20, 27*. According to these verses, are pastors and teachers really needed?

   14. _____

   Why (Hint: read *Ephesians 4:12*)?

   15. _____

   We are to listen carefully to God-appointed teachers; however, we are always to compare what any human being says with the Scriptures just as the Bereans evaluated what the Apostle Paul taught (see *Acts 17:11*). The believer can confidently depend on the Holy Spirit to provide accurate guidance for his own life even when humans teach error. Consequently, we should evaluate every teaching, depending on the Holy Spirit's illumination through His Word.

PRAYER IS VITAL

Not only is Scripture our authority and the Holy Spirit powerful in our lives, but prayer is vital.

A. Read *Principle 6* on Page 49 of the *Self-Confrontation* manual.

B. To expand on *Principle 6*, turn to **PRAYER PROVIDES COMMUNICATION WITH GOD** (*Self-Confrontation*, Pages 56-59).

   1. Read Section **I. Biblical truths about God's work** ....

   2. In Section **II. Observations from the Gospels about** ... on Pages 56 and 57, what do you particularly notice about Jesus' prayer life? List three things.

      16. _____

      _____

      _____

      Notice that consistency, diligence, and selflessness were essential ingredients of Jesus' pattern of prayer.

   3. In Section **III. Scriptural teaching to believers about prayer**, note the need for fervent, effectual prayer according to God's Word. Then, on Page 58, read the points under paragraphs C. How you are to pray, D. When you are to pray, and E. What you are to pray. What applies most to you in these paragraphs?

      17. _____

      _____

   4. In Section **IV. Unprofitable practices in your prayer life**, remember the need to pray meaningfully and to avoid unprofitable practices in prayer. We may even miss God's answers to our prayers because we have preconceived ideas about the answers we should get. Consider the following illustration:

> **ILLUSTRATION:** In a mountainous area, there was a severe rainstorm that started a flood. The water rose at such a rapid rate that only the roofs of some homes were visible. On one of these roofs sat a believer praying to God for help. Someone in a small boat approached and offered a ride to safety. But the man on the house refused, saying, "I'm praying to the Lord for help and I am confident that He will save me." As the water rose higher and covered his feet, a larger boat came along and offered to rescue him. Again the man refused, saying, "I'm praying to the Lord for help and I am confident that He will save me." Just as the water reached the man's chest, a helicopter let down a rope for him. But, again, he refused, saying the same thing. The man ultimately drowned.
>
> When the drowned man appeared before the Lord, he asked, "Lord, I asked you to save me and I believed that you would. Why didn't you?" The Lord replied, "What do you mean? I sent you two boats and a helicopter. You refused My answer three times."
>
> Even though this is a humorous story, the fact is that we may often fail to recognize God's answers to our prayers because they don't fit our expectations. We miss God's answers to prayer because we are looking for our own preconceived answers.
>
> Can you think of a case where God answered one of your prayers in a way you did not expect?
>
> 18. _____

Based on this section, list at least one way in which you could improve your prayer life.

19. _____

SCRIPTURE RECITATION

Recite *II Timothy 3:16-17* to someone at home, in class, or elsewhere. Also, recite one of the previous memory passages chosen by the listener. Put a check here (___) when you have accurately recited the verses.

ADDITIONAL HOMEWORK

Read **PREPARING A PERSONAL TESTIMONY** *(Self-Confrontation, Supplement 4)*. Every believer must be prepared to give an account for the hope that is within him *(I Peter 3:15)*. Write a brief sentence or two for each portion of your testimony (before conversion, conversion, after conversion). Write a testimony that you could give in thirty seconds or less following the suggested format of Supplement 4. Use a separate sheet of paper and read it to someone at home or elsewhere. If you are in a class, turn it in to the leader at your next meeting.

QUESTIONS

A. List and explain one Scripture passage that shows that God and His Word are sufficient to provide instructions to believers in dealing with the problems of life.

20. _____
_____
_____
_____

B. List at least two ways in which the Holy Spirit helps you live the Christian life.

21. _____
_____
_____
_____

C. What about Jesus' prayer life (see *Self-Confrontation*, Pages 56-57) can apply to your own? List at least one area.

22. _____
_____
_____
_____

D. What was the most significant truth you learned in completing this lesson?

23. _____
_____

PREVIEW OF NEXT LESSON

In Lesson 4, we will investigate some of the false philosophies that are presented by the world as "truth," and you will see the total inadequacy of the world's wisdom. You will also discover that the biblical view of self is diametrically opposed to what is being taught on this subject in many pulpits and so-called "Christian" counseling courses.

LESSON 4
MAN'S WAY AND GOD'S WAY (PART TWO)

OPENING PRAYER AND SCRIPTURE MEMORY

Before you begin this lesson, ask for God's help in understanding His Word and for wisdom and strength to apply what you learn in the power of the Holy Spirit.

Begin memorizing *II Corinthians 3:5-6*. Also, review the Scripture memory passages assigned in the previous lessons. Then, be prepared to recite them at the end of this lesson.

Also, in your own words, please write out the meaning of the new memory verses below:

_____
_____
_____
_____

INTRODUCTION TO THE LESSON

A. The first two lessons of the *Self-Confrontation* manual established a foundation for the entire Bible Study. In Lesson 3, emphasis was placed on three significant resources that God provides to the believer for daily living. As a review, list those resources here:

   1.
   _____
   _____
   _____

B. These resources are totally sufficient to enable the believer to face, deal with, and endure all of life's problems. However, you may still wonder whether the Bible, the Holy Spirit, and prayer are sufficient for the truly *serious* problems of life. We need to remember that God knows us better than anyone on this earth, and in His gracious love has provided all we need for a meaningful, fruitful life. How can we justify relying on the theories and "credentials" of the world for the difficult problems, and only rely on God's Word for the supposedly easy or routine ones? Is God not sophisticated or knowledgeable enough to understand our problems and to have made provision for us? Hopefully your confidence in God and His Word to deal with all of life's problems will greatly increase as we go through this lesson.

C. In this lesson, we will investigate some of the false philosophies that are presented in the world as "truth," "facts," or "the latest scientific research." You will see the total inadequacy of the world's wisdom as compared to the changeless, ageless, absolute wisdom of God.

Also, in this and subsequent lessons, we will follow a teaching technique exemplified in the Scriptures, that of contrasting God's way and man's way. Jesus often said, "You have heard that it was said ..., but I say unto you." He taught by contrast to encourage them to listen to what He was saying and to make His point clear.

D. Read the purposes of **LESSON 4: MAN'S WAY AND GOD'S WAY (PART TWO)** (*Self-Confrontation*, Page 64).

BIBLICAL PRINCIPLES

A. Highlight in your manual and read *Principle 7*, **BIBLICAL PRINCIPLES: MAN'S WAY AND GOD'S WAY (PART TWO)** *(Self-Confrontation*, Page 65) as background information for the lesson. Look up each of the three passages, *Proverbs 14:12; Isaiah 55:8-9;* and *I Corinthians 2:14*, and describe what they tell you about the *natural* man (man apart from Jesus Christ)

2. *Proverbs 14:12* —

Isaiah 55:8-9 —

I Corinthians 2:14 —

B. Read *Principle 8*. The natural man's problem is even worse than being inadequate; he is actually rebellious toward God. Also, note that partial obedience is just as unacceptable to God as deliberate rebellion. Read about the incident of King Saul and the Amalekites in *I Samuel 15:3-23*. Saul was the first King of Israel, and at first, he looked very good. But very early in his reign, he demonstrated that he already had an established pattern of disobedience before this incident. Saul gave excuses when he would disobey (as early as *I Samuel 13*). In *I Samuel 15*, then, God sends Samuel to give Saul a command for which there was no room for doubt.

1. In *verse 3*, God's command was very clear and specific. What was His command?

   3.

   Note that God had said much earlier (in *Exodus 17:14*) that He would utterly blot out the memory of Amalek from under heaven because of their continual attacks on the Israelites.

2. In *verses 8-9*, what did King Saul and the people fail to do with respect to God's command?

   4.

3. In *verse 13*, what did King Saul say he had done?

   5.

4. In *verse 14*, what did Samuel accuse Saul of?

   6.

5. In *verse 15*, what did Saul say in an attempt to justify himself?

   7.

6. Read *verses 22-23*. Even though Saul did most of what the Lord commanded, what did Samuel say about Saul's behavior?

   8.

   When Saul selectively chose which part of God's command he would follow and which part he would not follow, he was disobedient even though he accomplished almost all that God had commanded. The fact that Saul was selective meant that *he* maintained control over his life, and played God in his own life. To what did Samuel equate Saul's partial obedience?

   9.

   The key issue in Saul's actions was who is in control — himself or God. Saul chose to be the one in control; he decided when he would be obedient and when he would disobey. As a result, Saul bore significant consequences. He lost his position as king.

This is a valuable lesson for us. If we obey God in every aspect of our lives, but we purposely determine not to obey Him in one point, we are like King Saul. We are refusing to obey the Lord as though we disobeyed in all points *(James 2:10)*.

Think about an area in your life where you have yet to yield control over to the Lord. It may be a sin that no one else knows about. It may involve a failure to forgive someone else or a failure to carry out a responsibility you know you have. You do not need to write down the specifics here, but think about how you will demonstrate love for the Lord and others by doing what you know God would want you to do in this area. You can pause right now to pray, confess your sin to the Lord, and make a commitment to yield to the Lord's will in this area. Check here ____ when you have finished. You will have a chance later in the study to select a problem area to work on in more detail. It could be a problem area you are thinking of here, or something else.

C. Read *Principle 9*. Salvation is necessary for biblical change. Remember, you cannot walk before you are born.

MAN'S FAILURE

Now let's review the reasons that man is in such a lost state, by looking at the history of man's failure. Read **THE BIBLICAL MODEL OF MAN'S FAILURE** *(Self-Confrontation*, Pages 66-67). These two pages illustrate not only man's failure, but also his unwillingness to accept the responsibility for his failure.

BIBLICAL VIEW OF SELF

Turn to **THE BIBLICAL VIEW OF SELF** *(Self-Confrontation,* Page 68) to see just how far man has fallen.

A. Read Section **I. Sinless self to the sinful self** ... on Page 68 of the *Self-Confrontation* manual.

B. Read Section **II. Scripture speaks of the natural man's self-importance** on Pages 68-69. This portion points out the tremendous contrast between God and man. It deals directly with man's mistaken view of his self-importance and his ideas of worthiness in comparison to the worthiness of God. God says that, compared to Him, man is like dust, like a vapor, stupid and devoid of knowledge; yet the natural man esteems himself as significant and having unlimited potential in his human unsaved self. Many times, even as believers, it is easy to be prideful when we compare ourselves to other people rather than the Lord.

C. Read Paragraph A. under Section **V. You can be more than a conqueror** ... *(Self-Confrontation,* Page 70). Who provided the greatest example of dying to self?

10. _____

1. Read Subparagraph 1. on Page 70 about "self worth." Then, read *I Corinthians 1:26-31*. In *verses 26-28,* whom has God chosen?

11. _____
_____

2. Read Subparagraph 3. on Page 70 about "self-love." Then, read *II Timothy 3:1-2*. What is the primary characteristic of people living during the last days?

12. _____

Many have used *Matthew 22:39* (we looked at this passage in the introduction to the study) to justify what they call the "need" for self-love. In *Matthew 22:37-40,* Jesus lists only two laws (i.e., love God and love others), not three. God's implication here is that we already love ourselves. This will be explained in more detail in Lesson 9.

3. Read Subparagraph 6. on Page 71 about "self-esteem." Read *Philippians 3:7-11*. In *verse 9*, where does our righteousness *not* come from?

13. _____

Where does it come from?

14. _____

Note that the Scripture tells us to esteem (regard) God *(Malachi 3:16)* and others *(Philippians 2:4)*, but nowhere in Scripture are we told to esteem ourselves. The word "esteem" means to view highly, to put in a high place, as on a pedestal.

4. Read over the other "errors of man's way" on Pages 71 and 72 as you have time.

These views, popular in the world today, are a result of unscriptural approaches to personal problems. We will see why in the next section.

CONTRASTING VIEWS — MAN'S WAY VERSUS GOD'S WAY

A. Turn to the chart, **BASIC APPROACHES TO SOLVING PERSONAL PROBLEMS** (*Self-Confrontation*, Page 74).

The four columns under **MAN'S WAY** depict some of the most common humanistic philosophies of the world, when it comes to dealing with difficulties of life. The aim of this chart is to teach you to recognize the difference between truth (God's way) and error (man's way).

The methodologies shown on this chart are four major categories that describe hundreds of separate and distinct philosophies being advocated and practiced in the United States alone, all dealing with personal problems. The fact that there are so many different views (with the number increasing every year) indicates that these methodologies are not leading to the knowledge of truth about man. Nor are they scientific, as many claim. The scientific method involves five steps: 1) observation, 2) hypothesis, 3) experimentation, 4) theory, and finally, 5) law (for example, the law of gravity). A scientific search for truth would result in a gradual convergence (coming together) toward the central truth that stands as various theories were tested over many years of experiment. In contrast, man's ideas about how the mind works continue to diverge (go farther apart) year after year, and supposed solutions keep changing.

An important reason for pointing out these methodologies is to look at what underlies the various practices. You must ask yourself, "Where do these ideas come from?" and "What are the presuppositions on which these ideas are built?" At the top of the leftmost column on the chart, notice the phrase, **BASIC VIEW OF MAN**. Each approach is built on differing theories about what man is like mentally and spiritually. In order to understand any approach, it is important to understand the basic presuppositions upon which that theory is built.

Also, notice at the bottom of the leftmost column the words **COUNSELING FOCUS**. It is also very important to understand what the practitioners of that theory think is an appropriate goal for their treatment. You need to ask, "Where is the focus of this view, and where is it headed?" Then, it is fairly easy to understand how they progress from start to finish.

Since each of these approaches is based on a particular philosophy about what man is like and how he behaves, this lesson is really a contrast of faith systems. While the world does not label psychology as a faith system, it is important to recognize that any teaching on how a man thinks and how he should live implies a certain faith system. Because the brain is physical, it can be examined by specialists, but it is impossible to put the mind in a test tube. Therefore, any conclusion about how a person will respond in a particular situation is made on the basis of faith, and on the assumptions made by this faith system.

On the surface, some of the methods may seem to have points in line with Scripture. Sometimes, without knowing it, man discovers portions of God's truth (even a broken clock is right twice a day). However, they are based on an incorrect understanding of the very core of how people behave, and they are practiced with a totally unbiblical focus. And even if worldly counselors discover a truth, they either do not recognize, or they deny the source of that truth, which is God Himself. In doing so, they try to discredit the sufficiency of God's resources to overcome problems. We must not be misled by the wisdom of man, even when it seems to offer portions of God's truth. It becomes very difficult, in many cases, to distinguish truth from falsehood.

Many cults contain mostly truth, and the errors are concealed very carefully. Otherwise, there would be few followers. That is why it is so important to make a thorough evaluation. Let's illustrate.

> **ILLUSTRATION:** Suppose that you gave someone instructions on how to get to your home, and these instructions included ten changes in direction. Now suppose that you described all but one of the ten turns correctly. The result would be that, following your directions, he would never get to your home. He could easily end up going in the opposite direction, even though your directions were 90% accurate. In the same way, something that has a lot of truth in it, but also contains error, though seemingly small, may result in a large deviation from what Scripture actually teaches.

Furthermore, it is important to recognize that many of these worldly theories or beliefs directly contradict the Bible and, as a result, stand in direct competition with God's revelation. Some of the world's philosophies may make someone *feel* better, at least for a time, but they don't address the real problem. They only deal with symptoms of the problem. Consequently, it is vital that you heed God's warning not to integrate the world's philosophies with the Scriptures.

As you review each of these columns, you should be reminded about the error of man's way; however, the columns do not address individuals by name. Most counselors have a genuine concern for helping people, so intentions (motives) should not be questioned. The purpose is to distinguish between truth and error, not to question a person's motives or standing before the Lord. The encouragement to you is to be like the Bereans, whom God commended. What does *Acts 17:11* say the Bereans did?

15. _____

_____

B. Explanation of the method for evaluating man's way.

Each of the four columns under **MAN'S WAY** shows an unbiblical theory or philosophy. When reviewing the columns, follow each column completely down, beginning with the **BASIC VIEW OF MAN** and progressing to the **COUNSELING FOCUS**. Note that when an assumption is made about man, then the **CAUSE OF PROBLEMS**, the so-called **CURE**, the **COUNSELING TECHNIQUE**, and the **COUNSELOR'S TERMINOLOGY** must fit the **BASIC VIEW OF MAN**, even though it is an unbiblical theory or philosophy. Note also at the bottom of the chart, for each column under **MAN'S WAY**, the common focus is on *self*, not on God. This is true of all of man's approaches to life. As you study the columns, read the text for each below, and complete the brief exercise at the end of the discussion of each approach.

C. Review the column labeled, **Instinctual**.

INSTINCTUAL APPROACH

Note the **BASIC VIEW OF MAN** for the **Instinctual** approach. Under this view, you are assumed to be only another animal, having the same instincts and drives as animals. This assumption implies that like animals, people do not have souls.

According to the Instinctual approach, the **CAUSE OF PROBLEMS** is that your natural instincts and drives have been repressed or thwarted by society, family, or upbringing. The four drives identified are said to be to seek food, to fight, to flee from danger, and to seek sexual gratification. And since the supporters of this theory claim that you are born with these drives, it is not your fault that you have problems when these drives are frustrated.

This idea was not just introduced 100 years ago. It was a common belief even back in Ezekiel's day. The Israelites had a proverb that said, *"The fathers eat the sour grapes, but the children's teeth are set on edge."* In other words, they said that the reason the children turned out or acted in certain ways was because of what the parents did. God told them to get rid of that proverb because each person is responsible for his own actions *(Ezekiel 18:2-4, 20)*.

According to those who believe in the Instinctual approach, the so-called **CURE** must be to get you back to the place where you can once again follow your instincts. Proponents of this view say you must be released from all the constraints that prevent you from fulfilling your drives.

When considering the **COUNSELING TECHNIQUE**, the belief is that only a highly trained human being can interpret what are called your "subconscious," "irrational" thoughts and dreams. This technique focuses on delving intensely into the past of the counselee, and often even requires him to give over the control of his mind to the counselor through hypnosis. Note that even the terms describing the methods used are difficult to understand, thus necessitating a highly trained person to analyze you.

Because the counseling method is so difficult, the **COUNSELOR'S TERMINOLOGY** is also difficult to understand. However, notice how many of these terms have become part of our daily language, without our even questioning the philosophy behind them. For example, the term, "subconscious," has been used so often, many just assume there is such a thing even though it denies the Bible's claim that everyone is responsible for his deeds, i.e., thoughts, speech, and actions *(Ezekiel 18:20; Romans 2:5-10)*. We cannot justify ourselves by saying, "I just did it subconsciously." The Scriptures describe "conscious" (alert) and "unconscious" (asleep or unaware), but never a "subconscious" (irrational).

Finally, note the **COUNSELING FOCUS** of this approach has the goal of liberating self. According to *Philippians 2:3-4*, what should we do instead?

16. _____

_____

_____

D. Review the column labeled, **Behavioral**.

BEHAVIORAL APPROACH

Under this column, the **BASIC VIEW OF MAN** assumes you are a higher form of animal, having "conditioned" reflexes and responses, just like animals. Once again, the assumption is that you do not have a soul.

This approach says that the **CAUSE OF PROBLEMS** is that you have been wrongly influenced by others and the environment around you, and therefore, that you have been wrongly "conditioned." Once again, your problems are caused from outside you.

This also is not a new view. The Pharisees even in Jesus' day manipulated the people by focusing only on "right behavior" to consider a person as righteous. There was not an appeal to the heart transformation. Similarly, the behaviorists say that the **CURE** is to "reprogram" or "recondition" you to respond the right way. Regrettably, the counselor trained in this approach determines how you should be reconditioned, according to his beliefs, preferences, and training. Suppose his training or views are wrong. Then, according to this view, you must be reprogrammed once more.

This particular **COUNSELING TECHNIQUE** can lead many believers astray, since it can seem on the surface that "rewards" and "punishments" are the same practice used by God. This is an example of how man sometimes discovers a portion of God's truth. However, even here, the world's approach in dealing with reward and punishment is very different from God's way. The Behavioral approach teaches individuals to expect rewards for every correct action (instantaneous gratification) and to avoid punishment for every incorrect action (fear of punitive action). The Lord, on the other hand, blesses or rewards us according to His sovereignty and timing for patterns of obedience (not necessarily for every individual act of obedience). It is for the purpose of teaching us to live by the Lord's guidance, to produce Christlike character, not for "what do I get out of this?" He also disciplines us for the purpose of restoring us back to Him, not just for teaching us to avoid pain *(based on Colossians 3:23-24; Hebrews 12:11; James 1:22-25).* Even though the same words are used, the approach is completely different.

Because this counseling method is focused on eliciting the "right" response, the **COUNSELOR'S TERMINOLOGY** is focused on changing only the behavior, not on dealing with the heart.

Finally, note the **COUNSELING FOCUS** of this approach is once again on self. Look up *John 15:4-5*, and state what these verses say that are contrary to the philosophy of improving self.

17. _____

_____

E. Review the column labeled, **Positive Potential**.

POSITIVE POTENTIAL APPROACH

For the **BASIC VIEW OF MAN,** the Positive Potential approach states that everyone is basically good, and that within you is the capacity and potential to solve all your problems *(denying Jeremiah 17:9; Matthew 15:18; and Romans 3:10, 23).* This view happens to be one of the most ancient untruths, as seen by the statement Satan made to Eve to tempt her: *"... you will be like God ...."* This approach to life is still very popular just like it must have been during the time of the book of *Judges* when everyone did what was right in his own eyes.

This approach says that the **CAUSE OF PROBLEMS** is that you have had your inner potential and goodness blocked by negative thinking and all the negative influences around you.

According to those who believe in the positive potential of man, you must **CURE** the problem by releasing the positive potential within yourself. This is accomplished only from within yourself, by solving the problem yourself.

The **COUNSELING TECHNIQUE** therefore requires a passive counselor who does not give you answers. Instead his focus is to release the so-called goodness inherent in you by reflecting your own statements back to you, until you come up with your own answers based on the resources within you. This counseling method is focused on drawing out the counselee's own goodness and positive thinking.

The **COUNSELOR'S TERMINOLOGY** includes statements reminding the counselee of the potential and goodness within him, such as "the god within," "inner power," etc.

Because of this belief in the goodness of man, the **COUNSELING FOCUS** of this approach is on self as having utmost importance. Look up *Romans 3:10-18, 23* and state what these verses say that are contrary to the elevation of self.

18. _____

_____

_____

F. Review the column labeled, **Spiritist**.

SPIRITIST APPROACH

For the **BASIC VIEW OF MAN**, the Spiritist approach assumes that everyone is subject to the control of spirits without any hindrance *(denying I John 4:4)*.

This ancient untruth says that the **CAUSE OF PROBLEMS** is that everyone is under the control of, or committed to, spirits, demons, or ancestors. Once again, the problems within you are said to be caused by forces outside of you.

Therefore, this approach says you must **CURE** the problem of being controlled by spirits or ancestors by appeasing them or by casting out demons or spirits.

Thus, the **COUNSELING TECHNIQUE** involves mantras, chants, curses on the enemy, nullifying curses on self, contacting spirits, and the like *(violating Leviticus 19:31, Deuteronomy 18:10-11)*.

Because the counseling method here is focused on dealing with spirits, demons, and ancestors, the emphasis is on gaining power over or being delivered from evil spirits. Therefore, the **COUNSELOR'S TERMINOLOGY** includes words like "curses," "binding spirits," etc.

Note that once again the **COUNSELING FOCUS** of this approach is on self as needing deliverance or protection. Look up *I John 5:4-5*, and state what these verses say that are contrary to the release of self from bondage.

19. _____

_____

G. These false philosophies have certain things in common. God is not considered when individuals with problems are perceived to be victims. The blame is placed on society, family, heritage, the environment, and/or what is called chemical imbalance for a person's failure to overcome the problems of life.

Regarding chemical imbalance, it is true that certain chemical or hormonal changes in the body can make it more difficult to behave righteously. However, chemical changes in the body cannot *cause* someone to sin. God tells us in His Word that He will hold everyone responsible for his deeds (thoughts, speech, and actions) *(Romans 2:6)*. This does not, however, mean that anyone other than a medical doctor should suggest that a person stop taking prescribed drugs. Many of the psychotropic drugs can endanger life if taken in the wrong dosage or if the intake is ceased abruptly.

H. Review the column labeled, **GOD'S WAY**:

> ## GOD'S WAY
>
> This column shows the stark contrast between what God's Word says about man, and man's ideas about man from the **BASIC VIEW OF MAN** to the **COUNSELING FOCUS**. God's way is much higher than anything man can devise. God gives us tremendous hope in facing, dealing with, and enduring problems. His way remains a consistent standard and is not dependent on circumstances, others, or things around us.
>
> The foundational truth about man is that he was made in the image of God, has fallen into a depraved state, and is hopeless without Christ. Man looks on the outside (feelings, circumstances, etc.); God looks at the heart *(I Samuel 16:7)*. Man says, "I am not responsible." God says, "You are responsible."
>
> God tells us that the **CAUSE OF PROBLEMS** is that man is rebellious, unbelieving, and disobedient; and denies God's power.
>
> Therefore, God's **CURE** to man's problem is first, salvation, then walking in His way through the empowering of the Holy Spirit.
>
> Thus, the **COUNSELING TECHNIQUE** includes all that the Lord says believers are to do to help others live victoriously. A biblical discipler/counselor is to employ *all* the ways listed in this section in order to disciple/counsel effectively. Obviously, all aspects of biblical discipleship/counseling also include prayer *(Ephesians 6:18; I Timothy 2:1)* and comfort *(II Corinthians 3:5-6)*.
>
> Because God has given His perfect Word to show us how we are to face and deal with problems, the **COUNSELOR'S TERMINOLOGY** must consist of words consistent with the Scriptures, such as, "sin," "salvation," "putting off the practices of the old self and putting on the practices of the new self," etc.
>
> The **COUNSELING FOCUS** is in stark contrast to all of man's ways and involves denying self, pleasing God, and blessing others.

EXAMPLES OF DIFFERENCES

A. Read **EXAMPLES OF MAN'S WAY COMPARED TO GOD'S WAY** *(Self-Confrontation, Pages 75-76)*. List two of the areas that stand out to you as being areas where Christians are most tempted to go man's way.

20. _____

_____

B. You can see from this study that it is important to understand the difference between man's way and God's way. Thankfully, we can know the difference. Let's turn to the *Self-Confrontation* manual, Page 77.

KNOWING THE DIFFERENCE

Read **KNOWING THE DIFFERENCE BETWEEN MAN'S WAY AND GOD'S WAY** *(Self-Confrontation*, Page 77). It is important to realize that the way to distinguish truth from error is not primarily to study man's way. The key is to become intimately familiar with the truth. It is similar to how bank personnel are taught to recognize counterfeit money by studying and handling the genuine money so much that they will easily recognize the counterfeit. So spend more time in the Word, not in reading books that profess to expose error.

SCRIPTURE RECITATION

Recite *II Corinthians 3:5-6* to someone at home, in class, or elsewhere. Also, recite one of the previous memory passages chosen by the listener. Put a check here (___) when you have accurately recited the verses.

QUESTIONS AND CONCLUSIONS

A. The world has come up with many different explanations of man's problem. What does God say man's problem is?

21. _____

What does God say the solution is?

22. _____

B. Is partial obedience as unacceptable to God as deliberate sin?

23. _____

C. What was the most significant truth you learned in completing this lesson?

24. _____

D. Key Points:

1. Remember to compare anything you read or hear with God's Word. God has not promised to bless man's words; He has, however, promised that His Word will accomplish exactly what He intends *(Isaiah 55:11; I Peter 1:24-25)*.

2. Our environment, others around us, chemical changes in the body, etc. cannot *cause* someone to sin. God tells us in His Word that He will hold everyone responsible for his deeds (thoughts, speech, and actions) *(Romans 2:6)*.

3. Willfully holding back from God even one area of your life can seriously affect your relationship with God, as we saw with Saul.

4. You must be careful not to tear down individual authors, teachers, counselors, or particular techniques when you are discussing solutions to personal problems. Instead, you should concentrate your conversation on biblical principles found in God's Word.

PREVIEW OF NEXT LESSON

The next lesson starts a new phase of the Bible Study. Lesson 5 deals with the "life history" of problems (i.e., how they begin, how they progress, and how they can be overcome to the glory of God). We will also begin working on the **VICTORY OVER FAILURES PLAN**.

LESSON 5
BIBLICAL DYNAMICS OF CHANGE

OPENING PRAYER AND SCRIPTURE MEMORY

Before you begin this lesson, ask for God's help in understanding His Word and for wisdom and strength to apply what you learn in the power of the Holy Spirit.

Begin memorizing *I Corinthians 10:13*. Also, review the Scripture memory passages assigned in the previous lessons. Then, be prepared to recite them at the end of this lesson.

Also, in your own words, please write out the meaning of the new memory verse below:

___

SELECTING A PERSONAL PROBLEM

During this Bible Study you will have the opportunity to work on a problem area in your life that the Lord has brought to your attention. As you proceed, you will be provided with guidance from the Scriptures to make and apply a biblical plan to respond God's way. This plan is called a **VICTORY OVER FAILURES PLAN**. It replaces the **VICTORY OVER FAILURES WORKSHEET** located at Supplements 7 and 8 of the current *Self-Confrontation* manual published in 1991. The plan is a tool that has been developed to help you overcome any difficulty of life with the full expectation of complete and lasting victory. To live victoriously in a lasting, fruitful way, we first need to see how we have failed to live God's way, hence the phrase "victory over failures." By victory over "failures" we don't mean failures at business or failures in school. We mean having victory over failures to love biblically (what God calls sin) that keep us from having a joyful, vibrant, growing relationship with the Lord. Part of the process involves putting off the old manner of life and putting on new, righteous practices in their place *(Ephesians 4:22-24)*. The **VICTORY OVER FAILURES PLAN** describes how to do that in very practical ways and gives you a format you can follow.

The objective is to help you to rely wholly on the Scriptures and the work of the Holy Spirit Himself, rather than to rely on the superficial remedies of the world, or on your own strength. There are vast contrasts between God's way of dealing with problems and the world's way *(Isaiah 55:8-11)*. Only through applying God's principles can you expect lasting change. As you walk according to the biblical principles written in your **VICTORY OVER FAILURES PLAN**, you will develop Christlike character in your life. The changes will be enduring and meaningful, and you will be a faithful, fruitful vessel in God's hands.

You might ask the question, "Why should I actually have a plan written out to deal with a difficulty in my life?" One reason is found in a careful study of *I Corinthians 10:12-14*. In this passage, *verse 13* provides great hope that God will not allow a temptation or trial in your life that is more than you can handle. The previous verse, *I Corinthians 10:12*, warns that we must take heed (to our spiritual walk), or we might fall into sin. Isn't it interesting that in the very passage where God gives us a great promise of His sovereignty, He also tells us not to be presumptuous or arrogant about our ability to withstand temptation on our own? He tells us to "be careful" or "be prepared." The verb "take heed" has the idea of being watchful on a continuing basis in anticipation of a future event. It is the same word that Jesus used when He warned the disciples to stay alert in anticipation of His return. In the same way, we need to be alert to when we might be tempted and to be prepared to respond the way the Lord commands. Then in *I Corinthians 10:14*, we are told, "therefore" (referring back to *verse 13*), to "flee idolatry." In other words, in light of God's providing us with the way to endure trials, He tells us not to hesitate when tempted, but take immediate and decisive action. The **VICTORY OVER FAILURES PLAN** will help you to be prepared to take decisive, godly action when temptations come. Many temptations can be anticipated, especially where we have been tempted previously, and have yielded and sinned. Many times, we even put ourselves in the path of temptation unnecessarily. Making biblical plans ahead of time will help you to remember what to do when you face temptation, and will be an indication of your commitment before God to handle trials His way, in the power of the Holy Spirit.

You may ask yourself, "Will I need to make written plans all my life?" After you have become established in overcoming temptations through the development and practice of biblical plans, you will become more able to think through how to deal with sins in your life. This is because the **VICTORY OVER FAILURES PLAN** has become part of your life. Then it will only be occasionally that you might need to write out a **VICTORY OVER FAILURES PLAN** for complicated matters.

The **VICTORY OVER FAILURES PLAN** is based on biblical principles, and guides you to victory even in the midst of any trial, test, or temptation of life. The **PLAN** has four purposes:

A. To help you learn how to judge yourself biblically;

B. To help you recognize specific biblical "put-offs" and "put-ons" for daily living;

C. To help you develop and act upon specific plans for biblical change; and

D. To help you make your specific biblical changes part of your daily walk in every area of your life.

Guidelines for the new procedure will be explained starting in this lesson and continuing in the remaining lessons. Included will be explanations, blank forms for you to photocopy, and examples to show you how to complete each step of the process.

You will be working on this plan as part of your homework for each of the remaining lessons.

A. To develop a **VICTORY OVER FAILURES PLAN**, you must start by completing **Worksheet 1: Description of the Problem**. A blank copy of this worksheet is on Page W54.

1. Under the "**Ongoing problem area**" section, write down the problem area that is of greatest hindrance to your walk with God *(Hebrews 12:1-2)*. To make the selection, use the following guidelines:

    a. Focus on dealing with a problem that is ongoing, not on one that you experience only occasionally. You may wish to review the **SAMPLE LIST OF PROBLEM AREAS** located on Page W55. It contains a list of problem areas with references to relevant sections of the *Self-Confrontation* manual. Also listed are some key passages of Scripture to help determine possible areas of failure.

    b. Seek the Lord's wisdom in determining the problem area to choose. Concentrate on an area in your life that requires the most immediate change, even though it may be difficult. The Lord is primarily concerned about your commitment to Him, not how much you can accomplish easily. So, choose the pattern that the Lord is convicting you to develop. To do this, ask yourself, "In what ways do I continue to show that I fail to love God and others?" *(based on Matthew 22:37-40; John 13:34-35; 14:15, 20-21; I Corinthians 13:4-8a)*. Ask the Holy Spirit to bring to your mind the specific ways you have sinned against the Lord and others.

    One of your tendencies with sinful habits may be to identify only those areas *you* want to change. However, when you seek to change some area of your life according to your own perceptions, you may focus on something that seems easy to do or that appeals to self-centered accomplishments (for example, overcoming fear of flying motivated by pride).

2. Under the "**Short description of the problem**" section, summarize the problem in one or two paragraphs. See Page W56 for a sample of a description written by a fictitious person who is angry and bitter toward a co-worker. Subsequent samples represent how he might complete a **VICTORY OVER FAILURES PLAN** based on these guidelines.

Work on this project a little each day as you are doing your other homework. If you are studying this Bible Study as a part of a class or group study, the teacher or leader may be available to comment on your assignment, providing additional Scriptures that may apply or additional insights into the problem area. It could be a very helpful exchange for both you and your teacher or leader. Consider making arrangements with your leader to turn in this part of your homework. However, this is optional. If you decide to turn this in, make a copy for the leader so that you can continue working on the next steps during the following week. You will not be discussing your personal problem, or anyone else's problem, in your group.

Throughout this Bible Study, you will be learning and applying the biblical principles of how to face, deal with, and endure the problem you have selected. The general procedure for dealing with any other problem area will be the same; therefore this exercise will be very helpful in preparing you for dealing biblically with all problems that come your way in the future.

Worksheet 1: Description of the Problem

Ongoing problem area:

_____

_____

This portion should be the identification of the ongoing difficulty that is of greatest hindrance to your walk with God *(Hebrews 12:1-2)*.

Short description of the problem:

_____
_____
_____
_____
_____
_____
_____
_____
_____
_____
_____
_____
_____
_____
_____
_____
_____
_____
_____
_____

VOFP Worksheet 1 © Biblical Counseling Foundation

Permission is granted to reproduce this form for personal or ministry use

SAMPLE LIST OF PROBLEM AREAS

A sample set of problem areas is listed below. Scripture references containing biblical principles, "put-offs," and "put-ons" for these problem areas can be found in the indicated lessons of the *Self-Confrontation* manual. In some of the referenced lessons, the problem area may not be specifically listed, but the biblical principles and biblical references will apply.

Anger — Lesson 11

Bitterness — Lesson 11

Communication, sinful (lying, slander, arguing, cursing) — Lesson 13

Contentment, lack of — Lesson 6

Envy, jealousy, covetousness, greed — Lessons 9 and 10

Depression (despair, lack of fulfillment of responsibilities, total inactivity) — Lesson 18

Drug abuse — Lessons 20 and 21

Drunkenness — Lessons 20 and 21

Eating problems (Overeating; starving self, called "anorexia;" or binging on food and purging self, called "bulimia") — Lessons 9, 10, 20, and 21

Fear (including "panic attacks") — Lesson 19

Gambling — Lessons 20 and 21

Grief focused on self — Lessons 9, 10, 20 and 21

Lust — Lessons 9, 10, 20-21

Marriage problems — Lessons 14 and 15

Parent-child problems — Lessons 16 and 17

Reconciliation problems — Lessons 12 and 13

Relationship problems (marriage, relative, acquaintances, etc.) — Lessons 12-17, 20-21

Satanic influences — Lessons 20 and 21

Self-belittlement — Lessons 9 and 10

Self-exaltation — Lessons 9 and 10

Self-pity — Lessons 9 and 10

Sexual sins (adultery, fornication, homosexuality, pornography) — Lessons 20 and 21

Stealing (covetousness) — Lesson 9

Stewardship problems (body, time, material goods, abilities) — Lesson 10

Unforgiveness — Lesson 12

Worry (anxiety) — Lesson 19

Some key passages of Scripture to help determine possible problem areas:

Proverbs Chapters 15 and 18

Romans Chapters 12 - 14

I Corinthians 13:4-8a

Ephesians 4:22 - 6:9

Colossians Chapter 3

I Peter 2:11 - 3:17

Sample Worksheet 1: Description of the Problem

Ongoing problem area:

Anger and bitterness toward my co-worker

This portion should be the identification of the ongoing difficulty that is of greatest hindrance to your walk with God *(Hebrews 12:1-2)*.

Short description of the problem:

I have a very bad relationship with my co-worker at the office. We argue about almost everything. He criticizes my work all the time. He blames me for mistakes that I don't make and lies to the boss about me. I get so bitter that I can't concentrate on my work, and the situation gets worse. I am about to lose my job because of our arguments over responsibilities of projects that our boss has assigned. My co-worker takes the easy jobs and leaves the hard ones for me. I would like to quit, but I need the money. So I just get more angry and bitter.

NOTE: In order to make this description more accurate, please read the explanation for how to complete a list of specific failures in Lesson 6, Pages W67-W69). You will see an evaluation of this sample worksheet on Page W71.

VOFP Worksheet 1 © Biblical Counseling Foundation

INTRODUCTION TO THE LESSON

A. Turn to the **TABLE OF CONTENTS** on Page 6 of the *Self-Confrontation* manual. Remember that the first eight lessons are foundational to the rest of the Bible Study. In Lessons 1-4, we covered who you are in Christ and all that is available to you as a believer. We also saw the inadequacy of man's way as contrasted with the complete sufficiency of God's way in dealing with life.

Notice that Lessons 5-8 all have to do with change. They present a biblical methodology for change. Believers are to be undergoing a continuing process of change. What does *Romans 8:29* say about God's plan for believers?

1. _____

This means that the normal experience of the believer should be progressive change toward spiritual maturity. While God conforms, that is changes, believers into the image of Christ, He has provided in His Word specific guidance on how to put off the old sinful ways and put on the new ways of godliness.

Sadly, even many Christian counselors learn and practice secular methodologies for helping people change because they are not aware that the Scriptures present very specific and profound guidance for facing, dealing with, and enduring every problem of life.

Lessons 5-8 describe this very important process of change. Lesson 5 describes the "life history" of problems (i.e., how they begin, worsen, and end). Lessons 6-8 build on Lesson 5, describing the methodology for dealing with problems biblically.

B. This lesson demonstrates that a person's life will become progressively more set in sin with correspondingly graver consequences if he continues to live according to man's way (the downward spiral). It emphasizes the importance of doing God's Word, which will lead to lasting biblical change. The teaching on obedience to the Word also highlights that spiritual maturity will only come through an obedient walk of faith (the upward path).

The biblical principles in Lesson 5 fall under three major points: 1) how problems begin and worsen if not dealt with God's way (the downward spiral), 2) how to begin to overcome problems quickly (the upward path), and 3) how to walk in a manner worthy of the Lord's calling (being a doer of the Word).

It is important to emphasize that biblical change is based on salvation, a commitment to live each day in a manner that pleases God, and a constant reliance on God's resources.

C. Read the purposes of **LESSON 5: BIBLICAL DYNAMICS OF CHANGE** (*Self-Confrontation*, Page 82).

THE DOWNWARD SPIRAL

A. To discover what happens when we neglect God's way, read *Principle 10* on Page 83 of the *Self-Confrontation* manual. Then, turn to the first chapter of *Romans* in the Bible. This chapter gives a biblical example of the downward spiral. Highlight the reference to *Romans 1:20-32* in your manual and study this passage as follows:

1. Read *verses 18-20* and note that man's separation from God is not a matter of a lack of knowledge. So what is the issue?

   2. _____

   In *verse 19*, we see that God reveals Himself to mankind from within man by means of man's conscience, and in *verse 20*, God reveals Himself from outside man by means of God's creation. The issue is not how much you know about God — it is how you respond to what you know of Him that shows your focus. The fact is that man willfully rejects God.

2. Read *verses 21-23*. What are the consequences in people's lives when they reject God?

3. _____

_____

It seems incredible that people will worship animals and even images they have carved out of wood. Yet, this shows how foolish man can be when his primary objective is to create an idol that he can manipulate to achieve his own foolish desires. As long as man creates the idols he chooses to worship, he maintains control.

3. Note in *verses 24, 26*, and *28* that *"God gave them over"* to their own lusts and depravity. Why? Because often, the only thing that will get a fool's attention is consequences. God helps them see the consequences of their actions so that they may see their error and may be encouraged to repent.

ILLUSTRATION: In these verses, homosexual behavior is presented as a primary example of depravity. Notice that this illustration does not only apply just for the period of time when the book of *Romans* was written, but the same situation exists today.

Before and through the first half of the twentieth century, homosexuality was considered to be depraved and abhorrent. It was even declared to be a criminal act. There were hospitals and treatment centers where people were sent to deal with their homosexuality, but they had practically no success.

So, to deal with the lack of success, it was decided in the 1960s that homosexuality must merely be an "alternate lifestyle." The lifestyle was called "gay." But people still struggled and were defeated.

In order to justify their sin, homosexuals next claimed that they were not just following an alternate lifestyle, but that they were born with the tendency to be homosexual, and could not change. They argued that, since they were born to be homosexuals, they should celebrate and be proud of their behavior.

Now even young children are taught that homosexuality is a legitimate activity, and those who practice homosexuality should be protected by special civil rights and applauded for their lifestyle. You see the modern illustration of *Romans 1:24-32*.

---

4. In *verse 32*, how did they sink to the lowest depth?

4. _____

B. So you see that man has gradually sunk lower and lower. Let's look at this downward spiral in greater detail. Turn to **THE DOWNWARD SPIRAL: NEGLECTING OR REFUSING GOD'S WAY** (*Self-Confrontation*, Page 84).

1. First, let's see the context of the downward spiral by understanding the three levels of problems. In this lesson, we will introduce the three levels. In Lesson 6, we will describe them in more detail. Read the three paragraphs just below the box at the top. What are the names of the three levels typed in **boldface** print?

5. _____

_____

_____

2. In the paragraph beginning with, "Problems start in the **heart** ..." highlight in your manual and read *Matthew 15:18-19*. The "heart" in Scripture refers to the inner man (including the mind, intentions, and motives) where the real person is revealed. Where do all deeds (which include thoughts, speech, and actions) come from, according to *verses 18-19*?

   6. _____

   The heart is the source of all that is demonstrated in our lives.

3. In the paragraph beginning with, "Bad **feelings**," highlight in your manual *Genesis 4:6-7*. Also, write in *verse 5*. Then, read *Genesis 4:5*. Also read *I John 3:12*. What led to Cain's bad feelings?

   7. _____

4. The following illustration is an example of how a student might experience these three levels of a problem as he deals with his responsibility to study. ***NOTE:*** *See Page 84 of the Self-Confrontation manual.* The reason the illustration of a student was chosen is because all of us have been students or apprentices at some point in our lives.

ILLUSTRATION: Let's assume that this student just arrived at a boarding school and that this is the first time he is living away from home. His parents have provided funds for his schooling and they have exhorted him to study diligently.

During his first day of classes, each teacher also exhorted him to study diligently every evening. But when it was time to study, his roommates asked him to go with them to the student recreation center on campus. He remembered his responsibility to study; but because he was focused on self at the heart level, he soon decided to delay studying and, instead, went to the center with his roommates (doing level). He enjoyed himself so much that when he returned to the dormitory, it was too late to study.

The next day, he was anxious in class, but none of his teachers called on him for an answer. He was extremely relieved!

In the evening, it was a little easier to ignore his studies and, once again, to go to the recreation center with his companions. He was starting down the spiral as the focus of his sinful heart was being manifested by sinful deeds.

As a result of not studying, the student began to worry about failing the course. When his parents wrote and asked about his studies, he lied to them and told them he was doing fine. As you can see, he was sliding further down the spiral.

Finally, in desperation, he cheated on his exams and failed anyway. As a result, he felt guilty and depressed (at the feeling level).

In summary, this student's focus on self (heart level) led to the unbiblical deeds (the doing level). Each sin made it easier to commit another sin. As he continued to sin, he became depressed (the feeling level).

---

5. Now, suppose the student were to come to you for help when he was at the bottom of his downward spiral. Remember, you would not know immediately what led to his depression. What problem do you think he would present to you (put a check beside your answer below):

   ❏ a.   His feelings of being depressed;

   ❏ b.   The fact that he was lazy and cheated (the doing level); or

   ❏ c.   The fact that he is a sinful, self-centered person (the heart level)?

Most people in that situation would present their feelings of being depressed to you. This is where the Bible presents very different answers from the world's philosophies.

First, let's look at some of the ways that man would counsel the student. What the world would typically assume when the student presents the situation is that his depression is not his fault. Let's review some of man's approaches to dealing with this problem based on some of the columns under **MAN'S WAY** in the chart in Lesson 4 on Page 74 of the *Self-Confrontation* manual.

Followers of the first philosophy (the **Instinctual** approach) might say that no action should be taken until a thorough analysis of a person's history is conducted, often reaching back to early childhood. This analysis often takes months and even years.

Followers of the second philosophy (the **Behavioral** approach) would concentrate on reconditioning his behavior through positive and negative stimuli.

Followers of the third philosophy (the **Positive Potential** approach) would concentrate on fixing his feelings. They would encourage him to love himself more because they believe his depression is caused by low self-esteem.

Followers of the fourth philosophy (the **Spiritist** approach) would attempt to free the person from demonic bondage concentrating on prayer and deliverance rituals.

In contrast, the Bible assures the student that he can have victory quickly and completely by placing himself under the control of the Holy Spirit.

In the next section, we will determine from the Word of God what steps we must take to get out of the downward spiral and travel the upward path to victory.

BEGINNINGS OF BIBLICAL CHANGE

A. Read *Principle 11*, **BIBLICAL PRINCIPLES: BIBLICAL DYNAMICS OF CHANGE** (*Self-Confrontation*, Page 83).

The first and most important thing that you would do to help the student in the illustration is to examine whether or not he is saved. Why should you deal with salvation first?

8. _____

_____

If he is not saved, he will not be able to apply God's solutions in a lasting, meaningful way. If you present God's solutions without dealing with his salvation, he may apply biblical principles temporarily in his own strength, but you will not have dealt with his most significant problem. You must be careful not to help him be satisfied without the Lord.

If he is a believer, he needs to examine in what ways he is failing to love God and others. It would not be difficult for him to remember that he disobeyed God by not studying diligently, by lying to his parents, by cheating on the exam, etc. If he repents of these sins and obeys God, the Lord will provide not only the power to change quickly and completely, but also the contentment that only He can give.

B. Read the first sentence of *Principle 12*, **BIBLICAL PRINCIPLES: BIBLICAL DYNAMICS OF CHANGE** (*Self-Confrontation*, Page 83). Now, highlight in your manual and read *Ecclesiastes 12:13-14*. What does this passage tell you about commitment to the Lord?

9. _____

_____

W61

> **EXERCISE: IMPORTANCE OF FULFILLING DAILY RESPONSIBILITIES**
>
> Think of the activities that you typically dwell on or look forward to with eagerness and anticipation. Many of us think of unusual and infrequent events, such as job promotions, anniversaries, exciting events, retreats and seminars, vacations, or hobbies. Man tends to look to power, feeling-oriented pleasure, riches, recognition, etc., for contentment.
>
> In the book of *Ecclesiastes,* Solomon searched for contentment in all of these ways, and more, only to be frustrated over and over again. In fact, we tend to look at *Ecclesiastes* as the book of "vanities." But tucked within the book, Solomon states that he found the secret of contentment. He found fulfillment and satisfaction only in eating, drinking, and daily labor; in other words, in carrying out his normal, daily responsibilities (write next to *Principle 12* and read *Ecclesiastes 2:24, 3:12-13, 5:18*).
>
> Now, list at least six daily responsibilities that you have. These can be at home, work, school, church, etc.
>
> *10.* _____
> _____
> _____
> _____
> _____
> _____
>
> Now put a check mark (✓) to the right of the daily responsibilities in which you do not consistently find fulfillment and satisfaction.
>
> Our tendency is to focus on pleasurable things and events, but these are not normally where we have to make difficult choices to obey God or disobey Him. The difficult choices often come with the seemingly mundane tasks of life: taking out the garbage with cheerfulness, disciplining the children with patience and love, and so on. We can only have total satisfaction when we live in the way that God intended us to live. Remember, God created us to be content when we love Him and others sacrificially. Therefore, it is only when we are growing in love that we can be truly satisfied.
>
> When you think about it, the greatest opportunities to demonstrate sacrificial love are in the unpleasant situations of daily living. Why? Because it is in the daily tasks that we experience tests and trials, and it is in these same tests and trials that we must choose to love God and others or choose to focus on self. Do you remember the characteristics of love listed in *I Corinthians 13:4-8a*? The first characteristic mentioned is patience. There are many opportunities to practice patience when we are experiencing the trials of a typical day. So, it is in these tests and trials that significant growth in love results.
>
> Think about how this could revolutionize your life. Most of each day, and consequently most of life, involves fulfilling your daily responsibilities. Rather than begrudging the daily routine, you should look forward to each day's work finding great satisfaction as you grow in your love for God and your neighbor.
>
> The key to a victorious life is total commitment to the Lord through loving obedience in every area of life, whether ordinary and routine or extraordinary and unusual.

C. Read *Principle 13,* **BIBLICAL PRINCIPLES: BIBLICAL DYNAMICS OF CHANGE** *(Self-Confrontation,* Page 83). We must ask in faith for wisdom to live according to God's Word.

The place to begin the process of biblical change is within the present trial, temptation, or problem in your life. Highlight in your manual and turn to *James 1:5*. God says that He will give us answers. But many people will say, "I asked God for wisdom, but I didn't receive it." Why? Because they asked the wrong questions or had a wrong motivation.

For what situation does God promise wisdom? Notice the context of this passage. The first verses in *James, Chapter 1* are about trials. You see, the Lord will give us wisdom, but there are several conditions. First, it is for the current trial that you are to seek wisdom. You should not disconnect *verse 5* from *verses 2-4*. Second, God tells you in the sixth verse that you are to ask in faith without doubting. Third, God commands you in the twenty-second verse to obey, regardless of your feelings.

It is important to remember that you keep God's commandments in the present, not in the past or the future. Read *Hebrews 4:16*. At what time does God give you His grace?

11. _____

Your faith is tested in the present.

Answers to problems are not difficult to find if you focus on your present responsibilities. Remember that you only need to keep two commandments — love God and love your neighbor. Therefore, you only need to ask yourself, "In what way have I not been a loving person and how can I demonstrate love in the present situation?"

D. The procedures that the student should have followed are on Page 85 of the *Self-Confrontation* manual. Read **BEGINNINGS OF BIBLICAL CHANGE**. The steps in this section were included in the explanation of *Principles 11-13*. We have already looked at most of them.

THE UPWARD PATH

A. Read *Principle 14*, **BIBLICAL PRINCIPLES: BIBLICAL DYNAMICS OF CHANGE** (*Self-Confrontation*, Page 83). This points out that as you faithfully do the Lord's will, you will demonstrate Christlikeness in your life.

B. Read **THE UPWARD PATH: WALKING GOD'S WAY** (*Self-Confrontation*, Page 86). It is called the upward path because the Scriptures often refer to the believer's walk. This page should be read starting at the bottom and progressing upward; however, the list is not meant to be exhaustive nor in a rigid sequence.

DOING THE WORD

A. Note that in **THE UPWARD PATH**, there is a significant emphasis on keeping God's commandments, so let's look at **THE IMPORTANCE OF DOING THE WORD** on Page 87 of the *Self-Confrontation* manual.

On Pages 87 through 90, you will see many Scriptures on doing the Word (obedience to the Lord). You may be wondering why there are so many more Scripture verses on doing the Word than there are on explaining a believer's position in Christ. Which do you think is more difficult: understanding your position in Christ or consistently doing the Word?

12. _____

Scripture emphasizes doing the Word not because it is more important than understanding your position in Christ, but because doing the Word consistently is harder! The Lord in His grace typically gives us the most instruction in the very areas where it is the hardest to follow Him, or where we tend to go our own direction most. Do we struggle more with understanding and accepting God's goodness, or with denying self and living obediently?

13. _____

While it is important to know who we are in Christ, gaining understanding about our position in Christ does not require much explanation, and accepting this truth is not difficult. In contrast, doing the Word requires much more than understanding; it requires sacrificial love. This includes, for example, being patient when wronged, being kind, giving a blessing in response to insults, etc. Does doing the Word typically require following our feelings, or going against them?

14. _____

The Israelites had no difficulty in offering sacrifices on the altar. Their major problem was lack of obedience. For example, in Lesson 4 we read that Samuel told King Saul, *"Behold, to obey is better than sacrifice"* (I Samuel 15:22) and in *Proverbs 21:3* it is written, *"To do righteousness and justice is desired by the Lord more than sacrifice."*

In the New Testament, the Corinthian believers had an abundance of spiritual gifts, but they lacked obedience. As you read through both the Old and New Testaments, you realize that much of it is an exhortation to obedience.

With all the emphasis on living according to our feelings today, is it any wonder that believers need to be called back to a life of disciplined obedience?

Another point that needs to be made here is that doing the Word is not to be done blindly or for the wrong reason. Doing the Word is *not* being legalistic (unless one is doing it to obtain credit for self). Doing the Word is a loving response to God's love for us. Perhaps an illustration might be helpful.

ILLUSTRATION: A woman had a very unloving husband. Every day before he went to work, he would make a long list of tasks she was to complete before he returned home. No matter how hard she tried to complete the tasks, she never was successful. So, every night he would scold her for what he considered a very poor performance. Her life with this husband was very hard.

After a time, the husband died and a few years later she married another man who was kind and loving. They had a wonderful relationship and she was very happy.

One day as she was cleaning her home, she came across one of the lists of tasks that her former husband had written for her to do. As she looked at the list, she was amazed to discover that while she could not complete the list for the former husband no matter how hard she tried, she was now accomplishing *all* those things for her new husband.

The key application of this illustration is that before salvation, it was impossible to keep the Lord's commands consistently. When you are saved, you have a loving relationship espoused to the Lord. Following Him is not a matter of merely following a set of rules. Following His commands is not an exercise in legalistic do's and don'ts. It is not a way to earn our salvation or to gain favor with God to balance out our sin. It is a loving response to what God has so amazingly and marvelously done for us. It is now a matter of loving obedience in the empowering of the Holy Spirit.

B. Highlight in your manual and read the Scriptures referenced below. Write down your observations concerning doing the Word from each Scripture.

15. Ephesians 2:8-10 (in Section **I.** on Page 87): _____

_____

16. James 2:17-18 (in Section **I.** on Page 87): _____

_____

Note that it is inconsistent to claim that you have faith if you do not demonstrate your faith by good works.

17. *II Corinthians 5:10* (in the box on Page 87): _____

18. *I John 2:3-4* (in the box on Page 87): _____

19. *John 15:10-11* (in Paragraph C. on Page 89): _____

20. *James 1:25* (at the top of Page 90): _____

SCRIPTURE RECITATION

Recite *I Corinthians 10:13* to someone at home, in class, or elsewhere. Also, recite one of the previous memory passages chosen by the listener. Put a check here (___) when you have accurately recited the verses.

QUESTIONS AND CONCLUSION

A. What is God's plan for believers *(Romans 8:29)*?

21. _____

B. What are the three levels of problems dealt with in this lesson?

22. _____

C. Obedience often requires going against our:

23. _____

D. What was the most significant truth you learned in completing this lesson?

24. _____

Remember that obedience is not legalism. It is an act of love for God and our neighbor, in response to what God has done for us. Our obedience and love for God are demonstrated not so much in situations where it is easy to obey, but often in the routine, mundane, and seemingly unpleasant tasks of life.

PREVIEW OF NEXT LESSON

In the next lesson, we will introduce the four elements of how to face, deal with, and endure biblically the problems of life.

Also, we will cover the three levels of problems in more detail, and in so doing we will look into the place of feelings in our lives. You will learn how you can have hope, joy, and peace in *every* situation of life.

LESSON 6
BIBLICAL BASIS FOR CHANGE

OPENING PRAYER AND SCRIPTURE MEMORY

Before you begin this lesson, ask for God's help in understanding His Word and for wisdom and strength to apply what you learn in the power of the Holy Spirit.

Begin memorizing *Romans 8:28-29*. Also, review the Scripture memory passages assigned in the previous lessons. Then, be prepared to recite them at the end of this lesson.

Also, in your own words, please write out the meaning of the new memory verses below:

_____

_____

_____

_____

PERSONAL PLAN FOR CHANGE

How are you progressing in describing the problem on which you will be working? If God has already shown you the problem area on which He wants you to work at changing, you are ready to take the next step which is prayerfully to complete *Worksheet 2: Lists of Specific Failures to Live Biblically*. A blank form is shown on Page W70.

In order to know how God intends for you to change, you must first describe clearly *what* needs to be changed in your life. This worksheet helps you learn to judge yourself biblically.

First, read **Evaluation — Sample Worksheet 1: Description of the Problem** on Page W69. This will help you understand what needs correcting when completing *Worksheet 2*.

On *Worksheet 2*, list your unbiblical deeds related to the problem area you selected. For some problem areas, the unbiblical deeds may involve offenses to specific people. For others, it may involve sins only against God. Keep in mind that offenses against others are also sins against God.

Once you have worked through the plan with one person, you may find that there are others you have sinned against. You will need to use a separate sheet for each person you have offended in order to avoid confusion.

Keep in mind that you should list only your *own* failures, not another person's *(Matthew 7:5)*. God tells us to concentrate on our own sins first. Otherwise, we cannot even understand the other person's life accurately. We do not see clearly how to deal with our brother's sins until we have first dealt with our own sins.

A. Under the "**List of speech and actions related to the ongoing problem area**" section, write your sinful speech and actions (not your thoughts) committed against the person you have identified.

   NOTE: If the problem involves sins only against the Lord, you would only fill out the bottom of the worksheet.

B. Under the "**List of thoughts, speech, and actions against the Lord alone**" section, list your unbiblical thoughts, speech, and actions committed only before the Lord. These are failures that do not involve other people (for example, sinful thoughts — even about others, or sins of grumbling, shouting, or using curse words when you are alone, stomping your feet or slamming doors while no one else is around, not spending time in daily devotions, lusting, drug abuse when you are alone, etc.).

NOTE: Thoughts are not included in the first list since sinful thoughts are only committed against the Lord. However, if thoughts are communicated to the one offended, through speech or actions, these must be added to the first list.

C. In making your list, make sure it meets the following criteria:

1. **Be specific.** Write exactly how you demonstrated your failures in each situation.

   Why is it important to be specific in listing your failures?

   1. _____

   _____

   a. It is very important to be specific. Change takes place in specific ways, i.e., specific changes in thoughts, speech, and actions. Change does not take place in generalities. For example, you would not just say "I was angry." Rather, you would list the specific ways in which you have demonstrated your anger. List specific unbiblical thoughts (such as grumbling inside self, devising sarcastic responses, etc.), speech (including the tone and volume of your voice), and actions (including looks, gestures, etc.). These are the things you can change.

   b. Following are examples of the wrong and right ways to describe failures.

      1) *Wrong description:* "I get *angry* with my co-worker often." This is too general. Change is demonstrated only by acting in specific ways.

      2) *Correct description:* "I think about getting revenge" (thoughts); or "I speak loudly frequently to my co-worker with a harsh tone of voice" (speech); or "I glared at my co-worker, then stomped out of the room, slamming the door behind me" (actions).

   c. When developing your specific list, you should take into account the following:

      1) Do not include specific details about sinful thoughts that may present a stumbling block to you or others to whom you may need to show the list. It is enough to list the kinds of thoughts (e.g., grumbling, argumentative, reviling). Keeping a written record of exact words can serve as a reminder to keep you thinking those sinful thoughts.

      2) Do not identify emotions (i.e., feelings) because God does not hold you responsible for how you feel; in addition, you cannot change your feelings by a direct act of your will. Feelings, in themselves, are not sinful, since nowhere in the Scriptures does God command you to change them.

      3) It may be difficult for you to determine whether some activities are sinful, where the deed is not specifically named as sin in the Scriptures (e.g., modes of dress, certain items ingested, companions, activities, etc.). In these situations, ask yourself the following questions.

a) Is this profitable (in other words, does this contribute toward the development of godly traits or help to accomplish biblical responsibilities in my life or in the lives of others)? Read *I Corinthians 6:12* and write an example of something that is biblically permissible, but may not be beneficial.

2. _____
_____
_____

b) Does this bring me under its power or am I controlled by it in any way? Again, read *I Corinthians 6:12* and write an example of something that is biblically permissible, but could become an obsession.

3. _____
_____
_____

c) Is this an area of spiritual weakness (a stumbling block) in my life? Read *Matthew 18:8-9* and write an example of something that could be a stumbling block in a person's life.

4. _____
_____
_____

d) Could this lead another believer in Christ to stumble? Read *I Corinthians 8:9-13* and write an example of something that could be a stumbling block in another person's life.

5. _____
_____
_____

e) Does this edify (build up) others or, stated in another way, is this the biblically loving thing to do? Read *I Corinthians 10:23-24* and write an example of something that does not build up or edify.

6. _____
_____
_____

f) Does this glorify God? Read *I Corinthians 10:31*.

2. **Be thorough.**

For each situation in which you know you failed to love biblically, it is important to consider thoughts, speech, and actions. Remember that it is possible to sin in many ways in a very short period of time. For example, if you had an argument with another person, within seconds you might have:

a. Reviled and grumbled about the person in your mind (thoughts),

b. Shouted at the person, used a harsh tone of voice, called him/her tearing down names (speech),

c. Given hard looks, thrown objects, and slammed doors (actions).

3. **Do not shift blame.** When making your list, take care not to place blame on anyone else for your failures *(in light of Ezekiel 18:20; Matthew 7:5)*. Do not write such statements as "I slammed the door in my wife's face when she yelled at me." Instead say, "I slammed the door in my wife's face." Regardless of what the other person did, it is not an excuse for your sins. It is important that you do not use the list of your own sins as a way of pointing blame at the other person.

4. **Do not minimize or excuse sin.** In listing your failures, take care not to minimize or excuse away your sin *(based on Proverbs 28:13; Ezekiel 18:20; I John 1:5-9)*. Do not write such statements as "I told a little lie, but I was tired and couldn't think of anything better to say." Instead say, "I lied."

Page W69 provides an evaluation of the sample *Worksheet 1: Description of the Problem* from Lesson 5, Page W56. Note the blameshifting, etc. Then, notice that the sample of *Worksheet 2* on Page W71 is specific and thorough, and does not shift blame nor excuse sin.

*NOTE: It is important to repent and confess all sins to God as soon as you recognize them as sins (I John 1:8-10); however, before going to be reconciled with another human being, you must be careful to take proper precautions so that you do not place a stumbling block before the person you have offended. If you are not careful, even the way you approach reconciliation could be a stumbling block to them. It may be helpful to develop a biblical plan for change first. Putting the plan into effect is a practical way of demonstrating to the one you have offended how serious you are in your intention to change and not repeat the offense. A **"Forgiveness/Reconciliation" Plan** is described later in this Bible Study.*

Keep working on this list a little each day as you are doing your other homework.

This week, read *I Corinthians 13:4-6* as a reminder on how to love biblically. If you are specific and thorough, you should have no problem in listing at least ten failures.

Your list will not be discussed in class. But if you turn it in to your leader or teacher for evaluation, make a copy for yourself before you hand it in. You will need to refer to it for your homework in the next lesson.

Evaluation — Sample Worksheet 1: Description of the Problem

Ongoing problem area:
Anger and bitterness toward my co-worker

This portion should be the identification of the ongoing difficulty that is of greatest hindrance to your walk with God *(Hebrews 12:1-2)*.

Short description of the problem: *Blameshifting; justifying own sin*

I have a very bad relationship with my co-worker at the office. We argue about almost everything. (He criticizes my work all the time.) He (blames me for mistakes that I don't make and lies to the boss about me.) (I get so bitter) that I can't concentrate on my work, and the situation gets worse. (I am about to lose my job because of our arguments) over responsibilities of projects that our boss has assigned. (My co-worker takes the easy jobs and leaves the hard ones for me.) I would like to quit, but I need the money. So (I just get more angry and bitter.)

Not thorough   *Not specific*   *Blameshifting*   *Not specific; not thorough*

VOFP Worksheet 1

Worksheet 2:
Lists of Specific Failures to Live Biblically

List of speech and actions related to the ongoing problem area:

_____
_____
_____
_____
_____
_____
_____
_____
_____
_____
_____
_____
_____
_____
_____
_____
_____
_____
_____
_____

List of thoughts, speech, and actions against the Lord alone:

_____
_____
_____
_____
_____
_____
_____
_____
_____

Sample Worksheet 2:
Lists of Specific Failures to Live Biblically

List of speech and actions related to the ongoing problem area:

1. Often, I speak to my co-worker in an angry way. I speak with a loud voice using condemning and accusing words.

2. I argue with my co-worker every day, and I often speak with a harsh tone of voice and say tearing down words to my co-worker.

3. I gossip about my co-worker to my employer and others in the office saying tearing down things, and I complain to my family members about my situation at work.

List of thoughts, speech, and actions against the Lord alone:

1. I have bitter, vengeful thoughts toward my co-worker, not only at the office, but in many other places.

2. When I pray, I grumble and complain to the Lord about my situation at work.

3. When on my way home from work, I think and speak to myself about sharp, tearing down statements I might make to my co-worker.

© Biblical Counseling Foundation   VOFP Worksheet 2

INTRODUCTION TO THE LESSON

A. In Lesson 5, you saw how a person's life will become progressively more set in sin, with correspondingly graver consequences if he continues to live according to man's way (the downward spiral). The lesson emphasized the importance of obedience to God's Word to accomplish lasting biblical change, since spiritual maturity will only come through an obedient walk of faith (the upward path).

In Lessons 6-8 we will begin to study the upward path of lasting biblical change. These three lessons describe the four elements of how to face, deal with, and endure biblically the tests and trials of life. The four elements are: 1) biblical understanding, 2) biblical hope, 3) biblical change, and 4) biblical practice (doing the Word). These four elements are not listed in your manual, but because they form the structure for the remaining lessons, they will be repeated many times. These four elements were not selected arbitrarily. They are a summary of how God has dealt with His children throughout the Scriptures, starting with Adam and Eve.

This lesson covers the first two elements: biblical understanding, and biblical hope. We will cover the three levels of problems in more detail than last lesson and, in so doing, we will look into the place of feelings in our lives. We will also be reminded of the biblical hope that is available in every situation of life.

If you were to re-title this lesson, you might say that this is a lesson of re-defining terms. This is necessary because the world has polluted many terms that are used in Scripture and has changed their meanings completely. The church has then read those polluted meanings back into the Scriptures. As a result, there is much misunderstanding regarding what God's Word really teaches regarding such common words as "heart," "hope," "joy," "peace," etc. In this lesson, we will re-define these and other terms according to their biblical usage.

B. Read the purposes of **LESSON 6: BIBLICAL BASIS FOR CHANGE** (*Self-Confrontation*, Page 96). Also, read the box at the top of the page, and highlight the words, "you can count on."

BIBLICAL UNDERSTANDING

A. Read *Principles 15-19*, **BIBLICAL PRINCIPLES: BIBLICAL BASIS FOR CHANGE** (*Self-Confrontation*, Page 97). These principles address understanding our problems at the three levels.

B. Turn to **THREE LEVELS OF PROBLEMS** (*Self-Confrontation*, Pages 99-100). Biblical understanding at these three levels is the first of four elements for facing, dealing with, and enduring problems biblically. In order to understand the problem biblically, we need to examine each of the three problem levels. In Lesson 5, the three levels of the problem were listed in the order of the source of the problems, which is the heart level, followed by the doing and feeling levels. In this lesson, we begin with the feeling level, because typically that is the level at which people first become alert to the fact that they have problems.

1. **Feeling level**

a. Read Paragraphs A. and B. on Page 99 of the *Self-Confrontation* manual. How a person feels is not a reliable indication of the condition of a person's heart. In the example in Paragraph A., David experienced many horrible feelings (both in his emotions and in his body) while he tried to hide his sin with Bathsheba. On the other hand, as illustrated in Paragraph B., the Israelites rejoiced as they sinned while they became drunk, worshiped the golden calf, and committed sensuality and immorality. Can you think of situations in which a person may not have good feelings, and yet there is no sin involved?

7. _____
_____

Unpleasant feelings could be the result of an illness, such as the flu. A chemical or hormonal imbalance could cause feelings of gloom even though there may be nothing wrong at the heart level.

Feelings are involuntary. They are caused indirectly, not directly. Feelings are not willed into being. They are indicators, not instigators. Feelings, in and of themselves, are not sin.

How do we know that feelings are not sin and that God does not hold us responsible for changing our feelings? We are never commanded anywhere in the Scriptures to change them. God only commands us to change our deeds.

b. Read Paragraph C. on Page 99. Because most feelings are involuntary responses to a person's thoughts, speech, or actions that arise in the context of the circumstances of life, feelings may provide clues that a person is sinning. Therefore, feelings should not be ignored. Consider the following illustration.

> **ILLUSTRATION:** A good way to understand feelings is to compare them to the oil warning light in a car. The purpose of the warning light is to communicate that there is something wrong under the hood. When one is driving along on the highway and the oil light comes on, what types of things may be wrong?
>
> 8. _____
>
> Sometimes, the oil light itself may be malfunctioning. For all of these situations, even the one with the malfunctioning oil light, the light is a signal that the driver needs to examine the automobile and determine what the real problem is. Then, as necessary, he must take corrective action as a result of this examination. If the driver ignores or punches out the warning light because it is a nuisance, he may soon find himself sitting behind the wheel of a vehicle that has a serious problem.
>
> In the same way, if you ignore or merely soothe your feelings and do not correct the underlying problem, you may have more serious problems later. You may actually be putting a salve on a guilty conscience that is being pricked by the Holy Spirit.

c. God gave us feelings for our good. Feelings usually provide the first indication that we need to pay attention to what is happening, either good or bad. Keep in mind, however, that while feelings are helpful indicators, we are not to follow our feelings. God tells us to obey whether we feel like it or not, and He enables us to obey.

2. **Doing Level** — Read the lists in Section **II.** on Pages 99 and 100 of the *Self-Confrontation* manual. Deeds, not feelings, are the primary *observable* indicators of the inner person. Review *Matthew 15:18-19*. List all the sinful deeds you see in these verses, grouped by whether they are thoughts, speech, or actions.

   9. Thoughts: _____

   10. Speech: _____

   11. Actions: _____

   Deeds would include anything in these three categories. They can include sinful thoughts, sinful speech, or sinful actions. Notice in Section **II.** that the deeds listed in the third column (saying unkind words and being critical) are indicators of the heart problem of arrogance. We will cover each of these in more detail later.

3. **Heart level** — The world's focus regarding the heart is primarily on the emotions. But what do the Scriptures say about the heart? Section **III.** answers this question.

   a. Read Paragraphs A. and B. on Page 100 of the *Self-Confrontation* manual. Note that the use of the word "heart" in the Bible is often very different from the secular view of "heart."

   b. Before reading Paragraphs C. and D., read Paragraph F. on Page 100 and highlight in your manual and read *Jeremiah 17:9-10*. Who is the only one who can see a person's heart completely?

   12. _____

   Notice that in *verse 10*, though God knows our hearts fully, He deals with us at the "deeds" or doing level.

   c. Read Paragraph D. and highlight in your manual and read *Luke 5:22*. In this passage, to what does Jesus liken the heart?

   13. _____

   We see here that Jesus mentioned reasoning as being in the heart. Notice that Jesus associates the heart with the mind, not with feelings or emotions. Have you ever heard someone say, "I knew it in my mind, but it wasn't until it got to my heart that it became a part of my life?" The erroneous emphasis on feelings in the world today is a result of the misconception that the heart is primarily associated with feelings.

   Since the mind is closely associated with the heart, this should encourage us to evaluate our thought life carefully. What does *II Corinthians 10:5* say about our thoughts?

   14. _____

   How does this principle apply to your life? Ask the Lord to reveal where your thoughts need to be taken captive. Check here (__) when you have finished.

In summary, all three levels of an individual's problem are important to examine because they are interrelated: the basic heart attitude leads to deeds (thoughts, speech, and actions) and sometimes directly to feelings. Deeds, in turn, reveal to an individual, and often to others, a little bit about the spiritual condition of the heart. While all three levels are important to evaluate, only God knows the heart fully, and feelings are spontaneous. Therefore, the Scripture urges believers to concentrate on doing the Word (the doing level).

Remember, no one can *make* a person sin. We know this because when God gives us a command, He also gives us the capability to obey it. We always have a choice of whether or not to sin.

This is in sharp contrast to the world's emphasis on "fixing" the feelings.

In what ways do you see the world focusing on fixing feelings, rather than dealing with the doing level and heart level?

15. _____
_____
_____
_____

This brings us to the second element of how to face, deal with, and endure every problem of life: biblical hope. Let's turn to Page 101 of the *Self-Confrontation* manual.

BIBLICAL HOPE

A. Read the contents of the box at the top of Page 101 of the *Self-Confrontation* manual, entitled **BIBLICAL HOPE**. Then, highlight the first and third sentences. Hope is much more than a wish. It is a confident expectation of (a looking forward to) God's fulfillment of His promises in your life. No believer can legitimately say he has no hope, since God places His hope in you at salvation. You may grow and deepen in hope, but all believers already have hope, whether they recognize it or not. Read Pages 101-102. We will cover some of these Scriptures as we proceed further through this lesson.

B. For an explanation of biblical hope, please turn back to the biblical principles on Page 98 of the *Self-Confrontation* manual.

1. Read *Principle 20*. Then, highlight in your manual and read *Romans 6:6-7, 18*.

   Let's say that a person has a life-dominating practice of sin, such as drunkenness. Many in the world would say that drunkenness is an illness. The Bible calls drunkenness sin. How can it possibly bring hope to point out that this person is committing sin and is not subject to an illness?

   16. _____
   _____

   This is in sharp contrast with the world's approach to problems such as alcohol abuse. The world calls one who is controlled by alcohol an "alcoholic." This implies that he has a disease. Viewing the problem as a disease does not offer much hope because all you can do then is to cope with (which means to learn to live with, or merely to put up with) the problem of alcohol. Relieving the symptoms of drunkenness, anger, depression, etc. without dealing with sin is shallow and would, at most, only provide artificial and temporary comfort. This does not deal with the basic problem and, thus, does not provide biblical hope.

   No sinner is beyond the reach of God even though he may have placed himself under the control of sin for many years. After becoming a believer, he can stop his drinking immediately and live victoriously by God's power. This brings tremendous hope to someone who has been a drunkard for years and has tried many times to break his bondage to alcohol. Yes, he may still have strong cravings for some time to come, but he does not ever have to yield to temptation again. He is finally free and empowered by God to live in great victory.

Read *Romans 6:18*. What does God say about believers?

17. _____

In *verse 7* we read that you are set free from sin, but in *verse 18* you are a slave to righteousness. You go from being a slave to sin to being a slave to righteousness. Does that sound like freedom to you? Many would say it does not.

ILLUSTRATION: Think about a guitar or violin string. Sometimes a string breaks and you must replace it. When you get a new string it usually comes in a package coiled up all by itself. When you take it out of the package it looks free, but really it is only loose. It is not truly free until it is put on the instrument and the proper tension applied for it to sound on pitch. Only then is it finally free to fulfill its purpose and be played by the musician. In the same way, it is only when you are attached to the Lord (i.e., only when you are saved), that you are truly free. Only then are you able to live in the tension that God has designed for you, to respond in God's way, and to fulfill the purpose for which He created you.

Keep in mind that dealing with sin in a person's life is of first importance, because sin affects his relationship with God. When sin is confessed and repentance takes place, the deeper problem of the heart is dealt with, and biblical hope is immediate.

2. Read *Principle 21* on Page 98 of the *Self-Confrontation* manual. Then, highlight in your manual and read *I Corinthians 10:13*.

ILLUSTRATION: Because of greed, merchants for hundreds of years up to the late 19th century would send ships out as empty as possible to collect cargo and treasure. On the return trip, they would direct the captains to overload the ships. On the first leg of the journey, ships would be so light (with no load) that they would be tossed to and fro in storms and would be prone to capsize. On the return, the ships would be so full that they would sink in turbulent seas, riding too low in the water. As a result, Samuel Plimsoll, a member of the British Parliament, initiated a bill to require all ships to have a horizontal line painted on their hulls to show the ideal weight with which they should be loaded for safety. The bill became law, and even today, this line is still painted on ships. This "ideal weight" line is known as the "Plimsoll line."

In the same way, God places His own "ideal weight" line on every believer. Although a believer can be heavily burdened, God knows how much weight (trials) each one needs and can face; and no believer ever needs to be overcome by any "weight" of life that will cause him to sink spiritually. God will never allow anything into a believer's life that will cause him to fall to temptation and sin.

While *I Corinthians 10:13* provides great hope, it presents a warning at the same time. If a person gives in to a temptation, he cannot blame anything or anyone else for his sin.

It is also important to note that in *I Corinthians 10:13*, God states there is an escape. From what is the escape?

18. _____

_____

Note that the situation may not go away. It may even intensify. But God says that you will be able not only to face and deal with any difficulty of life, but also to endure it. Enduring the difficulty means to live in victory whether or not the difficulty disappears. This is a marvelous hope. But it is also sobering, because when you sin, it is not because circumstances are too much for you to bear. Instead, you sin because you choose to do so. To sin is a choice.

3. Read *Principle 22* on Page 98 of the *Self-Confrontation* manual. Then, highlight in your manual and read *Hebrews 4:15-16*. What characteristics of Jesus do you see in these verses?

   19. _____

   This is not a passive entering into our feelings. He understands each situation and actively works in our lives. Notice that God's help is provided at the time of need (literally "at the exact time"). For the believer, grace is promised at the exact time of need, not sooner nor later. Like a lifetime travel ticket, it is always available but applicable only when it is needed.

   > **ILLUSTRATION:** Have you ever said to someone something like, "I can't understand how Martha could possibly have peace in the midst of the pain she is experiencing with cancer?" It is not surprising that you would not understand because you are not in the midst of that trial and you do not need God's grace to deal with the situation that Martha is in. The Lord will give you exactly the grace you need at the time you need it, not before.

4. Read *Principle 23* on Page 98 of the *Self-Confrontation* manual.

   a. Highlight in your manual and look at *James 1:2-4*. What does God say in this passage about trials?

   20. _____

   God tells us that every trial is an *opportunity* to become more mature. Trials are not obstacles to spiritual growth when you respond to them in a biblical manner. Remember the "Plimsoll line"? God allows just enough trials to encourage maximum growth, neither too few trials nor too many.

   The phrase "counting (or considering) it all joy" in this passage is not dependent on feelings. It indicates an inner contentment and satisfaction that comes from God, independent of circumstances. A good example is found in *Hebrews 12:2*. What was the joy set before Jesus?

   21. _____

   Did Jesus feel good about going to the cross?

   22. _____

   Can you think of a verse in the Gospels that demonstrates this?

   23. _____

   As Jesus was going through His most difficult trial (the crucifixion and separation from His Father), His focus was on the end result — that He would be back with His Father.

   The word, "joy," is only one of many biblical words that the world has redefined. Other examples are the words, "heart," "hope," and "peace."

   b. Then, in *Principle 23* highlight and read *Romans 8:28-29*. Notice that God works all things together for good in your life. Many people have the wrong idea of what actually is good for them. They sometimes think that "good" means that circumstances and relationships work out according to the way they want them to work out. Often, they describe *experiences* as good or bad.

> **ILLUSTRATION:** Certain medicines include ingredients that, if taken separately or included in the medicine in the wrong amount, could kill a person. However, because these ingredients are mixed in the right amount, they are very beneficial. For example, if taken in the right amount nitroglycerin can be a lifesaver when a person is having a heart attack. It is also a powerful explosive that can destroy many lives.
>
> In the same way, God actively works out His plan and always does what is good for us even if He must discipline us in the process. We may view certain painful experiences as bad, but God always works them together for good to those who love Him and are called according to His purpose.

What is the "good" for us according to *Romans 8:29*?

24. _____

c. Finally, highlight in your manual and read *Genesis 50:20*. What were some of the trials Joseph faced? Read the following passages and list the trials and injustices that God allowed in his life:

25. *Genesis 37:23-28* — _____

26. *Genesis 39:11-20* — _____

27. *Genesis 40:12-14, 23* — _____

In all these, Joseph did not take revenge or complain. Rather, he trusted the Lord to use these events for good. He did not know exactly how they might be used in his life, but he knew that God was faithful.

List at least one example of a trial in your life which you now recognize that God used for your good, even though you may not have recognized it at the time.

28. _____

Trials not only mature you, but they also make you useful.

5. Read *Principle 24* on Page 98 of the *Self-Confrontation* manual.

   a. Highlight in your manual and read *Psalm 119:165*. What could be a cause of losing your peace or of your stumbling?

   29. _____

   You can easily lose peace and joy when you depend on some aspect of creation and not the Creator or His Word.

   b. Highlight in your manual and read *John 14:27*. How is the peace that Jesus gives different from the peace that the world gives?

   30. _____

The world says that you can have peace when everything is comfortable for you and going well. The promise to the believer is that he can have peace *regardless* of the circumstances. Also, read *John 16:33* and note that we will have tribulation in the world, but we can have peace anyway.

> **ILLUSTRATION:** An artist once won a contest with a painting entitled, "Peace," but most of the painting depicted a violent storm at sea. However, in the center of the stormy picture, in a small opening of a rock, was a little bird fast asleep.
>
> Anyone can have peace when everything is tranquil or progressing as he desires, but Jesus gives peace in the middle of the storm *(John 16:33)*.

    c. Highlight in your manual and read *John 15:10-11*. The Lord intends for His children to have joy on a continuing basis. Upon what is the believer's joy based?

31. _____

The believer's joy comes from his relationship with Jesus Christ and is found in keeping God's commandments. True joy is not dependent on circumstances.

6. Read *Principle 25* on Page 98 of the *Self-Confrontation* manual. Then, highlight in your manual and read *Ezekiel 18:1-20*. This passage concerns a false proverb that had arisen among the children of Israel. What was the erroneous proverb (see *verse 2*)?

32. _____

How have you heard that erroneous proverb being used today?

33. _____
_____
_____

What is God's response in *verses 3* and *4*?

34. _____
_____

Note that fathers cannot cause their children to sin. This is contrary to much of today's teaching in which parents are blamed for their children's sinful behavior.

God's point is that children are not doomed to sin because of what their parents did or how their parents treated them. This is tremendous hope. There is *nothing* that can keep us from having complete victory in the Lord — not family heritage, not the environment we grew up in, not circumstances, etc. On the other hand, children cannot use their parents, or other influences for that matter, as an excuse for their sin.

Have you ever heard someone say "His parents were like this, so is it any wonder that he is like this himself?" This is similar to the proverb that the Israelites were using in *verses 2-4*. In much of today's teaching and counseling, parents are blamed for their children's sinful behavior. Are parents responsible before God to be good parents? Of course they are! But even if they are not godly parents, the children are still responsible for their own sins.

To emphasize this point, God describes a righteous man in *verses 5-9* who has a violent son, as we see described in *verses 10-13*. Then we see in *verses 14-17* that this violent son, in turn, has a son who has observed all the evil acts that his father has done and yet rejects his father's behavior and lives a very righteous life. Notice that this son was present and saw all that his very wicked father did, yet he did not sin. Neither was he scarred for life.

Verse 20 indicates that we need not have false guilt for someone else's sin. It is important that parents do not live in defeat when their children go astray as adults.

Now, what about the Scripture passage that says the sins of the father will be visited on the children to the third and fourth generation? (See, for example, *Deuteronomy 5:9*.) God's Law clearly placed the blame for an individual's sins on himself only *(Deuteronomy 24:16)*. However, the *physical* consequences of an individual's sins are often experienced by others closely related to the offender. This is what is being discussed in *Deuteronomy 5:9*. What are some examples of sin reaping physical consequences to others not responsible for the sin?

35. _____

You may be wondering why God allows sinners to harm innocent people physically. If someone were to aim a pistol directly at you and pull the trigger, God would not necessarily stop the bullet in midair just because you are innocent. You see, God allows us to make choices either to obey or disobey Him. If He did not allow us to choose, we would merely be robots and incapable of love since love is a choice.

But the wonderful truth is that while God may allow us to experience *physical* consequences of someone else's sins, He will never allow anything or anyone to affect our *spiritual* condition, and our spiritual condition is far more important than our physical condition. God sovereignly protects us from spiritual harm.

Similarly, you may have heard people talk about "generational sins" or having a "genetic predisposition" to a particular sin, such as drunkenness or homosexuality. The Bible tells us that, because of Adam's sin we *all* have a predisposition to sin. But just because we may be tempted or weak in a particular area of our life does not mean that we must commit that sin. By God's grace we can say "no" to ungodliness and live in victory over sin.

7. Read *Principle 26* on Page 98 of the *Self-Confrontation* manual. Then, highlight in your manual and read *I John 1:9*. What hope about problems is offered in this verse?

36. _____

Isn't it wonderful to know that even when a person fails miserably, he can start afresh?

NOTE: For a more thorough explanation of peace and joy in the Lord, you may wish to read **BIBLICAL BASIS FOR PEACE AND JOY** *(Self-Confrontation,* Pages 103-105).

SCRIPTURE RECITATION

Recite *Romans 8:28-29* to someone at home, in class, or elsewhere. Also, recite one of the previous memory passages chosen by the listener. Put a check here (___) when you have accurately recited the verses.

QUESTIONS AND CONCLUSION

A. Of the three problem levels (feeling, doing, heart), which level are we to focus on as believers?

37. _____

B. How does it bring hope to a person to call a behavior the Bible designates as sinful a "sin," when the world excuses it as a disease or something caused by an outside force, such as heredity or another person?

38.

C. What hope has God provided in *I Corinthians 10:13*?

39.

D. How do trials represent an opportunity for us?

40.

E. What was the most significant truth you learned in completing this lesson?

41.

Sometimes Christians are afraid to deal with sin because they think that it will be discouraging or depressing. God says just the opposite. Taking responsibility for our sin and dealing with it is tremendously freeing and hopeful. Moreover, we can have hope in life's trials, because we know that God intends them for our good.

PREVIEW OF NEXT LESSON

The next lesson describes the process of change. This is often called progressive sanctification. We will learn that this is the process of putting off old sinful practices, renewing the mind, and putting on new righteous practices which continue for a believer's entire life.

LESSON 7
BIBLICAL STRUCTURE FOR CHANGE

OPENING PRAYER AND SCRIPTURE MEMORY

Before you begin this lesson, ask for God's help in understanding His Word and for wisdom and strength to apply what you learn in the power of the Holy Spirit.

Begin memorizing *Ephesians 4:22-24*. Also, review the Scripture memory passages assigned in the previous lessons. Then, be prepared to recite them at the end of this lesson.

Also, in your own words, please write out the meaning of the new memory verses below:

_____
_____
_____
_____

INTRODUCTION TO THE LESSON

A. Lessons 6-8 describe the four elements of how to face, deal with, and endure problems biblically: 1) biblical understanding, 2) biblical hope, 3) biblical change, and 4) biblical practice (doing the Word). These four elements form the structure upon which the remaining lessons are built. Lesson 6 covered the first two elements. Lesson 7 will cover the third element: biblical change. This process of change, which is sometimes called "progressive sanctification," is fundamental to spiritual maturity.

Thankfully, the Lord doesn't save us only to let us fend for ourselves spiritually and leave us to change into the likeness of Christ on our own. Read *Philippians 1:6*, then, write the reference next to the summary box on Page 110. Who completes the work God began in us?

1. _____

What is the work He is completing in believers? Refer to a Scripture verse that you memorized in a previous lesson.

2. _____

Imagine what it would be like for a mother to give birth to her child and then say to the child, "I've done my part — I've spent nine months carrying you and giving birth, so now you are on your own. Your diapers are over there on the shelf. Your milk is in the refrigerator. Your clothes and blankets are in the closet. I have provided all you need; however, if you have any problems, do not hesitate to ask me for wisdom any time." Now, doesn't that sound ridiculous?

Loving parents are intimately involved in caring for and bringing up their children. You can expect much more from your loving Father in Heaven, who will not leave you on the "delivery table." Not only does He save you, He nurtures you and trains you throughout your life on this earth.

The Lord uses His children to disciple newborn believers. Sadly, many churches leave newborn Christians on the delivery table and assume their work is finished after someone becomes a believer. Then, they are surprised when the new believer stumbles and falls, or goes back to his old ways.

Much of God's Word is about spiritual growth or change. Let's look at an example. The first half of *Ephesians*, Chapters 1-3, describes all that is true of us and available to us in Christ. In Chapters 4-6, God describes how we are to walk (or live) in light of Chapters 1-3. Notice the term *walk (or live)* in *Ephesians 4:1* and *17*. This is what we will talk about in Lesson 7.

B. To start this lesson, read the purposes of **LESSON 7: BIBLICAL STRUCTURE FOR CHANGE** (*Self-Confrontation*, Page 110).

BIBLICAL CHANGE — THE PROCESS

A. To gain an overview of biblical "put-offs" and "put-ons":

1. Read *Principle 27*, **BIBLICAL PRINCIPLES: BIBLICAL STRUCTURE FOR CHANGE** (*Self-Confrontation*, Page 111) and highlight the words "continuing progress" in the first sentence, and "put-off" and "put-on" in the third sentence. To understand that biblical change is a process, turn to Page 112. This portion expands on *Principle 27*.

   a. Under Section I. Paragraph A. of Page 112, highlight *Ephesians 4:22-32* and read *Ephesians 4:22-24*. Notice that at the beginning of *verse 22* we are told to deal with the *manner* of life of the old self. This passage describes the biblical principle of putting off the old way of living and putting on the righteous practices of the new self. While the new self has been put on at salvation, the old manner of life must be decisively put off (that is, laid aside completely and permanently). The words "put-off" are not telling us to remove temporarily, but the command is to "put away" sinful practices from our lives. At the same time, the righteous *practices* of the new self must be put on. *Verses 25* through *32* provide practical examples of how the principle works. This is a process that continues in the believer's life until death. Lasting change doesn't take place merely by putting off — both "put-ons" and "put-offs" must be practiced simultaneously.

   As you study the Word, you will discover many "put-offs" and "put-ons" in the Scripture passages. One way of keeping track of the "put-offs" and "put-ons" is to write a minus (-) symbol above each Scripture portion that lists a "put-off" and a plus (+) symbol above each portion that lists a "put-on."

   List below the various "put-offs" and "put-ons" you see in *Ephesians 4:25-32*. As you read each verse, place a minus (-) symbol above each "put-off" and a plus (+) symbol above each "put-on."

   Verse 25

   3. "Put-off": _____

   4. "Put-on": _____

   Is it possible for someone to put off lying and never put on speaking the truth? If so, how?

   5. _____

   Note that merely putting off falsehood does not necessarily mean that lasting change has taken place.

   Verse 28

   6. "Put-off": _____

   7. "Put-on": _____

If a robber has stopped robbing after stealing a million dollars, does that mean that he is no longer a robber?

8. _____

Note that to change completely, he must earn money by working for it and then share with those in need. Then, he has become a *giver* rather than a *taker*.

Verse 29

9. "Put-off": _____

10. "Put-on": _____

Note that this is very different from saying, "If you cannot say anything nice, don't say anything at all."

Verses 31-32

11. "Put-off": _____

12. "Put-on": _____

Notice the pattern in these verses; for each "put-off" in the Bible, there is usually a "put-on," and often it is in the same passage. This correspondence of "put-offs" and "put-ons" is present throughout the Bible. God does not just tell us what to refrain from doing; He tells us what to do instead. **WARNING:** *You must be careful not to try to match "put-offs" and "put-ons" from unrelated passages or make your own selection of a "put-on" for a particular "put-off" listed in the Scriptures. If you replace God's instruction with what seems good to you, you will have difficulties.*

2. Failure to accomplish lasting, biblical change may be the result of several errors. For example:

   a. There may be superficial change. A person may attempt to change superficially by selecting a convenient or easy solution. For example, a husband may buy flowers for his wife instead of asking forgiveness for sinning against her; or he may take pills to make himself feel better without following the biblical mandate related to his problem.

   b. There may be a "put-off," but no corresponding "put-on." Read *Ephesians 5:18*. A person may recognize that he should not get drunk and should not allow himself to be controlled by alcohol. However, to concentrate merely on quitting the consumption of alcohol without taking corresponding steps of placing one's self under the control of the Holy Spirit in everyday life only deals with the symptom. It does not deal with the cause. What must be done according to *Ephesians 5:18*?

   13. _____

   It is important to note that most of our failures to change old patterns are due to focusing on the "put-off" without practicing a biblical "put-on."

   c. A person may attempt to put on a righteous practice while maintaining the basic sinful pattern of his old life. For example, look at *Mark 2:21-22*. What is Jesus' warning here?

   14. _____

A person who reforms his life by starting to attend church, studying his Bible daily, etc. without dealing with his immoral behavior is only fooling himself into thinking he is pleasing God.

    d. Some believers justify not dealing with past sinful practices that affect their present lives or the lives of others by misusing the phrase "forgetting what lies behind" in *Philippians 3:13* (read this verse). The context of *Philippians 3* is placing no confidence in self, even for past accomplishments but, instead, concentrating on the upward call in Christ Jesus. So does past, unresolved sin need to be dealt with?

15. _____

A new believer who has committed an offense against someone must be reconciled to that person, even if the offense took place before the new believer received Christ. Because the relationship has never been reconciled, the offense remains in the present.

Remember, you do not eliminate a garbage heap by sprinkling perfume on it. Adding perfume only counters the odor for awhile; the basic problem remains. You must get rid of the garbage.

B. Read Paragraph A. of Section **I. Put-offs and put-ons** (*Self-Confrontation*, Page 112) as a review of the "put-offs" and "put-ons."

C. Read Paragraph B. Note that sins of *omission*, i.e., not putting on, are often overlooked. In *James 4:17*, when does God say we are guilty of sin?

16. _____

Sins of *omission* are just as serious as sins of *commission*. Read Subparagraphs 1.-5. under Paragraph B. (Page 112).

D. Prayer and action

We have seen so far that God conforms believers into the image of Christ on a continuing basis during our lives on earth. But whose responsibility is it to put off the old sinful practices and put on the new practices of righteousness?

17. _____

God provides us the power to change our practices; however, He does not promise that changing our ways will be easy. Now let's see what is required for lasting biblical change.

Read the contents of Section **II. Prayer and action** on Pages 112 and 113. Lasting change takes self-control, discipline, work, and time because it involves putting off the practices (habit patterns) of the old self, which is corrupted, and putting on the practices (habit patterns) of the new self, which has been created in righteousness and holiness of the truth.

God created us with the ability to develop habits (practices) in order to carry out our responsibilities effectively. If it were not for habit, we would never get to work, because we would be too busy making (first-time) decisions every morning about how to get dressed and how to eat breakfast, etc. Habits allow us to accomplish many routine responsibilities with little deliberation so that we can focus our attention on new matters in life.

Biblical change is difficult (at times, 'major surgery' must be performed in your life). Initially, changing from one practice to another may feel unnatural or strange. For example, riding a bicycle seems unnatural when you are first learning. However, after a while it becomes more and more a familiar practice (habit) of your life with fewer and fewer failures. Once a new habit is formed, it becomes easier to make progress in your spiritual walk. In what area have you seen God help you with putting off an old ungodly habit and putting on a new righteous practice?

18. _____

_____

NOTE: You will have an opportunity to work on the "put-offs" and "put-ons" for a current problem in your life as part of this Bible Study.

ILLUSTRATION: If you are sawing a piece of wood with a handsaw and mistakenly start a groove a few millimeters outside the mark, it is very difficult to start a new groove in the correct place. To insure that you cut exactly where you want, you must hold the handsaw very carefully with your thumb against the mark as a guide. Then, you must align the saw on the mark next to your thumb. And, finally, you must move the saw back and forth slowly at the new mark on the wood. Only after several strokes can you lift your thumb and speed up your sawing. After the groove is fairly deep, you hardly have to deliberate about what you are doing.

Also, compare learning how to walk physically with walking spiritually. Learning to walk may involve a number of failures initially, but the key to learning to walk well is getting up each time you fall. In the same way, changing any unbiblical practice (habit) requires continued work.

In conclusion, when changing from an ungodly practice to a righteous practice, you must be very careful and deliberate at first. Then, you must be persistent every time you fail to confess your sins, repent, and start again.

E. Read the text of Section **III. Failure and confession** on Page 113.

PERSONAL PLAN FOR CHANGE

In Lesson 6, you began a list of unbiblical thoughts, speech, and actions related to the problem you identified in Lesson 5. In developing this list, you have been concentrating on making sure that each failure to live God's way is specific, thorough, not shifting blame, and not minimizing or excusing sin. Continue working on *Worksheet 2* this week.

Keep working on your failures list a little each day as you are doing your other homework. Correct those failures that you have already listed from your Lesson 6 homework, and add to the list as the Lord reminds you. This week, read *I Corinthians 13:4-8a* as a reminder on how to love biblically.

Then, begin to complete *Worksheet 3: "Put-offs" and "Put-ons"* of your **VICTORY OVER FAILURES PLAN**. The form for the worksheet is shown on Page W89. This foundational worksheet is designed to help you learn how to find the biblical "put-offs" and "put-ons" associated with the personal problem you have chosen. To complete *Worksheet 3*, follow the steps below:

A. At the top of your worksheet in the space entitled, "**Ongoing problem area**," copy what you wrote as your ongoing problem area from *Worksheet 1: Description of the Problem* on Page W54, which you completed earlier.

B. Complete the first column of *Worksheet 3* by copying each item from your *Worksheet 2: Lists of Specific Failures to Live Biblically*, Page W70, which you have completed. *NOTE: Be sure to leave a little empty space between each failure in the first column so that you can relate the corresponding entries in the second and third columns to the appropriate failure.*

NOTE: *The reason you need to wait until now to copy the information into the first column is to make sure your list conforms to all the guidelines for completing Worksheet 2. This will save you from starting Worksheet 3 repeatedly.*

C. Complete the second and third columns of **Worksheet 3**.

    1. Search the Scriptures for the appropriate words to write in the second and third columns. The "put-off" (in the second column) is the biblical name given to the failure (listed in the first column); the "put-on" (in the third column) is the phrase in the Scriptures that corresponds to the "put-off" in the second column. In addition to the key passages of Scripture listed on the **SAMPLE LIST OF PROBLEM AREAS** on Page W55, it may be helpful to use a concordance and the *Self-Confrontation* manual to find the related passages. Generally, each pair of "put-offs" and "put-ons" is in the same Scripture passage.

    You may find a "put-off" without a related "put-on" in the same passage, such as *"You shall not bear false witness" (Exodus 20:16)*. In this case, find another passage that contains the same "put-off" along with an associated "put-on" such as *Ephesians 4:25* that designates a "put-on" of "speaking truth." You also may find "put-ons" without related "put-offs." Again, search for other passages where the "put-ons" and "put-offs" correspond to one another.

    2. List the "put-offs" along with the associated Scripture references in the second column, and list the "put-ons" along with the associated Scripture references in the third column. To make sure that you base each entry in the second and third columns only on Scripture passages, it is important that you place the scriptural reference next to each "put-off" and "put-on."

See the sample completed worksheet on Page W90.

D. For at least three unbiblical deeds on the list that you have developed in your previous homework, identify the associated "put-offs" and "put-ons" along with the biblical references.

Your worksheet will not be discussed in class. But if you turn it in to your leader or teacher for evaluation, make a copy for yourself before you hand it in. You will need to refer to it for your homework in the next lesson.

Worksheet 3: "Put-offs" and "Put-ons"

Ongoing problem area _____   Page ____ of ____

(1) My specific unbiblical deeds (thoughts, speech, and actions) *(based on Matthew 7:1-5; 15:18)*	(2) "Put-off" and biblical reference(s) *(Ephesians 4:22; Colossians 3:5-9)*	(3) "Put-on" and biblical reference(s) *(Ephesians 4:24; Colossians 3:10-17)*

VOFP Worksheet 3

Sample Worksheet 3: "Put-offs" and "Put-ons"

Ongoing problem area _Anger and bitterness toward my co-worker_   Page __1__ of __1__

(1) My specific unbiblical deeds (thoughts, speech, and actions) *(based on Matthew 7:1-5; 15:18)*	(2) "Put-off" and biblical reference(s) *(Ephesians 4:22; Colossians 3:5-9)*	(3) "Put-on" and biblical reference(s) *(Ephesians 4:24; Colossians 3:10-17)*
Often, I speak to my co-worker in an angry way. I speak with a loud voice using condemning and accusing words.	*Bitterness, wrath, anger, clamor, malice (Ephesians 4:31)* *Unwholesome words (Ephesians 4:29)* *Harsh words (Proverbs 15:1)* *Hot temper (Proverbs 15:18)* *Evil speech (Proverbs 15:28)*	*Kindness, tender-heartedness, and forgiveness (Ephesians 4:32)* *Edifying words that give grace to the hearer and are appropriate to the need (Ephesians 4:29)* *Gentle words (Proverbs 15:1)* *Patience (Proverbs 15:18)* *Pondering before answering (Proverbs 15:28)*
I argue with my co-worker every day, and I often speak with a harsh tone of voice, and say tearing down words to my co-worker.	*Bitterness, wrath, anger, clamor, malice (Ephesians 4:31)* *Unwholesome words (Ephesians 4:29)* *Harsh words (Proverbs 15:1)* *Hot temper (Proverbs 15:18)* *Evil speech (Proverbs 15:28)* *Quarrels (arguments) (II Timothy 2:23-24)*	*Kindness, tender-heartedness, and forgiveness (Ephesians 4:32)* *Edifying words that give grace to the hearer and are appropriate to the need (Ephesians 4:29)* *Gentle words (Proverbs 15:1)* *Patience (Proverbs 15:18)* *Pondering before answering (Proverbs 15:28)* *Kindness, patience, gentleness (II Timothy 2:24-25)*
I gossip about my co-worker to my employer and others in the office saying tearing down things, and I complain to my family members about my situation at work.	*Gossip (talebearing) (Proverbs 11:13)* *Unwholesome words (Ephesians 4:29)* *Evil speech (Proverbs 15:28)*	*Keeping a secret (Proverbs 11:13)* *Edifying words that give grace to the hearer and are appropriate to the need (Ephesians 4:29)* *Pondering before answering (Proverbs 15:28)*
I have bitter, vengeful thoughts toward my co-worker, not only at the office, but in many other places.	*Bitterness, wrath, anger, clamor, malice (Ephesians 4:31)*	*Kindness, tender-heartedness, and forgiveness (Ephesians 4:32)*
When I pray, I grumble and complain to the Lord about my situation at work.	*Grumbling and disputing (Philippians 2:14)*	*Holding fast the Word of God and rejoicing (Philippians 2:16, 18)*
When on my way home from work, I think and speak to myself about sharp, tearing down statements I might make to my co-worker.	*Unwholesome words (Ephesians 4:29)*	*Edifying words that give grace to the hearer and are appropriate to the need (Ephesians 4:29)*

VOFP Worksheet 3 © Biblical Counseling Foundation

Student Workbook for the Self-Confrontation Bible Study
- Lesson 8 -

THE EFFECTS OF UNBIBLICAL THOUGHTS, SPEECH, AND ACTIONS

Review the page entitled **THE EFFECTS OF UNBIBLICAL THOUGHTS, SPEECH, AND ACTIONS** *(Self-Confrontation*, Page 114). You can see that if you refuse to change biblically you will become worse, and the effects can hinder your spiritual growth. While unbiblical deeds (thoughts, speech, and actions) often lead to physical problems, there are other causes for these same physical problems. For example, you should not hastily assume that the reason behind someone's ulcers is sin.

THE "PUT-OFFS"

Let's look now at what is involved in putting off sinful habits by turning to *Principle 28*, *(Self-Confrontation*, Page 111).

A. It is important to identify and concentrate on those areas in your life that God requires you to change, even though they may be difficult. When you seek to change some area of your life according to what seems good to you (via human wisdom or desires), you may focus on something that seems easy to do or that appeals to self-centered accomplishments.

B. After you identify your sinful practice, it must be dealt with quickly or it will become worse. Read just the beginning part of *II Timothy 2:22*. What does this Scripture say about what we are to do with youthful lusts?

19. _____

Fleeing is a term that indicates urgent flight from something that is dangerous. God tells us in *Genesis 4:7* that sin is crouching at the door if we do not do well. The implication is that, given a chance, sin will attempt to master you. Clearly, the Scriptures indicate that it is dangerous to play with sin or hesitate when temptation comes.

The *II Timothy 2:22a* example leads us to *Principle 29*.

THE "PUT-ONS"

Read *Principle 29*, **BIBLICAL PRINCIPLES: BIBLICAL STRUCTURE FOR CHANGE** *(Self-Confrontation*, Page 111). This principle deals with putting on righteous deeds (thoughts, speech, and actions).

What are we to put on in the place of youthful lusts according to the second half of *II Timothy 2:22*?

20. _____

Can you think of an example of how to apply this passage to a specific type of sin?

21. _____
_____
_____

Concentrating on the "put-on" will often make the "put-off" much easier to master. Read *Galatians 5:16*. If you walk by the Holy Spirit, what will you not do?

22. _____

Notice where the emphasis is. If you walk by the Spirit (in other words, as you put on living by the Holy Spirit), you will not carry out the desires of the flesh. When you focus your attention on the "put-on," your mind is not easily distracted to do wrong. When you focus your attention only on the "put-off," the temptation to do wrong is always before you. To illustrate this, try this exercise.

> ### EXERCISE: GETTING RID OF THE LION
>
> Let's do an exercise to illustrate the importance of focusing on "put-ons." Think of a large, ferocious, and hungry lion crouched on a rock just above you and ready to pounce on you. After reading this paragraph, close your eyes to eliminate distractions. Concentrate on the lion for at least 15 seconds after you close your eyes. Then, as quickly as possible, stop thinking of the huge lion. After a few seconds, open your eyes.
>
> Now, do the exercise.
>
> Were you immediately able to get rid of the mental picture of the lion?
>
> 23. _____
>
> How were you able to get rid of the lion?
>
> 24. _____
>
> The most effective way to get rid of the picture of the dangerous lion is to focus on thinking of something not dangerous, like a dove. In the same way, placing your focus on "put-ons" makes it easier to accomplish "put-offs" as well.
>
> Isn't it interesting that the world's focus is just the opposite? Most worldly therapies focus primarily on the "put-off." The reason that we often fail to change in a permanent way is that we focus on the "put-offs" and neglect to put attention on the "put-ons."

RENEWING YOUR MIND

As you put off the old practices of sin and put on the new practices of righteousness, God renews your mind. This is explained in **RENEWING YOUR MIND** (*Self-Confrontation,* Pages 115-116). Now, read Section **I. The renewal of your mind with regard to your growth in Christ** on Page 115.

- A. Start by reading **I. A.** and **B.** In **I. A.**, highlight and then read *Colossians 3:9-10*. Who renews the believer's mind?

    25. _____

    It is important to note that God the Holy Spirit sovereignly renews our minds continuously as we obey Him.

    According to *II Corinthians 4:16,* when does God renew us?

    26. _____

    This does not mean that we should sit back and not work on thinking biblically. It is *our* responsibility to develop biblical ways of thinking, speaking, and acting as the Holy Spirit renews our minds.

- B. Read the text of Section **II. The renewal of your mind with regard to your personal responsibilities**. Who is responsible for disciplining their thought lives and learning God's Word?

    27. _____

Particularly note Paragraph B. What are the five aspects listed that relate to developing a Christlike way of thinking?

28. _____

_____

_____

_____

_____

SCRIPTURE RECITATION

Recite *Ephesians 4:22-24* to someone at home, in class, or elsewhere. Also, recite one of the previous memory passages chosen by the listener. Put a check here (___) when you have accurately recited the verses.

QUESTIONS AND CONCLUSION

A. Lasting biblical change comes from not only putting off the old, unrighteous behavior, but also:

29. _____

in the power of the Holy Spirit.

B. Give examples of "put-offs" and "put-ons" in *II Timothy 2:22*.

30. "Put-off": _____

31. "Put-on": _____

_____

C. Regarding "put-offs" and "put-ons," remember that:

1. "Put-offs" and "put-ons" must be biblical.

2. Wherever there is a "put-off" in the Scriptures, usually, but not always, a corresponding "put-on" will be present in the same passage.

3. Some biblical "put-ons" exist without corresponding "put-offs."

4. Placing emphasis on the "put-on" will often make the "put-off" easier.

D. What was the most significant truth you learned in completing this lesson?

32. _____

_____

PREVIEW OF NEXT LESSON

The next lesson completes coverage of the four elements of how to face, deal with, and endure problems biblically. It covers the fourth element: biblical practice. Also covered are the very important subjects of discipline, tests, and temptations.

LESSON 8
BIBLICAL PRACTICE ACHIEVES LASTING CHANGE

OPENING PRAYER AND SCRIPTURE MEMORY

Before you begin this lesson, ask for God's help in understanding His Word and for wisdom and strength to apply what you learn in the power of the Holy Spirit.

Begin memorizing *Hebrews 5:14* and *James 4:17*. Also, review the Scripture memory passages assigned in the previous lessons. Then, be prepared to recite them at the end of this lesson.

Also, in your own words, please write out the meaning of the new memory verses below:

_____
_____
_____
_____

PERSONAL PLAN FOR CHANGE

In Lesson 7, you began to complete *Worksheet 3: "Put-offs" and "Put-ons"* of your **VICTORY OVER FAILURES PLAN**. As you review your work, make sure that the failures you have listed in the first column are specific, thorough, not shifting blame, and not minimizing or excusing sin.

Then, continue to complete the second and third columns of *Worksheet 3* during the remainder of the week.

Your worksheet will not be discussed in class. But, if you turn it in to your leader or teacher for evaluation, make a copy for yourself before you hand it in. You will need to refer to it for your homework in the next lesson.

INTRODUCTION TO THE LESSON

A. Remember that in Lessons 6-8, we are studying the four elements of facing, dealing with, and enduring problems biblically. As a review, list the four elements below.

1. _____
_____
_____
_____

This lesson covers the fourth element: biblical practice (doing the Word). You can understand the problem, have hope, know how to change, but if you do not *practice* the Word, you will be worse off.

Biblical practice is the element that makes the difference between being just a "hearer of the Word" and being a "doer of the Word." Let's look at *Hebrews 5:12-14*, which was taught in Lesson 2. What happens without the practice of God's Word?

2. _____

You will not stay at the same place in your spiritual life. What does God say in *James 1:22* will happen if you are not a doer of the Word?

3. _____

Notice that you delude *yourself*. No one else deludes you, or takes you unaware. You are not "robbed" of your peace and joy; you put yourself in that state.

This lesson will develop the **VICTORY OVER FAILURES PLAN** which is designed to help you become a doer of the Word. You will be using this tool throughout the remainder of this Bible Study to develop a specific plan for change in dealing with the particular problem that you selected in Lesson 5.

B. Read the purposes of **LESSON 8: BIBLICAL PRACTICE ACHIEVES LASTING CHANGE** (*Self-Confrontation*, Page 122).

1. Let's look at the biblical principles on establishing biblical practice in our lives by turning to Page 123.

    a. Read the first sentence of *Principle 30* on Page 123, highlight *Revelation 2:4-5* in your manual, and turn to *Revelation 2:1*. To which church is this passage addressed?

    4. _____

    Now read *Revelation 2:2-3*. This is the same church that received much powerful teaching from the Lord, through the Apostle Paul, on their riches in Christ and the process of biblical change (note the discussion of the book of *Ephesians* in Lesson 7). As stated in *Revelation 2*, the Ephesian church seemed to be doing the Word but for the wrong reasons. Thus, all of their deeds were unacceptable. What does *verse 4* say happened to them?

    5. _____

    In *verse 5*, Jesus showed the Ephesians that their problem was not a lack of knowledge. Then, Jesus not only showed what was wrong (leaving the first love for the Lord), He showed the Ephesian church how to return to that love. Note that part of returning is to *remember* from where they had fallen. Jesus counseled the Ephesians to begin again to live the same way they did during the period of their first love.

    b. Read the first sentence of *Principle 31* on Page 123. Highlight *I Timothy 4:7-11* in your manual, and turn to *I Timothy 4:7-8*. Can you identify the "put-off" and "put-on" in *verse 7*?

    6. "Put-off": _____

    7. "Put-on": _____

    At first glance, the "put-off" and "put-on" do not seem to fit. But when the New Testament was written, the ones who were considered wise and experienced in developing remedies for daily problems of life were the older women who had gained much experience. This is actually a high view of old women because they were the experienced ones in dealing with life. Nonetheless, in the letter to Timothy, the Lord, through the Apostle Paul, was pointing out that wisdom based on worldly experience was not to be relied upon in becoming godly. The problem with worldly experience or knowledge is that sometimes it is correct and at other times it is false.

    Also, the "put-on," which is "discipline" in the New American Standard Bible, "train" in the New International Version, and 'exercise' in the King James Version, means to exercise vigorously as athletes do.

Now, think about where the world tells you to find answers. Man emphasizes that we should live according to experience or our feelings while God tells us to be disciplined in obeying His Word.

In summary, God says we are not to have anything to do with the world's experience or knowledge, which is often false. On the other hand, our focus is to be toward godliness, which requires discipline (going against our inclinations, and going toward what is right).

 c. Read the first sentence of *Principle 32*. Highlight in your manual, then read *I Corinthians 15:58*. Maturing in biblical practice requires steadfastness and perseverance in the midst of trials, tests, and temptations.

TESTS AND TEMPTATIONS

A. In order to establish biblical change in your life, you must learn to recognize how trials can be either tests or temptations in your life. Turn to Page 124 of the *Self-Confrontation* manual and read the box at the top of the page. Then, study Section **I. The difference between tests and temptations.**

 1. Read Paragraph A. Highlight in your manual, then read *I Peter 1:6-7*. What is more precious than gold?

  8. _____

  a. The word in this passage for "test" means to be proved, such as metals are tried by fire and thus are purified. The word "prove" does not mean to show to be true or false, but it means to "show forth." The emphasis in this passage is to prove someone good and acceptable.

  b. Read *I Peter 4:12*. Write the reference next to the first sentence of Paragraph A. on Page 124 of the *Self-Confrontation* manual. What does God say about trials in this passage?

   9. _____

  c. Can you think of any trials that you have been "surprised" by in your life?

   10. _____

  What does this passage tell you about that trial?

   11. _____

  We should not be surprised when trials come, even when they are intense and seem fiery.

> **ILLUSTRATION:** Years ago when Amy Carmichael was ministering in India as a missionary, she went to a goldsmith to find out how gold was purified so that she could understand how God "tests" or "proves" us. The goldsmith placed in the pot old jewelry, gold bars, and ore, which all seemed to have varying degrees of purity. She watched as the gold was being melted in a pot placed over an intense fire. As the material in the pot heated, smoke began to rise from the pot. The goldsmith explained that if she would look down into the pot, Amy would notice scum floating on the surface. The scum, he explained, is called "dross" and must be burned off. At one point, Amy asked the goldsmith how he would know that the gold was purified. He answered that the gold would be pure when he could look down into it and see a perfect reflection of his face.
>
> In the same way, God tests or proves believers so that they may reflect the image of Christ in their lives.

> Looking beyond the illustration of Amy Carmichael's experience, remember that the goldsmith is not finished with the gold, even when it has been purified. He then molds, forms, pounds, and etches the gold to make it into something useful and beautiful. God does not necessarily remove us from a circumstance, but while we are being purified, He continues His work in our lives to make us useful vessels for His service.

We are going to study about trials much more, but if the Lord so leads you right now, pause and give Him thanks for the trial or trials you are now facing and how He is using it in your life.

2. Read Paragraph B. of Section I. on Page 124 of the *Self-Confrontation* manual. Then, highlight in your manual and read *James 1:13-14*. Who is *not* the source of temptation?

   12. _____

   What *is* a source of temptation?

   13. _____

   It is important to note that temptations, in and of themselves, are not sins. We know this because we read in *Hebrews 4:15* that Jesus was tempted, but did not sin.

   Secondly, the source of the temptations in this passage is not Satan but our own lust (or evil desires). Remember, when we read *James 1:22* at the beginning of this lesson, we saw that we delude ourselves when we do not obey the Word.

   Believers often criticize worldly counselors because of their tendency to blame failures to function victoriously on external influences such as a harsh environment and abusive people. Yet, believers often do exactly the same thing when they excuse their own behavior by blaming Satan, demons, curses, etc. for their failures.

3. Read Paragraph C. of Section I. on Page 124 of the *Self-Confrontation* manual. Every circumstance is a test from God or is used by our fleshly desires or Satan as a temptation to sin. So in every difficulty, your choice is either to stand firm and grow in Christlikeness or to sin and suffer the consequences. To respond biblically to the circumstance, do not focus on trying to discover if it is a test or a temptation. Rather, focus on pleasing God in every circumstance.

B. Read Paragraph B. under Section II. **God and tests** on Page 124 of the *Self-Confrontation* manual.

C. Read Section III. **Satan and temptations to self-gratification** on Page 125. Then, in Paragraph B., highlight in your manual and read *I John 2:16*. What are the three areas of temptation listed here?

   14. _____
   _____
   _____

D. Read Paragraph B., Subparagraph 3. on Page 125. Notice how the three categories are illustrated in the temptation of Jesus.

   Tests and temptations are opportunities to respond in a godly way, but we should not merely wait for trials in order to grow in the Lord. We need to investigate how to approach all of life in a godly way.

PLANS FOR VICTORY OVER FAILURES

The next topic in your *Self-Confrontation* manual, **PRACTICAL STEPS FOR ACHIEVING BIBLICAL CHANGE** (Pages 129-131), has been replaced by the procedure for completing the **VICTORY OVER FAILURES PLAN** that you began working on in Lesson 5. So, let's review the guidelines.

A. Remember, the purpose of the **VICTORY OVER FAILURES PLAN** is to help you overcome sinful patterns in your life and, as you apply the plan to your life, to have complete and lasting change.

B. Keep in mind that the Scriptures are the sole standard and authority for your life and the only lasting hope is promised in the Bible.

C. Review what you have done so far in working on your problem.

   1. Since you completed *Worksheet 1: Description of the Problem*, are you becoming more alert to specific ways you sin in the problem you selected to work on?

      15. _____

   2. As you completed *Worksheet 2: List of Specific Failures to Live Biblically*, did you insure that all the entries were specific, thorough, not blameshifting, and not minimizing or excusing sin?

      16. _____

   3. As you completed *Worksheet 3: "Put-offs" and "Put-ons,"* were all of the "put-off"/"put-on" pairs from the same passage of Scripture?

      17. _____

D. In future lessons, you will develop specific plans to face and deal with the difficulties that you have described so far. Upon completion of *Worksheet 3: "Put-offs" and "Put-ons,"* you may need to develop up to three kinds of plans in parallel with one another. They are, the *"Daily Practices" Plan*, the *"Overcoming Temptations" Plan*, and the *"Forgiveness/Reconciliation" Plan*.

   The purpose of the *"Daily Practices" Plan* is to help you put off a particular ongoing pattern of unrighteous behavior and to put on the appropriate biblical pattern of righteous deeds instead. It includes changes that must be made throughout the day. You will begin working on this plan during Lesson 9.

   The purpose of the *"Overcoming Temptations" Plan* is to help you respond in a godly manner to situations where you have been tempted and have fallen repeatedly. It is for you to use only at the time the temptation occurs, but it is prepared in advance of the temptation so that you will be better prepared to deal with the temptation when it occurs. You will begin working on this plan during Lesson 11.

   The purpose of the *"Forgiveness/Reconciliation" Plan* is to help you deal with relationships that are not reconciled. You will begin working on this plan during Lesson 12.

SCRIPTURE RECITATION

Recite *Hebrews 5:14* and *James 4:17* to someone at home, in class, or elsewhere. Also, recite one of the previous memory passages chosen by the listener. Put a check here (___) when you have accurately recited the verses.

QUESTIONS

A. What happens when you understand your problem biblically, have hope, know how to change but do not practice God's Word?

18. _____

B. Man emphasizes that we should live according to experience or our feelings. In contrast, what does God say?

19. _____

C. List the purpose of each of the first three worksheets of the **VICTORY OVER FAILURES PLAN**:

20. In *Worksheet 1:* _____

_____

21. In *Worksheet 2:* _____

_____

22. In *Worksheet 3:* _____

_____

D. What was the most significant truth you learned in completing this lesson?

23. _____

_____

PREVIEW OF NEXT LESSON

The next two lessons will be about a preoccupation with self. They are extremely important because they show how your view of self affects how you approach all problems of life. It is particularly important to understand what the Bible teaches concerning this subject because there is so much confusion within the body of Christ surrounding the subject of self (e.g., "self-worth," "self-esteem," "self-image," "loving one's self," "forgiving one's self," etc.).

LESSON 9

DEALING WITH SELF (PART ONE)

OPENING PRAYER AND SCRIPTURE MEMORY

Before you begin this lesson, ask for God's help in understanding His Word and for wisdom and strength to apply what you learn in the power of the Holy Spirit.

Begin memorizing *Luke 9:23-24*. Also, review the Scripture memory passages assigned in the previous lessons. Then, be prepared to recite them at the end of this lesson.

Also, in your own words, please write out the meaning of the new memory verses below:

_____
_____
_____
_____

PERSONAL PLAN FOR CHANGE

Last lesson, we introduced three plans. You are now ready to complete your *Worksheet 4: "Daily Practices" Plan*. The form for the worksheet is shown on Pages W103-W104. Remember, the purpose of the *"Daily Practices" Plan* is to help you put off a particular ongoing pattern of unrighteous behavior and to put on the appropriate biblical pattern of righteous deeds instead. It includes changes that must be made throughout the day.

NOTE: You do not need to develop a separate plan for each person against whom you have sinned, as long as your pattern of sin is the same as on your lists of sins against the others.

A. Complete the two items in the top portion of the page (based on what you entered into *Worksheet 3: "Put-offs" and "Put-ons"*).

   1. Under "**Sin pattern that I need to change**," list the "put-offs" from the second column of *Worksheet 3*.

   2. Under "**Righteous pattern to be established**," list the "put-ons" from the third column of *Worksheet 3*.

   3. Begin work on the section entitled, "**My plan to live righteously**." In this section, specify what you will do to practice the righteous pattern starting with when you awaken in the morning and proceeding through the entire day. Since the basic problem is habitual, it reveals itself in many ways throughout each day. Your plan will be adjusted and added to as there is need.

NOTE: A very important portion of this section is a detailed description of your plans for daily devotions and Scripture memory. Review the biblical basis for daily devotions and Scripture memory in the Self-Confrontation manual, Pages 38-40.

It is important to recognize that devotional time spent in God's Word and memorizing God's Word should directly relate to the very areas in your life where God has your attention.

This week, complete your plan only up to breakfast time. Use the sample plan on Pages W105-W106 as a guide. Work on this assignment a little each day as you are doing your other homework. In future lessons, you will receive additional help.

Your homework will not be discussed in class. But if you turn it in to your leader or teacher for evaluation, make a copy for yourself before you hand it in. You will need to refer to it for your homework in the next lesson.

Worksheet 4: "Daily Practices" Plan

My plan not to repeat this sin and, instead, to respond biblically (James 1:22-25)

Page _____ of _____

Sin pattern that I need to change *(as seen from the second column of Worksheet 3)*:
_____
_____
_____

Righteous pattern to be established *(as seen from the third column of Worksheet 3)*:
_____
_____
_____

My plan to live righteously:
_____
_____
_____
_____
_____
_____
_____
_____
_____
_____
_____
_____
_____
_____
_____
_____
_____
_____

© Biblical Counseling Foundation

VOFP Worksheet 4 a

Permission is granted to reproduce this form for personal or ministry use

Student Workbook for the Self-Confrontation Bible Study
- Lesson 9 -

Worksheet 4: "Daily Practices" Plan (Continued)

My plan not to repeat this sin and, instead, to respond biblically (James 1:22-25)

Page _____ of _____

My plan to live righteously *(continued)*:

_____
_____
_____
_____
_____
_____
_____
_____
_____
_____
_____
_____
_____
_____
_____
_____
_____
_____
_____
_____
_____
_____
_____
_____
_____
_____
_____
_____

VOFP Worksheet 4 b　　　　　　　　　　　　　　　　　　© Biblical Counseling Foundation

Permission is granted to reproduce this form for personal or ministry use

Student Workbook for the Self-Confrontation Bible Study
- Lesson 9 -

Sample Worksheet 4: "Daily Practices" Plan

My plan not to repeat this sin and, instead, to respond biblically (James 1:22-25)

Sin pattern that I need to change (*as seen from the second column of* **Worksheet 3**):
Anger: bitterness, wrath, clamor, malice, unwholesome words, harsh words, hot temper, evil speech, quarrelling, gossiping, grumbling, disputing

Righteous pattern to be established (*as seen from the third column of* **Worksheet 3**):
Kindness, tender-heartedness, and forgiveness, edifying words that give grace to my co-worker and are appropriate to the need, gentle words, patience, pondering before answering, keeping a secret, holding fast the Word of God, rejoicing

My plan to live righteously:

A. When rising from bed:
   1. Thank the Lord for His grace, mercy, and comfort, and express my desire to please Him today.
   2. Thank God for the privilege of ministering to my co-worker and ask the Lord for guidance throughout the day.
   3. Ask the Lord to reveal to me, as I go through the day, areas of my conduct that are sinful, and in need of change.

B. During morning devotions:
   1. In my study of God's Word:
      a. Using a concordance, keep listing additional Scripture verses relating to kindness, tender-heartedness, and forgiveness, especially those that show me practical changes to make. Then, incorporate into this plan what I should apply to my life in relationship with my co-worker based on key verses.
      b. On my list of verses I have looked up, put an asterisk by the verses I should memorize. Continue writing these verses on cards, so I can carry them around to memorize.
   2. In my prayer time:
      a. Pray about what I just studied and acknowledge my dependence upon the Lord for wisdom and strength to apply what I learned.

© Biblical Counseling Foundation

VOFP Worksheet 4 a

Sample Worksheet 4: "Daily Practices" Plan (Continued)

My plan not to repeat this sin and, instead, to respond biblically (James 1:22-25)

Page __2__ of __2__

My plan to live righteously (*continued*):

        b. Pray about the items on my prayer list that relate to my co-worker.

  C. In my Scripture memory:

        a. Write down my Scripture memory verses on cards (from my list that relates to the problem).

        b. From my list, memorize at least one new Scripture verse a week and daily review the verses I have already learned.

        c. Carry the memory verse cards with me everywhere I go and review them often during the day, especially when I do not have responsibilities that fully occupy my mind.

  D. During breakfast and preparation for work:

        1. Thank the Lord for the current situation regarding my co-worker.

        2. Ask the Lord to reveal to me the opportunities to show kindness and tenderheartedness toward my co-worker, especially as they show me areas of my life in which the Lord is maturing me.

        3. Ask the Lord's help in dealing with my speech around others.

  E. At work:

        1. When opportunities arise, show kindness and tenderheartedness toward my co-worker.

        2. Offer help to my co-worker when he is having difficulty accomplishing his tasks.

VOFP Worksheet 4 b   © Biblical Counseling Foundation

W107

INTRODUCTION TO THE LESSON

A. Turn back to Page 7 in the **TABLE OF CONTENTS** of the *Self-Confrontation* manual. Lesson 9 begins the second phase of this Bible Study. The first eight lessons concentrated on the basic principles for living God's way. Notice that after Lesson 8, you see a new subtitle, "Application to Specific Problem Areas." The next 13 lessons under this subtitle provide biblical teaching and guidance on how to face, deal with, and endure certain commonly experienced problems.

B. The order of these 13 lessons is important. Dealing with self, or what could be called a preoccupation with self, is taught first because your view of self affects how you approach *all* problems of life. Failure to deal with self in a biblical manner will greatly hamper success in facing and dealing with anger, bitterness, depression, worry, etc.

The most important truth of this lesson is that the natural man pays too much attention to self, not too little. Therefore, in order to put off the old practices and begin to live God's way, the believer must put off preoccupation with self and instead must regard the Lord and others as more important than himself.

Having a biblical understanding of self is also important because there is so much interest and confusion within the body of Christ regarding this subject. The terms "self-worth," "self-esteem," "self-image," "loving one's self," and "forgiving one's self" have been used so commonly that they are often accepted as valid wording even among believers.

This is the first of two lessons dealing with a preoccupation with self. This lesson covers the first two elements of dealing with self. What are the first two elements?

1. _____

_____

The next lesson covers the last two elements. Do you remember what they are?

2. _____

_____

C. Read the purposes of **LESSON 9: DEALING WITH SELF (PART ONE)** (*Self-Confrontation*, Page 136).

MAN'S WAY

A. Following the method exemplified by Jesus when He contrasted God's way and man's way, let's start with the "you have heard that it was said …" part by reviewing man's way of dealing with problems related to self by turning to **SELF-BELITTLEMENT, SELF-EXALTATION, AND SELF-PITY** (*Self-Confrontation*, Page 139).

1. Read the text in the box at the top of Page 139 and also read Section **I. Man's view.** Highlight the last sentence in the paragraph, beginning with "All of these views …."

2. Read Section **II. Some of man's mistaken explanations for a low view of self.** List at least two of the mistaken explanations that you have heard in conversations or through the media of radio, printed matter, or television.

3. _____

_____

Student Workbook for the Self-Confrontation Bible Study
- Lesson 9 -
© Biblical Counseling Foundation

3. From Section **III. Some of man's futile ways** ..., list at least two of man's futile ways of building up self that you have heard in conversations or through the media of radio, printed matter, or television.

4.
_____
_____

The wisdom of this world states that a sense of inferiority or failure is a result of not loving yourself enough, so it is taught that you need to learn how to love yourself more. Sadly, even in the body of Christ, we hear unbiblical viewpoints taught as truth.

4. Section **IV. Some unbiblical viewpoints about "self" being taught in some churches today** lists actual quotes from some popular preachers and teachers. These views have no biblical support; in fact, they contradict God's Word. Remember that our purpose is not to demean others, but to distinguish biblical truth from error, just as the Bereans did *(Acts 17:11)*.

   Now, in contrast to man's ideas that elevate self and shift blame, let's go on to the "but I say unto you ..." part by studying God's way.

5. Read Section **V. God's view** (Page 140). God's truth is diametrically opposed to man's way. Highlight in your manual and read *II Timothy 3:1-7*. What is the first characteristic cited in the list in *verse 2*?

5.
_____

Note from *verse 1* that loving self will be a characteristic prevalent in the last days, an illustration of mankind falling deeper into sin. Notice that all the other evidences of the last days in *verses 2-7* are just other demonstrations of mankind's love for self.

BIBLICAL UNDERSTANDING ABOUT MAN'S PREOCCUPATION WITH SELF

A. Let's continue our study of God's way by turning to *Principle 33* on Page 137 of the *Self-Confrontation* manual. Read the first sentence of *Principle 33*.

   1. Highlight in your manual and read *Ephesians 5:29a*. What does this verse say about our selves?

   6.
   _____

   Many times, people claim that they do not know how to love another person (e.g., husbands sometimes claim this toward their wives). But in this verse, the Lord says that we know *how* to love because we *already* love ourselves. We demonstrate love for ourselves by nourishing and cherishing ourselves. In other words, we place a lot of attention on ourselves. For example, when someone shows you a picture of a large group that includes you, at whom do you look first?

   > **ILLUSTRATION:** You might be wondering about someone who seems to hate himself. Someone like that often talks much of his failures and says such things as, "I can't do anything right" or "I am just no good." But where is this person's attention, and with whom is he preoccupied?
   >
   > *7.*
   > _____
   >
   > He is demonstrating how much he loves (gives attention to) himself because the subject of his discussion is himself. The problem is not how low or high he sees himself, the problem is how *much* he thinks about himself. The total focus of his life is on himself.
   >
   > As an example, think about the young man who stands off in a corner by himself during a school activity while everyone else is in a group engaging in friendly conversation with the other

students. He is invited into the group but declines, thinking, "I don't know how to talk to anyone. I'm a failure. I'll just say something stupid." Does he hate himself? No, just the opposite, he loves himself so much he is not willing to mix with the others for fear he might make a mistake and be laughed at.

If that person really hated himself, he would jump into the middle of the group, make a fool of himself, and then invite them to ridicule him so that they could participate in degrading him. But instead, he does not want to be embarrassed because he loves himself and seeks only to be accepted.

2. Highlight in your manual and turn to *Matthew 22:37-39*. How many commandments did Jesus give in this passage?

   8. _____

   Is there a third commandment in this passage?

   9. _____

   Some would say that this passage also encourages love of self since Jesus commands you to love your neighbor as yourself. This cannot be correct since *verse 40* refers only to two commandments. In this passage, Jesus is not encouraging you to love yourself. Instead, He commands you to love others in the same way that you already love yourself.

   Jesus states not only what to do but how to do it. According to *Matthew 7:12*, in what way are you to treat (love) others?

   10. _____

   No one needs to be taught how he would like others to treat him. Even a small child knows how he would like to be treated. Therefore, to love we need merely to reverse the focus from ourselves to God and others. God made it very simple to understand. Make a list of some of the ways you like to be treated:

   11. _____
   _____
   _____
   _____
   _____

   It is easy to think of these things, isn't it? God says treat others in this same way.

3. Read the second sentence of *Principle 33*, then highlight in your manual and read *Luke 9:23-24*. In this passage, Jesus gives you His basic focus for living. You are to deny self, that is, take your focus off self. Notice that Jesus tells you to take up your cross daily. What is the cross a symbol of?

   12. _____

   Now, what is the "put-on" in this passage?

   13. _____

   How does a person find (or save) his life?

   14. _____

In *verse 24*, we see how important this command is. If you concentrate on finding (or saving) your life, you will lose it. To understand the significance of this statement, let's consider how God created you to live.

In the book of *Genesis*, God tells you that He created man in His image. In other words, He created you to be like Him. Since God is Spirit, He did not make you like Him physically; this must mean that He made you to be like Him spiritually. He is a God of love; and therefore, He has created you to love. So, when you love God and your neighbor (the two great commandments) you are behaving according to the way you were created. You are content because you were created to function in love. On the other hand, when you take your focus off serving the Lord and others, you become dissatisfied and miserable.

> ***ILLUSTRATION:*** Suppose a locomotive had a personality and decided one day that life was too restrictive. As it traveled, the locomotive noticed that animals were roaming about the beautiful countryside. In comparison, it was restricted very narrowly to traveling along two very rigid railroad tracks. It said to itself, "I want to be free from this boring life. I want to escape from these tracks and travel through the countryside like those animals."
>
> Suppose that the locomotive were able to leave the tracks. What would happen?
>
> **15.** _____
>
> Rather than being free, it would soon not be able to move at all. The point is that the locomotive was designed to function most efficiently when it was restricted to the tracks. In the same way, we function best as God intended and are completely fulfilled only when we die to self and serve God and others.

4. Let's look at a parallel passage to *Luke 9:24* to see another way that Jesus explained this truth. Read *John 12:24*. Jesus compares our lives to grains of wheat. Now, just imagine a grain of wheat lying in a storage bin. It is dry and warm and comfortable with many other grains of wheat to keep it company, but it is not fulfilling its purpose. Not until it is placed in the cold, dark ground without other grains nearby to keep it company, and not until it dies does it bear fruit and multiply.

   Now read *John 12:25*. Jesus is not just talking about grains of wheat. What is He talking about?

   16. _____

   In other words, He is pointing out how important it is not to be preoccupied with self but, instead, to focus our attention on the Lord and others.

B. The truths in *Principle 33* are life-changing. Just think, if we truly were to die to self, nothing could hurt us. When we say that someone has hurt us, we really mean, "I am angry and bitter about what happened to me, and I don't like it." A dead body is not hurt no matter how much it is kicked. It is when we die daily that we can have contentment in the midst of even the most difficult circumstances.

C. At this point, let's review some of the major contrasts between man's way and God's way.

   1. In Lessons 4 and 5, we learned that:

      a. Man focuses on feelings; God requires obedience in spite of feelings, and

      b. Man denies responsibility for his problems; God holds man responsible.

   2. In this lesson, we have seen that man concentrates on finding (or saving) his life; God shows us that contentment comes from losing your life for Jesus' sake.

| SOME EXAMPLES OF FOCUS ON SELF |

A. Turn to the *Self-Confrontation* manual, Page 141, **ENVY, JEALOUSY, COVETOUSNESS, AND GREED**. People, even in the church, often minimize or accept these sins as normal, as revealed by statements such as, "I sure envy your clothes," or "I am so jealous you get to do that ministry." When a person is focused on self, he also tends to compare himself with others and becomes envious, jealous, covetous, or greedy. "To focus on" means "to place all attention on," "to be set on." While we are to look at our lives biblically, we are not to be preoccupied with ourselves.

1. Read Section **I. Characteristics of envy, jealousy, covetousness, and greed** on Page 141.

    a. In Paragraph A., God's Word clearly shows the extreme self-focus of these sins. In addition, it is clear that they are focused on harming or tearing down others and are contrary to biblical love.

    b. Paragraph B. emphasizes the importance of accepting God's sovereignty for what you receive. Read the parable Jesus told in *Matthew 20:1-16*. What did the workers who were hired first say when the other workers, who worked fewer hours, were paid the same wage?

    17. _____

    _____

    What was the sin exhibited by the workers who were hired first?

    18. _____

    As you consider your own life, think of any situations in which you became envious. Pray right now and ask the Holy Spirit to reveal to you anything you should confess to the Lord in this area of your life. Place a check here (__) after you have examined yourself in this way. And remember one of the "put-ons" for envy is contentment (see *I Timothy 6:4-8* — we are told to be content with whatever we have). Food, covering, and shelter are enough, and God has promised to provide those.

2. Read Section **II. Some common thoughts, words, and actions that reveal envy, jealousy, covetousness, or greed** on Page 141.

3. In Section **III. Recognizing the difference between godly jealousy and sinful jealousy**, read Paragraph B. on Page 143. Then read the content of **PLEASING SELF OR PLEASING GOD** (*Self-Confrontation*, Pages 145-146).

    Page 145 illustrates the importance of a person's focus. In each of the examples, the same word in the original language describes sinfulness or godliness, depending on the context of the passage. For example, in Section **I.**, the same word in the original language is translated "worry" and "anxious" to indicate a focus on pleasing self, while it is translated "concern" and "care for" to indicate a focus on pleasing God.

    As we continue to study the various problem areas, we will see how important it is to examine the focus of life.

4. Now go back to Page 143 and read Section **IV. God's view of envy, jealousy, covetousness, and greed**. Especially focus on each of the definitions indicated within parentheses in Paragraphs A. and B.

Write a statement that you have heard or said demonstrating:

19. Envy: _____

Jealousy: _____

Covetousness: _____

Greed: _____

God describes these sins as very serious.

OUR INHERITANCE IN CHRIST

Now, let's return to the biblical principles on Page 137 of Lesson 9. Read *Principle 34*. Highlight in your manual and read *Romans 8:14-17*. What kind of relationship do believers have with God?

20. _____

What will believers inherit?

21. _____

Is there anything about this that we have earned or deserved?

22. _____

In this passage, the King of kings and Lord of lords says that we have been chosen by Him to be His children. This means that you and I, as believers in the Lord Jesus Christ, are princes and princesses. We are joint heirs with Jesus Christ. We can't even comprehend the magnitude of this wonderful truth.

There are whole courses concentrating on what the Bible says about who we are in Christ. People study those topics for weeks and months at a time. Yet, if you look at the verses in the Bible that deal with who you are in Christ, you could read them all in a very short time. To remain focused on simply contemplating who we are in Christ may be a subtle way in which we deceive ourselves into maintaining a preoccupation with self. God has already told us who we are in Him, and He has already done all that is necessary for us to be members of His royal family, so we do not need to focus our attention on who we are in Christ. That is easy to learn. Rather, the Lord wants us to focus on losing our lives (getting the focus off self) and to focus on Jesus, as we studied in *Luke 9:23-24*.

> **ILLUSTRATION:** For example, in the British royal family, the princes and princesses know from a very early age that they are royalty. That is why their education and training focuses not on *who* they are as princes and princesses, but rather, it focuses on how to *live* like royalty.

THE PEACE AND JOY OF JESUS CHRIST

Read *Principle 35*, (*Self-Confrontation*, Page 137). Read *Psalm 119:165*, *Isaiah 26:3*, and *John 14:15, 21, 23-24*.

Now take a few minutes to go back and review the first column of your personal *Worksheet 3*. As a result of what you have studied in this lesson so far, what other failures to live God's way have you discovered that need to be added in this column?

23. _____

NOTE: *These may or may not be related to the personal problem you have chosen. In fact, as you go through the Bible Study, the Lord may show you the need to choose another problem area instead. So, add* *the new failures to your list in the first column. Then write "put-offs" and "put-ons," associated with the new failures in the second and third columns. Give special attention to those aspects that focus on self (for example, self-belittlement, self-gratification, self-pity, self-love, self-exaltation, envy, jealousy, covetousness or greed).*

BIBLICAL HOPE

Turn to Section **II. Your Hope** (*Self-Confrontation*, Page 138). Read *Principle 36.* Since it is God who has made us as we are, we are not to take any credit nor are we to degrade what God has created. Instead, we are to thank Him for our physical condition and mental capabilities. God does not regard anyone as being disadvantaged, no matter what his physical condition.

The world calls certain people "handicapped," "disabled," or "impaired." Someone could infer from these words that such a person is hindered from completely fulfilling God's plan for his life. But a person's mental or physical capabilities will never hinder him from being everything that God wants him to be. For example, if the Lord allows your arms or legs not to work the way others' do, then He does not intend for you to use your arms or legs to glorify Him the way others use them. You are never hindered from being fully content in glorifying God in your life even though your body may be different from others'. If your legs do not work, you can focus on using the other parts of your body to serve and glorify Him.

Most believers with the problem of "low self-esteem" are already familiar with the fact that they are fearfully and wonderfully made by God *(Psalm 139:13-14).* Merely knowing that fact does not change people because their problem is not just an intellectual misunderstanding. Rather than thanking God, as David did, they continue to focus on self instead.

Read *Principles 37* and *38* and the note under *Principle 38.*

SCRIPTURE RECITATION

Recite *Luke 9:23-24* to someone at home, in class, or elsewhere. Also, recite one of the previous memory passages chosen by the listener. Put a check here (___) when you have accurately recited the verses.

QUESTIONS AND CONCLUSION

A. How do we demonstrate love for ourselves according to *Ephesians 5:29?*

24. _____

B. What are the two greatest commandments?

25. _____

C. How did Jesus tell us to love others in a practical way according to *Matthew 7:12?*

26. _____

D. What does *Luke 9:23-24* say in your own words?

27. _____
_____
_____

E. What was the most significant truth you learned in completing this lesson?

28. _____
_____

In summary, the most important truth of this lesson is that the natural man pays too much attention to self, not too little. Therefore, in order to put off the old practices and begin to live God's way, the believer must take the focus off himself and regard the Lord and others as more important than himself.

PREVIEW OF NEXT LESSON

In the next lesson, we will continue this study by covering the second two elements of dealing with a preoccupation with self: biblical change and biblical practice. Included in the lesson will be two very important subjects — stewardship and spiritual gifts, God's special provision to believers for serving others.

LESSON 10

DEALING WITH SELF (PART TWO)

OPENING PRAYER AND SCRIPTURE MEMORY

Before you begin this lesson, ask for God's help in understanding His Word and for wisdom and strength to apply what you learn in the power of the Holy Spirit.

Begin memorizing *Romans 6:12-13*. Also, review the Scripture memory passages assigned in the previous lessons. Then, be prepared to recite them at the end of this lesson.

Also, in your own words, please write out the meaning of the new memory verses below:

_____

_____

_____

_____

PERSONAL PLAN FOR CHANGE

Continue to work on your personal **VICTORY OVER FAILURES PLAN**. Review each of the columns in *Worksheet 3: "Put-offs" and "Put-ons"* and make corrections based on what you will be learning this week. The Lord may bring to your mind more failures to live biblically that should be added to the first column. This would then affect your entries in the second and third columns.

Also, continue to add to your *Worksheet 4: "Daily Practices" Plan*. Refine your plan up to breakfast time, which you completed in Lesson 9, and then add to it to cover the rest of your typical day. You can use the sample plan on Pages W105-W106 as a guide.

Work on this assignment a little each day as you are doing your other homework. Remember that the purpose of the *"Daily Practices" Plan* is to become a consistent doer of the Word, having victory over the problem area you identified originally in Lesson 5. Continue to ask the Lord for wisdom as you add to your plan.

Implement your plan. This will include:

1. Conviction and sorrow to the point of repentance *(II Corinthians 7:9)*. This is not an intellectual exercise. You must commit yourself to change from a pattern of disobedience to God (which demonstrates your lack of love for Him) to a new pattern of godliness.

2. Self-control and discipline. Old habits are difficult to put off, and putting on new habits often feels unnatural initially.

3. Acknowledging and repenting when you fail. This involves confession of your sins, placing yourself back under the control of the Holy Spirit, changing your plan, if appropriate, and starting again to implement your plan.

INTRODUCTION TO THE LESSON

A. In Lesson 9, we introduced the subject of dealing with a preoccupation with self. We concentrated on the first two elements of how to face, deal with, and endure problems biblically: biblical understanding, and biblical hope. We learned that man's basic problem is that he pays too much attention to self, not too little. The primary teaching of Jesus on how to truly live is to deny self (take the focus of life off self), die daily, and follow Him.

This lesson covers the last two elements of how to face, deal with, and endure problems related to a preoccupation with self. The first two were, "biblical understanding" and "biblical hope." What are the third and fourth elements?

1. _____

This lesson describes *how* to get your focus off self and onto the Lord and others.

B. In this lesson, we will learn *how* to treat others as more important than ourselves. Included will be two very important characteristics of a faithful believer: stewardship (how we manage what God has put in our care) and servanthood (including the use of spiritual gifts, God's special provisions to believers for effectively serving others).

C. Read the purposes of **LESSON 10: DEALING WITH SELF (PART TWO)** (*Self-Confrontation*, Page 154).

BIBLICAL CHANGE — DEALING WITH SELF

Turn to **BIBLICAL PRINCIPLES: DEALING WITH SELF (PART TWO)** (*Self-Confrontation*, Pages 155-156).

A. Read *Principle 39,* then, highlight in your manual and read *Philippians 2:3-8*. How did Jesus demonstrate His servanthood?

2. _____

What are the "put-offs" and "put-ons" in *verses 3-4?*

3. "Put-offs:" _____

"Put-ons:" _____

_____

Give three specific examples of how you can be a servant to those around you.

4. _____

_____

_____

B. Read *Principle 40,* then, highlight in your manual and read *Psalm 37:1-9*. Identify at least three "put-offs" and "put-ons" in this passage.

5. "Put-offs:" _____

"Put-ons:" _____

C. Read *Principle 41,* then, highlight in your manual and read *I Corinthians 4:1-2*. What is required of stewards?

6. _____

Isn't it wonderful to know that God does not say that we are responsible for results? Our responsibility is to be faithful in the present; God takes care of the results in the present and future. Understanding and applying this truth can eliminate much anxiety about how situations turn out. We are to be faithful parents, but the Lord is in control of how our children turn out. We are to be faithful employees, but God is in control of our employment situation. We are to be faithful students, but God is in control of the resulting grades. In what area or areas are you anxious about the results, when you should be just focusing on your faithfulness and trusting that the Lord is in control?

7. _____

Remember that the Lord is in *control,* but He does not promise that things will turn out according to our desires. He is working things out for our ultimate good.

D. Read *Principle 42,* then, highlight in your manual and read *Galatians 6:3-4.* This passage warns that you are not to compare yourself to others, but you are to seek to please God in all that you do. List examples, if appropriate, where you have compared yourself to someone else.

8. _____

E. Read *Principle 43,* then, highlight in your manual and read *II Corinthians 12:7-10.* Note that, while Paul was buffeted by a messenger of Satan, he focused on the Lord, not on battling Satan. Thank God for what you cannot change about yourself (such as bodily or intellectual limitations) and correct those deficiencies that hinder you from serving God and others (such as lack of knowledge about how to present the salvation message, not having learned to read in order to study the Word, etc.).

1. In what areas of your life are you tempted to complain about things you cannot change?

9. _____

2. In what areas of your life do you lack knowledge or skill that you need to change?

10. _____

F. Read *Principle 44.*

BIBLICAL PRACTICE — STEWARDSHIP

All of the above principles are important to keep in mind when learning about stewardship. So let's turn to **BIBLICAL PRINCIPLES OF STEWARDSHIP** on Page 157 in the *Self-Confrontation* manual.

A. Under Section **I. God is sovereign over every facet of His creation** ….

1. Read Paragraphs A. and B. Then, highlight the reference in your manual and read the parable of the talents in *Matthew 25:14-30.*

   In *verse 15,* how did the master determine the number of talents to give to each servant?

   11. _____

   According to *verses 21* and *23,* on what basis was each person commended?

   12. _____

   Note that each servant was not commended on the basis of the amount he gained or the number of his talents (or his abilities). Every believer is to be a faithful and trustworthy steward, regardless of his ability.

B. Under Section **II. Your motivation to be a faithful steward is to be centered on God and His objectives instead of a preoccupation with self:**

1. Read Paragraph A. As a caretaker you are to delight in (to give all your attention to, to exalt in) doing all to glorify God. According to *II Corinthians 5:17-20* (highlight this reference in your manual), what is one of our greatest responsibilities as believers?

   13. _____

   Your caretaking and testimony are important to keep in mind in all areas of stewardship. In Paragraphs B. through E., we will examine four areas of stewardship: spiritual gifts, time, the physical body, and material goods.

2. Read Paragraph B. Although the use of spiritual gifts, talents, and abilities is introduced in this paragraph, this subject requires much more in-depth teaching. We will cover this topic in great detail in the next section (**BIBLICAL PRACTICE — SERVING OTHERS**).

3. Read Paragraph C., then, highlight in your manual and read *Ephesians 5:15-16*. What are you to be careful to do?

   14. _____

   In the language of the New Testament, there are two different words translated "time." One word focuses on linear time or the amount of time (the seconds, minutes, hours, days, etc.). The other word, which is the one used in this passage, focuses on the "opportunity" (or what we are given to do within the time allotted to us). God tells us we are to make the most of the opportunities that He has given us. The issue is not the number of seconds or days we live, but how faithful we have been with the opportunities God has provided within the time that He has given us on this earth.

   In what area or areas are you not using time as effectively as you ought to?

   15. _____
   _____

   How can you make the most of your opportunities in those situations?

   16. _____

4. Read Paragraph D., then, highlight in your manual and read *Romans 6:12-13*. To whom do our bodies belong?

   17. _____

   Even our bodies are not our "own property" (they belong to the Lord as temples of the Holy Spirit) and all that is done with the body, in public or in private, is to be for the glory of the Lord. What are some specific responsibilities we have in being stewards of our bodies?

   18. _____
   _____
   _____

   While the world's focus regarding the body is to draw attention and give glory to self, the motivation of biblical stewardship of the body is to have energy and stamina to love and serve the Lord and others more fully.

5. Read Paragraph E., then, highlight in your manual and read *Luke 16:10-13*. What is the important message of *verse 10*?

19. _____

_____

The important lesson is that we are to establish faithfulness in our current responsibilities. We can not just wait for the "big, important jobs" to demonstrate our faithfulness. It is sobering to realize that if a person is not faithful in the little things, God says that he is also not faithful in the big things.

Very often, we think of the word "mammon" in *verse 11* merely in terms of money. In actuality, the word "mammon" indicates the sum total of all the material goods in our care.

As you read the subparagraphs in Paragraph E., keep in mind that material goods include not only money, but also dwelling places, household goods, toys, work equipment, vehicles for transportation, and any other things we typically tend to think of as our own possessions.

Also read *Matthew 6:19-21* and identify the "put-offs" and "put-ons."

20. "Put-offs:" _____

"Put-ons:" _____

What we think about most frequently is a good indication of where our treasure is. Our level of attachment to material things in this world is usually indicated by how we think, speak, or act if we lose them. This gets back to our focus of life.

| BIBLICAL PRACTICE — SERVING OTHERS |

During the first part of the lesson, we learned that as God's stewards, we are to be faithful to carry out His instructions using His resources. These resources include the spiritual gifts, time, body, and material goods that He has put in our care.

Now let's turn to Page 160 of the *Self-Confrontation* manual and look at how we can die to self by using God's resources in serving others.

A. Read Section **I. As a believer in Jesus Christ, you have been given all the provisions you need for ministry**. From this section, what are the three provisions God provided to us for ministry?

21. _____

_____

B. Read Section **II. God has a unique plan of ministry for you and for every other believer to fulfill**.

1. Read Paragraph A. According to *I Peter 4:10* (highlight this reference in your manual):

Whom has God gifted spiritually?

22. _____

When does a person receive the gifting?

23. _____

What is the purpose of the gifts?

24. _____

Student Workbook for the Self-Confrontation Bible Study
- Lesson 10 -
© Biblical Counseling Foundation

NOTE: The word for "gift" in this passage should more accurately be translated "gifting" or "giftedness" — not a specific kind of gift.

There is much controversy about spiritual gifts within the body of Christ, even to the point of division in some Christian circles. Much of the controversy would be eliminated if we would simply remember three basic facts: 1) we are to use our gifting to serve others, not to serve ourselves; 2) God, in the person of the Holy Spirit, has gifted every believer at the time of spiritual birth; and 3) the gifts are distributed according to God's will in our lives, not according to our preferences. Therefore, all believers are to use whatever gifting they have received from the Lord to serve others. The focus, then, is not to be on oneself, but rather on blessing others. The following illustration may help to understand the value of using spiritual gifts to minister to others:

ILLUSTRATION: An elderly believer was becoming weary and even weak in his faith as he neared death. He began to have so many doubts that he even wondered if there were a heaven and a hell, and if so, what was the difference?

One day, the man saw an artist's depiction of both places. Observing the depiction of hell, the believer was surprised to see a huge vat of his favorite stew with many people standing at the rim trying to eat the stew. All of them were starving and miserable in spite of being so close to the food. They had long spoons permanently attached to their wrists, and the spoons were 18 inches (half a meter) longer than the distance from their wrists to their mouths. Thus, they could dip into the stew, but they could not feed themselves. That was hell.

Observing the depiction of heaven, the believer saw a similar scene with many people with the same type of spoons attached to their wrists. However the people were healthy and completely satisfied. Why? They were feeding each other.

You see, the people in hell would never think of ministering to others. In fact, if one of them suggested to another that they feed each other, they might still fail because they would not agree on who provides the first spoonful.

---

2. Read *I Corinthians 12:7-11*. Who determines what gifts believers receive?

   25. _____

   For whose good does He distribute them?

   26. _____

3. Read Paragraphs B.-D.

4. Read Section **III. As a believer in Jesus Christ, you need to minister and are needed in ministry by the rest of the Body of Christ** (Page 161). Especially note the six guidelines in Paragraph C.

   Pay special attention to Subparagraph 4. The Lord will make clear, through your serving others, in which ministry you should spend more time.

   You do not discover your gifts by simply sitting and waiting for them to be revealed to you, or by taking a spiritual gifts test. In fact, the results of a spiritual gifts test can present a temptation to pride if you think you have a particularly desirable gift. You may also be tempted to answer questions in a way that disposes you toward a certain favored gift. Alternatively, if a spiritual gifts test indicates a lack of gifting in a particular area, you may be tempted to excuse yourself for not doing what God commands on the grounds that it is not your gift, even though God commands every believer to practice all of the ministering gifts (such as giving, serving, mercy, teaching, etc.).

You discover what your gifts are by simply serving and having the Lord direct you in the areas where you are most effectively used in the body of Christ. It is through your doing the work of ministry that the Lord will reveal to you where you will be most effective in using the spiritual abilities He has granted you.

> ***ILLUSTRATION:*** When a ship is in a docking slip, it will not change direction no matter how much the rudder moves. However, once the ship is out of the dock and moving, even the slightest movement of the rudder changes the course of the ship.
>
> So too, the Lord directs our lives as we are obedient to Him. Since the ministering gifts are also commands, God requires that we be diligent to practice all of them. For example, we are to give, whether or not we have the gift of giving; we are to show mercy, whether or not we have the gift of mercy. Therefore, it is as we are being doers of the Word that we are able to discern God's will in exercising the gifts He has given us.

Also, in Subparagraph 4., note that you should take opportunities to keep you in a Christlike servant attitude before others. You are not to choose to be a servant only in areas you enjoy. It is only when you are *treated* as a servant that you begin to know what kind of servant you really are.

PLAN FOR OVERCOMING A PREOCCUPATION WITH SELF

A. The remainder of this lesson provides guidance on how to have lasting victory over a preoccupation with self. You may wish to review the remaining pages in Lesson 10 of the *Self-Confrontation* manual; however, your primary concentration should be to incorporate the truths you have learned in this lesson into your personal plan for change.

B. When adding to your **"Daily Practices" Plan**, consider *Romans 6:12-13* and *Philippians 2:3-4* since these verses are about putting off the habitual pattern of preoccupation with self and putting on godliness.

NOTE: We will study about the "overcoming temptations" plan and the forgiveness/ reconciliation" plan in future lessons.

SCRIPTURE RECITATION

Recite *Romans 6:12-13* to someone at home, in class, or elsewhere. Also, recite one of the previous memory passages chosen by the listener. Put a check here (__) when you have accurately recited the verses.

QUESTIONS AND CONCLUSION

A. According to *I Corinthians 4:1-2*, what is required of stewards?

27. _____

B. For what results are you responsible?

28. _____

Wonderfully, God takes care of all results.

C. When we complain that we don't have enough material things or abilities that others have, whom are we blaming ultimately?

29. _____

D. Whom has God gifted spiritually?

30. _____

E. Whom are you to serve using your spiritual gifting?

31. _____

F. What is the best way to determine how God may have gifted you?

32. _____
_____

G. What was the most significant truth you learned in completing this lesson?

33. _____
_____

H. In conclusion, read *Ephesians 4:16* and consider the following illustration:

> ***ILLUSTRATION:*** Consider what it would be like if parts of your body did not cooperate with one another. Suppose that you were eating and just as your hand was bringing a bite of food to your mouth, your head decided not to cooperate and turned to the side. Or suppose that you were in the process of sitting down in a chair and just as you were about to be seated, your hand decided not to cooperate and pulled the chair out from under you. These would be extremely unusual reactions because the various parts of the body cooperate with one another.
>
> So it should be in the body of Christ. It is a wonderful, vibrant church where everyone serves one another as Jesus Christ has commanded. We must not wait for someone else to serve us. We need to take the initiative to serve others, without expecting anything in return. It is vital that we in the church heed *Ephesians 4:16*.

PREVIEW OF NEXT LESSON

In the next lesson, you will learn about the problems of anger and bitterness. This lesson immediately follows the lessons on dealing with self because anger and bitterness are so widespread, particularly among those with a strong focus on self.

Anger is probably the most common type of sin known to man. Some even accept it as proper, but is it ever proper to be angry? We'll answer that question in the next lesson.

LESSON 11
ANGER AND BITTERNESS

OPENING PRAYER AND SCRIPTURE MEMORY

Before you begin this lesson, ask for God's help in understanding His Word and for wisdom and strength to apply what you learn in the power of the Holy Spirit.

Begin memorizing *Ephesians 4:31-32* and *James 1:19-20*. Also, review the Scripture memory passages assigned in the previous lessons. Then, be prepared to recite them at the end of this lesson.

Also, in your own words, please write out the meaning of the new memory verses below:

_____
_____
_____
_____

PERSONAL PLAN FOR CHANGE

In Lesson 10 you completed the *"Daily Practices" Plan*. Now, you are ready to proceed to *Worksheet 5: "Overcoming Temptations" Plan*. The form is on Pages W126-W127. Remember that the purpose of an *"Overcoming Temptations" Plan* is to help you to respond in a godly manner to situations where you have been tempted and have fallen repeatedly. It is implemented only at the time the temptation occurs, but it is prepared in advance of the temptation so that you will be better prepared to deal with the temptation when it occurs. The plan is then put into practice at the time of the temptation.

A. Complete the first section of the form entitled, *Worksheet 5: "Overcoming Temptations" Plan*. If you wonder about the importance of having a *written* plan, review the first page of Lesson 5.

  1. Under **"Type of situation in which I previously have been tempted and sinned"** describe the type of situation in which you have been repeatedly tempted and have not had victory (for example, suppose you have a weekly appointment at a location that requires you to travel through heavy traffic congestion. Suppose that in the past, you have given way to angry feelings each week, and have reviled others, honked the horn at others, and have forced your way ahead of others). Normally, these types of temptations are associated with the major pattern written at the top of *Worksheet 4: "Daily Practices" Plan*.

  2. Under **"Ways in which I sinned in this situation"** list the deeds from the first column of *Worksheet 3* that are associated with the type of situation you selected.

  3. Under **"Righteous pattern to be established"** list the godly traits from the third column of *Worksheet 3* that you recognize need to be developed in your life.

B. Complete the section entitled, **"My plan to respond righteously the next time a similar temptation arises."** Write a specific plan that you will implement when you are tempted. To help you write a biblical plan, review the following guidance:

  1. Deal with yourself first *(based on Matthew 7:5)*.

   a. Immediately ask for God's help *(I Thessalonians 5:17; Hebrews 4:15-16; James 1:5)*.

b. Repent and confess to God any sinful thoughts you dwelt upon, even for a short period of time *(I John 1:9)*.

c. Review the biblical basis for hope in the situation.

1) Review *Romans 8:28-29* and remind yourself that God causes all things to work together for good to those who love Him and are called according to His purpose.

2) Review *I Corinthians 10:13* and remind yourself that God will not allow you to be tested or tempted beyond what you can bear.

3) Review *James 1:2-4* and remind yourself that regardless of your feelings or circumstances, the situation is an opportunity for further spiritual maturity.

4) Review *Philippians 4:13* and remind yourself that you can do all things through Christ who gives you strength.

5) Review *Ezekiel 18:20* and remind yourself that you are not responsible for changing the hearts of others.

d. Thank God for the opportunity to serve Him and trust Him for wisdom to deal victoriously with the present situation, no matter how intense the temptation *(Ephesians 5:20; I Thessalonians 5:18)*.

e. Review the Scripture passages you have memorized that relate to the type of sin *(based on Psalm 119:9, 11)*. Include verses showing hope and giving practical guidance for how to change.

f. Write the specific thoughts, speech, and/or actions you will change based on the "put-offs" in the second column and the corresponding "put-ons" in the third column. Recognize that in most cases, thinking, speaking, and acting biblically are almost simultaneous, or within a very short time period.

2. After dealing with yourself, when others are involved:

a. Listen to all sides first; make no prejudgments *(based on Proverbs 18:2, 17; James 1:19)*. Ask questions to get the facts and to gain understanding, not opinions *(based on Proverbs 13:10; 18:13, 15; II Timothy 2:23)*.

b. Formulate and state your evaluation carefully and slowly *(based on Proverbs 18:13; James 1:19)*, while

1) Judging yourself first *(Matthew 7:1-5)*.

2) Evaluating the observable deeds (speech and actions) of others, not their apparent motives *(based on I Samuel 16:7; Jeremiah 17:9-10)*.

c. Describe the situation and the biblical solution — speak at the appropriate time and only with words that edify *(Ephesians 4:29)*; speak the truth (i.e., biblical truth) in love with a gentle and humble spirit *(based on Proverbs 15:1; Ephesians 4:1-3, 15; I Peter 3:8-9)*.

d. Act in a way that demonstrates your love for the other person(s) who are present.

e. Then, deal with the deeds of others. Seek ways to edify others by serving them, not yourself, in this situation *(Romans 14:19; Ephesians 4:29; Philippians 2:3-4)*. Bless the people who are involved *(I Peter 3:8-9)*. Focus on restoration, not condemnation *(Galatians 6:1; II Timothy 2:24-26)* nor revenge *(Romans 12:19)*.

See the sample *"Overcoming Temptations" Plan* on Pages W128-W129.

Work on this assignment a little each day as you are doing your other homework.

A. When adding to your *"Daily Practices" Plan*, consider *Ephesians 4:31-32* and *Colossians 3:8, 12-14* since these verses are about putting off the habitual pattern of anger and bitterness and putting on godliness.

B. When working on your *"Overcoming Temptations" Plan*, consider *James 1:19* and *Ephesians 4:26-27* since these verses are about taking steps to deal with situations that occur suddenly and you need to take immediate steps to control your anger.

NOTE: *You will study these passages of Scripture and their application as you work through this week's lesson.*

Worksheet 5: "Overcoming Temptations" Plan

My plan not to repeat this sin and, instead, to respond biblically at the time of temptation (II Timothy 2:22)

Page _____ of _____

Type of situation in which I previously have been tempted and sinned:
_____

Ways in which I sinned in this situation *(as seen from the first column of Worksheet 3)*:
_____
_____

Righteous pattern to be established *(as seen from the third column of Worksheet 3)*:
_____
_____

My plan to respond righteously the next time a similar temptation arises:
_____
_____
_____
_____
_____
_____
_____
_____
_____
_____
_____
_____
_____
_____
_____
_____
_____
_____
_____

VOFP Worksheet 5 a © Biblical Counseling Foundation

Permission is granted to reproduce this form for personal or ministry use

Student Workbook for the Self-Confrontation Bible Study
- Lesson 11 -

Worksheet 5: "Overcoming Temptation" Plan (Continued)

*My plan not to repeat this sin and, instead, to respond biblically
at the time of temptation (II Timothy 2:22)*

Page _____ of _____

My plan to respond righteously the next time a similar temptation arises (continued):

_____
_____
_____
_____
_____
_____
_____
_____
_____
_____
_____
_____
_____
_____
_____
_____
_____
_____
_____
_____
_____
_____
_____
_____
_____
_____
_____
_____
_____
_____
_____
_____
_____
_____
_____

© Biblical Counseling Foundation

VOFP Worksheet 5 b

Permission is granted to reproduce this form for personal or ministry use

Sample Worksheet 5: "Overcoming Temptations" Plan

My plan not to repeat this sin and, instead, to respond biblically at the time of temptation (II Timothy 2:22)

Page __1__ of __2__

Type of situation in which I previously have been tempted and sinned:
When my co-worker loads his work onto me

Ways in which I sinned in this situation (*as seen from the first column of* **Worksheet 3**):
I spoke in an angry way, with a loud, harsh tone of voice using condemning and accusing words. I quarrelled with my co-worker and said tearing down words to him.

Righteous pattern to be established (*as seen from the third column of* **Worksheet 3**):
Kindness, tender-heartedness, and forgiveness, edifying words that give grace to the hearer and are appropriate to the need, gentle words, patience, pondering before answering

My plan to respond righteously the next time a similar temptation arises:

A. Deal with myself first. I will:
   1. Immediately, ask for God's help.
   2. Repent and confess to God any sinful thoughts that I purposely held onto beyond the immediate temptation.
   3. Review the biblical basis for hope in the situation.
      a. Recite Romans 8:28-29 and thank God for using this trial for my good.
      b. Recite I Corinthians 10:13 and thank God for giving me the strength to bear this temptation.
      c. Recite James 1:2-4 and thank God that this situation is an opportunity for further spiritual maturity.
      d. Recite Philippians 4:13 and remind myself that I can do all things through Christ Who gives me strength since my adequacy is from God and not from any natural inner strength.
      e. Recite Ezekiel 18:20 and thank God that it is not my responsibility to change my co-worker, only to bless him.
   4. Thank God for the opportunity to serve Him and trust Him for wisdom and grace to deal victoriously with the present situation.
   5. Review verses I have memorized that relate to anger.

VOFP Worksheet 5 a © Biblical Counseling Foundation

Sample Worksheet 5: "Overcoming Temptation" Plan (Continued)

My plan not to repeat this sin and, instead, to respond biblically at the time of temptation (II Timothy 2:22)

Page __2__ of __2__

My plan to respond righteously the next time a similar temptation arises (continued):

B. Deal with my co-worker:

   1. Listen to him attentively and ask questions about the work to gain understanding.

   2. Repeat back what he said to make sure I understand and that he knows I've listened to him.

   3. If the work is really his to do, and it is too much for him, tell him I will ask our supervisor how best to redistribute the responsibilities and help him accordingly so we can accomplish the work together.

   4. If he needs to do the work himself, tell him that I am willing to help him as appropriate.

C. Return to my daily tasks rather than dwell on evil thoughts.

D. When temptations arise in my thought life about my co-worker:

   1. Pray for my co-worker, and ask the Lord to remind me of ways to bless him.

   2. Actively turn my thoughts to blessing.

   3. If necessary, make a list (or add to the existing list) of ways to bless my co-worker, using Romans 12:9-21 as a guideline.

© Biblical Counseling Foundation

VOFP Worksheet 5 b

INTRODUCTION TO THE LESSON

A. This lesson on the problems of anger and bitterness immediately follows the lessons on dealing with self because anger and bitterness are so widespread, particularly among those individuals with a strong preoccupation with self.

Anger and bitterness are often accurate indicators of an individual's lack of sensitivity to sin. Anger especially is accompanied by strong feelings and is often wrongly excused by making it seem as:

- Righteous — "It is enough to make *anyone* mad!"
- Unimportant — "I have *always* had a quick temper."
- Not sinful — "I get angry fast but I get over it just as fast."

Anger is probably the most common type of sin known to man. It is even accepted as proper by many who cite that Jesus was angry when He healed a man's hand on the Sabbath. But is it ever proper for human beings to be angry? We'll answer that question a little later.

B. Read the purposes of **LESSON 11: ANGER AND BITTERNESS** (*Self-Confrontation*, Page 172).

BIBLICAL UNDERSTANDING ABOUT ANGER AND BITTERNESS

A. The biblical principles in Lesson 11 cover all four of the elements of how to face, deal with, and endure any temptation to anger or bitterness. What are the four elements?

1. _____

Read *Principle 45*, **BIBLICAL PRINCIPLES: ANGER AND BITTERNESS** (*Self-Confrontation*, Page 173) and *Galatians 5:19-21*. Notice that anger is demonstrated in several ways in *verse 20*. Though we are saved by grace through faith, this Scripture passage shows that continuing outbursts of anger could be an indication that a person is not a believer. You cannot continue in sin as an ongoing pattern and legitimately claim to have the empowering of the Holy Spirit to change (i.e., be saved).

B. There are many ways that we demonstrate anger. Let's look at some of them by turning to **UNBIBLICAL RESPONSES TO ANGER AND BITTERNESS** (*Self-Confrontation*, Page 175).

1. Read Paragraphs A., C., and F. under Section **I. Some examples from Scripture** ..., Page 175.

2. Under Section **II. Some unbiblical ways** ..., Page 175:

    a. Read Paragraph A.

    b. Read Paragraph B. Some people try to justify expressing their angry thoughts outwardly without physically harming the person they hate. What is wrong with this approach? Read *Matthew 5:22*.

    2. _____

    c. Now read the rest of Section **II**. Note that secular treatments for anger often focus only on helping a person *feel* better.

3. Turn to Section **III. Some unbiblical justifications** ....

    a. Read Paragraph A. Remember that each person is totally responsible for his own sins (*Ezekiel 18:20*).

    b. Read Paragraph B. and *Matthew 15:18-19*. Where does anger come from?

    3. _____

> *ILLUSTRATION:* When a cup full of water is shaken, water spills out. When a cup full of milk is shaken, milk spills out. Why water out of one, and milk out of the other? Because only what is in the cup can come out when it is shaken. If a person is full of anger, anger spills out when he is shaken. It is not legitimate to say, "He made me angry," since no one and no circumstance can make a person angry. Angry reactions only reveal what is in the heart already.

C. In contrast to these unbiblical views, we see the biblical understanding of anger in **A BIBLICAL VIEW OF ANGER** (*Self-Confrontation*, Pages 177-180).

 1. Read each point under Section **I. Anger of God** and Section **II. Anger of Jesus** on Page 177.

 2. Read Section **III. Anger that is not sinful** …. Then compare *Ephesians 4:26-27* and *James 1:20*. You might wonder how to reconcile these two verses, since *Ephesians 4:26-27* seems to indicate a non-sinful aspect of anger, and *James 1:20* states that the anger of man is not righteous.

    The primary message of the *Ephesians 4:26-27* passage is that anger can be dangerous if not dealt with quickly. It is important to recognize that anger has two components: feelings and deeds. To see this, let's turn to *Psalm 4:4*, from which this passage is referenced. The first phrase of this verse can be translated "tremble," "quiver in fear or awe," "be agitated," "quake," or "be perturbed." These are strong emotions.

    What happens in your body when you experience very strong emotions? What do you notice first? Usually with anger or fear, your body tenses up and you start trembling. With anger you may also get hot, or feel a surge of energy. That physical response of trembling, which is mentioned in *Psalm 4:4*, is what gets your attention. So, God is saying to you through *Ephesians 4:26-27* that as soon as you recognize the strong bodily responses (feelings), take care that you do not sin. You may find your palms moist, and your voice trembling, but you can still do the loving thing.

    Because the passion associated with anger is so volatile if not brought into check quickly, the angry person can easily go out of control. The *Ephesians* passage is an appeal to deal with anger quickly and thoroughly, before the temptation to sin becomes monumental, so that the devil does not gain an opportunity to create havoc.

    It is important to differentiate between angry deeds (thoughts, speech, and actions) and the emotions (or feelings) associated with anger. You are totally responsible for changing your thoughts, speech, and actions, but you are not held responsible for your feelings because they are involuntary. However, you need to pay close attention to the feelings associated with anger because very often, they are the first indication that anger is coming on. Therefore, when you first detect that you are getting angry, while you are still in the temptation phase, you had better deal with it quickly before it becomes sin.

 3. Under Section **IV. Sinful anger**, Page 177:

    a. Read Paragraph B. and *Proverbs 29:11*. What is the difference between the foolish and wise man in this passage?

    4. _____

    "Outbursts of anger" and "immediate anger" are always condemned in Scripture. Even when someone is "slow to anger," he must not violate any other portion of Scripture and must still portray Christlike characteristics, which is to exhibit biblical love.

    b. Read the first four subparagraphs in Paragraph G. A person can be angry without sinning if he is totally loving at the same time, which implies that he is not in any way preoccupied with himself.

In summary, man concentrates on "ventilating" and thus, sinning in thoughts, speech, and actions, but God requires a disciplining of thoughts, speech, and actions in the midst of — or in spite of — strong emotions.

BIBLICAL HOPE

So far, we have seen that anger can be very volatile, and if the anger is not brought into check quickly, the angry person can easily go out of control. The Scriptures state that we must deal with anger quickly and thoroughly so that the devil does not gain an opportunity to create more havoc. But can a person always control anger? In other words, is there hope for dealing with anger in a godly way?

A. Read *Principle 46*, **BIBLICAL PRINCIPLES: ANGER AND BITTERNESS** (*Self-Confrontation*, Page 173). The Lord gives believers power to overcome anger and bitterness.

Lest you think it is not possible to control anger, can you think of a time when you were having an argument with someone and the phone rang? How did you answer the phone?

5. _____

Just think of how even unbelievers can change their tone of voice very quickly even in the midst of an angry quarrel. We can change our demeanor and become very sweet-sounding if we choose to do so. Since this is an act of the will in spite of emotions, there is great hope that we can change.

B. Read *Principle 47*, **BIBLICAL PRINCIPLES: ANGER AND BITTERNESS** (*Self-Confrontation*, Page 173). When you are bitter, the very person you want to suffer may be free while *you* pay the consequences. When you are bitter, you stay miserable and your mind and body pay a price.

BIBLICAL CHANGE

Now that we have seen our hope in dealing with anger, let's see how we can put off the practice of anger and bitterness and put on the biblical practice of righteousness. Read *Principle 48*, **BIBLICAL PRINCIPLES: ANGER AND BITTERNESS** (*Self-Confrontation*, Page 173).

A. Re-read *Ephesians 4:26-27* and read *Proverbs 16:32; 25:28*. Remember that it is important to deal with anger quickly. When one gives over control of his spirit to the powerful emotions of anger, angry deeds can get out of control very easily.

B. Dealing with the temptation to explosive anger.

   1. Read *James 1:19*. What is the "put-off" in this verse?

   6. _____

   What are the "put-ons?"

   7. _____

> **ILLUSTRATION:** Consider this example of how *James 1:19* applies. Suppose a mother walks into the kitchen and discovers milk spilled on the floor. Since her children have spilled milk before, her temptation is to get angry and accuse one of the children.
>
> However, her first action should be to listen carefully, ask questions to get the facts, and make no pre-judgments or hasty decisions. Without making accusations, she should ask the children if any of them knows how the milk was spilled.
>
> Only after considering all the possibilities, should she then announce her tentative conclusions about how the milk could have been spilled speaking deliberately and gently.

> Being careful to deal with the deeds, not the children's motives; she then decides what to do about the problem.

2. Read the procedure outlined in Subparagraph 5. on Page 187 of the *Self-Confrontation* manual for more details. As you can see, the *James 1:19* passage describes how to deal with a specific temptation to sin in anger. In contrast, the last half of *Principle 48* explains how to deal with an ongoing pattern of anger toward others.

C. Dealing with the habitual pattern of anger and bitterness.

1. Read *Ephesians 4:31-32* and note the "put-offs" and "put-ons."

    What are the "put-offs"?

    8. _____

    What are the "put-ons"?

    9. _____

    Kindness, tenderheartedness, and forgiveness must be toward the same individual with whom you were angry. You must not avoid the person with whom you are having difficulty. Instead, you are especially to minister to that person by demonstrating kind deeds in a tenderhearted way, showing that you have forgiven that person in your heart.

2. Read *Colossians 3:8, 12-14* and note the "put-offs" and "put-ons."

    What are the "put-offs"?

    10. _____

    What are the "put-ons"?

    11. _____

3. You *can* be kind, tenderhearted, compassionate, etc. toward someone in spite of your feelings since these are commands, and you can carry out God's commands no matter how you feel.

    You may think, "But that is hypocritical." Remember that you are not a hypocrite if you are being obedient while going against your feelings. You would be a hypocrite if you say that you enjoy doing it, even though you do not. Being disciplined to obey in spite of your feelings just means that you are being victorious over the flesh, in the power of the Holy Spirit. This is something the Lord both commands and enables us to do.

PLAN FOR OVERCOMING ANGER AND BITTERNESS

The remainder of this lesson provides guidance on how to have lasting victory over anger and bitterness. You may wish to review the remaining pages in Lesson 11 of the *Self-Confrontation* manual; however, your primary concentration should be to incorporate the truths you have learned in this lesson into your personal plan for change.

SCRIPTURE RECITATION

Recite *Ephesians 4:31-32* and *James 1:19-20* to someone at home, in class, or elsewhere. Also, recite one of the previous memory passages chosen by the listener. Put a check here (___) when you have accurately recited the verses.

QUESTIONS AND CONCLUSION

A. What Scripture verse shows that if anger is not dealt with quickly, it can gain control and give the devil a foothold?

12. _____

B. From where does anger come?

13. _____

There is no excuse for sinful anger since no one else and no situation can make a person angry.

C. Is a person responsible for angry feelings?

14. _____

It is important to differentiate between angry deeds (thoughts, speech, and actions) and the emotions (or feelings) associated with anger. You are totally responsible for your thoughts, speech, and actions, but you are not held responsible for your feelings because they are involuntary.

D. Can a person be angry without sinning?

15. _____
_____

A person can be angry without sinning if he is totally loving at the same time, which implies that he is not in any way focused on self.

E. What are some key verses for use in developing a *"Daily Practices" Plan* regarding anger?

16. _____

F. What are some key verses for use in developing an *"Overcoming Temptations" Plan* regarding anger?

17. _____

G. What was the most significant truth you learned in completing this lesson?

18. _____

PREVIEW OF NEXT LESSON

In the next two lessons, you will learn about subjects that relate to interpersonal relationships. We will start by covering biblical forgiveness, the key to the reconciliation of all broken relationships.

LESSON 12
INTERPERSONAL PROBLEMS (PART ONE)
(LEARNING HOW TO LOVE YOUR NEIGHBOR)

OPENING PRAYER AND SCRIPTURE MEMORY

Before you begin this lesson, ask for God's help in understanding His Word and for wisdom and strength to apply what you learn in the power of the Holy Spirit.

Begin memorizing *Matthew 5:23-24*. Also, review the Scripture memory passages assigned in the previous lessons. Then, be prepared to recite them at the end of this lesson.

Also, in your own words, please write out the meaning of the new memory verses below:

_____
_____
_____
_____

PERSONAL PLAN FOR CHANGE

Continue to work on your *Worksheet 5: "Overcoming Temptations" Plan* that you started in Lesson 11. Implement your plan. This will require:

A. Conviction and sorrow to the point of repentance *(II Corinthians 7:9)*. This is not an intellectual exercise. You must commit yourself to change from a pattern of disobedience to God (which demonstrates your lack of love for Him) to a new pattern of godliness.

B. Self-control and discipline. Old habits are difficult to put off and putting on new habits often feels unnatural with failures initially.

C. Acknowledging and repenting when you fail. This involves confession of your sin, recommitment to place yourself back under the control of the Holy Spirit, changing your plan, if appropriate, and starting again to implement your plan.

You can also make changes and corrections to the other worksheets of your **VICTORY OVER FAILURES PLAN** based on what you will be learning this week. In addition, as you progress through this study, you will be shown how to begin working on a **"Forgiveness/Reconciliation" Plan**.

INTRODUCTION TO THE LESSON

A. This is the first of two lessons dealing with interpersonal problems. This lesson addresses the first two elements of how to face, deal with, and endure problems biblically. Please list them below.

1. _____

In the next lesson, **INTERPERSONAL PROBLEMS (PART TWO)**, we will cover the last two elements. Please list them below.

2.
___

Because of interpersonal problems, many believers have poor testimonies, many families are in conflict, and many local churches are ineffective. Some churches are completely divided. While the body of Christ should be a testimony of love and unity, believers, even in leadership, refuse to forgive and be reconciled with each other. This is in direct violation of Jesus' statement that the way the world can recognize His disciples is by their love for one another.

B. This lesson focuses on the subjects of forgiveness and reconciliation as necessary for repairing broken relationships. You will learn the biblical principles and procedures involved in forgiving someone for the sins he has committed against you.

We will also distinguish between forgiving another and releasing the one forgiven from the consequences of their unbiblical conduct. This will include: 1) forgiving in your heart before being asked and 2) granting forgiveness when asked.

Also, you will learn biblical principles and procedures for asking someone to forgive you when you are the offender.

C. Read the purposes of **LESSON 12: INTERPERSONAL PROBLEMS (PART ONE) (LEARNING HOW TO LOVE YOUR NEIGHBOR)** (*Self-Confrontation*, Page 194).

BIBLICAL UNDERSTANDING OF INTERPERSONAL PROBLEMS

A. Read the first sentence of *Principle 51*, **BIBLICAL PRINCIPLES: INTERPERSONAL PROBLEMS (PART ONE) (LEARNING HOW TO LOVE YOUR NEIGHBOR)** (*Self-Confrontation*, Page 195). Also read *I John 4:20-21*. According to this passage, what is true of those who say that they love God, but do not love their brother?

3.
___

Love for God and love for others are inseparable. What does this tell you about the seriousness of *any* relationship problem with someone else? Take a moment to think through and pray about relationships in your life. Are there any deeds in which your failure to show love has resulted in strained, broken relationships?

We will talk about what to do about these as we go through these two lessons.

B. Read the second sentence of *Principle 51* and note that forgiveness is *not an option* for a child of God; it is a matter of obedience. Highlight in your manual and read *Matthew 6:14-15*. This is another serious admonition about our relationship with others. What is the consequence if someone will not forgive those against whom he has taken offense?

4.
___

C. Note that this passage comes right after the prayer that Jesus taught the disciples (often called "The Lord's Prayer"), and that the only responsibility given to believers in that prayer is the responsibility to forgive. You can see that lack of forgiveness is very serious. It is so serious that if a believer does not forgive the one against whom he has taken offense, God will not forgive him. This does not mean that he has lost his salvation, since, in this passage, God is still referred to as his heavenly Father. However, his fellowship with God is hindered, and he can expect to be disciplined by the Lord.

D. Read *Principle 52*, **BIBLICAL PRINCIPLES: INTERPERSONAL PROBLEMS (PART ONE) (LEARNING HOW TO LOVE YOUR NEIGHBOR)** (*Self-Confrontation*, Page 195). Because this principle establishes the importance of dealing with sin according to biblical standards, which has already been covered in detail elsewhere, you do not need to spend much time looking up the referenced verses.

BIBLICAL UNDERSTANDING OF FORGIVING

Since forgiveness is so important to the Lord, let's spend some time on this subject. To start this study, turn to Page 196 of the *Self-Confrontation* manual.

A. Under Section **I. Understanding God's forgiveness**:

1. Read all of Paragraph B. Then, highlight in your manual the reference to *Hebrews 10:14-18* and read *Hebrews 10:17* which is cited in Subparagraph 4. at the top of Page 197. It is important to note that the phrase, "not to remember" is an accounting term which means "not to charge against" in the sense of counting a debit, or placing a mark against you. It does not mean "to forget" or "wipe from memory." If God were to forget whenever He forgives:

    a. We would be without much of the Bible. For instance, God forgave David's sin with Bathsheba, but He did not wipe it from memory, since He recorded it in Scripture. God did not record David's sin in order to charge it against him or to accuse him, but to instruct us *(see I Corinthians 10:1-11)*.

    b. God would not be omniscient. In *Ecclesiastes 12:14* and *Romans 2:5-6*, what deeds will God bring to judgment?

    5. _____

    If God were to remove your sins from His memory, He would not be able to judge every deed.

    c. The Holy Spirit could not remind us of our past sins in order to convict us of a need to change from a habitual pattern of sin to a consistent pattern of righteousness. It is a loving and gracious work of God to remind us of our past sins so that we can learn not to repeat the same sins over and over again.

    This is a very important truth. Have you ever heard someone say, "When God forgives, He forgets"? This can be a great stumbling block to someone who can not forget, but is aware that the Bible commands us in *Ephesians 4:32* to *"forgive each other, just as God in Christ also has forgiven you."* The truth is that we cannot will ourselves to wipe an event from our memory and God does not require that we do so. However, we can cease from remembering (or holding) something against someone; and this is what God does with us.

2. In Paragraph **I. B. 4.**, highlight in your manual and read *Isaiah 38:17*. The word "back" in this verse connotes the small of the back. Let's try an experiment.

> **EXERCISE:** Make one hand into a fist and place it in the small of your back. Now, turn around and try to look at your fist. It is impossible to see. Now bring the fist to your front. In the same way, when God forgives you, He puts your sins out of His sight (i.e., removes the reminders of your sins); however, when it is good for you or others, God will remind you of the sinful pattern you need to eliminate. For example, read *I Corinthians 10:6, 11*. For what reason are the sins of the Israelites recorded in the Scriptures?
>
> 6. _____
>
> In the same way, when we forgive someone, we are not to hold it against him any longer. Just because we remember that the event occurred does not mean that we have not forgiven him. However, it is possible, and expected by God, that we not hold the offense against the offender.

> Forgiveness is possible even for the gravest offenses, through the power of the Holy Spirit. Continuing to focus (in an accusing way) on what a person did is a good sign that we are still holding it against him. In addition, there is a difference between forgiving someone and having to deal with the consequences of his sin, as we will see in the next section.

B. In Section **II. Responding to God's forgiveness** (*Self-Confrontation*, Page 197):

   1. Read Paragraph A.; then, highlight in your manual and read *Ephesians 4:32*. Then, read the six subparagraphs.

      a. How are we to forgive according to *Ephesians 4:32*?

7. _____

      b. Notice in Subparagraph 6. on Page 197 of the *Self-Confrontation* manual that it is important to distinguish between forgiveness and the release of consequences. Forgiveness is an act of mercy that reestablishes fellowship with the offender. In other words, there is no longer an estrangement between the offender and the one offended. On the other hand, consequences should be an encouragement to the offender to change. For example, you may have forgiven a child for breaking a window. But he may be required to replace the window partly or fully with his own money. This will remind him of the importance of not repeating the offense.

   2. Read Paragraph B., then, highlight in your manual and read *Mark 11:25*. Are there any conditions that would preclude forgiving another person?

8. _____

Should you go to a person to tell him that you forgive him even if he has not asked for forgiveness?

9. _____

You are to forgive in your heart even *before* the offender asks for forgiveness. Your telling him that you forgive him, when he has not requested forgiveness, can be construed as your accusing him of sin when he may not yet recognize the conviction of the Holy Spirit. Telling him prematurely could actually be a stumbling block to him. Telling him is not necessary for you to carry out your responsibility to forgive. There may be an appropriate time to admonish a fellow-believer in love if he continues in sin, but do not presume that you need to go to that person to tell of your forgiveness of him. You must forgive him in your heart. Also keep in mind that the penalty for sin is removed at salvation, but sin (such as lack of forgiveness) by a child of God hinders fellowship with the Father.

C. In Section **III. Reviewing principles of forgiveness** (*Self-Confrontation*, Page 197):

   1. Read Paragraphs A.-D.

   2. Read Paragraph E. To see how important forgiveness is, let's first look at *Luke 17:3-10*.

      a. In *verses 3-4*, what did Jesus say about how many times we are to forgive someone who offends us frequently?

10. _____

In some situations, consequences may be appropriate to help that person not to continue in sin, but we are always to grant forgiveness.

In *verse 5*, what was the response of the disciples?

11. _____

b. Notice Jesus' response in *verses 6-10*. He tells them a story to illustrate the real problem. What was their basic problem?

12. _____

_____

When we are unwilling to forgive, it is because we are protesting that we have the "right" not to be treated a certain way. An unwillingness to forgive is an indication of pride, not an inability to forgive. We are not willing to consider ourselves as unworthy slaves.

D. Section **IV. Refusing to forgive**, Paragraph B. presents another passage that helps us to understand the consequences of a lack of forgiveness. Highlight in your manual and read *Matthew 18:21-35*.

Notice in *verse 21*, Peter brings up the subject of forgiveness. It's as though he was still thinking about how difficult it is to forgive. It seems his hope was to get the number of times reduced.

What was Jesus' answer in *verse 22*?

13. _____

Then Jesus tells the story of the wicked slave who was forgiven 10,000 talents by his master, yet he would not forgive another slave 100 denarii.

What was the message Jesus was delivering (see *verse 35*)?

14. _____

Just think of the comparison that Jesus was making. A denarius was a normal day's wage. Ten thousand talents were worth millions of days of wages.

The message to us is that Jesus Christ has paid the penalty for all the sins of a believer's life, which are many; surely, the believer should be willing to forgive the relatively few sins committed against him.

Notice also from this passage the importance of sincere forgiveness (from the heart). Not to forgive is extremely serious.

FORGIVENESS/RECONCILIATION PLAN

Now let's take a look at the **"Forgiveness/Reconciliation" Plan**. The purpose of this plan is to help you deal with relationships that are not reconciled, with emphasis on long standing broken relationships or ones in which there is a serious rift. In these cases, you will want to be especially prepared to be reconciled in a godly way by writing out what you will do. This will help you to think through how to be reconciled with that other person in a biblical manner.

Depending on your situation, you may need to include in the plan:

- Steps you will take to *demonstrate* forgiveness. Jesus said in *Mark 11:25* that we need to forgive and demonstrate forgiveness whether or not the offender requests forgiveness. Remember that your forgiveness of another is much bigger than just your relationship with the other person. Your forgiveness of others is essential to unbroken fellowship with your heavenly Father (*Matthew 6:12-15*). *Worksheet 6a: My Plan for Demonstrating Forgiveness* will help you develop this part of your plan. The form for this worksheet is located on Page W141.

- Steps you will take and the words you will use for *asking* forgiveness. *Worksheet 6b: My Plan for Asking Forgiveness* will help you develop this part of your plan. The form for this worksheet is located on Page W150.

A. To complete *Worksheet 6a: My Plan for Demonstrating Forgiveness*, follow the steps below:

1. Complete the first section of *Worksheet 6a: My Plan for Demonstrating Forgiveness* by listing the name of the person you need to forgive, and the offenses you need to forgive at the top of the page. *(See the sample on Page W142.)*

2. Complete the section entitled "**Steps I will take to:**" The subparagraphs in this section are aspects of biblical forgiveness presented in Lesson 12 of the *Self-Confrontation* manual.

   As God in Christ has forgiven us *(Ephesians 4:32; Colossians 3:13)*, we are to:

   a. Not dwell on the offense suffered *(based on Isaiah 38:17)*. We are not to keep account of any wrongs suffered *(I Corinthians 13:5)*. We should not dwell on the evil done to us, but consider how to give a blessing instead *(based on I Peter 3:9)*.

   b. Not remind the forgiven person of his sin in an accusing manner *(based on Hebrews 10:17)*. There may be times when you will need to remind the person of his sin even after you have forgiven him. For example, if that individual develops a pattern of repeating the sin, you are to exhort that person to repent. But the difference now is that you are to make your appeal in a spirit of gentleness, not in an accusing manner *(based on Galatians 6:1)*.

   c. Not gossip to others about the offense suffered *(II Corinthians 12:20)*. You may need to bring up someone's sins to others but only with the focus on helping the person who is sinning, not to tear him down. For example, parents often need to discuss the sins of their children between themselves first in order to determine how to discipline them.

   d. Remove all reminders of the offense that are stumbling blocks, as much as it is physically possible *(based on Matthew, 18:7-9)*.

   e. Restore fellowship with the forgiven person, as far as is biblically possible *(based on Romans 12:18; II Corinthians 2:6-8)*. Even if the person has not come to ask forgiveness, you must still forgive and stand ready to grant forgiveness if asked.

   NOTE: *None of the steps listed above is based on how a person feels. Forgiveness is an act of the will. We are to discipline ourselves to obey God, not act according to our feelings.*

   Also, when you forgive someone, it is important to distinguish between forgiveness and the release of consequences. Forgiveness is an act of obedience to the Lord (Luke 17:3-10) that gives the offender what he needs rather than what he deserves (based on Psalm 103:10; Romans 5:8). Consequences, on the other hand, are meant to encourage the offender to change his way (based on Psalm 119:67, 71). For example, a parent may have to allow his child to suffer the consequences of his sin even though the parent has already forgiven the child.

   See the sample on Page W142.

Work on this assignment a little each day as you are doing your other homework. Even if you do not need to demonstrate forgiveness to someone at this time, you will still find it helpful to develop a plan for demonstrating forgiveness of someone who may commit an offense against you in the future.

You will work on *Worksheet 6b: My Plan for Asking Forgiveness* in Lesson 13.

Worksheet 6a:
My Plan for Demonstrating Forgiveness

Name of person I need to forgive:
_____

Offenses I need to forgive:
_____
_____
_____
_____

Steps I will take to:

A. Not dwell on the offense suffered:
_____
_____
_____
_____

B. Not remind the forgiven person of his sin in an accusing manner:
_____
_____
_____
_____

C. Not gossip to others about the offense suffered:
_____
_____
_____
_____

D. Remove all reminders of the offense suffered:
_____
_____
_____
_____

E. Restore fellowship with the forgiven person, as far as is biblically possible:
_____
_____
_____
_____

© Biblical Counseling Foundation

Permission is granted to reproduce this form for personal or ministry use

Student Workbook for the Self-Confrontation Bible Study
- Lesson 12 -

Sample Worksheet 6a:
My Plan for Demonstrating Forgiveness

Name of person I need to forgive:
My co-worker

Offenses I need to forgive:
His yelling at me

His saying unwholesome words to me

Steps I will take to:

A. Not dwell on the offense suffered:
When temptations come, I will concentrate on how to bless my co-worker; and I will pray for him. I will concentrate on how I can resolve the difficulties between us, rather than focus only on the differences.

B. Not remind the forgiven person of his sin in an accusing manner:
If I must remind my co-worker of a sin that I have forgiven, I will first take any log out of my own eye, formulate how I can show him how to overcome the sinful pattern, find out if he is open to my help, and then, lovingly and gently provide counsel.

C. Not gossip to others about the offense suffered:
If I should commit gossip, I will ask forgiveness of my co-worker and the ones to whom I gossiped. I will concentrate on only saying building up things about him.

D. Remove all reminders of the offense suffered:
Not applicable

E. Restore fellowship with the forgiven person, as far as is biblically possible:
I will honor and respect my co-worker. I will remove stumbling blocks from him by not glaring at him, not speaking loudly with unwholesome words, and not using a harsh tone of voice. I will come alongside and help him, and I will look for opportunities to bless him.

QUESTIONS AND ANSWERS ABOUT BIBLICAL FORGIVENESS

The section on **QUESTIONS AND ANSWERS ABOUT BIBLICAL FORGIVENESS**, (*Self-Confrontation*, Pages 202-206) has more information about the subject of forgiveness. We have already studied some of this information. Read the following for supplemental study:

A. Under Section **I. Is it possible** ..., read Paragraph C.

B. Under Section **II. Will all the consequences** ..., read Paragraph B.

C. Under Section **V. Is it necessary** ..., read Paragraph B.

Now let's take a look at an opposite situation where you are the offender and need to ask forgiveness of someone else.

RECONCILIATION

Read *Principle 53*, **BIBLICAL PRINCIPLES: INTERPERSONAL PROBLEMS (PART ONE) (LEARNING HOW TO LOVE YOUR NEIGHBOR)** (*Self-Confrontation*, Page 195). Highlight in your manual and read *Matthew 5:23-24* which is the memory passage for this lesson. In this passage, what does the Lord say for us to do?

15. _____

Notice the importance of believers contacting quickly the individual who has something against them. However, it is vital that asking forgiveness is done in a biblically loving way. Guidance for a specific plan will be described in the next lesson.

In your relationships, what are ways you may be able to tell that your brother has something against you? List at least two ways.

16. _____

_____

So far, we have studied the importance of forgiving others. This is so important that if we do not forgive, God will not forgive our transgressions. And we can forgive as an act of our will because God gives us the power to do so.

BIBLICAL HOPE

This brings us to the second element of how to face, deal with, and endure interpersonal problems — biblical hope. So turn to Page 195 of the *Self-Confrontation* manual and read *Principle 54*, **BIBLICAL PRINCIPLES: INTERPERSONAL PROBLEMS (PART ONE) (LEARNING HOW TO LOVE YOUR NEIGHBOR)**. Love and forgiveness are acts of the will. They are not based on feelings but rather on faithful obedience to God's commands regardless of feelings. There is great hope because God enables us to carry out whatever He commands us to do. Read *Romans 12:18*. What does this verse say about being at peace with all men?

17. _____

Can you control the response of others?

18. _____

Are you responsible for the response of others?

19. _____

But you are responsible to God to love and be reconciled to others.

It is marvelous to know that months and years of counseling are not needed to restore relationships. Relationships can be immediately restored by applying the principles of forgiveness and reconciliation despite our feelings. Sometimes God rewards that obedience with changes in feelings, but we should not be dependent on nor necessarily expect these changes. The person to whom we desire to become reconciled may not want to respond in love. But we know that we have peace with God independent of the other person's response if we obediently forgive and ask forgiveness.

SCRIPTURE RECITATION

Recite *Matthew 5:23-24* to someone at home, in class, or elsewhere. Also, recite one of the previous memory passages chosen by the listener. Put a check here (___) when you have accurately recited the verses.

QUESTIONS AND CONCLUSIONS

A. What does God say is true of those who say that they love God, but do not love their brother?

20. _____

B. What is the consequence if someone will not forgive those against whom he has taken an offense?

21. _____

C. When we forgive, does God require us to forget (that is, erase the event from our memories)?

22. _____

D. What did Jesus say about how many times we are to forgive someone who offends us frequently?

23. _____

E. Does that mean you are necessarily to release the offender from the consequences of his sin?

24. _____

F. Is it possible or ever necessary for you to forgive yourself?

25. _____

G. Is it possible or ever necessary for you to forgive God?

26. _____

H. Who should take the initiative to be reconciled with another person?

27. _____

Remember that if you are harboring unforgiveness, you are in serious trouble. You need to forgive others as God has forgiven you. You do not deserve His forgiveness, but He has forgiven you of far more than anything you would need to forgive.

If you have committed a wrong toward a person and need to ask for forgiveness, you should make a specific biblical plan to do so. Then meet with that person to ask for forgiveness. Remember, you are only responsible for your obedience to the Lord; you are not responsible for the other person's response.

I. What was the most significant truth you learned in completing this lesson?

28. _____

_____

PREVIEW OF NEXT LESSON

In the next lesson, you will learn about the last two elements of how to face, deal with, and endure interpersonal-relationship problems. You will learn about biblical love and biblical communication which are very different from the world's understanding of these subjects.

W146

LESSON 13
INTERPERSONAL PROBLEMS (PART TWO)
(LEARNING HOW TO LOVE YOUR NEIGHBOR)

OPENING PRAYER AND SCRIPTURE MEMORY

Before you begin this lesson, ask for God's help in understanding His Word and for strength to apply what you learn in the power of the Holy Spirit.

Begin memorizing *Ephesians 4:29* and *Philippians 2:3-4*. Also, review the Scripture memory passages assigned in the previous lessons. Then, be prepared to recite them at the end of this lesson.

Also, in your own words, please write out the meaning of the new memory verses below:

_____

_____

_____

_____

PERSONAL PLAN FOR CHANGE

Continue to work on your personal **VICTORY OVER FAILURES PLAN** and make corrections based on what you will be learning this week. Also begin to work on the second part of your *"Forgiveness/Reconciliation" Plan*. A blank *Worksheet 6b* is located on Page W150.

A. Complete the first section of *Worksheet 6b: My Plan for Asking Forgiveness* by:

  1. Listing the name of the person of whom you need to ask forgiveness under "**Person of whom I need to ask forgiveness.**"

  2. Listing the offenses for which you need to ask forgiveness under "**Offenses for which I need to ask forgiveness.**"

  (See the sample on Page W151.)

B. Complete the second section of *Worksheet 6b: My Plan for Asking Forgiveness*. When you have sinned against another person, you need to reconcile with that person. Read *Matthew 5:23-24* which is the memory passage for Lesson 12. If, when you are in prayer, you remember that your brother has something against you, what becomes your first priority?

  1. _____

  This is part of preserving the unity of the Spirit (*Ephesians 4:3*). If you do not know for sure, but think it is possible that fellowship with that person may be broken, go anyway to determine whether you may have committed an offense unknowingly. *NOTE: You may be tempted to wait for a more convenient time. God says not to wait. However, you must be careful to take the proper steps or you could become a stumbling block to the other person.*

  When reconciling, you should:

1. Make restitution whenever appropriate *(based on Leviticus 5:15-18, 6:2-5; Numbers 5:5-8; Proverbs 6:30-31; Luke 19:8-9)*. Under "**A. Restitution I need to make to the person offended**" in *Worksheet 6b*, list how you plan to make restitution if appropriate.

2. Demonstrate repentance *(Psalm 51:12-13; Matthew 3:8; Acts 26:20)* by writing and implementing a plan for change. Therefore, under "**B. Specific steps I will take to put off the old pattern of sin and put on the new righteous behavior**," write your plan for change. Include in this section a description of the specific steps you are taking to put off the old pattern of sin and to put on the new pattern of righteousness based on your *"Daily Practices" Plan* and your *"Overcoming Temptations" Plan*.

3. Ask forgiveness. Under "**C. Words I will use when asking forgiveness**," write words to use when asking forgiveness. You should include:

   a. Admission of sin against God and the offended person *(James 5:16; I John 1:9)*.

   b. An expression of repentance which includes:

      1) An expression of sorrow for the sin *(Psalm 51:16-17; II Corinthians 7:9-10; James 4:8-10)*,

      2) An intention not to repeat the sin,

      3) The specific steps you are taking to change.

(See the sample on Page W151.)

C. Prepare yourself for various responses from the other person and plan how to respond biblically. Make sure you communicate your serious intent to change and to be reconciled. Write out what you would do and say if the other person replies:

1. "Oh, that's all right" or "Don't worry about it" or "People do that all the time." You might say, "Even though what I did may not have bothered you, I realize that my actions toward you were unloving, contrary to Scripture, and not pleasing to God. Since my desire is to be a Christlike person and to love you God's way, I ask for your forgiveness."

2. "I won't forgive you." You might respond with, "I am deeply sorry that I have so offended you, and greatly regret my unloving actions. I have made a commitment to the Lord to bless you, and will be praying that our relationship can soon be restored."

3. "I'll forgive you but I won't forget it." You might say, "I sincerely regret being part of such a painful memory in your life. My behavior was very unloving and I am committing myself to the Lord. I make the same commitment to you, to act in a biblically loving way toward you in the future. God does not require you to forget. To forgive only requires you to refrain from purposely bringing the offense up in the future."

D. After completing your plan, go to each individual against whom you have sinned in the following manner:

1. At a time when the other person is not busy or occupied, ask if you may talk with him about your failure in the relationship. If that time is not appropriate for the other person, ask if you may set an appropriate time to meet with him and confess the failures that you have committed against him *(based on Proverbs 25:11; Philippians 2:4)*.

2. When you meet with the one you sinned against, confess your sin *(James 5:16)* and ask for forgiveness according to your plan.

This concludes the guidelines for developing the **VICTORY OVER FAILURES PLAN**. Diligent application of these guidelines to the problem area you selected for this study will equip you to follow biblical principles for other problems in your life as well. You need not fear that some future situation might overwhelm you. Using the same biblical approach, you can have confidence that you can face, deal with, and endure any difficult situation that may confront you in the future.

Also, you should have confidence that you can guide others including your family members and those you are discipling to victory over any failures they might experience.

This week, continue to work on a plan for asking forgiveness. Work on this assignment a little each day as you are doing your other homework. Even if you do not need to ask forgiveness of someone at this time, you will still find it helpful to develop a plan for asking forgiveness of someone against whom you may commit an offense in the future.

Worksheet 6b: My Plan for Asking Forgiveness

Person of whom I need to ask forgiveness:
_____

Offenses for which I need to ask forgiveness:
_____
_____
_____
_____

Steps I will take and words I will use when asking forgiveness:

A. Restitution I need to make to the person offended:
_____
_____

B. Specific steps I will take to put off the old pattern of sin and put on the new righteous deeds (thoughts, speech, and actions):
_____
_____
_____
_____
_____
_____
_____
_____

C. Words I will use when asking forgiveness:
_____
_____
_____
_____
_____
_____
_____
_____
_____
_____
_____

VOFP Worksheet 6b © Biblical Counseling Foundation
Permission is granted to reproduce this form for personal or ministry use
Student Workbook for the Self-Confrontation Bible Study
- Lesson 13 -

Sample Worksheet 6b: My Plan for Asking Forgiveness

Person of whom I need to ask forgiveness:
My co-worker

Offenses for which I need to ask forgiveness:
I spoke loudly to my co-worker with malicious words, a harsh tone of voice, and a glaring look.

Steps I will take and words I will use when asking forgiveness:

A. Restitution I need to make to the person offended:
Not applicable

B. Specific steps I will take to put off the old pattern of sin and put on the new righteous deeds (thoughts, speech, and actions):
Pray for my co-worker every day, whenever he comes to mind, and when situations come up that involve us both.
Speak only those things that give honor and respect to him; respond with a soft and gentle voice and only after carefully thinking about how to answer.

C. Words I will use when asking forgiveness:
I recognize that I have sinned against the Lord and you by speaking loudly to you with unwholesome words and a harsh tone of voice. I am sorry for having offended the Lord and you. It is my intention never again to repeat this offense against you. By God's grace I will change by speaking only those things that show honor and respect to you. I will respond to you with a soft and gentle voice and only after carefully thinking about how to answer. I will focus on helping you in whatever way I should. I would also appreciate your pointing out to me if I sin in this way again. I have asked the Lord to forgive me, and I want you to know that I desire your forgiveness as well. Will you please forgive me?

© Biblical Counseling Foundation

INTRODUCTION TO THE LESSON

A. This is the second of two lessons on interpersonal problems. This lesson deals with the final two elements of how to face, deal with, and endure problems biblically. What are they?

2. _____

In this lesson, we will address some of the most important practices within the body of Christ. We will learn: 1) the meaning of biblical love, which is an act of the will in obedience to God and is not dependent on feelings; 2) restoration/discipline in the local church, which is practiced rather rarely in these times; and 3) biblical communication, which is a major area in which both believers and unbelievers sin frequently.

B. Read the purposes of **LESSON 13: INTERPERSONAL PROBLEMS (PART TWO) (LEARNING HOW TO LOVE YOUR NEIGHBOR)** *(Self-Confrontation,* Page 214).

Because all the biblical principles for this lesson are explained later in the lesson in great detail, let's go directly to the first subject, biblical love. So, turn to **THE MEANING OF BIBLICAL LOVE** *(Self-Confrontation,* Page 217).

MEANING OF BIBLICAL LOVE

A. Read Section **I. All of God's directives** ... and Section **II. Love is giving** .... Biblical love is not just the giving of things, but giving of one's very self.

B. Read Section **III. Love has specific characteristics** .... These descriptions of love are from *I Corinthians 13:4-8*. Each of the phrases illustrates the giving up of selfish desires and putting God and others first. Love is particularly tested when we do not *feel* like being loving. Choose from the list (on Pages 217 to 219) three of the specific actions of biblical love that you have difficulty demonstrating.

3. _____

_____

_____

C. Read Paragraph E. of Section **IV. Love characterizes the life of a disciple of Christ** .... Biblical love is not a matter of merely making other people feel good either about themselves or their circumstances. Rather, biblical love involves *blessing* others. This may mean that in practicing biblical love, it is sometimes necessary to do that which is difficult, unpleasant, or perhaps downright grievous. For example, parents sometimes must tell children "no," or speak in a firm manner, or discipline as necessary in obedience to *Ephesians 6:4* out of love for their children. These deeds are not necessarily easy or pleasant, but they are loving when done to bring children up in God's way. We will study this further in Lessons 16 and 17.

RESTORATION/DISCIPLINE

One of the most difficult acts of love in the local church is church restoration/discipline; so let's spend some time on this subject. First, turn to **RESTORATION/DISCIPLINE (YOUR BIBLICAL RESPONSE TO THE SIN OF ANOTHER BELIEVER)** *(Self-Confrontation,* Page 220).

A. Read the box at the top of Page 220, then, highlight in your manual and read *Matthew 18:15-17*. Also, to one side of the summary box, write in the reference, *Matthew 18:12-14*.

B. Before studying the *Matthew 18:15-17* passage in detail, let's look at the rest of the chapter first, as this provides us with the context. Most of this chapter emphasizes the importance of helping others to live godly lives — first, in *verses 1-11*, by not placing stumbling blocks in the way and second, in *verses 12-14*, by pursuing one who has fallen (as seen by the picture of the shepherd pursuing the straying sheep). The latter part of the chapter addresses the issue of forgiving the one who sins. The instruction of *Matthew 18:15-17* is placed in the middle of an entire passage concerning forgiveness and restoration.

Often, church leaders (in dealing with the sheep gone astray) say, "Well, I have 99 others to care for. They are important." Clearly they are. And yes, they should be put in a safe place. But we are to concentrate on restoring the ones who have gone astray.

Sadly, many churches do not practice church restoration/discipline at all, or they do not carefully follow the procedure described by our Lord. Some are harsh and unloving in the process and, sometimes, shun people in an unbiblical way. No wonder the world sometimes sees church discipline as a harsh, unloving action. Yet, church restoration/discipline that is carried out according to *verses 12-14* is clearly a supreme act of love; we are to care for the straying brothers or sisters so much that we go after them. When the shepherd finds the lost sheep, he does not demean or berate the sheep, but He restores the sheep back to the fold and rejoices that the sheep has been restored.

C. Now, let's look at the church restoration/discipline process as described in *Matthew 18:15-17*.

1. First, read the paragraph just below the box at the top of Page 220. Before reproving someone who has sinned, it is important to discern whether or not this procedure should be initiated. The church restoration/discipline procedure is so serious that if the offender does not change, he is ultimately to be treated as an unbeliever. So, the primary issue is not that the person has sinned (which believers do from time to time), but that he is continuing in sin, is unrepentant, and is not willing to change.

    The restoration/discipline process applies to the one who claims to be a believer but who has made it a practice to continue sinning in direct defiance of the Lord's commands and other believers' continued exhortations to go God's way.

    Also notice in the paragraph just below the box on Page 220, that before you go to reprove someone, you must properly prepare yourself by doing two things. What are they?

    4. _____

    _____

2. Highlight in your manual and read *Matthew 18:15* and the sentence beginning with, "If a fellow-believer sins ...." along with the next two paragraphs. Remember that you must restore gently with love *(Galatians 6:1-2)*. Also, highlight *Galatians 6:1-2* at the end of the fourth paragraph under the box.

    From the teaching in the third paragraph, if he repents, what three things are you to do?

    5. _____

    _____

    _____

3. Read *Matthew 18:16* and the sentence on Page 220 beginning with, "If he chooses not to repent ...." Then, note that if he repents, the response is the same.

    Normally, several appeals may need to be made before taking this second step because it is important to discern whether or not the person is deliberately continuing to practice the sin. The kind of sin is not the primary problem; the lack of repentance is the major issue.

According to *I John 3:8-10*, what does the evidence point to for a person who deliberately continues to practice a sin without repentance?

6. _____

4. Read *Matthew 18:17a* and the sentence on Page 220 of the *Self-Confrontation* manual beginning with, "If a fellow believer remains unrepentant ...." Again, note that if he repents, the response is still the same — he returns to full fellowship. Remember, repentance must be demonstrated by deeds appropriate to repentance *(Acts 26:20)*, not merely words.

5. Read *Matthew 18:17b* and note that if he remains unrepentant after the church has appealed to him to be restored to the Lord, he is to be treated by the believers according to the way he is living — as someone who does not belong to the family of God. But even the last step is taken in order to encourage repentance and restoration and perhaps, if he is truly an unbeliever, to help him see his need for salvation.

D. Also, read *II Thessalonians 3:6, 13-15* (highlight the reference after the second bullet point on Page 221) and note that this is how we conduct ourselves while we are going through the procedure. The process can become harsh and unloving unless we watch ourselves.

1. We are to persist in doing good. No matter how long it takes, we are not to grow weary in doing good.

2. We are to take special note, which means that we are to pay special attention to the one involved, with the view of making a prayerful effort to restore the person. This does not mean that we are to shun the individual, but we are to highlight (as with a marker) his need for restoration.

3. We are to love the sinning person as a brother by consistently praying for him and appealing to him to repent.

E. The remainder of Pages 220-224 provides more details on the church restoration/discipline procedure. All of these steps are aimed toward bringing about reconciliation and restoration, not punishment, and they are to be carried out with love. Additionally, the one who has been restored will often need to be discipled/counseled from the Scriptures in order to be helped to develop a consistent pattern of biblical living. The purpose of the restoration/discipline process is two-fold: first, the discipline/restoration of the fellow-believer who sins; and second, to maintain the unity and purity of the body of Christ.

BIBLICAL COMMUNICATION

We have been talking about the biblical definition of love. We see that love is an act of obedience to sacrificially give up oneself for another. Love is not dependent on feelings. As a matter of fact, an act of love such as being patient goes against our feelings. We also have seen that one of the most difficult demonstrations of love is carrying out restoration/discipline in the local church.

Now let's look at one of the most common failures to love — the failure to communicate biblically. Turn to **BIBLICAL COMMUNICATION** (*Self-Confrontation*, Page 225).

A. Read Section **I. What do your words reveal?**, Paragraphs A. through C. After reading Paragraph C., highlight the reference to *James 3:1-6* in your manual and read *verses 5-6*. What does *verse 6* tell you about the tongue?

7. _____

Often, we may evaluate a believer's spiritual maturity by his involvement in church activities; but here the Scripture speaks of spiritual maturity gauged by the way he speaks.

Read Paragraph D.

B. In Section **II. To whom should you speak?**, read Paragraphs A. through C. After reading Paragraph C., highlight in your manual and read *Proverbs 9:7-9*. What two types of people does this passage refer to?

8. _____

The Bible provides guidance on how to treat both. You should counsel a wise person because he is open to correction and will change, but you should not attempt to counsel a scoffer or a foolish person (one who is not open to change) because he will merely insult you and misuse the information. Therefore, you should first discern whether a person is open to counsel before talking to him about what he needs to change in his life. This may only be determined over a number of contacts with the other person. You must not reach conclusions hastily.

Jesus emphasized this truth regarding talking to unbelievers. He said in *Matthew 7:6*, *"Do not throw your pearls before swine, lest they trample them under their feet, and turn and tear you to pieces."* The word "swine" was commonly used in Jesus' day to describe unbelievers (pigs being creatures not to be used by Jews for food since they were considered unclean). The reason Jesus taught this is because unbelievers cannot apply God's truth God's way. They will misuse it.

Read Paragraphs D. through F.

C. Read Section **III. When should you speak?** After reading Paragraph A., highlight in your manual and read *Proverbs 18:13*. What does this verse say about the way we should not communicate with others?

9. _____

Describe a situation when you did not practice this principle with an individual at home, church, or school.

10. _____

Is this something for which you need to ask forgiveness?

11. _____

We often sin in our communication with others when we have not taken time to seek out the facts of a matter. We often pre-judge others and, thus, do not bother to listen.

1. Read Subparagraph 1., then, highlight in your manual and read *Proverbs 18:2*. What is the fool interested in?

   12. _____

   Instead, what should we do as a believer?

   13. _____

   Often, the only reason we are willing to listen to another person is because we know that it is our turn next.

   Read Subparagraph 2., then, highlight in your manual and read *Proverbs 18:17* (referenced in Subparagraph 2.). When we hear one side of the story first, what are we tempted to conclude?

   14. _____

   What should we do before drawing a conclusion and taking action?

   15. _____

Student Workbook for the Self-Confrontation Bible Study
- Lesson 13 -
© Biblical Counseling Foundation

2. Read Paragraphs B. and C. at the top of Page 226

D. Turn to Section **IV. How should you speak?** (Page 226)

1. Read Paragraph A., then, highlight in your manual and read *Ephesians 4:15*. How are we to speak the truth?

   16. _____

   It can be said that speaking the truth without love is like doing surgery without an anesthetic.

2. Read Paragraph D., then, highlight in your manual and read *Colossians 4:6*. We must "speak with grace."

3. Read Paragraph E., then, highlight in your manual and read *I Peter 3:9*. Notice the "put-off" and the "put-on."

   17. "Put-off:" _____

   "Put-on:" _____

   Giving a blessing is doing what is good for a person (i.e., helping him to be godly).

E. Turn to Section **V. What should you not say?** on Page 226. Read Paragraphs A. through D.

1. Highlight in your manual and read *Ephesians 5:4*. What are the "put-offs" and "put-on"?

   18. "Put-offs:" _____

   "Put-on:" _____

   Coarse joking often tears others down. You must always consider others as more important than yourself.

2. Read Paragraph E., then, highlight in your manual and read *I Timothy 6:20*. What are the "put-off" and "put-on"?

   19. "Put-off:" _____

   "Put-on:" _____

   Believers should avoid the irreverent babble and empty arguments about spiritual controversies.

3. Read Paragraph F. at the top of Page 227, then, highlight in your manual and read *Proverbs 10:19*. What are the "put-off" and "put-on"?

   20. "Put-off:" _____

   "Put-on:" _____

   It is the fool who loves to speak his mind with many words.

4. Read Paragraphs G. and H., then, highlight in your manual and read *Proverbs 20:19; 26:20*. What should you not do?

   21. _____

Gossip involves giving out information (often tearing someone down) without seeking to build up or restore, and often creates dissension. But, it is important to understand that speaking to someone about another person's faults is not always sinful. For example, parents should speak to one another about the misdeeds of their children and come to agreement about how to deal with their misdeeds before going to them. This is not gossip, because the parents plan to go to their children to discipline and instruct them. If their talk was idle chatter and they did not intend to deal with the children in a responsible way, *then* it would be gossip.

F. Read Section **VI. What should you speak?** on Page 227.

1. Read Paragraphs A. and B., then, highlight in your manual and read *Isaiah 55:8-11*. Identify what you should speak:

    22. _____

2. From Paragraph C., what does *Ephesians 4:29* say about what to speak?

    23. _____

BIBLICAL RELATIONSHIPS

The commandment to love one another is repeated often in the New Testament. On Pages 228-231, **BIBLICAL RELATIONSHIPS (LOVING EACH OTHER IN THE BODY OF CHRIST)**, you see many references to this subject. Merely scan this section. You can read and study it in more detail when you have time. As you study, you'll find that God often explains the blessings believers receive when they follow His commands and directives.

PLAN FOR OVERCOMING INTERPERSONAL PROBLEMS

A. The remainder of this lesson provides guidance on how to gain lasting victory over interpersonal problems. You may wish to review the remaining pages in Lesson 13 of the *Self-Confrontation* manual; however, your primary concentration should be to incorporate the truths you have learned in this lesson into your personal plan for change.

B. When adding to your:

1. *"Daily Practices" Plan*, consider *Proverbs 18:2, 13, 17; Ephesians 4:29;* and *I Peter 3:8-9*.

2. *"Overcoming Temptations" Plan*, consider *James 1:19* and *Ephesians 4:26-27*.

3. *"Forgiveness/Reconciliation" Plan*, consider *Matthew 5:23-24; 18:15-17*.

SCRIPTURE RECITATION

Recite *Ephesians 4:29* and *Philippians 2:3-4* to someone at home, in class, or elsewhere. Also, recite one of the previous memory passages chosen by the listener. Put a check here (___) when you have accurately recited the verses.

QUESTIONS

A. God commands you to love biblically; does He require you to feel good about it?

   24. _____

B. For you to act in a loving way toward another person, must that other person feel good about it?

   25. _____

C. Before reproving someone else, what two things are you required to do first?

   26. _____

D. What is likely to happen if you try to counsel someone who does not want counsel, according to *Proverbs 9:7-9*?

27. _____

E. According to *Proverbs 10:19*, what is sure to happen if we use many words?

28. _____

F. What was the most significant truth you learned in completing this lesson?

29. _____
_____

PREVIEW OF NEXT LESSON

In the next two lessons, you will learn about the marriage relationship. Since this is the most intimate of all human relationships, what you have learned in the past two lessons will help you face, deal with, and endure marriage problems.

LESSON 14
THE MARRIAGE RELATIONSHIP (PART ONE)

OPENING PRAYER AND SCRIPTURE MEMORY

Before you begin this lesson, ask for God's help in understanding His Word and for wisdom and strength to apply what you learn in the power of the Holy Spirit.

Begin memorizing *Ephesians 5:21-22, 25*. Also, review the Scripture memory passages assigned in the previous lessons. Then, be prepared to recite them at the end of this lesson.

Also, in your own words, please write out the meaning of the new memory verses below:

_____
_____
_____
_____

PERSONAL PLAN FOR CHANGE

Continue to work on your personal **VICTORY OVER FAILURES PLAN** and make corrections based on what you will be learning this week.

INTRODUCTION TO THE LESSON

A. This is the first of two lessons on marriage problems. This lesson addresses the first two elements of how to face, deal with, and endure problems biblically: biblical understanding and biblical hope.

B. Apart from the Lord, marriage can be a disaster. Marriage tends to reveal sinful practices that have been present for years but have never been overcome. Even if they have been next-door neighbors, any two people who marry each other often will have grown up with very different ideas about family life and decision-making. They are truly strangers in many ways.

For example, decisions regarding finances, assignment of responsibilities among family members, the training of children, times of relaxation, maintenance of the home, ministry in the church, family devotions, etc., are often based on previous experience rather than on the Scriptures. The parents of one of the spouses may have spent money freely, while the parents of the other spouse may have been very thrifty. In one home, the children may have been disciplined harshly, while in the other home, discipline was very lax. Is it any wonder that we often hear the statement, "Opposites attract"? The reality is that all couples are made up of individuals who are very different from each other in many ways and therefore seem opposite to each other.

When two people who have lived as singles for many years are joined together in marriage, the natural result can often be conflict. When two self-centered people live in the close quarters of a common home, the result can easily be explosive.

These two lessons on marriage are very valuable for those who are single as well. For most of their waking hours, married couples deal with the same tests and trials in life as do single people.

Since these lessons are about how to live a godly life, most of the teaching points in Lessons 14 and 15 are also very applicable to singles.

C. Read the purposes of **LESSON 14: THE MARRIAGE RELATIONSHIP (PART ONE)** (*Self-Confrontation*, Page 244).

BIBLICAL UNDERSTANDING ABOUT THE MARRIAGE RELATIONSHIP

A. Read *Principles 60-61*, **BIBLICAL PRINCIPLES: THE MARRIAGE RELATIONSHIP (PART ONE)** (*Self-Confrontation*, Page 245).

B. For more information on the biblical understanding of marriage, let's turn to **THE BIBLICAL MODEL FOR MARRIAGE** (*Self-Confrontation*, Page 246).

1. Read the box at the top of the page. Write the reference to *Proverbs 5:15-19* next to the box. It may be a surprise to you to note that there are relatively few passages in Scripture on marriage. With the addition of the *Proverbs* passage, all of the verses clearly describing God's commands and guidelines concerning the marriage relationship (except for examples of *Song of Solomon*) are listed in the box. References to the *Song of Solomon* are not included because that book is primarily a description of romantic delight in marriage. It does not contain commands related to marriage.

    As a point of comparison between the number of verses on marriage and the number of verses dealing with an individual's walk with Christ, it is obvious that there are many more verses directed toward an individual's life before God than those addressing marriage. In fact, a single person deals with most of the same temptations and tests as does a married person. The hundreds of verses focusing on one's personal life, whether single or married, illustrate the primary focus of God's Word. Thus, as mentioned before, most of the instruction in these two lessons is just as applicable to single people.

    To understand God's plan for marriage, let's look at God's model for marriage.

2. Go to Section **I. God has ordained marriage**, on Page 246.

    a. Read Paragraph A., then highlight in your manual and read *Malachi 2:14*. According to this passage, is the marriage agreement a contract or a covenant?

    1. _____

    A contract can be dissolved by agreement of both parties. On the other hand, a covenant is never to be broken except by death. Read *Mark 10:6-9*. God did not design the marriage relationship to be dissolved.

    NOTE: A study about divorce is outside the focus of this lesson. The emphasis of this lesson is on how to have and maintain a marriage that brings honor to the Lord. God's plan for marriage is that it reflect the relationship between Jesus Christ and His church, which is the topic of the next point.

    b. Read Paragraph B. in Section **I.** on Page 246, then, highlight in your manual and read *Ephesians 5:24-27*. What is the marriage relationship compared to?

    2. _____

    _____

    From this passage, list some aspects of the relationship between Christ and His church.

    3. _____

    _____

3. Turn to Section **II. God has established the character of marriage** on Page 246.

   a. Read Paragraph A. Each person is to live to please the Lord, not simply to please the spouse. It is important to keep in mind that the Lord must always come first. In pleasing the Lord, the spouses will bless one another. Also, recognize that blessing the spouse may not always mean pleasing the spouse, but it always will be what is best for the spouse.

   b. Read Paragraph B., then, highlight in your manual and read *Genesis 2:24*. The phrase, "one flesh," means much more than being one physically. Often, even in wedding ceremonies, people associate the two becoming one flesh with the physical relationship, but the phrase "one flesh" refers to much more than that. For example, when God said, *"I will pour out my spirit on all flesh" (Joel 2:28),* He was not talking about bodies, but about people's souls. Therefore, the phrase "one flesh," means that the two spouses are united as one person. God's intention is for the husband and wife to complement one another; both are needed to make up the whole unit.

   c. Read Paragraph C., then, highlight in your manual and read *Galatians 3:28*. What does God say about men and women in terms of spiritual status?

   4. _____

   Even though the husband is head of the home, God does not prefer the husband over the wife (or any one human being over another). God has no favorites. One is not inherently more godly or more important to God than the other, nor does one have a better connection to the Lord than the other. Spiritually, each person is equally responsible before the Lord.

   This does not take away from the husband's responsibility to lead and protect his wife and children and to manage the household. However, the only One Who can be the spiritual head is the One Who can change the heart. Therefore, only Jesus is the spiritual head of each person, regardless of gender.

   d. Read Paragraph D., then, highlight in your manual and read *I Corinthians 1:10*. God's Word is the ultimate authority in the home, and each spouse is to carry out his or her responsibilities as to the Lord. This verse is in the context of the church, and would also apply to the relationship of believing husbands and wives. What is the emphasis of this verse?

   5. _____

   If there is not agreement regarding a decision, you can defer the decision until you study God's Word to see what principles, commands, and precepts He has for how to make the decision. Since most decisions you must make as a couple are not urgent, it is not necessary to make a decision just for the sake of making a decision. It is far more important to study together how to make that decision. The unity you demonstrate as you work through the decision-making process is often more important than the actual decision itself. The necessity for immediacy in decision-making is relatively rare. Unity in marital decisions should always be the goal.

   After reading Subparagraph 2., highlight in your manual and read *Romans 12:10b*. What does this verse say that we should do with respect to our desires?

   6. _____

   In summary, in making decisions, the authority is the Bible. Where God's Word gives specific commands, both spouses are to seek agreement on their understanding of the

Scriptural principles and follow them. Where it is a matter of opinion (like what to eat at the next meal) and biblical principles are not violated, spouses should defer to one another.

These guidelines do not in any way diminish the husband's responsibility to lead in the home. In fact, they demonstrate that the husband and wife are to act as one under the headship of the Lord.

Now think about your own life in this area. If you are married, identify any of the important decision-making areas where you know you do not have unity with your spouse. If you are not married, think of others within the church or at home with whom you believe the Lord would want you to be more unified in specific areas. Don't focus on areas where it is a matter of opinion, as discussed above, but where commands of Scripture are involved. You may list those areas here or on a separate piece of paper. Also list at least one Scripture passage that applies to that area of decision-making.

7. _____

_____

_____

e. Read Paragraph G., then Subparagraphs 1. through 3. on Page 247. Then, after Subparagraph 3., highlight in your manual and read *Mark 10:43-45*. What are you to do if you are to be highly regarded in God's kingdom?

8. _____

Each spouse is to serve the other following the example of self-sacrifice given by Jesus.

f. Backing up to Subparagraph 1., highlight in your manual and read *I Corinthians 7:3-4* as an example of servanthood. To whom should the wife give her body?

9. _____

g. To whom should the husband give his body?

10. _____

Many times, physical intimacy is the last holdout in marriage. A wife might say to herself, "I have to do all the other things for him, but no way will I give in to him with my body." Or the husband might say to his wife, "This is my right." But God says our bodies are not our own. We are to serve one another, even in the physical relationship. We are not to be focused on self-gratification.

4. Read Section **IV. God has designed some to receive the blessing of remaining single** on Page 247. It is important to note that God does not favor marriage over singleness. Each condition is determined according to God's will. If you are not content as a single person, you will not be content as a married person. We are told in *I Corinthians 7* not to seek marriage or to change our marital status. What does Paul say that he learned? (Read *Philippians 4:11*.)

11. _____

This would include our marital status. So if you are single, you should not be searching for a spouse. If the Lord has someone for you, nothing can keep you from meeting your future spouse. You never need to look. Instead, you are to focus on serving the Lord with all of your heart. In the process of serving the Lord, He may lead you to the one who is to be your husband or wife. But you are not to have that search be the focus of your life. You are to be content in the circumstances into which God has placed you, and delight in serving the Lord with all your energy.

MARITAL CONFLICTS

Turn to: **MARITAL CONFLICTS (MAN'S WAY VERSUS GOD'S WAY)** (*Self-Confrontation*, Page 248).

A. Read Section **I. When living to please self** .... Remember that, apart from the Lord, marriage can be a disaster. Blaming the spouse for problems is a natural outgrowth of a self-focus.

B. Read Paragraphs A., B., C., and H. of Section **II. When a husband and wife live to please themselves** .... This list presents some of the more common solutions offered by counselors, even Christian counselors. Note that all of the solutions are focused on pleasing self either through direct confrontation or manipulation.

C. Read Paragraphs A., B., and C. of Section **III. God desires that problems in marriages be solved for the good of each spouse** .... Two key principles for living as a spouse can be found in the following passages. From Paragraph C., read the Scripture references below and then state the principle in:

12. II Corinthians 5:9 —

Philippians 2:3-4 —

Even if the marriage partner is disobedient to the Word, the godly spouse is to follow these same two principles.

D. Read Paragraphs A. and B. of Section **IV. Spouses are to be drawing closer to God, especially during times of conflict**. Lesson 15 expands on this subject. Now to see our biblical hope in dealing with marriage problems, let's turn back to the biblical principles on Page 245.

BIBLICAL HOPE

A. Read *Principle 62*, **BIBLICAL PRINCIPLES: THE MARRIAGE RELATIONSHIP (PART ONE)** (*Self-Confrontation*, Page 245). State how you can have hope even in a difficult marriage relationship, based on the following verses. You have seen these before in Lesson 6.

13. Psalm 119:165 (highlight the reference in the middle of the principle) —

Remember that your peace and joy are to be dependent only on the Lord as you obediently trust Him.

14. Ezekiel 18:20 (highlight the reference in the last sentence of the principle) —

Also, remember that you are not responsible for changing the heart of your spouse.

You can have a life filled with peace and joy before God, regardless of the circumstances. The circumstances may be extremely difficult. Your spouse may even be completely unloving, uncaring, or uninterested in the relationship. Regardless of that, your relationship with the Lord can still be victorious. Your relationship with the Lord is not under the control of your spouse. You can still love God and your neighbor, even your closest neighbor (your spouse), through the power that God gives you.

If you are in what you would call a difficult marital relationship, pause and ask the Lord right now for the strength and wisdom to apply the principles of godly love and servanthood that you have been learning. He does not allow the situation by accident. He is providing you with an opportunity to become more like Christ. If you are in a relationship that is going well, pause and thank the Lord for His blessing on you and ask for God's continued grace to serve Him, your spouse, and those around you.

B. Read *Principle 63*. We have already studied these truths.

SCRIPTURE RECITATION

Recite *Ephesians 5:21-22, 25* to someone at home, in class, or elsewhere. Also, recite one of the previous memory passages chosen by the listener. Put a check here (___) when you have accurately recited the verses.

QUESTIONS AND CONCLUSION

A. Does God establish a marriage by contract or by covenant?

15. _____

B. What is the only time a covenant can be broken?

16. _____

C. What is the ultimate authority for principles of decision-making in the home?

17. _____

D. What should a husband and wife work toward when making decisions in the home?

18. _____

E. How do spouses make decisions when none of God's commands directly apply to the matter?

19. _____

F. Who is the human leader in the home?

20. _____

G. Who is the ultimate head of all in the home?

21. _____

H. Should you ever allow your spouse (or anyone or anything) to control your relationship with the Lord?

22. _____

You can still have peace and joy in the Lord, regardless of how difficult your circumstances may be. Also, remember that you do not need to seek for a spouse or despair if you do not find one. Be content in your current state. If God brings His choice of a spouse along, He will make that known to you as you seek to serve Him.

I. What was the most significant truth you learned in completing this lesson?

23. _____

PREVIEW OF NEXT LESSON

In the next lesson, we will learn about the last two elements of how to face, deal with, and endure marriage problems. The lesson will include a study of biblical submission, which is vital to a proper understanding of Lessons 12-17. You will also be introduced to a practical plan by which marital problems can be dealt with in a manner that pleases the Lord.

LESSON 15
THE MARRIAGE RELATIONSHIP (PART TWO)

OPENING PRAYER AND SCRIPTURE MEMORY

Before you begin this lesson, ask for God's help in understanding His Word and for strength to apply what you learn in the power of the Holy Spirit.

Begin memorizing *I Peter 3:1, 7*. Also, review the Scripture memory passages assigned in the previous lessons. Then, be prepared to recite them at the end of this lesson.

Also, in your own words, please write out the meaning of the new memory verses below:

_____
_____
_____
_____

PERSONAL PLAN FOR CHANGE

Continue to work on your personal **VICTORY OVER FAILURES PLAN** and make corrections based on what you will be learning this week.

INTRODUCTION TO THE LESSON

A. This is the second of two lessons dealing with marriage problems. This lesson addresses the final two elements of how to face, deal with, and endure problems biblically. What are the two elements?

   1. _____

B. The lesson will include a study of biblical submission, which is vital to a proper understanding of Lessons 12 through 17. Biblical submission is often thought of as a subject mainly for women. In dealing with marriage problems, wives are often counseled to focus on submission and husbands are told to focus on love. This approach is based on an overemphasis of certain Scripture passages to the exclusion of others. For example, wives are told that since *Ephesians 5:22* only mentions that wives are to submit to their husbands and does not mention anything about loving their husbands, wives must uniquely have difficulty submitting and no difficulty loving. Conversely husbands are told that since *verse 25* only mentions that husbands are to love their wives, husbands must uniquely have difficulty loving. As a result of this unbalanced emphasis in the body of Christ, there are many husbands who lack submissiveness, and many wives who fail to be loving.

C. We will find in this lesson that servanthood is a very important characteristic of all loving relationships, and applies to both the husband and wife.

D. Start by reading the purposes of **LESSON 15: THE MARRIAGE RELATIONSHIP (PART TWO)** *(Self-Confrontation*, Page 256).

BIBLICAL CHANGE

A. Turn to **BIBLICAL PRINCIPLES: THE MARRIAGE RELATIONSHIP (PART TWO)** (*Self-Confrontation*, Page 257).

1. In *Principle 64*, name the "put-offs" and "put-ons" for husbands (place a minus above each "put-off," and a plus above each "put-on"):

    2. "Put-offs": _____

    "Put-ons": _____

2. In *Principle 65*, name the "put-offs" and "put-ons" for wives (place a minus above each "put-off," and a plus above each "put-on"):

    3. "Put-offs": _____

    "Put-ons": _____

3. In *Principle 66*, name the "put-offs" and "put-ons" for spouses (place a minus above each "put-off," and a plus above each "put-on"):

    4. "Put-offs": _____

    "Put-ons": _____

These principles emphasize the need for constantly depending on the Lord and dying to self. Remember that God enables the believer to fulfill His commandments regardless of feelings. Note that for both the husband and the wife, the common "put-on" is love, which is exemplified by biblical submission and dying to self. As you can see, biblical submission is essential in a marriage, so let's study this subject in more detail.

B. Turn to **BIBLICAL SUBMISSION** (*Self-Confrontation*, Page 258).

1. Read the box at the top of the page. Note that biblical submission is voluntary, and is not imposed on another. In addition, submissiveness does not mean placing yourself under the *control* of another.

2. Read Section **I. You are to be like the Lord Jesus Christ** …. Then, highlight in your manual and read *Matthew 20:26-28*. What does this passage say about the purpose of Jesus' coming to earth?

    5. _____

    Keep in mind that He knew that He was the King of kings, and worthy of great praise and honor. Jesus deserves the ultimate respect, yet he was willing to serve and to give.

    After reading Paragraph A. of Section **I.**, highlight in your manual and read *John 5:30*. Though Jesus was a servant, He did not place Himself under the control of any human being. There is a big difference between being submissive (demonstrated by servanthood), and being under the control of someone. Being under the control of someone implies that you will do what they want no matter what, without question. In the Gospels, although Jesus was perfectly submissive and served others, you do not see Him being controlled by others. Nor did He obey others when they violated God's will for Him. Whose will did Jesus seek exclusively?

    6. _____

    In the same way, we are to seek the Father's will (that is, be under only God's control) but to be a servant to others.

3. Turn to Section **II. God's Word requires you to submit without a contentious spirit** ... on Page 258 of the *Self-Confrontation* manual. Paragraphs A. through G. of this section refer to various verses within the *Ephesians 5:18 - 6:9* Scripture passage. To the left of Section **II.**, write in *Ephesians 5:18 – 6:19*. Notice that the structure of this passage is similar to the structure of *Ephesians 4:22-32*. Both passages present a general principle (*Ephesians 4:22-24* and *5:18-21*), and then give examples to illustrate the principle in action (*Ephesians 4:25-32* and *5:22 – 6:9*). In *Ephesians 5*, the general principle is that believers are to put off placing themselves under the control of anything or anyone else and are to put on being filled with the Spirit (i.e., to place themselves under the control of the Holy Spirit).

In *verse 18* what are the "put-off" and "put-on"?

7. "Put-off": _____

"Put-on": _____

Notice that *verse 18* is a command, not an option. You are not to place yourself under the control of anything (for example, wine) other than the control of the Holy Spirit. The ways in which you then *demonstrate* that you are filled with the Holy Spirit (i.e., under the control of the Holy Spirit) are listed in the verses following *Ephesians 5:18*.

a. Read Paragraph A. under Section **II**. In *Ephesians 5:19-20*, what will be some of the personal evidences of one who submits himself to the control of the Holy Spirit?

8. _____

_____

b. Read Paragraph B. What is the interpersonal evidence described in *Ephesians 5:21*?

9. _____

c. Read Paragraph C. What are some examples of the interpersonal evidences of submitting to one another under the control of the Holy Spirit, as described in *Ephesians 5:22, 25*?

10. _____

_____

Submission has nothing to do with decision-making in the family. God has established that the husband should be the leader in the home, but the ultimate authority in the home is the Lord. Remember from the study of God's Word in Lesson 14 that unity is to be sought in decision-making under the guidance of the Holy Spirit and the Word of God.

Submission is a one-way voluntary giving up of oneself for another regardless of how the other acts. Submissiveness is shown through servanthood. As believers, we are to be serving one another always considering the other person as more important than ourselves (*Philippians 2:3-4*).

Remember, we learned in Lesson 14 that even in decision-making, when the Scripture is not applicable to a particular situation (such as what to eat at the next meal), family members should defer to one another rather than insist on their own preferences (*Romans 12:10*).

d. Read Paragraph D. on Page 258. In *Ephesians 6:1-2* (highlight in your manual), what are some of the evidences of submissiveness under the control of the Holy Spirit?

11. _____

e. Read Paragraph E. According to *Ephesians 6:4* (highlight in your manual), what are some of the evidences?

12. _____

Parents who are under the control of the Holy Spirit will sacrifice themselves for their children by doing for them what is needed in their training without consideration of personal desires. Remember, this does not mean that parents allow children to do what they want. Parents are to bless their children by doing what is *good* for them whether or not they appreciate it.

f. Read Paragraph F. According to *Ephesians 6:5*, what is another evidence of being submissive under the control of the Holy Spirit?

13. _____

g. Read Paragraph G. What is an evidence described in *Ephesians 6:9*?

14. _____

Many of the ways believers demonstrate that they are under the control of the Holy Spirit are by submissiveness in responsibilities and interpersonal relationships.

BIBLICAL PRACTICE

A. Now turn back to Page 257 in the *Self-Confrontation* manual, **BIBLICAL PRINCIPLES: THE MARRIAGE RELATIONSHIP (PART TWO)**.

1. Read *Principle 67*, then, highlight in your manual and read *Proverbs 3:5-6*. On whose understanding are we *not* to rely?

15. _____

Rather, we are to do what?

16. _____

2. Read *Principle 68*. This is an expansion of *Revelation 2:4-5* which was covered in Lesson 8.

B. Turn to **YOU CAN LEARN HOW TO SHOW LOVE TOWARD YOUR SPOUSE** (*Self-Confrontation*, Page 259) and read the box at the top of the page. God enables the believer to show love toward others even if he has never known or practiced biblical love. Remember that marriage is not merely a covenant to live together in the same place, it is a covenant of companionship and service to your spouse.

1. Read Paragraphs A. and B. under Section **I. Your marriage is to be a covenant before the Lord to a lifetime of companionship** .... This is a review of previous material. Also read the *NOTE* under Paragraph B. List one or two areas in which you have to go against your feelings to carry out a God-given responsibility in your relationship with your spouse, someone else in the family, a work associate, or someone else. Do not mention anyone by name.

17. _____
_____

Just remember that doing what is right in spite of your feelings does not make you a hypocrite; it demonstrates your faithfulness to follow the Lord in the midst of difficulties.

2. Read Paragraphs A. and B. of Section **II. God's solution to problems in your marriage** ... on Page 259 of the *Self-Confrontation* manual. This is also a review of previous material.

3. Turn to Section **III. Diligently practice biblical love** ... on Page 260 of the *Self-Confrontation* manual.

   a. Read Paragraph B. Note that "edify" means to build up in the Lord (i.e., to help another become more Christlike). It does not mean to "puff-up" (to invite to pridefulness).

   b. Read Paragraph D. on Page 260, then, highlight in your manual and read *Romans 12:20-21*. How are we to treat others even when we regard them as our enemies?

      18. _____

      What are we not to be doing?

      19. _____

      Often in reading the phrase "heap burning coals" the temptation is to say, "If I do what this passage says, this will really burn him up!" as though it were an indirect way of getting revenge. This opinion is contrary to the rest of the passage. The context of *Romans 12:20-21*, beginning at *verse 14* is on blessing others. In *verse 17*, we are to put off getting revenge, and in *verse 18* we are to put on living in peace.

      The picture of "heaping burning coals" comes from the fact that in the Ancient Near East, people had to keep burning coals in their homes at all times for warmth and for cooking. If the coals died, the people did not have matches or other convenient methods of relighting fires. So, if the coals were extinguished, someone from the household had to search for burning coals, often using a container carried on his head for the new supply. If you see your enemy looking for this necessity, God says that the loving thing to do is not to ignore him or to give him merely the bare minimum number of coals. Rather, you are to heap the burning coals on, far more than he would expect, even from a friend. You are to "heap" on the blessings.

      Notice that this Scripture never says your enemy asks you for help, or thanks you, or even notices that you blessed him. This may be true of your relationship with your spouse even when your spouse treats you as an enemy.

   c. Read Paragraph E. on Page 260. Then highlight in your manual the reference to *I Peter 3:1-9* and read *I Peter 3:8-9*. What are the "put-offs" and "put-on" in this passage?

      20. "Put-offs": _____

      "Put-on": _____

      These verses summarize the teaching on submission, which begins in *I Peter 2:13*. In the left margin of Paragraph E., write the passage *I Peter 2:13 – 3:9*.

      In *I Peter 2:13*, to whom are we to be in submission?

      21. _____

      In *verse 18*, to whom are we to be in submission?

      22. _____

      In *verse 20*, when we patiently endure suffering for doing what is right, what do we find?

      23. _____

Student Workbook for the Self-Confrontation Bible Study
- Lesson 15 -
© Biblical Counseling Foundation

Notice how important this is in *verse 21*. We are called for this very purpose, and then we are given our ultimate example of how to respond. Who is our example?

24. _____

We see in *verse 23* that Jesus did not revile in return; He uttered no threats. What did He do instead?

25. _____

What an example that is to us! Have you been in a position of leadership or responsibility where you thought that you were due more respect, or where you thought you were being treated unjustly?

26. _____

How did you respond?

27. _____

If you did not respond in a godly way, what should you have done instead?

28. _____

Jesus focused not on His enemies, but rather on His loving Father. We should do the same.

Considering *I Peter 3:1* in light of the above passages, how are wives to live?

29. _____

Wives are to respond in the same way that Jesus responded when He faced harsh treatment at the hands of unjust men. Wives are to demonstrate submissiveness to their husbands (through their chaste and respectful behavior) out of obedience to the Lord even if the husbands are disobedient to the Word and unreasonable. This does not mean that the wife will commit sin in order to demonstrate submissiveness to her husband.

Also, in *I Peter 3:7*, how are the husbands to respond?

30. _____
_____

NOTE: The words "in the same way" (in I Peter 3:1) or "likewise" (in I Peter 3:7) do not just refer back to instructions for wives. It goes further back to the general topic of submission in I Peter 2:13-25.

Husbands should protect their wives and care for them as they would a delicate and precious vase.

ILLUSTRATION: In most countries there are at least two different kinds of containers: common clay, base metal, stoneware, or wooden vessels which are rough, durable, and require no special treatment; and precious vessels, which are much thinner and more delicate and fragile. Because the delicate vessels are so fragile and precious, you treat them with special care. You do not treat them roughly or shake them to see if they will break. Husbands are, in the physical

> sense, to treat their wives with the same kind of tenderness and care with which they would treat a fragile vessel. In addition, *verse 7* says a husband is to grant his wife honor since she is a fellow-heir (i.e., spiritually, she is no less strong or responsible than the man). The husband is not only to treat his wife with tender care physically, but he is also to put his wife in a place of special honor.

    Now, review *I Peter 3:8-9*. Notice that God not only tells us what to do, but He also tells us why it is good for us. As each spouse is submissive, not returning evil for evil, but blessing instead, regardless of the response of others, both the husband and the wife will be fulfilling the purpose for which they were called and, in the process, they will inherit a blessing from God.

4. Read Section **IV. You can respond biblically to an "irritating" spouse** ... on Page 260 of the *Self-Confrontation* manual. It is important to understand that *no one*, not even your spouse, can make you act in an ungodly way. Your reaction to anything your spouse says or does only reveals what is already in your heart. Your peace and joy is to be only in the Lord.

THE FAMILY CONFERENCE TABLE

When relationship problems exist in a marriage, as well as in other relationships, there is usually a need to establish biblical communications. Let's look at one way of establishing biblical communication by following the procedure for conducting a family meeting or "conference table." Turn to **OVERCOMING PROBLEMS THROUGH BIBLICAL COMMUNICATION (USING A CONFERENCE TABLE FOR RECONCILIATION)** (*Self-Confrontation*, Page 261).

A. Read Section **I. Overall purposes of conference tables**. The conference table is a highly structured exercise designed to help initiate biblical communication (even when relationships are very poor). However, its format is useful for making any family or group decisions even when relationships are good.

B. Read all the paragraphs under Section **II. Prerequisites to conducting a first conference table**.

C. Read each portion of Section **III. Procedures for the first conference table** on Pages 262-264.

SCRIPTURE RECITATION

Recite *I Peter 3:1, 7* to someone at home, in class, or elsewhere. Also, recite one of the previous memory passages chosen by the listener. Put a check here (__) when you have successfully recited the verses.

QUESTIONS AND CONCLUSION

A. Under whose complete control are we to place ourselves?

31. _____

B. To whom should we submit ourselves as servants?

32. _____

We have seen in this lesson that each spouse has many opportunities in a marriage to die to self and to be a servant. Spouses should not insist on their own way but seek together to find God's will in every matter.

Most problems come about between spouses because either one or both are seeking their own way. As a consequence, problems compound themselves over time and divisions increase.

Also, remember that no one, not even your spouse, can make you act in an ungodly way. Your reaction to your spouse only reveals what is in your heart already. This is a great hope, as you can live a godly life no matter what your spouse does. But it is also a challenge to you to live God's way regardless of the behavior of your spouse.

   C. What was the most significant truth you learned in completing this lesson?

   33. _____

_____

PREVIEW OF THE NEXT LESSON

In the next two lessons, we will look at parent-child relationships. Few parents are biblically prepared to train up their children to live in God's way, according to the Scriptures. The Scriptures provide a wealth of guidance on proper training of children, and yet, so many rely on the notions of the world or their own experiences when they were growing up. These two lessons are vital to parents. They are also very helpful to people without children, since most of the principles and teaching points also apply to discipleship of others.

LESSON 16
PARENT–CHILD RELATIONSHIPS (PART ONE)

OPENING PRAYER AND SCRIPTURE MEMORY

Before you begin this lesson, ask for God's help in understanding His Word and for strength to apply what you learn in the power of the Holy Spirit.

Begin memorizing *Ezekiel 18:20* and *Ephesians 6:4*. Also, review the Scripture memory passages assigned in the previous lessons. Then, be prepared to recite them at the end of this lesson.

Also, in your own words, please write out the meaning of the new memory verses below:

_____
_____
_____
_____

PERSONAL PLAN FOR CHANGE

Continue to work on your personal **VICTORY OVER FAILURES PLAN** and make corrections based on what you will be learning this week.

INTRODUCTION TO THE LESSON

A. We began Lesson 14 by recognizing that apart from the Lord, marriage can be a disaster. Often, this happens because decisions are based on previous experience rather than the Scriptures. It is the same with training children. To make matters worse, many parents, even Christian parents, look to the world for wisdom, often not realizing that the Scriptures provide a wealth of guidance on the proper training of children. In fact, the entire Bible describes how God, our heavenly Father, trains His children.

Also, most of the principles related to training children are applicable to discipling any believer. Read *I Thessalonians 2:7-11*. Write in the reference to the left of the summary box on Page 272 of the *Self-Confrontation* manual. What example did the Apostle Paul give to describe how he discipled the Thessalonians in *verse 7*?

1. _____

In *verse 11*?

2. _____

As you can see, even if you are not a parent, you are to approach discipleship in the same way parents disciple (train) their children. You will find these next two lessons valuable as you train up others in the Lord.

As mentioned before, these lessons build on one another as the Bible Study progresses. The previous seven lessons are particularly important for a full understanding of these two lessons on parent-child relationships. This lesson deals with the first two elements of how to face, deal with, and endure problems biblically: biblical understanding and biblical hope. The next lesson will cover the last two elements: biblical change and biblical practice (doing the Word).

B. Read the purposes of **LESSON 16: PARENT-CHILD RELATIONSHIPS (PART ONE)** (*Self-Confrontation*, Page 272).

MAN'S VIEW

Following the method exemplified in the Scriptures of contrasting God's way and man's way, let's start with the "you have heard that it was said ..." part by looking at some of man's theories on how to train children. Turn to **MAN'S THEORIES AND PRACTICES FOR REARING CHILDREN** (*Self-Confrontation*, Page 274).

A. In Section **I. Characteristics of man's theories** ..., note that the major characteristics focus on self-exaltation and on feelings.

B. In Section **II. Some of man's mistaken explanations** ...,

1. Under Paragraph A.:

    a. Read Subparagraph 1. The world teaches parents techniques for training children according to the latest findings or research rather than according to God's standard.

    b. In Subparagraphs 2.-11., note that all the explanations place the emphasis on blaming circumstances or others rather than on dealing with self.

2. Under Paragraph B.:

    a. Read Subparagraph 3. This false teaching about self (as described in Lessons 9 and 10) is prevalent due to an emphasis today on justifying or excusing problems (i.e., not taking responsibility for them).

    b. Read Subparagraph 8. This mistaken explanation teaches and encourages children to be preoccupied with self.

C. You do not need to spend much time on Section **III. Some of man's futile attempts** ... (*Self-Confrontation*, Page 275). To summarize, the world's answers focus on reducing or eliminating symptoms and on preoccupation with self rather than on dealing with the true problem.

D. Turn to Section **IV. Some unbiblical views within the church regarding the bringing up of children** on Page 276 of the *Self-Confrontation* manual. In Paragraph A.:

1. Read Subparagraph 1. This is one of the most frequent mistaken practices in the body of Christ. In many Sunday school classes, Bible Studies, and seminars, students are taught on the basis that we must go outside God's Word to gain a full intellectual understanding of how to train children, or we need to depend upon the opinions of those who have much experience in training children.

2. Read Subparagraph 6. This presents a backwards view. Parents *cannot* be the role model of the Lord, since only God's Word contains the description of the heavenly Father, and only Jesus was the embodiment (or "model") of God. While parents cannot represent the perfection of Christ, they are to be examples of the believer. Remember that Jesus is the only perfect example to follow. Even when the Apostle Paul said, "Follow me," he pointed beyond himself by adding, "as I follow Christ."

> **ILLUSTRATION:** To view parents as role models of the Lord would be similar to your looking at the moon and saying, "How beautifully the moon glows! The sun must be marvelous." Instead, you ought to be considering the source, the sun, and then saying, "Look at how powerful and brilliant the sun is! No wonder the moon glows so beautifully!"

| BIBLICAL UNDERSTANDING ABOUT PARENT-CHILD RELATIONSHIPS |

A. Now, in contrast with man's theories and practices for training children which focus on self-exaltation and living according to feelings, let's go to the "but I say unto you …" part by studying what the Bible says about training children. Turn to *Principle 69* on Page 273, **BIBLICAL PRINCIPLES: PARENT-CHILD RELATIONSHIPS (PART ONE)**.

1. Read the first sentence of *Principle 69*, then, highlight in your manual the reference to *Psalm 127:3* and read *verses 3-4*. Note that children are not possessions of the parents. They are gifts from the Lord, and are like arrows.

> *ILLUSTRATION:* The picture here is of an arrow in the hands of a warrior. A warrior does not keep the arrow in his quiver, but he carefully places it in the bow, takes aim, and then releases the arrow so that it can make an impact. Parents are to prepare their children to go forth into the world to make an impact for the Lord.

2. Read the remainder of *Principle 69*, then, highlight in your manual and read *Proverbs 22:6*. Parents are responsible to train each child in the way or plan that God has for him, not according to their personal opinions, desires, or ways. Parents are to know the Scriptures and each child, observing how the child responds to God's work in his life. Note that this verse is not an assurance to parents that if they train their children biblically, the children will be saved and live in godly ways *(this teaching is in violation of Ezekiel 18:20 and other passages)*. This Scripture teaches that, in general, the biblical training provided by parents will follow their children wherever they go even if they choose to be ungodly.

> *ILLUSTRATION:* The indication of a child not being able to depart from the training *"when he is old"* can be described like this: On a sunny day when you can see your shadow, you can turn away from your shadow or even try to run away from it, but you cannot depart from your shadow. Similarly, no matter how hard a child tries to run from his biblical training, he cannot get away from it.

What does *Isaiah 55:11* say about God's Word?

3. _____
   _____

Do you remember the teaching on being a faithful steward in Lesson 10? The responsibility of parents is to be faithful stewards. But only God is responsible for results.

Parents are responsible to help their children learn the Word, develop godly habits, be available to them for godly counsel, etc., but parents cannot ultimately control the choices their children make in their own relationship with the Lord. Parents cannot change the hearts of their children. Parents who are faithful to train their children in God's way need not suffer false guilt because one of their children is not living a godly life. Even God has rebellious children!

3. Training up children is a very serious responsibility. Parents need to study the Scriptures diligently so that they know how to train their children according to God's directives.

B. Read *Principle 70*, **BIBLICAL PRINCIPLES: PARENT-CHILD RELATIONSHIPS (PART ONE)** (*Self-Confrontation*, Page 273).

Principles 69 and *70* provide the basis for the biblical guidelines beginning on Page 278.

GUIDELINES FOR DISCIPLING CHILDREN

A. Turn to **GUIDELINES FOR TRAINING CHILDREN** (*Self-Confrontation*, Page 278).

1. You do not need to spend much time on Sections **I. A parent's commitment to the Lord**, **II. A parent's commitment to the Word of God**, and **III. The commitment of parents to each other**, since we covered these subjects in the lessons on marriage.

2. Turn to Section **IV. The commitment of believing parents to their children** (*Self-Confrontation*, Page 279).

   a. Read Paragraph A. Note that parents are:

   1) To be *godly examples*, and they are to point to Jesus Christ as the ultimate example. While parents sin and are not perfect, Jesus never sinned and He has provided the only perfect example to follow. Write, "godly examples" in the margin next to Subparagraph 1.

   2) To be *godly servants* and regard their children as more important than themselves. Write, "godly servants" in the margin next to Subparagraph 2.

   3) To be *godly disciplers*. Write, "godly disciplers" in the margin next to Subparagraph 3. Highlight in your manual and read *II Timothy 2:24-26*. What characteristics of discipleship are contained in this passage?

   4. _____

   _____

   b. Read Paragraph B. Note that parents are held just as responsible as children to obey God's Word. This includes confessing to their children the sins they, as parents, commit against them.

   c. Paragraph C. covers overlooked information concerning the training of children.

   1) Read the first sentence of Paragraph C., then, highlight in your manual and read *Ephesians 6:4*. What are the "put-off" and "put-ons" in this passage?

   5. "Put-off": _____

   "Put-ons": _____

   2) Also read the **WAYS THAT PARENTS PROVOKE THEIR CHILDREN TO ANGER** (*Self-Confrontation*, Pages 281-283). The ways of provoking children listed in this section can be summarized in one phrase: "not loving them God's way or considering them as more important than self" (*in violation of Philippians 2:3-4*).

   3) Now, go back to Paragraph C. on Page 179. Highlight in your manual and read *Deuteronomy 6:5-7*.

   a) In *verses 5* and *6*, what is the primary responsibility of parents in training their children?

   6. _____

   Children watch their parents very carefully to see how they will deal with various situations of life.

   b) In *verse 7*, what is your responsibility to your children?

   7. _____

Parents are to be training their children at all times whenever they are with them. Parents are to teach them God's ways as they go about experiencing the situations of life. This is the way Jesus taught His disciples.

The most important training that children (as well as others we disciple) can receive is how to demonstrate love toward God and others (i.e., how to be a loving person). Biblical love is often difficult since it goes against the flesh; however, helping children be loving in the midst of difficulties is crucial. Therefore, parents should not necessarily take children out of difficult situations, but rather, help them to have victory in the midst of difficulties. It may be God's will that they learn important biblical lessons by staying in the situation.

It is important to note that children tend not to remember what they are taught in a classroom setting nearly as well as truths they learn through experience, particularly when they are confronted with difficulties. When they are in the midst of difficult situations, children are much more attentive to instruction.

List some examples of where and when you can be teaching your children in the course of a normal day.

8.

3. Read Sections **V. The commitment of children to the Lord** and **VI. The commitment of children to their parents** (*Self-Confrontation*, Page 280).

B. Turn to **UNDERSTANDING BIBLICAL INSTRUCTION OF CHILDREN** (*Self-Confrontation*, Pages 284-287).

1. In Section **IV. What are you to teach your children?**, read the first line of Paragraphs A. through D. on Page 285.

2. In Section **V. How are you as a believer to receive instruction …?**, read Paragraph H. (*Self-Confrontation*, Page 286) and *Proverbs 14:15*. What is the difference between a wise or prudent person and a naïve or simple person?

9.

3. In Section **VI. How are you to instruct your children?**:

   a. Read Paragraph F. (*Self-Confrontation*, Page 287), then, highlight in your manual and read *I Thessalonians 2:8*. Paul was pleased to not only give them the Gospel, but what else?

   10.

   What does this tell you about how we are to regard our own children?

   11.

   b. Paragraph G. (*Self-Confrontation*, Page 287) describes how to train children using the example of how Jesus trained the disciples. Each step of Subparagraph 2. is important and distinct. Although all the Gospels show how Jesus taught and trained the disciples, we will learn His discipleship principles using the book of *Mark*.

1) In the margin to the left of Subparagraph a., write in the title *"Teaching them what and why."* Highlight in your manual and read *Mark 1:17*. Jesus told the disciples *what* to do, which was to:

   12. _____

   He also told them *why*, which was to make them:

   13. _____

2) In the margin to the left of Subparagraph b., write in the title *"Showing them how."* Note that in Chapters 3 - 6 of *Mark*, Jesus showed the disciples *how* to minister. He demonstrated it first-hand.

3) In the margin to the left of Subparagraph c., write in the title *"Getting them started."* Turn to *Mark 6:7*. Jesus sent the disciples out to minister. How did He send them out?

   14. _____

4) In the margin to the left of Subparagraph d., write in the title *"Keeping them going."* Note that in the remainder of *Mark*, Jesus kept encouraging the disciples to keep on in spite of difficulties.

5) In the margin to the left of Subparagraph e., write in the title *"Training them to teach others."* In the last chapters of *Matthew* and *Mark*, Jesus instructed the disciples to teach/disciple others.

Children are often not trained properly because parents fail to carry out one or more of these steps. See the following illustration:

ILLUSTRATION: We can illustrate these steps by describing how to teach a child to make his bed.

Step 1: *Teach him what and why.* Start out by explaining, "It is important that you learn how to make your bed because you will learn how to be a faithful steward by caring for what God has provided for you" (I Corinthians 4:2). "This will also help you become disciplined in carrying out your responsibilities even when you do not feel like it" (I Timothy 4:7).

What are some additional Christlike characteristics that would be developed by making the bed every day?

15. _____

_____

_____

Step 2: *Show him how.* Show him how by making the bed properly and explaining each step.

Step 3: *Get him started.* Assign the responsibility to the child and give him a certain time period to complete the task. At first, you may even be providing a great deal of help.

Step 4: *Keep him going.* Remind him to make the bed and correct any errors, teach him as appropriate, and correct him if he does not finish properly in the allotted time. When the time comes to change the bed sheets, he may need additional training and help.

Step 5: *Train him to disciple others* (for example, teach his younger brother or sister, etc. how to make their beds).

Whether you are training children or discipling other believers, you would apply the same biblical principles.

BIBLICAL HOPE

This brings us to the second element, biblical hope. Let's turn to Page 273 of the *Self-Confrontation* manual.

A. Read *Principle 71,* then, highlight in your manual and read *Proverbs 3:5-6.* As a parent, whose is the only wisdom you can trust to be perfectly reliable?

16. _____

B. Read *Principle 72,* then, highlight in your manual and read *Ephesians 6:2-3.* Note that being obedient is the right thing to do; this is itself a blessing. Remember that God's command stands even if the parents are not godly. The child is to honor his parents, but his ultimate authority is the Lord, so the child would not obey if his parents demand that he sin.

SCRIPTURE RECITATION

Recite *Ezekiel 18:20* and *Ephesians 6:4* to someone at home, in class, or elsewhere. Also, recite one of the previous memory passages chosen by the listener. Put a check here (___) when you have successfully recited the verses.

QUESTIONS

A. What are three of the things parents are to be toward their children (see the section of this *Workbook* on **GUIDELINES FOR DISCIPLING CHILDREN**)?

17. _____
_____
_____

B. What are five steps of discipleship Jesus used that can also be applied to bringing up children?

18. _____
_____
_____
_____
_____

C. What was the most significant truth you learned in completing this lesson?

19. _____
_____

PREVIEW OF THE NEXT LESSON

The next lesson completes coverage of the four elements of how to face, deal with, and endure parent-child relationship problems biblically. You will discover that training children requires planning, diligence, and practice. We will study how to train children to be faithful and how to discipline them biblically.

LESSON 17
PARENT–CHILD RELATIONSHIPS (PART TWO)

OPENING PRAYER AND SCRIPTURE MEMORY

Before you begin this lesson, ask for God's help in understanding His Word and for strength to apply what you learn in the power of the Holy Spirit.

Begin memorizing *Ephesians 6:1-3*. Also, review the Scripture memory passages assigned in the previous lessons. Then, be prepared to recite them at the end of this lesson.

Also, in your own words, please write out the meaning of the new memory verses below:

_____

_____

_____

_____

PERSONAL PLAN FOR CHANGE

Continue to work on your personal **VICTORY OVER FAILURES PLAN** and make corrections based on what you will be learning this week.

INTRODUCTION TO THE LESSON

A. In the last lesson, you looked at the first two elements of how to face, deal with, and endure parent-child relationship problems, which are: biblical understanding and biblical hope. This lesson will cover the last two elements: biblical change and biblical practice (doing the Word).

Teaching and help on child discipline and family devotions are included in this lesson. These are very important in bringing up children; and yet, few parents understand how to carry out either of these so that effective training takes place.

B. Read the purposes of **LESSON 17: PARENT-CHILD RELATIONSHIPS (PART TWO)** *(Self-Confrontation, Page 292)*.

C. Read *Principle 73*, **BIBLICAL PRINCIPLES: PARENT-CHILD RELATIONSHIPS (PART TWO)** *(Self-Confrontation, Page 293)*, then, highlight in your manual and read *Ephesians 6:4*.

What are the "put-off" and "put-on" in the passage?

1. "Put-off:" _____

"Put-on:" _____

D. We will cover the truths of the other principles relating to biblical change and biblical practice during the rest of the lesson. Let's look into the subject of training children to be faithful disciples by turning to *Self-Confrontation*, Page 295.

DISCIPLESHIP IN THE HOME

Turn to **TRAINING CHILDREN TO BE FAITHFUL (BIBLICAL DISCIPLESHIP IN THE HOME)** *(Self-Confrontation, Page 295)*. This section is particularly valuable for discipling others, whether one has children or not. These principles apply to all who need to be trained to become faithful, mature disciples of Christ.

- A. In Section **I. Principles for training children to be faithful** ...:
  1. Read Paragraph A. on Page 295. Parents need to study the Word of God diligently and then teach their children according to God's way, not according to their own human wisdom or their children's inclinations. Highlight *Proverbs 22:15a* and *Jeremiah 17:9* after the first sentence. What does *Proverbs 22:15a* say is the tendency of a child?

     2. _____

     What does *Jeremiah 17:9* say about even a child's heart?

     3. _____

     Notice that these verses contradict the Positive Potential approach studied in Lesson 4, which states that each person is intrinsically good. By nature, we are all foolish and tend to go our own way. Because of this truth, it is the responsibility of believing parents to provide biblical guidance and discipline from the earliest age on.

  2. Read Paragraph B. on Page 296. Each child is to be treated individually, according to his or her own God-given characteristics. Some children may readily go God's way, once they understand it. Others may be resistant or outright rebellious. Whatever the discipline may be, children should always be shown that your desire for them, and your motivation for discipline, is to help them to know the Lord and to become more like His Son, Jesus.

  3. Read Paragraph C. on Page 296. Even in their first year, children should begin to be taught to deny themselves daily and to follow the Lord and serve and build up others. What are some examples of ways that children could be taught this in their early years?

     4. _____
     _____
     _____

     People often erroneously begin by letting children have their own way, letting them avoid responsibility, focusing on following their feelings, and then, later endeavor to do just the opposite at some point in the child's growth. This confusing double standard is unbiblical.

- B. Read Section **II. Areas of your children's lives** ..., on Page 296. Parents are to train their children to live faithfully before the Lord in every area of their lives. This training doesn't start at the age of 3 or 10 or 16, but instead, begins in infancy and continues until they are adults. Biblical principles do not change and so are the same for children and adults.

BIBLICAL DISCIPLINE

So far, we have looked at the importance of discipleship in training children. Parents are to begin discipling their children the moment they come into the world. Children are to be trained in the way that God commands them to live, not according to the philosophies of man. In this section, you will study how parents are to discipline their children when they resist biblical training. Turn to **UNDERSTANDING BIBLICAL DISCIPLINE** on Page 299 in the *Self-Confrontation* manual.

- A. Read Section **I. What does discipline mean?** on Page 299. Instruction and discipline in the Scripture are very closely intertwined.

- B. In Section **II. Why is discipline necessary?**, read Paragraph B., then, highlight and read *Hebrews 12:10-11*. There is a distinction in this passage between what we might feel like doing and what we know to be in the long-term interest of the child. What does God say about the short term feelings associated with discipline?

5. _____

This should be true not only for the child, but also for the parent. It is also grievous (sorrowful) to the Lord when we sin *(based on Ephesians 4:30)*.

C. Read the paragraph immediately under the section title, **III. How and when is discipline carried out?** on Page 299. Note that parental discipline is to be carried out in love and is designed to produce Christlike character.

Parents are to *discipline* their children, not punish them. There is a big difference. Discipline is for *restoration,* while punishment is for carrying out a sentence (like a judge does in a courtroom). When children are disobedient, they are out of fellowship with the Lord and others. They need to be restored to fellowship and to return to being a doer of the Word. Punishment, on the other hand, is only for the purpose of paying a penalty.

The next paragraphs in Section **III.** of the manual contain a biblical step-by-step procedure for disciplining children.

1. Read Paragraph A., then, highlight in your manual and read *Genesis 2:16-17.* How many commands did the Lord give Adam and Eve?

    6. _____

    What was the command?

    7. _____

    The command was simple, but very important. It was a test to demonstrate their love for God through obedience. The number of God's commands only increased as man's disobedience continued. Make sure the instructions to your children are clear, not too complicated, and focused on developing obedience.

2. Read Paragraph B., then, highlight in your manual and read *Exodus 31:18.* The commandments were very clear and written down so that they would not be forgotten or misunderstood. Where there are persistent problems of disobedience, it may be especially appropriate to write down the instructions.

3. Read Paragraph C., then, highlight in your manual and read *Deuteronomy 11:26-28.* What will bring blessings?

    8. _____

    What will bring curses?

    9. _____

    God told the Israelites ahead of time what He would do as a result of their obedience or disobedience. Likewise, children who are having difficulty with obedience should know in advance that there will be consequences for disobedience.

4. Read the first part of Paragraph D. on Page 300 and Sub-paragraph 1. Notice the emphasis on the "put-on" for the purpose of restoration.

    a. Highlight in your manual and read *Ecclesiastes 8:11* and Subparagraph 2. When does God say that the discipline should be administered?

        10. _____

Why is that important for the child?

11. _____

The principle in *Ecclesiastes 8:11* is violated when parents send their disobedient child to his room for a period of time for the purpose of thinking over what he has done with the hope that he will repent. Instead, this kind of action often encourages bitter thoughts and is a temptation to do evil.

    b. Highlight in your manual and read *Proverbs 22:15* and Subparagraph 2. a. on Page 300. What is the purpose of the rod of discipline?

12. _____

    c. Read Subparagraph 2. b. Parents must be very careful to use the rod (the most stern form of discipline) only when the child is acting like a fool, that is, he is in willful, deliberate rebellion.

Highlight in your manual and read *Matthew 21:28-31*. What does this tell you about responding to your children?

13. _____
_____

Parents should be careful not to conclude too quickly that a child is rebellious just because he says, "No," initially.

Proverbs 9:7-9 states that a fool is not open to counsel. That is why the rod is used to get his attention. But if the child is not rebellious at the moment, he is open to counsel and to appropriate training tailored to the situation.

    d. Read Subparagraph 2. c. Even when the child is rebellious, the rod should be applied only until the child is sorrowful and repentant. The rod must never be administered for the purpose of inflicting harm, but out of love, with sorrow, to help a rebellious child see his sin and repent of it *(Proverbs 13:24)*.

5. Read Paragraph F. then, highlight in your manual and read *Matthew 5:23-24*. What does this passage indicate that you must do when you have sinned against someone?

14. _____

Are you exempt from asking forgiveness of your children just because you are their parents?

15. _____

Confession to your children is necessary when you have sinned against them. This is not only a responsibility you have to God, but it is a demonstration to your children of how relationships can be restored. This includes asking forgiveness for the manner in which discipline may have been administered (e.g., if it was administered in vengeance or anger). But parents must still carry out discipline even though they are to ask forgiveness for the sinful *manner* in which they previously administered discipline.

FAMILY DEVOTIONS

Another very important practice in training children is family devotions. Turn to **FAMILY DEVOTIONS AND WORSHIP (GUIDELINES AND SUGGESTIONS)** *(Self-Confrontation,* Page 302). As the word "devotions" suggests, family devotions should help all family members to become more devoted to the Lord. There are many ways of having family devotion times, but the purpose should be to become more devoted to God and one another as a family, just as personal devotions are to help us become more devoted to God personally.

A. Read Section **I. Matters to consider when planning family devotions**, then, highlight in your manual and read *Acts 2:42-47*, referenced in Subparagraph C. According to this passage, in what ways did the first century believers demonstrate their devotion to God?

16. _____
_____

B. Read Section **II. Family devotions** ... on Pages 302 and 303. Note that these areas of devotion to the Lord and one another are taken from *Acts 2:42-47*.

Devotions should not be focused exclusively on reading the Word and praying. Families can also use devotional times as opportunities to serve others, as a family, in the church, neighborhood, school, etc. In this way, children not only learn *what* they should do but are involved in *applying* it as well.

C. Read Section **III. When family devotional times should take place** on Page 303. It is important to establish a regular time when all are alert and all can attend consistently.

D. In Section **IV. Suggested topics and activities for family devotions and worship** (Pages 304 and 305), read the introduction to each paragraph and the first sentence of each subparagraph.

E. Section **V. Suggested plans and structures for family devotions and worship** (Pages 305 and 306) lists some ways that devotions can be organized. There are many possibilities. Based on one of these suggestions, or on other ideas discussed with your family or roommates, write down a plan for family devotions that you can realistically commit to, or write down the plan you are already using.

17. _____
_____
_____
_____
_____
_____
_____

Then, work with your family (or others in your living situation, as appropriate) to carry out the plan and be prepared to modify it based on their input.

F. Read Section **VI. Conclusion about family devotions and worship**.

SCRIPTURE RECITATION

Recite *Ephesians 6:1-3* to someone at home, in class, or elsewhere. Also, recite one of the previous memory passages chosen by the listener. Put a check here (___) when you have successfully recited the verses.

QUESTIONS

A. What are some of the commandments that apply to adults that should also be taught to children?

18. _____

B. What is the difference between discipline and punishment?

19. _____

C. Which approach (discipline or punishment) should parents use with their children?
20. _____

D. What should parents do if they sin against their children?
21. _____

E. What are some of the results of conducting regular family devotional times?
22. _____
_____
_____
_____

F. What was the most significant truth you learned in completing this lesson?
23. _____
_____
_____

PREVIEW OF THE NEXT LESSON

In the next lesson, we will cover the important subject of depression. The wonderful truth from the Scriptures is that no matter how hopeless and how depressed a believer is, he can carry out all the responsibilities that God has given him.

LESSON 18
DEPRESSION

OPENING PRAYER AND SCRIPTURE MEMORY

Before you begin this lesson, ask for God's help in understanding His Word and for strength to apply what you learn in the power of the Holy Spirit.

Begin memorizing *Genesis 4:7* and *James 1:22*. Also, review the Scripture memory passages assigned in the previous lessons. Then, be prepared to recite them at the end of this lesson.

Also, in your own words, please write out the meaning of the new memory verses below:

_____

_____

_____

_____

PERSONAL PLAN FOR CHANGE

Continue to work on your personal **VICTORY OVER FAILURES PLAN** and make corrections based on what you will be learning this week.

INTRODUCTION TO THE LESSON

A. This lesson teaches how to deal with the problem of depression, which is often misunderstood by many believers. The world focuses on dealing primarily with the symptoms associated with depression. Many powerful and dangerous drugs are prescribed freely by physicians to eliminate or reduce feelings of depression, but the person often remains defeated by unresolved, underlying problems.

In this lesson, we will look at all four elements of how to face, deal with, and endure the problem of depression. Let's review them: biblical understanding, biblical hope, biblical change, and biblical practice.

B. Read the box at the top of Page 318 of the *Self-Confrontation* manual. Then read purposes A., B., and C. of Section I. on Page 318. Note that nowhere in the Scriptures is the term "depression" used explicitly. However, many of the symptoms currently associated with feelings of depression are in the Scriptures, and none of these is described as a disease. Describing depression as a disease is the world's view, however. The importance of making this distinction will become evident as we look further into the Scriptures.

BIBLICAL UNDERSTANDING ABOUT DEPRESSION

A. Let's start with the first purpose, which deals with understanding depression. Turn to **UNDERSTANDING DEPRESSION** (*Self-Confrontation*, Page 321).

1. Read Paragraph A. of Section **I. What is "depression"?** Depression has both deeds and feelings associated with it. Many people think that getting rid of depression is equivalent to getting rid of certain unwanted feelings. You learned from God's Word taught in Lesson 6

Student Workbook for the Self-Confrontation Bible Study
- Lesson 18 -
© Biblical Counseling Foundation

that you are responsible before God for your deeds, but not for your feelings. It is especially important for you to remember this as we examine the subject of depression.

2. Read Paragraph C. of Section I. This description by David is a powerful picture of how bad one can feel, both in emotions and in the body. What reason did David give for his depressed feelings?

   1. _____

3. Read Section **II. Who can experience feelings of depression?** and note that various individuals in the Bible experienced what would today be called feelings of depression because of a preoccupation with self. What did Elijah experience in *I Kings 19:1-4*?

   2. _____

   What did Jonah experience in *Jonah 4:1-11*?

   3. _____

4. Turn to Section **III. What are possible factors that may lead to "depression"?** (*Self-Confrontation*, Page 322).

   a. First read the paragraph immediately under the topic sentence.

   b. Read Paragraph A. Although depression-like feelings associated with these conditions are not sinful, they cannot be used as an excuse for sin in thoughts, speech, or actions. Note the cautions in the italicized paragraph.

   c. Read Paragraphs B. through D.

5. Turn to Section **IV. What is the biblical perspective on factors contributing to "depression"?**

   a. In Paragraph A., read Subparagraphs 1. and 2.

   b. In Paragraph B., read Subparagraph 2. and the note in italics. All of this is summarized in *Principles 78* and *79* on Page 319.

B. Read *Principles 78-79*, **BIBLICAL PRINCIPLES: DEPRESSION** (*Self-Confrontation*, Page 319). There is a difference between the *feelings* associated with depression and the *sinful deeds* associated with depression. We are not responsible for our feelings, but we are responsible for our deeds.

| BIBLICAL HOPE |

There is great hope for a person who is depressed. God will not allow him to be tempted beyond what he can bear.

A. Read *Principle 80* on Page 319 of the *Self-Confrontation* manual.

1. Highlight in your manual and read *I Corinthians 10:13*. Remember (from Lesson 6) that while the temptation to be overcome by feelings is common to man, God is faithful and places His own "ideal weight" line on every believer. Although a believer can be heavily burdened, God knows how much weight (trials) each one needs and can face; and no believer ever needs to be overcome by any "weight" of life that will cause him to sink spiritually. God will never allow anything into a believer's life that will cause him to fall to temptation and sin. Take a moment now to think about problems that you are having or another believer is having that might seem, from a human perspective, to be too difficult to bear. If you wish, write them down here.

   4. _____

   _____

   Then, take a minute and thank the Lord that, if you are a believer, the promise of *I Corinthians 10:13* is true and applies to the very problems about which you are thinking.

   Also, while *I Corinthians 10:13* provides great hope, it presents a warning at the same time. If a person gives in to a temptation, he cannot blame anything or anyone else for his sin. A depressed person may need to be reminded of this verse very often. One who is feeling very low and living by his feelings may still say, "I can not" when reminded of his responsibilities. What he is really saying is, "I will not." He is making a choice. A person who feels depressed can still respond to the Lord, and, if he is a believer, can be obedient to the Lord and can carry out his responsibilities *despite* his feelings.

2. Another aspect of hope is that God does not judge us by our feelings; He judges us on the basis of our obedience. It is marvelous to know that, even when we feel miserable, God is pleased if we do what He commands us to do. The aim must be to please God in thoughts, speech, and actions, not merely to be rid of the feelings associated with depression. We are responsible for our thoughts, speech, and actions, but not our feelings. Feelings are not at issue. Love for the Lord and love for others (the two great commandments) are the keys to victory and pleasing God.

   It is important to distinguish between the feelings that are associated with depression and failure to live a responsible life. God holds us responsible for keeping His commandments regardless of how we feel. It is greatly encouraging to recognize that we can keep His commandments regardless of how we feel. This is living in victory.

B. Read *Principle 81*.

   Highlight in your manual and read *II Corinthians 1:3-5*. Where does the believer's comfort come from primarily?

   5. _____

   Is depression exempted from this promise?

   6. _____

   The passage says that God comforts us in *all* our afflictions. Other believers may or may not provide comfort, but our peace and joy are dependent only on the Lord.

   WARNING: In *II Corinthians 1:4*, we see that *any* godly believer is able to comfort those who are in *any* kind of affliction. While this passage provides great hope to biblical counselors, it is often used wrongly to present false hope. People are wrongly encouraged to specialize in counseling those who are experiencing the same kinds of problems that they have previously overcome. Consequently, former drunkards are encouraged to concentrate on helping drunkards. Godly believers do not need to experience any sin, such as drunkenness, in order to counsel someone with that problem. Therefore, we do not need to have experienced a particular problem in order to provide completely adequate biblical counsel.

Encouraging people to counsel others with primarily the same kinds of problems is a dangerous practice because Scripture warns us to flee temptation *(II Timothy 2:22)*. For example, associating with individuals while they are involved in drinking alcohol could be a stumbling block to a former drunkard.

Another temptation to those who counsel others with similar problems is to counsel from experience rather than the Word of God. The counselor may be tempted to excuse sinful behavior. He may also be tempted to suggest solutions from his own personal experience rather than to study the Scriptures for answers.

BIBLICAL CHANGE

A. Read *Principle 82*, **BIBLICAL PRINCIPLES: DEPRESSION** *(Self-Confrontation, Page 320)*.

B. Highlight *Genesis 4:7* in your manual, then read *Genesis 4:3-8*. What does *verse 5* say was Cain's problem?

7. _____

What does the Lord say in *verse 7* that Cain should do about it?

8. _____

It is important to note some of the differences among translations of this passage. The phrase translated *"will not your countenance be lifted up"* in the **New American Standard Bible (NASB)** is translated *"will you not be accepted"* in the **New International Version (NIV)** and the **King James Version (KJV)**. Many people who read the **NASB** conclude that if one obeys God *(does well)*, then he will no longer have feelings of depression *(i.e., his countenance will be lifted up)*. In the original language (Hebrew) the wording indicates that you will be accepted by the Lord, which means that your face will be lifted to God's without a barrier.

> **ILLUSTRATION:** To understand what God means by an uplifted countenance, think of a little child who knows he has done something wrong. He usually hangs his head and looks at the floor, but does not look at his parent's face. The barrier of his wrong is between him and his parent. It is only when he does what is right that a child freely looks at his parent's face. His countenance is lifted to his parent. In other words, a child can lift up his face to his parent's face without shame.

Note also in *verse 7* the importance of doing well. God warns you that if you do not do well, *"sin is crouching at the door; and its desire is for you."* Also, note that *you*, not God, must master it. Since it is a command to "do well," God provides you with the capability to obey Him regardless of your feelings.

C. As we saw in Lesson 8, *I Timothy 4:7-8* emphasizes the importance of discipline. Discipline, by definition, involves going against your feelings. *(**NOTE:** Instead of the word "discipline," the NIV uses the word "train" and the KJV uses the word "exercise." The word in the original language means to exercise vigorously as athletes do.)*

It is important to be obedience-oriented, not feeling-oriented. A depressed person allows feelings to lead his life. The problem is not a lack of understanding or capability. The issue is the willingness to do God's will and faithfulness in doing it.

BIBLICAL PRACTICE

A. Read *Principle 83*, **BIBLICAL PRINCIPLES: DEPRESSION** *(Self-Confrontation,* Page 320). After the first sentence, highlight in your manual the reference to *Ephesians 5:15-17* and read *Ephesians 5:15-16*. In this passage, what does God say we are to do with our time?

9. _____

After the second sentence in *Principle 83*, highlight in your manual and read *Colossians 3:23-24*. What does this passage tell us about *how* we are to be doing what we do?

10. _____

What does *James 4:17* tell us about responsibilities we know that we should be doing? Highlight this passage in your manual (after the first sentence).

11. _____

Omitting responsibilities is a very common problem associated with depressed people. They know what they should be doing, but choose to follow their feelings, rather than being obedient to God even when they do not feel like it (e.g., staying in bed or watching TV instead of doing their tasks).

B. Individuals who are depressed need first to identify their sins, repent, and confess them to the Lord and to those offended. Then, they need to discipline themselves to practice righteousness *(based on Hebrews 5:14 and James 1:22)*. They may need to start by completing a **VICTORY OVER FAILURES PLAN**.

Typically, people who have been depressed for an extended period of time have experienced downward spirals — one sin has led to another taking them further and further into depression. (See the downward spiral described on Page 84 of the *Self-Confrontation* manual.) In the process, they have neglected many of their God-given responsibilities. Thus, they may need to reorder their entire lives. To do this, it may be helpful to establish a new weekly schedule based on all of their God-given responsibilities. A procedure for developing a biblical schedule is provided in Lesson 22, Section **III. Incorporating God's standards into your life** *(Self-Confrontation,* Page 405). We will explain this procedure in detail when we get to Lesson 22.

As a depressed person is in the process of evaluating his life, he may be tempted to become overwhelmed with all the changes he needs to make. He may have lost hope of being able to function fully. It is important for him to remember that he is only required to take one step at a time. The issue is faithfulness. Wisdom for succeeding steps will come as the depressed person begins to establish faithfulness. A person who is faithful in a little thing is also faithful in much *(Luke 16:10)*.

SCRIPTURE RECITATION

Recite *Genesis 4:7* and *James 1:22* to someone at home, in class, or elsewhere. Also, recite one of the previous memory passages chosen by the listener. Put a check here (__) when you have successfully recited the verses.

QUESTIONS

A. There is a difference between the feelings associated with depression and the sin associated with depression. We are not responsible for our

12. _____

of depression, but we are responsible for our

13. _____

   B. List two reasons why there is hope for a depressed person:

14. _____
_____

   C. If you are being responsible to do what the Lord commands you to do, does God promise that your feelings will change?

15. _____

   D. What was the most significant truth you learned in completing this lesson?

16. _____
_____

PREVIEW OF THE NEXT LESSON

In the next lesson, we will cover the subjects of fear and worry. Worry is so common in the body of Christ that many believers do not even consider it to be a sin.

LESSON 19

FEAR AND WORRY

OPENING PRAYER AND SCRIPTURE MEMORY

Before you begin this lesson, ask for God's help in understanding His Word and for strength to apply what you learn in the power of the Holy Spirit.

Begin memorizing *Matthew 6:33-34* and *I John 4:18*. Also, review the Scripture memory passages assigned in the previous lessons. Then, be prepared to recite them at the end of this lesson.

Also, in your own words, please write out the meaning of the new memory verses below:

_____
_____
_____
_____

PERSONAL PLAN FOR CHANGE

Continue to work on your personal **VICTORY OVER FAILURES PLAN** and make corrections based on what you will be learning this week.

INTRODUCTION TO THE LESSON

A. The sins of fear and worry are often treated very lightly among Christians. You may recall from Lesson 4 that according to man's way, the term "phobia" is used instead of "fear," implying that you are a victim of a disease for which you are not responsible. Even many believers have come to accept fear and worry as a normal part of life. For example, if a group of Christians were to be asked to raise their hands if they had been fearful or worried in the last month, many hands would probably go up. You see, sins such as fear and worry are considered socially acceptable and so we tend to minimize them.

Also, because people cannot see our thoughts, we tend to treat the sins of fear and worry lightly. Yet Scripture admonishes us to discipline our thought lives *(II Corinthians 10:5; Philippians 4:8; Colossians 3:2)*. In fact, Jesus taught that sinful thoughts are just as serious as unrighteous speech and actions *(Matthew 5:28)*. Thus, you can see that it is important to eliminate sinful thought patterns, such as fear and worry, from our lives.

B. Read the purposes of **LESSON 19: FEAR AND WORRY** *(Self-Confrontation, Page 336)*.

BIBLICAL UNDERSTANDING ABOUT FEAR AND WORRY

A. There are many temptations to fear and worry. Let's look at some of them in **TEMPTATIONS TO FEAR AND WORRY** *(Self-Confrontation, Page 339)*.

1. Read Section **I. Situations that tempt you to fear and worry** .... What do you think are some of the more common situations where Christians are tempted to worry? (List at least two.)

   1. _____

   _____

   Note that fear and worry are typically centered on some perceived unpleasant experience that may happen in the future. The external situation does not cause fear or worry; the condition of your heart causes these problems.

   > **ILLUSTRATION:** Picture in your mind three people standing near a road talking to one another. Suddenly, there is a terrible crash as two vehicles traveling in opposite directions collide and a fire breaks out with a passenger trapped inside one of the vehicles.
   >
   > The three individuals observing the accident may each respond in different ways. One may flee in fear; the second may stand still as if he is paralyzed in place; and the third may immediately dash toward the flaming vehicle to rescue the passenger.
   >
   > All three observed the same event, but the response depended on what was taking place in their hearts. It was the third person who responded biblically.

2. Fear and worry often are accompanied by very strong feelings. Though you may be tempted to act according to these feelings, you must remember they are caused by your own reaction in thought, speech, and action to your circumstances. *(We are not here talking about emotions caused by chemical or hormonal imbalances, etc.).* The only real solution is to obey God in thought, speech, and action in spite of any feelings to the contrary.

3. Read Section **II. Your biblical response to situations that tempt you to fear and worry** .... Note that that at times we are commanded to fear and at times we are commanded not to fear, depending upon the focus of the fear.

B. Read *Principle 84*, **BIBLICAL PRINCIPLES: FEAR AND WORRY** (*Self-Confrontation*, Page 337).

1. After the first sentence, highlight in your manual and read *Matthew 25:25-26* and *I John 4:15-19*. In *I John 4:18*, with what is fear connected?

   2. _____

   Fear comes out of a concern about what will happen to me. The focus is on self.

2. In *Matthew 25:25-26*, what did the "one-talent" man say was the reason he did not make more money for his master?

   3. _____

   What did the master say was the man's problem?

   4. _____

   The master understood that the slave's real problem was laziness and disobedience since he had given the slave the talent according to his ability. For both fear and worry, the problem is preoccupation with self.

3. After the last sentence in *Principle 84*, highlight in your manual and read *II Corinthians 11:28*. What was Paul's concern in this verse?

   5. _____

His focus was not on himself but on caring for others.

C. The difference between God's way and man's way is further clarified on Page 341 of the *Self-Confrontation* manual. Read Section **I. The contrast between love and fear (sample list)** under **LOVE VERSUS FEAR (GOD'S WAY VERSUS MAN'S WAY).**

BIBLICAL HOPE

A. Read *Principle 85,* regarding fear, under **BIBLICAL PRINCIPLES: FEAR AND WORRY** (*Self-Confrontation,* Page 337), then, highlight in your manual and read *II Timothy 1:7.* Notice that the spirit of fear does not come from God; He has given the believer the power to love with a sound mind.

B. Read *Principle 86,* regarding worry, under **BIBLICAL PRINCIPLES: FEAR AND WORRY** (*Self-Confrontation,* Page 337). Refer to *Matthew 6:33-34.* What does the one who worries forget?

6. _____

Sinful worry is a self-centered focus on future events over which we have no control. Thus, when we worry we often assume responsibilities that God never intended us to have. It is important to remember that we are not responsible for results; we are only responsible for faithfulness.

While fear and worry focus on the future, the emphasis in the Word of God is on loving God and others in the *present.* Now that we understand biblical hope, let's see how we are to change biblically.

BIBLICAL CHANGE

A. Read *Principle 87,* under **BIBLICAL PRINCIPLES: FEAR AND WORRY** (*Self-Confrontation,* Page 337). What are the "put-off" and "put-ons" in *II Timothy 1:7* (highlight this passage in your manual)?

7. "Put-off": _____

"Put-ons": _____

What are the "put-off" and "put-on" in *I John 4:18* (highlight this passage in your manual)?

8. "Put-off": _____

"Put-on": _____

B. Read *Principle 88.* What are the "put-off" and "put-ons" in *Matthew 6:33-34* (highlight this passage in your manual)?

9. "Put-off": _____

"Put-ons": _____

It is important to differentiate between deeds and feelings. We are totally responsible for our thoughts, speech, and actions, but we are not responsible for our feelings because they are involuntary. There are very strong emotions associated with fear and worry; however, we can think, speak, and act in godly ways no matter how we feel.

It is also important to remember that our focus for living — either to please self or to please God — is revealed by our responses to life's situations. For example, worry is sinful because it is a focus on self, but concern (which is the same word as worry in the original language of the

New Testament) is godly because it is a focus on serving others. Review Section **I.** on Page 145 of the *Self-Confrontation* manual for more details.

BIBLICAL PRACTICE

This brings us to the final element — biblical practice.

A. Your practice concerning fear

Read *Principle 89*, under **BIBLICAL PRINCIPLES: FEAR AND WORRY** (*Self-Confrontation*, Page 338), then, highlight in your manual and review *I John 4:18*.

Note that the emphasis in *I John 4:18* is on the "put-on," perfect love. The key is to concentrate on biblical truth when we experience a temptation to fear and then, to act in love. To the extent that we do this, the fear will be cast out. In effect, fear being cast out is a by-product of the love of Christ being perfected in us.

Do you remember the "lion" illustration from Lesson 7? The illustration demonstrates that often concentrating on the "put-on" makes the "put-off" much easier. This is clearly seen from *I John 4:18* when dealing with fear. For example, when a person considers whether or not to travel by air, he must make his decision on the basis of doing (putting on) the loving thing, not on the basis of putting off fear. Then, throughout the trip, he needs to concentrate continually on the reasons for his act of love, not the harm that may come his way.

On another note, it is important that you do not try to eliminate a particular fear just so that you can prove your bravery. For example, you should not walk through a graveyard at night just so that you can boast to others that you overcame your fear. Many worldly counselors tell you to do the very thing you are fearful to do, just so you can feel better about yourself. This is focus on self and is a demonstration of pride.

B. Your practice concerning worry

Read *Principle 90* on Page 338 of the *Self-Confrontation* manual then, highlight in your manual and read *Philippians 4:6-9*. What is the "put-off?"

10. _____

There are several "put-ons." What are they?

11. _____
_____
_____

It is important to note that all three "put-ons" are necessary. Also, note in *verse 6* that prayer and supplication are to be *with thanksgiving*, and in *verse 7* God not only tells us what to do, but He also tells us why it is good for us.

In *verse 8*, note that each thought must satisfy all of the characteristics listed, not just one or two. In other words, it may be true that your boss is a cruel person, but you are not to think this way since that thought is not also honorable, pure, lovely, etc. Also, the thoughts should be relevant to the current situation, not some indefinite think list that is disconnected from the problem. It is necessary to think about the current situation, not just from the view of the problem, but in terms of what is the true, honorable, right, pure, etc. way to respond in the very situation.

Verse 9 is often neglected as a "put-on" for anxiety. Overcoming anxiety is not just a matter of prayer or controlling the thought life, it is a matter of practicing the Word. And from it comes the peace of God.

Also, remember that God only holds us responsible for keeping His commandments which are always kept in the present. The procedure below is a practical way to concentrate on the present.

EXERCISE: DEVELOPING A "TO DO" LIST

At the beginning of each day, or the night before, list all of the tasks that you believe should be accomplished in that day. (This is often called a *"To Do" List.*) Then, list them according to the sequence in which they should be carried out. It is clear that some tasks need to be done before others; however, remember that all tasks are important and are to be carried out to please the Lord.

At the start of the day, focus *only* on the first task and do it heartily as to the Lord. Then, carry out the second task. The key here is to focus only on the current task, not on the ones down the list. Continue working in the same fashion until the end of the day. If all tasks are not accomplished, remember that God may have sovereignly redirected a portion of your day and that you are only responsible to be faithful; God takes care of the results. If all tasks are not accomplished in one day, evaluate if you were disobedient at times or if you need to modify your expectations for the next day's tasks. If you do this, you will not have time to worry!

QUESTIONS AND CONCLUSION

A. Cite a verse that indicates that sinful thoughts are just as serious as unrighteous speech and actions:

   12. _____

B. What causes fear or worry; the external circumstances or the condition of the heart?

   13. _____

C. Where is the focus of someone who is fearful?

   14. _____

D. In dealing with fear and worry, it is important to remember that we are not responsible for results. However, we are responsible to be:

   15. _____

We can be faithful to do what God requires us to do despite our feelings and regardless of the way the situation may turn out. We need to entrust the results to our heavenly Father, who loves us and has promised to care for us. Remember that He may not give us what we want, but will lovingly give us what we need.

E. What can be the value of a "To Do" List in dealing with worry?

   16. _____

It is important to distinguish between the feelings associated with fear and worry and the sinful deeds of fear and worry. We are not responsible for our feelings, but we are responsible for what we think and say and how we act. We can do what God requires at all times regardless of how we feel.

Remember that anger, depression, fear, and worry are all associated with strong feelings. Those who practice these sins tend to live by their feelings, rather than in a disciplined way. In addition, one who is committing these sins is focused on the difficulties of life rather than the sovereignty of God.

F. What was the most significant truth you learned in completing this lesson?
17. _____
_____

SCRIPTURE RECITATION

Recite *Matthew 6:33-34* and *I John 4:18* to someone at home, in class, or elsewhere. Also, recite one of the previous memory passages chosen by the listener. Put a check here (__) when you have successfully recited the verses.

PREVIEW OF THE NEXT LESSON

In the next two lessons, we will cover life-dominating practices of sin. We will also look at how Satan's power can be broken immediately if a person is willing to trust in the power of Jesus Christ provided at salvation and, subsequently, to live in obedience to God's Word.

LESSON 20
LIFE-DOMINATING PRACTICES OF SIN (PART ONE)

OPENING PRAYER AND SCRIPTURE MEMORY

Before you begin this lesson, ask for God's help in understanding His Word and for strength to apply what you learn in the power of the Holy Spirit.

Begin memorizing *Romans 6:22* and *Ephesians 6:10-11*. Also, review the Scripture memory passages assigned in the previous lessons. Then, be prepared to recite them at the end of this lesson.

Also, in your own words, please write out the meaning of the new memory verses below:

_____
_____
_____
_____

PERSONAL PLAN FOR CHANGE

Continue to work on your personal **VICTORY OVER FAILURES PLAN** and make corrections based on what you will be learning this week.

INTRODUCTION TO THE LESSON

A. In this lesson, we will look at sinful practices that dominate a person's life. The characteristic that distinguishes a life-dominating practice of sin from other sins is not the severity or nature of the sin but rather its repeated practice. In fact, a person can continue sinning to the point that he becomes known by the name of his sinful practice. For example, someone can be called an "angry person" when he is habitually angry. He has continued sinning in the same way until his life is dominated by that sinful practice. Name at least three other examples of life-dominating practices of sin from those listed in *I Corinthians 6:9-10*. Write *I Corinthians 6:9-10* in the left margin next to the summary box.

1. _____
   _____

Because these types of difficulties seem to be overwhelming, the world searches, with little or no success, for special methods and techniques to help people caught up in these types of problems. How does this compare to a Scriptural approach? Should believers seek unusual methods outside of the Scriptures when they are seeking to overcome life-dominating practices of sin?

As we study these next two lessons, you will see that the Scriptures provide great hope and instruction on how to overcome these practices quickly and completely. Also, you will see a great contrast from the many popular secular methods.

We will also look at the way Satan tries to influence our lives. While it is important to understand the seriousness of allowing a sinful behavior to dominate a person's life, it is also important to recognize that Satan's hold can be broken immediately if a person is willing to trust in the power that is given him when he receives Jesus Christ.

B. Read the purposes of **LESSON 20: LIFE-DOMINATING SINS (PART ONE)** (*Self-Confrontation*, Page 354). In this lesson we will cover the first two elements of how to face, deal with, and endure problems biblically. So for biblical understanding, first let's see how to recognize life-dominating practices of sin.

RECOGNIZING LIFE-DOMINATING PRACTICES OF SIN

A. Turn to **RECOGNIZING LIFE-DOMINATING SINS** (*Self-Confrontation*, Page 356).

1. Read Section **I. Characteristics of a life-dominating sin**. As you read, highlight in your manual and write down words you find in this section that characterize life-dominating practices of sin (for example, "practice," or "repeatedly" could be listed from Paragraph A.).

   2. _____

   Note that any sin can dominate your life if you give yourself over to it.

2. Read Section **II. Man's view of life-dominating sins** on Page 357. Note that the world tends to excuse people from their responsibility for life-dominating practices of sin and thus merely helps them to "cope with" (which often means to put up with, not overcome) their problems. Secular programs address the symptoms, not the basic cause. Merely "coping" with a problem falls far short of God's purpose. Believers are to live as overwhelming conquerors and overcome their problems, not just "put up" with them.

3. Turn to Section **III. Some of man's erroneous explanations for life-dominating sins** on Page 357.

   a. Read Paragraph A. Scripture describes man as predisposed to sin; however, he does not *have* to sin. Sin is a choice.

   b. Read Paragraph B. Calling something a disease when the Scripture describes it as a sin is a serious error. Many believers replace the biblical word, "*drunkenness,*" with the term, "*alcoholism,*" or the biblical word, "*drunkard,*" with the term, "*alcoholic.*" In doing so, they do not realize that they are using the world's way of designating as a disease what the Bible calls sin. (The world often uses the ending, "*-ism*" or "*-ic*" to designate a disease.) This change of terminology is a deception because it indicates that a person is not responsible for his sin. We are not responsible for a disease; but God holds us accountable for sin, since we choose to sin.

   c. Read Paragraph C. All the disciples had different personalities, but Jesus gave them all the same guidance on how to live a godly life.

   d. Read the remaining paragraphs in Section **III**.

4. Turn to Section **IV. Some of man's attempts to deal with problems that enslave individuals** on Page 358.

   a. Read Paragraph A. along with the note.

   b. Read Paragraph B. along with the note. Not only do many of these therapies not acknowledge the Bible; they also do not follow the biblical methodology for change. They focus primarily on stopping the undesired practice instead of placing prime attention on putting on what they should be doing instead. Yet, believers often fall into the trap of seeking worldly counsel. What does God say in *Galatians 5:16* about how you can be enabled not to carry out the desires of the flesh?

   3. _____

God makes it very clear that we should concentrate on the "put-on," (i.e., obedience to Him). When we walk by the Spirit (obey Him), we will not need to be concerned about the "put-off," (i.e., carrying out the desires of the flesh).

    c. Read Paragraph C. with the note.

    d. Read Paragraphs D. and H. on Page 359.

5. Read Section **V. Some results of remaining enslaved by sin** on Page 360.

B. In order to help someone who is living a life dominated by a particular practice of sin, you must evaluate every aspect of his life. Turn to Page 361 to see how a life-dominating practice of sin can affect every aspect of life. Give some examples of how a life-dominating practice of sin such as drunkenness could affect the areas displayed in the diagram.

4. _____

_____

_____

BIBLICAL UNDERSTANDING ABOUT LIFE-DOMINATING PRACTICES OF SIN

A. With this as background, let's now contrast man's ideas with the biblical understanding about life-dominating practices of sin. We will look at the "but I say unto you ..." part by going back to the biblical principles on Page 355. First read the box at the top of the page.

1. Highlight in your manual and read *I John 3:4, 8-10*. Note that a believer is not characterized as practicing (holding on to) sin.

2. In the margin to the left of the summary box, write the reference *Galatians 5:19-21*, then, read it. Note that even anger, strife, and factions can be life-dominating practices of sin. In fact, it is important to realize that the practice of any sin can be life-dominating. If a person deliberately continues to commit a sin as a pattern of his life, is not repentant, and is not willing to take steps to stop the practice, he is dominated by sin and has reason to doubt the genuineness of his salvation.

Also, note that each person is responsible for his own life and cannot blame anyone or anything else (such as a demon or a spirit). In the world, people shift blame and excuse their life-dominating practices of sin.

B. Read *Principle 91* on Page 355 of the *Self-Confrontation* manual, then, highlight in your manual and read *Romans 6:16*. How does someone become controlled by sin?

5. _____

You can focus on yourself and be a slave to sin unto death or you can focus on God and be a slave of obedience unto righteousness. You become a slave to whomever you present yourself.

BIBLICAL HOPE

Read *Principle 92* on Page 355 of the *Self-Confrontation* manual, then, highlight in your manual and read *Romans 6:17-18*. In *Romans 6:17-18*, what were we freed from?

6. _____

Also, highlight in your manual and read *I Corinthians 6:9-11*. In this passage, what does God say happens to those who have been controlled by a life-dominating practice of sin when they become believers?

7. _____

This truth is in great contrast to a popular teaching, mentioned earlier, that once a person has been dominated by (or addicted to) a sinful practice, he is doomed to have to deal with that incurable disease which will plague him the rest of his life. He may have intense craving, but he does not have to give in to the temptation.

GOD HAS BROKEN SATAN'S POWER

Someone may ask, "What about Satan's power?" Thankfully, God has broken Satan's power.

A. Turn to Section **I. Satan's characteristics and power** on Page 362 in the *Self-Confrontation* manual.

   1. Read Paragraphs A. and B. Then, in Paragraph B. 3., highlight the reference to *II Corinthians 11:14* and read *verses 14-15*. According to these verses, how does Satan present himself?

   8. _____

   Believers need to be aware that not everyone who says he is a believer or uses the Bible is in fact a believer. Even though Judas was with the disciples daily for three years, the disciples did not detect his treachery. Judas did everything just as the other disciples did, including going out in twos and even being involved in healings and other miracles.

   Also read *John 13:21-22*. Write this reference to the left of Paragraph B. in your manual. Did the disciples have any suspicion that Judas was going to betray Jesus?

   9. _____

   Also, believers need to be aware that temptations of Satan are not always clearly presented as evil. For example, believers may wrongly give money to a lottery with the justification that if they win, they can donate part of their winnings to the church.

   2. Read Paragraph C., Subparagraphs 1.-4.

B. Turn to Section **II. Satan's limitations and judgment** on Page 363. Though Satan is powerful and deceptive, his power is limited. Do you remember as children playing the game of opposites? Let's try it. State the opposite of the following:

10. Opposite of "high": _____

Opposite of "hot": _____

Opposite of "white": _____

Opposite of "God": _____

Many people will write "Satan" as the opposite of God. However, Satan is a created being; therefore, he *cannot* be the opposite of God. God has no equal; therefore, He has no opposite. Satan is in opposition to God, but he is not the equal and opposite of God. Satan's power is limited by God, as further explained in the following Scriptures.

   1. Read Paragraph A., on Page 363, then, highlight in your manual and read *Colossians 2:9-10*. How much control does the Lord have?

   11. _____

   Even Satan is under subjection to Jesus Christ.

   2. Read Paragraph B., then, highlight in your manual and read *Job 1:7-12*. According to *verse 12*, how much can Satan do?

   12. _____

3. Read Paragraph C., then, highlight in your manual and read *John 16:11*. What is Satan's fate?

   13. _____

4. Read Paragraph D., then, highlight in your manual and read *I John 3:8*. What was one of Jesus' purposes for coming to earth?

   14. _____

5. Read Paragraph E., then, highlight in your manual and read *Hebrews 2:14-15*. How did Jesus take away Satan's power of death?

   15. _____

6. Read Paragraph F., then, highlight in your manual and read *I John 4:4*. What is the main truth of this Scripture?

   16. _____

   A believer can defeat Satan in every temptation by being obedient to the Lord and not sinning. It is also important to recognize that evil spirits *cannot* control a believer against his will. *I Peter 5:8-10* (highlight the reference in your manual in Paragraph F. 2.) describes Satan as being like a roaring lion. Just like the old lion that has a fierce voice but has little power, Satan has no power to harm believers. Satan attempts to scare God's children, but believers are told to stand firm. What are believers to do according to *James 4:7* (highlight in your manual the reference in Paragraph F. 2.)?

   17. _____

   What will be the result?

   18. _____

7. Read Paragraph G., then, highlight in your manual and read *Romans 8:35-39*. We can expect opposition from Satan, but what are believers promised in *verse 37*?

   19. _____

C. Read Section **III. Satanic associations are to be discarded from your life** on Page 364 and *Matthew 18:7-9*. In the left margin next to Section **III.**, write the reference, *Matthew 18:7-9*. If some possession tempts us to stumble, what are we to do?

   20. _____

   While physical objects do not have power in themselves *(from Jeremiah 10:3-5)*, you are to remove or destroy any objects and avoid any persons or places that may hinder you from fleeing temptations or resisting the devil. Since they can serve as reminders of your sinful practices, you must remove or avoid them. Your relationship with God is so important that you may need to take dramatic action to remove stumbling blocks, as we will see in Lesson 21.

SCRIPTURE RECITATION

Recite *Romans 6:22* and *Ephesians 6:10-11* to someone at home, in class, or elsewhere. Also, recite one of the previous memory passages chosen by the listener. Put a check here (__) when you have successfully recited the verses.

QUESTIONS AND CONCLUSION

A. List some examples of life-dominating practices of sin.

   21. _____

A life-dominating practice of sin could be any sinful practice that has become habitual. It usually affects many other areas of life as well. In a life-dominating practice, a person can even become known by his sinful practice (e.g., an impatient person, a gossip, etc.).

B. What is the problem with calling something a disease when, according to God, it is actually a sin?

22. _____

C. What hope does a person have by calling a life-dominating practice, "sin"?

23. _____

People may think that they are being compassionate by not calling these practices, "sin." On the contrary, it is compassionate and of great hope to identify sin for what it is, because sin can be dealt with quickly and decisively.

D. How can you be enabled not to carry out the desires of the flesh according to *Galatians 5:16*?

24. _____

E. What was the most significant truth you learned in completing this lesson?

25. _____

PREVIEW OF THE NEXT LESSON

In the next lesson, we will complete our coverage of life-dominating practices of sin. In that lesson, you will learn how to develop a thorough plan for overcoming any life-dominating practice of sin, including how to put on the full armor of God. We will also be looking at how to respond biblically to someone else who is enslaved by a life-dominating practice of sin.

LESSON 21
LIFE-DOMINATING PRACTICES OF SIN (PART TWO)

OPENING PRAYER AND SCRIPTURE MEMORY

Before you begin this lesson, ask for God's help in understanding His Word and for strength to apply what you learn in the power of the Holy Spirit.

Begin memorizing *Ephesians 5:18* and *Ephesians 6:12-13*. Also, review the Scripture memory passages assigned in the previous lessons. Then, be prepared to recite them at the end of this lesson.

Also, in your own words, please write out the meaning of the new memory verses below:

_____

_____

_____

_____

PERSONAL PLAN FOR CHANGE

Continue to work on your personal **VICTORY OVER FAILURES PLAN** and make corrections based on what you will be learning this week.

INTRODUCTION TO THE LESSON

A. In the last lesson, we learned that each person is responsible for his own life and cannot excuse away even life-dominating practices of sin. We also saw that God has already broken Satan's power and that believers do not need to be enslaved to sin.

In this lesson, we will look at what to do in order to overcome these life-dominating practices of sin.

B. Read the purposes of **LESSON 21: LIFE-DOMINATING SINS (PART TWO)** (*Self-Confrontation*, Page 370).

BIBLICAL CHANGE

A. Read *Principle 93*, **BIBLICAL PRINCIPLES: LIFE-DOMINATING SINS (PART TWO)** (*Self-Confrontation*, Page 371), then, highlight in your manual and read *Ephesians 5:18*. This verse states that we are not to do what?

1. _____

_____

But rather we are to do what?

2. _____

As a review, state what it means to be filled with the Spirit (see **BIBLICAL SUBMISSION**, *this Workbook*, Page W168-W170).

3. _____

Also, remember from the last lesson that a life-dominating practice of sin affects *every* area of life. Thus, there is a need to *change* in every area of life. Review **THE EFFECTS OF LIFE-DOMINATING SINS (THE CIRCLE OF LIFE)** *(Self-Confrontation,* Page 361).

As you can see, the biblical methodology for overcoming a life-dominating practice of sin is basically the same as in overcoming any problem; but there are two important emphases to keep in mind. First, the changes must take place very thoroughly (i.e., in every area of life).

The second emphasis is evident in *II Timothy 2:22*. Write the reference, *II Timothy 2:22*, in the margin to the left of *Principle 93*. What are the "put-off" and "put-ons" in this verse?

4. "Put-off":

"Put-ons":

Explain what the words "flee" and "pursue" imply with regard to dealing with life-dominating practices of sin:

5.

These words indicate that changes are to be made very quickly and decisively. Also, note at the end of *verse 22* the phrase, *"with those who call on the Lord from a pure heart."* The person who has repented from his life-dominating practice of sin needs to spend substantial time with other fervently committed believers. What would be the value of this to a person controlled by a life-dominating practice of sin according to *Proverbs 27:17?*

6.

Sadly, while the body of Christ is best suited to help people with life-dominating problems, often believers shun those who have the greatest needs. It is sometimes said that the church is the only army that shoots its wounded.

Name a person in the Scriptures who practiced this principle of fleeing sin and pursuing righteousness.

7.

Describe the situation.

8.

Name a person in the Scriptures who did *not* practice this principle, and it led to spiritual defeat.

9.

Describe the situation.

10.

BIBLICAL PRACTICE

A. Read *Principle 94*, **BIBLICAL PRINCIPLES: LIFE-DOMINATING SINS (PART TWO)** (*Self-Confrontation*, Page 371), highlight in your manual *I John 3:6-9*, then, read *I John 3:7-10*. What does this Scripture say is possible of one who continually practices sin?

11. _____

We are saved by grace through faith and not by our works. But works are an evidence of our faith (or lack of faith), and they can be indicators of whether we may or may not be believers. In other words, we need to take life-dominating practices of sin, in ourselves or in others, very seriously. If we have been dominated by a particular practice of sin to the point where it has become a pattern of life, we need to seek the Lord earnestly as to whether or not we are in the family of God. If we seem to lack the power to overcome the life-dominating sin, it may be that God's power is not in us.

B. Read *Principle 95*, **BIBLICAL PRINCIPLES: LIFE-DOMINATING SINS (PART TWO)** (*Self-Confrontation*, Page 371), then, highlight in your manual and read *Ephesians 6:10-18*. From *verses 10-13*, how would you summarize the purpose of putting on the full armor of God?

12. _____

In this teaching about spiritual warfare, the first part of *verse 10* indicates that this passage is not dealing with a new subject, but rather it is a summary of the previous verses and chapters — who we are and what is true about us as believers and how we are to live or walk, putting off the sinful practices and putting on the righteous practices. Sadly, many people focus only on *verse 12*, ignoring the context, and come up with different teachings and practices focusing on spirits and Satan. The believer is to focus on God, stand firm, and faithfully put on the full armor of God.

Since putting on the full armor of God is vital for resisting sin and standing firm against Satan, let's take a look at each piece of the armor. First, list the armor that you see in the following passages:

13. *Ephesians 6:14* — _____

Ephesians 6:15 — _____

Ephesians 6:16 — _____

Ephesians 6:17 — _____

C. Turn to **PUTTING ON THE FULL ARMOR OF GOD** (*Self-Confrontation*, Page 373).

1. As background on the armor of God, read: Section **I. The purposes of the armor of God**; Section **II. The need for putting on the armor of God**; and Section **III. Your confidence in the spiritual battle**.

2. Now let's describe each piece of the armor of God and see how it applies to your life. Turn to Section **IV. Your responsibility to put on the full armor of God** on Page 374.

    a. Read the initial paragraph under A. Note the emphasis on putting on the *full* armor of God (i.e., every piece of the armor). If you neglect just one piece, you are vulnerable to the enemy's attack.

    b. Read *Ephesians 6:14a* and Paragraph A. 1. "*… having girded your loins with truth ….*" Note the importance of evaluating your ways according to the truths of Scripture, not according to your own opinion or the opinions of others. To know the Scriptures well requires that you spend time in the Word on a daily basis with a great focus on learning and practicing the Word in the very areas where you are weak. God tells us in Scripture to hear, read, study, memorize, and meditate on the Word (see Page 115 of the *Self-Confrontation* manual for references).

As you spend time in the Scriptures, it is particularly important to focus on evaluating specific areas of weakness or temptation, and developing a biblical plan to overcome them so that you do not risk defeat because of a vulnerable area in your life.

c. Read *Ephesians 6:14b* and Paragraph A. 2. *"... having put on the breastplate of righteousness."* If you are a believer, you have been declared righteous through Christ's death, but you are responsible to live righteously. Does the way you live your life daily reflect the position of righteousness that is yours by being in Christ?

Read *Matthew 18:7-9*. What does this Scripture passage tell you about the importance of dealing with sin?

14. _____

With a life-dominating practice of sin, radical surgery is needed to remove all stumbling blocks to righteous living. The key here is to leave no room for doubt that a major change has taken place.

ILLUSTRATION: If you saw a person walking down the road whose hand had been amputated, you would never need to ask him if a change had taken place in his life. The change would be obvious. In doing "drastic surgery" for a life-dominating problem, major changes are necessary. For example, a man who has been a child molester may not minister to children again or be around children alone again, even if he is not tempted, in order to leave no room for doubt about his testimony. In other words, permanent changes should be obvious, even to others.

Develop and faithfully maintain a biblical plan for living that will please the Lord in all things and be a blessing to others, especially in your daily responsibilities and specific areas of service and ministry. If you are having difficulty maintaining consistent victory in a particular area of sin, consider completing a **VICTORY OVER FAILURES PLAN**.

d. Read *Ephesians 6:15* and Paragraph A. 3. *"and having shod your feet with the preparation of the gospel of peace."* Every believer is commanded by Jesus to make disciples. What are the two parts to this commandment (see *Matthew 28:19-20*)?

15. _____

_____

_____

Read *II Corinthians 5:18-20*. As an ambassador of Christ, what is every believer's ministry?

16. _____

If you do not yet know how to lead someone to Christ, you may want to study the basic elements of the plan of salvation in Sections **IV.** and **V.** on Pages 21-22 of the *Self-Confrontation* manual.

We are also to be peacemakers. To be a peacemaker, you need to be at peace with others as far as it depends on you.

e. Read *Ephesians 6:16* and Paragraph A. 4. *"in addition to all, taking up the shield of faith with which you will be able to extinguish all the flaming missiles of the evil one."* Believers are to live by faith, not by sight (or man's wisdom). Read *Colossians 2:5-8*. According to *verse 8*, how does the world distract the believer from living by faith?

17. _____

_____

Faith is demonstrated by faithfulness. According to *I Corinthians 4:2* what is to be the main characteristic of a steward?

18. _____

What did the master say about faithfulness to his slaves in *Matthew 25:21* and *23*?

19. _____

Your faithfulness will be of benefit also to the body of Christ.

    f. Read *Ephesians 6:17a* and Paragraph A. 5. *"And take the helmet of salvation ...."* In the same way that the helmet protects the brain, the believer needs to protect his thought life from thoughts that would hinder growth (working out his salvation) in Christ. This is vital since all sin is a matter of choice and, therefore, sin begins as a thought. The key to disciplining the thought life is to concentrate continually on what you should be thinking, rather than allowing your thoughts to stray out of control. Thoughts that distract from or hinder this focus are to be rejected. That is why it is so important to memorize and review Scripture during spare moments of the day.

    g. Read *Ephesians 6:17b* and Paragraph A. 6. *"... and the sword of the Spirit, which is the word of God."* The Word of God pierces one's life. It must be handled accurately and effectively in both defensive and offensive warfare. The Word is not only to be studied but also to be obeyed. What warning does *James 1:22* give?

20. _____

  3. In Section **V. Practical help for putting on the full armor of God** ..., note that this section provides many practical ideas on how to put on the armor of God. These are directly related to the content of Section **IV.**, covered above.

D. Read *Principle 96*, **BIBLICAL PRINCIPLES: LIFE-DOMINATING SINS (PART TWO)** (*Self-Confrontation*, Page 372). Add *verses 2-3* to the reference to *Psalm 1:1*. Then, highlight in your manual the references to *Psalm 1:1-3* and *II Timothy 2:22* and read both passages. As mentioned earlier, not only must the armor be put on completely, but it must also be put on quickly. Give an example of a specific action, based on the above verses that could be taken by someone enslaved by a life-dominating practice of sin (for example, gambling).

21. _____

_____

_____

This may require dramatic steps. God says in *Psalm 1:1* that sin is to be taken so seriously that the places and persons where temptation occurs must be avoided. So if, for instance, you struggle with gambling and your route to work takes you by the casino where you have gambled with others in the past, then your plan may need to include a new route to work or some other way of not "standing in the path of sinners." If you are tempted to watch pornographic movies on TV in the hotel room, you could commit to unplugging the TV when you check into your room. The specific action needs to be between you and the Lord. But if you are "caught in a trespass," as stated in *Galatians 6:1*, the action needs to be decisive, often dramatic, and leave no doubt to others that you have committed to living a holy life. If your "friends" really care about you, they will not only be understanding, but will help you avoid temptation in the future. If they criticize you for it, then it becomes clear that they don't really care about you as much as you may have thought. Your action may actually help them to see their own need to change and the power of God's principles and the Holy Spirit to change a person's life.

Then what does *Psalm 1:2* say to put on in the place of the old, sinful way of life?

22. _____

Putting off the old, sinful habits often leaves additional time to spend in God's Word.

Finally, what does *Psalm 1:3* say will be the result?

23. _____

In summary, the method for dealing with life-dominating practices of sin is essentially the same as dealing with any problem of life. The major differences are that the problem must be dealt with quickly and thoroughly.

E. Read *Principle 97*, **BIBLICAL PRINCIPLES: LIFE-DOMINATING PRACTICE OF SINS (PART TWO)** (*Self-Confrontation*, Page 372), then, highlight in your manual and read *II Peter 1:2-11*. In *verse 3*, what has God granted to us?

24. _____

Do you remember the three resources provided by God that are listed back in Lesson 3? As a review, list them below:

25. _____

Is there anything lacking in God's resources that would make us incapable of having victory over any area of sin?

26. _____

In *verse 8*, what does God say should be happening in our lives with regard to the spiritual qualities listed?

27. _____
_____

In other words, we should be growing to become more like Christ. In *verse 9*, what does God say is one of our problems if this is not happening?

28. _____

Have you forgotten how much God has done for you in providing for your salvation? He loves you more than you can possibly imagine, and you owe Him *everything*. Is there an area of your life that you have been resisting yielding to Him? You can deal with that right now, by decisively putting off the old, sinful practice and putting on the new righteous deeds. If you have not already done so, use the **VICTORY OVER FAILURES PLAN** to apply the appropriate biblical principles to this area of your life.

| HELPING THE ENSLAVED |

Suppose that you are living with a family member or know someone whose life is dominated by a practice of sin. How do you help such a person? Turn to **BIBLICALLY RESPONDING TO SOMEONE WITH A LIFE-DOMINATING SIN** (*Self-Confrontation*, Page 389).

A. Read Section **I. Life dominating sins of others give you an opportunity to examine yourself biblically.** Note that God holds you responsible for how you think, speak, and act no matter how sinfully another person behaves. You must concentrate on dealing with your own sins even if they seem very small in comparison.

Section **I.** has to do with the need and manner in which you are to deal with your own life. When you go to the other person, you must first help him to see the situation as it really is, as you see in Section **II.**

B. Read Paragraph A. of Section **II. Believers or unbelievers need to learn the effects of their life-dominating sin** on Pages 389 and 390 and the *NOTE* at the end of Paragraph B. at the top of Page 391. The *NOTE* is particularly important because often the only way to get the attention of the one whose life is dominated by sin is for him to experience the consequences of his actions. God, through the book of *Proverbs,* makes it clear that only consequences will get a fool's attention.

C. Read the *NOTE* under Paragraph B. of Section **III. You are to use all biblical resources** ... on Page 391. In helping a person with a life-dominating practice of sin, one of the most loving things you can do is to hold him responsible for his actions. It is very important that you do not take on his responsibilities. If you do, then he may become dependent on you, rather than on the Lord. Also, read the notes under Paragraphs E. and F.

SCRIPTURE RECITATION

Recite *Ephesians 5:18* and *Ephesians 6:12-13* to someone at home, in class, or elsewhere. Also, recite one of the previous memory passages chosen by the listener. Put a check here (__) when you have successfully recited the verses.

QUESTIONS AND CONCLUSION

A. You have seen that dealing with a life-dominating practice of sin requires essentially the same approach as when dealing with any other type of sin. But what two things especially need to be emphasized in dealing with a life-dominating practice of sin?

   29. _____

B. What does *Matthew 18:7-9* tell you about the importance of dealing with sin?

   30. _____

C. What is the purpose of putting on the full armor of God?

   31. _____

D. Why would it be important that you not take on the responsibilities of another person with a life-dominating practice of sin?

   32. _____
   _____

E. What was the most significant truth you learned in completing this lesson?

   33. _____
   _____

PREVIEW OF NEXT LESSON

In the next lesson, we will look at how to establish a guide for every aspect of daily living, not just those areas where problems exist. In Lesson 22, you will learn how to develop, in an organized way, a plan for living your whole life in a manner that pleases the Lord.

LESSON 22
GOD'S STANDARDS FOR LIFE

OPENING PRAYER AND SCRIPTURE MEMORY

Before you begin this lesson, ask for God's help in understanding His Word and for strength to apply what you learn in the power of the Holy Spirit.

Begin memorizing *Galatians 5:22-25*. Also, review the Scripture memory passages assigned in the previous lessons. Then, be prepared to recite them at the end of this lesson.

Also, in your own words, please write out the meaning of the new memory verses below:

_____
_____
_____
_____

INTRODUCTION TO THE LESSON

A. The purpose of Lessons 9-21, which you have just completed, is to describe how to face, deal with, and endure problems in specific areas of life, such as anger, depression, etc. However, success in dealing with these areas does not give us a complete picture of the Christian's walk with the Lord.

Many believers mistakenly think they are living godly lives just because they are not experiencing serious problems. They live by their feelings, often are not active in ministry, and do not really evaluate their lives in the light of God's Word. Or they are so busy doing "good" activities that they struggle with determining what is most important for their lives in God's sight.

This lesson will help you recognize the need to evaluate every area of your life to see if you are living in a godly manner. And it will help you recognize your need to eliminate any lawful, but unnecessary, activities in order to add profitable activities into your life *(I Corinthians 10:23)* by 1) describing a typical week's activities; 2) comparing these activities with God's standards; and 3) establishing a new plan.

Actually, this lesson is designed to help all believers because each person needs to evaluate himself continually to see if every aspect of his life is bringing glory to God.

B. Read the purposes of **LESSON 22: GOD'S STANDARDS FOR LIFE** (*Self-Confrontation*, Page 400).

PERSONAL PLAN FOR CHANGE

This week, you will be conducting a very important exercise that will help you to evaluate every area of your life and, if necessary, to reorder your life according to God's standards. So that you can be working on this exercise every day, we will immediately jump to Section **III. Incorporating God's standards into your life** on Page 405 of the *Self-Confrontation* manual. The exercise described in this section of the manual is similar to the one we conducted in Lesson 18, but it is more thorough.

> **EXERCISE: INCORPORATING GOD'S STANDARDS INTO YOUR LIFE**
>
> Starting immediately, follow the instructions in Paragraph A. of Section **III. Incorporating God's standards into your life.** Make a copy of **MY PRESENT SCHEDULE** (*Self-Confrontation*, Supplement 14, Page 473) and start filling it in from the time you get up each day until you go to bed. If you do not have a copier, you can prepare your own sheets with the same information. Continue each day this week to fill in the form immediately after you complete each activity.
>
> This form should be completed as you progress through a typical week, not an unusual week. Do not try to complete the form from memory of some previous week or estimate what you will be doing in the future. You may be surprised by the difference between your memory of how time was spent as compared to how time was actually spent in practice.
>
> *NOTE: The remaining steps of this exercise will be explained at the end of this lesson.*

BIBLICAL UNDERSTANDING ABOUT GOD'S STANDARDS FOR LIFE

A. Read the box at the top of **BIBLICAL PRINCIPLES: GOD'S STANDARDS FOR LIFE** (*Self-Confrontation*, Page 401). Then, highlight in your manual and read *Ecclesiastes 12:13-14*. What is the conclusion stated in *verse 13*?

1. _____

The key to victorious living is total commitment to the Lord through loving obedience in every area of life.

B. Read *Principle 98*, **BIBLICAL PRINCIPLES: GOD'S STANDARDS FOR LIFE** (*Self-Confrontation*, Page 401). God's commands are changeless. They are not dependent on whims or changing theories.

C. Read *Principle 99*, **BIBLICAL PRINCIPLES: GOD'S STANDARDS FOR LIFE**, then, highlight in your manual and read *Romans 2:9-11*. God's standards are the same for everyone, regardless of age, gender, or culture. All the disciples were very different one from the other, yet Jesus gave them all the same guidance for how to live a godly life.

D. Read *Principle 100*, **BIBLICAL PRINCIPLES: GOD'S STANDARDS FOR LIFE**, then, highlight in your manual and read *Psalm 111:10*. When a person fears God and keeps His commandments, he gains wisdom. This is one of the central teachings of the Scriptures and is an important theme often repeated in the Self-Confrontation Bible Study.

BIBLICAL HOPE

A. Read *Principle 101*, **BIBLICAL PRINCIPLES: GOD'S STANDARDS FOR LIFE** (*Self-Confrontation*, Page 401), then, highlight in your manual and read *Jeremiah 29:11-13*. Note that God's plans are for your benefit.

B. Read *Principle 102*, **BIBLICAL PRINCIPLES: GOD'S STANDARDS FOR LIFE** (*Self-Confrontation*, Page 401), then, highlight in your manual and read *Matthew 11:28-30*. Jesus invites us to come to Him when we are weary and heavy laden. God's standards are not burdensome.

Also highlight in your manual and read *Isaiah 40:25-31*. Not only are His resources vast, but they are continually available to us. God promises that our needs will be provided for, but He does not promise that we will be free of problems. Rather, as we have learned throughout this Bible Study, we should *expect* to encounter difficulties. As much as we might not want to go through these difficulties, they help to bring about our maturity as we respond to them God's way. This is a radical difference in perspective from the world's view. Understanding this and living according to it will give you a peace and comfort that transcends human understanding.

BIBLICAL CHANGE

A. Read *Principle 103*, **BIBLICAL PRINCIPLES: GOD'S STANDARDS FOR LIFE** (*Self-Confrontation*, Page 402*)*, then, highlight in your manual and read *Romans 13:12-14*. *verse 14* is a powerful statement of a "put-off" and "put-on." What are we to put off?

2.

Whom are we to put on?

3.

The context of this passage (read beginning from *Romans 13:8*) has to do with our obedience to God's commands. How are the commandments summed up in *verses 9* and *10*?

4.

If we are busy loving our neighbor, focusing on what is good for them, God says we will be fulfilling the law. Will it be inconvenient at times? Yes. Will it be humbling? Yes. Will it sometimes be unappreciated? Very likely. Will it be noticed by others? Often not. But this is what living a godly life is all about. We live for the Lord, not for earthly recognition or praise. It may be that the Lord is the only One who will ever know about a sacrificial act of kindness or about our not responding harshly when we are tempted to believe we are justified in doing so. As a believer, we have no guaranteed rights on earth, but we have great benefits. And one of the blessings is in knowing that we have been pleasing to the Lord. To do this, we must take the focus off ourselves and, instead, put it on others. God made this very easy to figure out. What many call "The Golden Rule" states it powerfully, and succinctly. Restate it here from *Matthew 7:12*.

5.

B. Read *Principle 104*, **BIBLICAL PRINCIPLES: GOD'S STANDARDS FOR LIFE** (*Self-Confrontation*, Page 402*)*, then, highlight in your manual and read *I Peter 4:12-19*. What does God say that we are to expect as part of life?

6.

What is their purpose?

7.

The book of *I Peter* is full of references to trials, including the example of how Jesus dealt with greater tests and injustices than we will ever face. *I Peter 4:12* indicates that these are not strange, unexpected things. We should be prepared for trials and even rejoice in them, as stated in *verse 13*. Applying this truth to your life will be revolutionary.

BIBLICAL PRACTICE

A. Read *Principle 105*, **BIBLICAL PRINCIPLES: GOD'S STANDARDS FOR LIFE** (*Self-Confrontation*, Page 402*)*, then, highlight in your manual and read *Galatians 5:22-23*.

B. Pages 403 to 405 present many of the principles or standards we have learned in this Bible Study. Let's review some of them.

1. Read through the list in Section **I. What you are to do (a sample list)** as a review of truths covered in previous lessons. None of these statements is new. The list is also not exhaustive. Note that the principles in Paragraph A. apply to every believer, while the standards in

Paragraphs B. through I. apply to specific areas of responsibility. As you go through the list, write down at least three of the standards that have made a particular impression on you in this Bible Study.

8. _____
_____
_____
_____

2. Read Section **II. How you are to obey God's standards**. Also, do you remember the illustration about the woman with an unloving husband? Following God's commands is not an exercise in legalistic do's and don'ts. It is not a way to earn our salvation or to gain favor with God to balance out our sin. It is a loving response to what God has so amazingly and marvelously done for us. It is now a matter of loving faithfulness in the empowering of the Holy Spirit. We must never forget that obeying with the wrong motives is hypocritical. On the other hand, loving God is demonstrated by obedience.

3. Follow the procedure outlined in Section **III. Incorporating God's standards into your life**.

   NOTE: You have already started the first step of this exercise at the beginning of the week. It is repeated in the first three paragraphs of the exercise below for reference.

EXERCISE: INCORPORATING GOD'S STANDARDS INTO YOUR LIFE

Follow the instructions in Paragraph A. of Section **III. Incorporating God's standards into your life**. Make a copy of **MY PRESENT SCHEDULE** (*Self-Confrontation*, Supplement 14, Page 473) and start filling it in from the time you get up each day until you go to bed. If you do not have a copier, you can prepare your own sheets with the same information. Continue each day this week to fill in the form immediately after you complete each activity.

This form should be completed as you progress through a typical week, not an unusual week. Do not try to complete the form from memory of some previous week or estimate what you will be doing in the future. You may be surprised by the difference between your memory of how time was spent as compared to how time was actually spent in practice.

When you have completed applying the first step for a week, follow the remaining steps. *NOTE: You will probably not have enough time to complete this exercise this week, so it will be continued next week.*

Read Paragraph B. and review the Scriptures referenced after each question. Then, draw a line through every activity on your present schedule that should be discontinued. An example of an activity that may need to be reduced is the amount of television watched, which may be hindering you from doing other responsibilities.

Read Paragraph C. Now list on a separate sheet of paper all the new activities that you should add to your schedule based on the responsibilities you should be practicing. Use the sample list under **GOD'S STANDARDS FOR YOU** (*Self-Confrontation*, Pages 403-405) as a guide.

Read Paragraph D. This combines the first three steps into one worksheet. Now complete **MY PROPOSED BIBLICAL SCHEDULE** (*Self-Confrontation*, Supplement 15, Page 474) using the information gathered in the first three steps. If you did not draw a line through enough activities in the second step to make room for carrying out the new activities listed in the third step, you need to consider deleting more of your present activities that are not absolutely necessary. God grants great freedom to take part in many activities, but there may not be

> enough time for some otherwise good activities because time is needed to carry out clearly identified, God-given responsibilities.

This exercise should be repeated every few weeks until your typical weekly schedule becomes biblically responsible. At a later time, you may wish to conduct this exercise with others in your household. In that case, it should not be conducted independently. It is a great opportunity for you to work together as a family or set of roommates to come up with a schedule that is good for both your own growth and that of your other household members. It is a good opportunity for you to demonstrate your love and care for them.

SCRIPTURE RECITATION

Recite *Galatians 5:22-25* to someone at home, in class, or elsewhere. Also, recite one of the previous memory passages chosen by the listener. Put a check here (__) when you have successfully recited the verses.

PREVIEW OF THE NEXT LESSON

In the next lesson, you will have an opportunity to write down a testimony of what you have learned in this Bible Study.

W220

LESSON 23
TESTIMONY OF
HOW GOD HAS USED THIS STUDY IN YOUR LIFE

INTRODUCTION TO THE LESSON

The primary purpose of this lesson is to provide you an opportunity to present your personal testimony of how God has used the Self-Confrontation Bible Study in your life.

Answer the question below. Then, if you are in a group study, be prepared to talk about what you have learned and how you have changed when you get together with your group.

How has God used His Word during this Bible study in your personal walk with Him?

SCRIPTURE RECITATION

Recite three of the previous memory passages chosen by the listener. Put a check here (__) when you have successfully recited the verses.

PREVIEW OF THE NEXT LESSON

The following lesson introduces biblical discipleship/counseling. It covers basic procedures you can use to help others and provides a transition to Biblical Discipleship/Counseling Course II.

LESSON 24
INTRODUCTION TO BIBLICAL DISCIPLESHIP/COUNSELING TRAINING

OPENING PRAYER AND SCRIPTURE MEMORY

Before you begin this lesson, ask for God's help in understanding His Word and for strength to apply what you learn in the power of the Holy Spirit.

Begin memorizing *I John 5:3-5*. Also, review the Scripture memory passages assigned in the previous lessons. Then, be prepared to recite them at the end of this lesson.

Also, in your own words, please write out the meaning of the new memory verses below:

_____

_____

_____

PERSONAL PLAN FOR CHANGE

Continue to work on your personal **VICTORY OVER FAILURES PLAN** and make corrections based on what you will be learning this week.

INTRODUCTION TO THE LESSON

A. The last 23 lessons of this Bible Study have taught you how to take the log out of your own eye. When you have faithfully applied the biblical principles covered in this Bible Study, you will have completed the first step in preparing yourself to be a part of a very significant ministry in the body of Christ. The last part of *Matthew 7:5* says, *"And then you will see clearly to take the speck out of your brother's eye."* Not only do you have the privilege, but you also have the responsibility to disciple others. Taking the speck out of your brother's eye does not just enable you to point out the problems that exist in other people, but actually it prepares you to restore them.

You may remember from the introduction to this Bible Study that God has commanded every believer to make disciples. Turn to *Matthew 28:19-20*. Biblical discipleship is God's plan for reaching the world. As disciple makers, what did Jesus say in *verse 20* that we should teach?

1. _____

The focus is on helping others to be doers of the Word, not merely hearers. The word *"all"* in *verse 20* indicates that discipleship is very thorough. Biblical discipleship deals with every aspect of a person's life. It is not just a call to evangelism, though evangelism is essential. Jesus talked about prayer, about going into all the world and bringing other people to Himself. He also talked about the importance of God's Word, and the importance of fellowship. But, teaching people to observe all that Jesus commanded is much bigger even than that. It is a call to help people live according to every principle of life contained in the Scriptures. It is a call to help people grow in their relationship with Christ and to become more like Him.

As you have recognized during the Self-Confrontation Bible Study, Jesus taught the disciples how to have victory in the midst of the daily trials and tests of life. The primary focus of the Self-Confrontation Bible Study has been to teach you how to have victory in every area of your life.

However, as you have seen, biblical discipleship is more than teaching a person how to live a godly life, because the one being discipled is also commanded to make other disciples. The Apostle Paul instructed Timothy to train faithful men who would train others, as expressed in *II Timothy 2:2*. There are four generations of disciples identified in this verse. Can you list them?

2. _____
_____
_____
_____

So you are to be trained up not only to live your own life in a godly way. You are to train others to be faithful to the Lord to the point that they can turn around and train or teach others. God intends to use believers powerfully in the lives of other people.

B. This brings us to the purpose of the next course which is to teach you how to disciple someone else — how to help your brother take the speck out of his eye. It is based on the biblical principles taught in this Bible Study and additional biblical principles relating to discipling others.

Since discipleship is a matter of helping a person to grow, you cannot just teach discipleship as you would a college course where you focus only on academics. You are to be involved in the life of the one you are discipling.

Biblical discipleship/counseling belongs in the local church under the oversight of the elders and the pastors of the church whose responsibility is to oversee the spiritual growth of people. The local body of believers is the best group to be involved in that person's life.

For this reason, Level II is designed to train the student as a biblical discipler/counselor within the *local* body of believers. The course is taught in such a way that *every* believer, regardless of educational level or experience, can learn how to disciple/counsel others. Jesus chose disciples with little or no formal education to continue His vital ministry. He calls every believer to follow His example.

C. Read the purposes of **LESSON 24: INTRODUCTION TO COURSE II: BIBLICAL COUNSELING TRAINING** (*Self-Confrontation*, Page 416).

WHAT DOES BIBLICAL DISCIPLESHIP/COUNSELING INVOLVE?

Turn to Page 417 of the *Self-Confrontation* manual and read the box at the top of the page.

You will notice the title of this lesson is **INTRODUCTION TO COURSE II: BIBLICAL COUNSELING TRAINING**.

Yet, instead of "biblical counseling" you may have noticed the phrase, "biblical discipleship/counseling" used above. There is a reason for this change of wording. When BCF originally wrote this material, "biblical counseling" was a unique term. But now, many people who call themselves biblical counselors also mix in worldly teaching. So, we needed to make more clear what biblical counseling is.

As you have seen in the previous lessons, biblical counseling is not just a matter of getting somebody over a problem. Many counselors meet with people only until their lives seem calmer; and then, they end the counseling. The person who comes for counsel learns to deal with that one problem and is fine, until the next problem comes along. Then he asks, "How do I now handle this new problem?" As a result, people come back to counselors over and over again. This often goes on for years. But true biblical counseling is in-depth discipleship. It is a matter of training someone how to live faithfully in God's way every day in consistent victory for the rest of his life.

In addition, many church leaders have polluted the meaning of the term "discipleship." When you say you are going to have a "discipleship course," people say, "Well we already have a discipleship course in our church. We meet for four weeks and we learn about the importance of studying the Scriptures, having a daily devotional time, having fellowship with one another, church attendance, telling others about Jesus Christ, and Scripture memory." All those things should be taught when discipling someone, but biblical discipleship is much more than those basic practices.

Also, the world has excluded the term "counseling" from the ministry of discipleship by laying claim to a whole field of study called "counseling." The world then says to the church, "You cannot use the term 'counseling' anymore because 'counseling' can only be practiced by people who have degrees after their names, and have been trained for years."

Because both terms "discipleship"' and "counseling" have been polluted, BCF uses another term, "biblical discipleship/counseling," so that you understand that counseling is an integral part of biblical discipleship. Biblical discipleship is helping people to follow the whole counsel of God. So we use the term "biblical discipleship/counseling."

Therefore, this next course is actually biblical discipleship/counseling training, and you will also see this term in BCF's further courses, from Level II on. They are called "biblical discipleship/counseling."

Now let's look at what biblical discipling/counseling is.

A. Read Section **I. What is biblical counseling?**

   1. Read Paragraph A. and highlight the word "restoration" and the reference, *Galatians 6:1-2*.

      In the second line of Paragraph A., please cross out the word "gentle confrontation." The only time the word "confrontation" is used in any of the courses beyond Level I is in dealing with ourselves. So, please change "gentle confrontation" to "gentleness."

      You are to help others deal with the battle within (the battle between the flesh and the spirit). You are to confront the sin in a person's life, not the person. You do not do battle with the person. You only help him to deal with himself. You cannot convict anybody of sin. You are not the Holy Spirit. It is the Holy Spirit's responsibility to convict concerning sin, and righteousness, and judgment *(John 16:8)*.

   2. Read *Galatians 6:1*.

      You may remember from the study of this passage in Lesson 2 that the word for "caught" here does not have the sense of "Aha! I caught you." Instead, some versions convey the sense of the word better by translating it, "caught up in" or "enmeshed in." In other words, the person is tangled up in his problems and he is having difficulties. If he is tangled up in or caught up in a trespass, then what are you to do?

   3. _____

      Who is to do the restoration?

   4. _____

      Who is the one who is spiritual? *(Refer to Galatians 5:16, 25.)*

   5. _____

      In other words, those who are walking according to the conviction and illumination of the Holy Spirit are the ones who are spiritual. They are dealing with their own lives God's way.

If you are not walking in God's way, you are not fit to restore anybody. If you do not deal with the sins in your own life, you can come out of a Bible study knowing what the Bible says about people's problems, but, at the same time, be a very judgmental, harsh, demeaning person, because all you do is point out people's sins without restoring them. The ones who are dealing with themselves are the ones who are fit to restore others.

Notice that the discipler/counselor helps the fallen one to change. The word "restore" in the original language, is the same word that fishermen used when they were mending nets. It means "to mend," "to put back together." The nets would tear from time to time, or the knots would come untied. This word describes the process of mending that net back to wholeness and usefulness. You are to bring that person back to wholeness in his walk and to usefulness in his life with others. You are not just to get him over the problem, but to restore him to being a useful member of the body of Christ. So, the goal is change.

Now, list some characteristics of how to help someone caught in a trespass according to *Galatians 6:1-2*.

6. _____

_____

Restoration is to be accomplished with gentleness.

What is the warning as you are restoring another?

7. _____

In other words, God says that you are not exempt from sinning just because you are helping somebody else. You are always to be looking to your own life. You must be careful even about the kinds of things you find out about somebody else's problems while you are helping him. For example, if you are dealing with helping somebody with a problem of adultery, it is enough that you know that that person committed adultery. You do not need to know, and you should not know, all the details of how it was committed. So, be very careful. God says that you are to be looking to yourself, *'lest you too be tempted.'* It is a great warning to us.

3. What is the law of Christ referred to in *verse 2*?

8. _____

We are to love as Jesus loved. That is why it is called the law of Christ. It is not just the law of the Old Testament, where God says to love God and love your neighbor. But the law of Christ is to love as Jesus loved *(John 13:34-35)*.

You are to bear one another's burdens. In other words, you are to come alongside that person and help him through the difficulty that he is having.

> **ILLUSTRATION:** Suppose you were walking along a road and saw someone lying in a ditch. You would not just stand over that ditch and say to that person, "I noticed you are lying in that ditch. You really should not be in there. You really need to get out." Of course, the person already knows that he is stuck in the ditch. Bearing one another's burdens means that you get down into that ditch and help him out.

You support him as much as he needs until he is strong enough to deal with the matter on his own. You help him, with whatever principles are necessary, go through the difficulty God's way. That is part of bearing one another's burdens.

But then, how much and how long do you bear one another's burdens?

4. What is the overall goal, according to *verse 5* (highlight in Paragraph B.)?

9. _____

> The aim is for that person to know as soon as possible how to deal with his life without always having to come to you for help. He should learn where to go to carry his load. That is, he should learn to go to God's Word, and to the Lord, depending on the Lord alone rather than always being dependent on another human being.
>
> This makes biblical discipleship/counseling very different from worldly counsel. In most worldly counseling, the counselee becomes more dependent on the counselor as time goes on, not less dependent, to the point that it is almost like the weekly fix. The counselee has to go to his counselor so he can feel better and face the rest of the week. That is not biblical counseling.
>
> Biblical discipleship/counseling is helping somebody to develop a pattern of life so that he learns how to depend on the Lord completely, and to live in a godly way without any human counselors getting in the way. That is what *verse 5* is all about.
>
> This leads us to the next subject.

B. Turn to Section **II. Why train believers to counsel biblically?** In your manual, substitute the phrase "every believer" for "believers" in this question. This one question is really a combination of four questions centered on the key words, "biblically," "counsel," "believers," and "train." We are going to look at each of these questions individually below.

1. *Why use only the Bible?*

   Write the question "Why biblically?" beside Paragraph A. and then read the paragraph. The Bible is under attack and increasingly ignored in many Christian churches even though it is the only completely sufficient source for facing, dealing with, and enduring the problems of life in a practical, victorious way.

   More and more people are adopting worldly ways in local churches. They say, "The Bible is good for dealing with every-day matters of life, but we must look elsewhere for answers to the really difficult problems." It is time that believers take to heart the claims in *II Timothy 3:16-17*, that all Scripture is inspired by God and is profitable so that the man of God may be adequate, equipped for every good work.

2. *Why is individual discipleship/counseling needed in the church?*

   Write the question "Why counsel individuals in the church?" beside Paragraphs B. through D.

   a. Read Paragraph B.

      Some church leaders do not believe in counseling in the local church because they are convinced that it is enough to preach the Word of God from the pulpit and classroom on a continuing basis. They believe it is sufficient to provide the truths of God's Word on a mass basis.

      Remember from Lesson 2 that God shows us in *Hebrews 5:12-14* that merely understanding biblical truths intellectually will not produce maturity. It is the personal practice of the truths that brings maturity. Also, you may remember that in *James 1:22*, God tells us that if we merely hear the Word, we delude ourselves. Throughout the Old and New Testament, we observe the children of God being defeated and miserable even though they were very much aware of God's commands. It is futile merely to hear the Word.

   b. Read Paragraph C.

Note that part of the discipleship/counseling process is evangelism. If an unbeliever comes to you for counsel on how to deal with a severe problem, such as deep depression, his greatest need is salvation. Of course, once he is saved and has the empowering of the Holy Spirit, it will be relatively easy to help him have peace and joy in his life. Therefore, it is important not to bypass the presentation of the plan of salvation in counseling.

    c. Read Paragraph D. Especially new believers need guidance to distinguish between truth and error.

3. *Why should **all** believers be involved?*

    a. Write the question "Why every believer?" beside Paragraphs E. and F.

    b. Read Paragraph E., then, highlight in your manual and read *Romans 15:14*. What does this verse say about the responsibilities of believers toward one another?

10.

At the time the Apostle Paul wrote this letter to the Romans, he had never met the believers who lived in Rome. Yet, he says, "*I myself also am convinced that you are full of goodness, filled with all knowledge, and able also to admonish one another.*" How could the Apostle Paul possibly say that to all the Roman believers who read this letter? The reality is that it was not *their* goodness; it was not *their* enabling; and it was not *their* knowledge. It was *God's* goodness, *God's* enabling, and *God's* knowledge. Because the Holy Spirit is in every believer, he can count on the fact that God, through His Word, makes him adequate to minister to others. Every believer who is walking in the Spirit is able to admonish (or counsel) one another, and as we studied earlier in *Galatians 6:1*, he is commanded to do so.

    c. Read Paragraph F.

Training in biblical discipleship/counseling greatly improves a person's ability to approach individuals as a caring friend and, thus, to show how the plan of salvation relates to the unbeliever's current problem. We see this in the approach of Jesus.

Jesus' approach was similar to that of a physician when people come to him for help. Jesus asked pertinent questions that showed His desire to minister to them in a meaningful way. His messages and actions were tailored to their needs.

For example, in *John Chapter 3*, Jesus ministered to Nicodemus in a totally different way from the way He ministered to the Samaritan woman at the well in the very next chapter, *John Chapter 4*. Nicodemus started his conversation with Jesus by asking questions in the intellectual realm. Jesus totally dispelled Nicodemus' preconceived notions. That is what led Nicodemus to say, "How can a man be born again and go back into his mother's womb?" He made clear to Jesus that he did not understand. Jesus started where Nicodemus was already sensitive.

On the other hand, the woman at the well only saw her need for physical water. Jesus used that symbol to show her she needed living water. We need to start where people are already sensitive to the need in their lives, and then, show them their need for the Lord.

ILLUSTRATION: What does a loving, caring physician do when you describe your problem? He takes the time to investigate to see what your real need is. He might take your temperature. He might take your blood pressure, or look in your ears, or examine all kinds of things that do not even seem like they relate. He checks out your overall body to see if anything else is affected. He might actually have you go through blood tests, or other tests, that may be quite painful. And he may even have to take out a scalpel and do some surgery. Does that hurt? Absolutely. But what is the whole focus? The purpose is to help heal you from the inside out, not just to put a bandage on something to make you feel better temporarily. He is not going to prescribe a cure until he knows the depth of the problem.

In the same way, you need to be trained like a physician. You need to learn how to take seriously people's problems, and ask the kinds of questions that bring out the depth of the problem. Then, you are to apply God's Word in a manner appropriate to the depth of the problem.

4. *Why **train** believers to counsel biblically?*

   Write the question "Why train?" beside Paragraph G.

   Members of a local church often expect the pastor to do the work of ministry, especially in matters of counseling. They say, in effect, "Pastor, you must be the primary person to do the counseling, because that is what we pay you for."

   a. Read Paragraph G. Then, highlight in your manual and read *Ephesians 4:11-12*. What is a primary purpose of pastors and teachers in the local church?

      11. _____

      _____

   It is not the responsibility of pastors to do the ministry; it is the responsibility of the pastor and the elders to train up people to counsel. The pastor is certainly to be involved in restoring others, but that is not his primary ministry; all believers are to be trained to disciple/counsel.

   b. Read Subparagraph 1., then, highlight in your manual and read *Exodus 18:13-26*.

   We see in this passage that Moses was the judge over the Israelites, who were in the wilderness at this point. Moses would be like the equivalent of our pastor within our local assemblies. He was responsible for the spiritual oversight of these millions of people.

   This is the first incident in the Scriptures where we see a person who is responsible for teaching others spiritual truths.

   1) In *verses 13 and 16*, what did Moses do?

      12. _____

      _____

   Notice that when Moses judged according to God's Word, people came to him with their difficulties. Also, notice that the task was enormous. People stood around from morning till evening. Moses was busy all day long.

   2) In *verse 14*, what did Jethro ask Moses?

      13. _____

   3) In *verse 15*, what was Moses' response to Jethro's question?

      14. _____

      _____

Moses' response is similar to how many people, especially pastors, respond when they have an overwhelming task of counseling others: He says, "they come to me." In other words, Moses ministered alone because he saw the need and the people came to him. The task is still enormous, especially when it is very clear that you are giving out God's answers, and people are being helped by God's Word. Yet we still tend to try to handle it ourselves.

4) In *verses 17* and *18*, what was Jethro's evaluation of what Moses was doing?

15. _____

Moses' father-in-law did not say, "Oh, Moses, you are such a good spiritual leader! You are so effective, and God is using you so powerfully, and this is such a good problem to have!" Instead, he pointed out that not only was the task too difficult to handle alone, but the people were not served well.

Moses' father-in-law said, "this is not a good thing that you are doing." Then he tells why it is not a good thing. First, he will wear himself out. It is too much for him. And second, the people will wear out. They are going to say, "I am never going to get my answers. I will never get this solved because all these other people are in line ahead of me."

5) In *verse 19*, Jethro offers Moses counsel, which is the first time the word "counsel" occurs in the Scripture.

6) In *verse 20*, what did Jethro tell Moses to teach?

16. _____

We see that Jethro counsels Moses to teach God's statutes and laws to the people, but he also counsels Moses to appoint certain ones to help him. Notice the qualities of those whom he is to choose in *verse 21*. Did he say that they must have studied psychology for eight years and have degrees? or that they must have been believers for many decades? or that they must have a seminary education?

7) In *verse 21*, what were the qualifications Moses was to use to select the leaders?

17. _____

Notice that Moses was to divide the task of counseling. He was to choose people to whom he could give the responsibility of judging.

The qualifications for the counselors were based on their character of life. The ones chosen were to be people of proven character.

In contrast, often in the church, the qualifications for counselors are based either on their level of education, their ability to quote Scripture, the number of classes they took, their communication skills, or their intelligence.

BIBLICAL PRACTICES

The **BASIC BIBLICAL COUNSELING PROCEDURES** on Pages 419-421 of the *Self-Confrontation* manual was written in 1991. It was the beginning of developing a plan for how to help somebody. Since then, the chart has been revised many times in attempts to explain the discipleship/counseling process in a practical way. So, instead of looking at the chart in the *Self-Confrontation* manual, you can use **BIBLICAL PRACTICES FOR FACING, DEALING WITH, AND ENDURING PROBLEMS** *(this guide, Supplement 3, Pages 309-322).*

The **BIBLICAL PRACTICES** chart is designed to help you plan and conduct biblical discipleship/counseling so that you not only know how to help someone face, deal with, and endure the tests and trials of life, but also so that you can help him progressively mature in Jesus Christ. You can also show him this chart so that he can see a well thought out, complete plan to help him deal with all problems he may face in the future.

This methodology will be a major focus in the second and third levels of your training. Let's look at the chart in more detail.

A. The **BIBLICAL PRACTICES** chart consists of the three pages which contain 18 boxes. Notice on the first page, the title at the top is, "**The Foundation for Biblical Discipleship/Counseling**."

   1. Boxes 1-5 are about gathering information. You must find out where that person's difficulty is, what he sees needs to change in his life right now, where his attention is, and what he has tried to do about his problems. In Level II, you will be taught how to gather information, what kinds of information to gather, and what kinds of information not to gather.

   2. Box 6 deals with salvation. You cannot help somebody to learn to walk in God's way unless he is first part of God's family. Obviously, the basic foundation to helping somebody walk in God's way is to receive Jesus Christ as Lord and Savior.

   3. Notice in Box 7, that once you present the plan of salvation, if they receive Christ, you deal with the need for continual commitment to the Lord and His Word.

   4. In Box 8, you deal with consistent reliance on the Lord. In Boxes 7 and 8, you see the basic topics that most people call discipleship: Willingness to please the Lord in all things, relying on the power of the Holy Spirit, obeying God's Word, prayer, fellowship, etc. But these matters are just the beginning of the whole discipleship/counseling process. They form the foundation.

B. Notice the second page is entitled, "**Biblical Reconciliation with God and Man**." Once you have established the foundation for being a disciple of Christ, then you need to deal with reconciliation, both with God and man. In other words, you need to examine and remove the logs from your own life. That is the whole process given to you on the second page.

   Boxes 9-14 describe how to establish a biblical structure for change. In this Self-Confrontation Bible Study, you have already been introduced to the primary tool indicated on this page, the **VICTORY OVER FAILURES PLAN**.

C. The third page of the Biblical Practices chart is entitled, "**The Maturing Disciple of Jesus Christ**." It contains Boxes 15-18, which provide guidelines for practicing the plans established previously and persevering daily as a faithful servant of God. It describes the believer who is reordering his entire life to conform to what God desires and is beginning to minister to others, thus fulfilling the Great Commission to make disciples. From this point on, most of the counsel will be to prepare the disciple/counselee for continuing his growth in discipleship after the structured discipleship/counseling phase ends.

As you can see, the **BIBLICAL PRACTICES** chart simply takes all those things that you learned from God's Word for how to deal with the matters of life, and puts them in a short format for how to help other people. In Level II, you learn how to follow this plan in a systematic way.

| FURTHER TRAINING |

You have learned how to obey the first part of Jesus' command in *Matthew 7:5*, which is to:

18. _____

What does the second part of the verse say that you will then be prepared for?

19. _____

Read *I Peter 3:15-16*. We see that, as believers, we are to be prepared to give an answer to everyone who asks of the hope we have in Christ, and we are to live righteously before the world. As you may remember, the Self-Confrontation Bible Study provides a foundation to do this. Now, you need to learn better how to disciple/counsel others.

Here are some ways to get additional training:

1. We strongly recommend that you attend the full Self-Confrontation course in a more formal teacher-student setting. This will help you learn the biblical principles in the *Self-Confrontation* manual in more depth and with more structured explanations. Many people have taken the course multiple times, finding that God gives them additional insights and challenges them in different ways each time.

2. After completing a weekly or Concentrated Course, you can attend the next level of training. The purpose of the second course is to equip you to use the Scriptures to help others face, deal with, and endure the problems of life and to have complete, total, and enduring victory.

   a. Course II will teach you in a practical way:

      1) How to develop biblical plans for each discipleship/counseling meeting with the disciple/counselee;

      2) How to practice and teach the Scriptures as your only authority for faith, conduct, and counsel;

      NOTE: *This truth alone can revolutionize your ministry. You never need to worry whether your opinion is correct because you should never be stating your opinion to someone you are discipling/counseling anyway. You should only be pointing the disciple to God's Word. It is God's Word, not yours, that will accomplish God's purposes (Isaiah 55:11).*

      3) How to gain and provide biblical understanding of problems at the feeling, doing, and heart levels;

      4) How to emphasize biblical hope for any test or trial of life;

      5) How to observe, evaluate, and address biblically the speech and actions of a disciple/counselee;

      6) How to evaluate and encourage commitment to the Lord; and

      7) How to assign biblical homework to help establish lasting biblical change.

   b. In addition to the 105 biblical principles in the Self-Confrontation Bible Study, Course II provides another 32 biblical principles for how to disciple/counsel others. It consists of thirteen lessons, usually taught in two-hours once a week. Included in these lessons are practice role-plays in which students actively participate as assistant and lead disciplers/counselors on a team.

   c. You will also be introduced to the *Handbook for the Ministry of Biblical Discipleship/Counseling*. The *Handbook* is a reference for biblical disciplers/counselors and for all BCF training courses starting with Biblical Discipleship/Counseling Course II. It has been developed to help the biblical discipler/counselor maintain his biblical focus in ministering to those with problems.

3. You can also attend BCF's Teacher Training Course. The Teacher Training Course is very different from courses taught by the world because teaching based on biblical principles is very different from secular teaching. The course follows the example of Jesus in training His

disciples. Most of the course consists of practical exercises where each of the students practice-teach one of the Self-Confrontation course lessons using the *Course I Instructor's Guide*. Then, they are evaluated and given guidance on how to improve their teaching. Also, the students are given teaching tips and warnings about pitfalls.

During the course, you will become familiar with the *Course I Instructor's Guide*. It contains specific guidance in how to teach each lesson of the *Self-Confrontation* manual. It walks you through the important points to make, provides you with illustrations, and transitions that will make it easy to teach the Self-Confrontation course. It also helps you to focus on the essential portions of the manual and the key scripture verses.

The Biblical Counseling Foundation offers each of these courses in a one-week concentrated format. When the courses are taught in the concentrated format, they are called 'Tracks.' The content is largely the same as in the courses, but you will not have time to do the homework. Concentrated courses are conducted eight hours a day for five consecutive days. Concentrated courses for all BCF levels of training are scheduled for different locations around the U.S. and elsewhere, usually several times a year. You can find more information about concentrated courses by visiting the BCF website, www.bcfministries.org and clicking on the Courses menu or by calling the BCF Office at 760.773.1667.

YOUR ONGOING MINISTRY

Disciple others using the *Student Workbook*

You may have been used of the Lord to lead someone to a saving knowledge of Jesus Christ and are wondering how best to help him become established in his or her walk with the Lord. You can begin immediately to disciple that person using the materials that you just completed. Also, you may be a ministry leader responsible for training others in a small group, or you may have children whom you are responsible to disciple.

In any of the above cases, a *Leader's Guide for the Self-Confrontation Bible Study* is available to assist you in leading a small group through the Self-Confrontation Bible Study. The *Leader's Guide* contains the same material as the *Student Workbook* but provides additional instructions for how to lead your group (or someone you may be discipling) through the study. Instructions for the leader are inserted on the left side, opposite the corresponding *Student Workbook*. Answers to the fill-in-the-blank questions are also provided on the appropriate pages.

Teach a regular Self-Confrontation course in a classroom setting

Prepare yourself to teach the regular 24-week Self-Confrontation course. The first step would be to attend the course yourself. If this course is offered in your local area, you can review the homework assignments in your *Student Workbook* instead of following the instructions listed at the end of each lesson in the *Self-Confrontation* manual. The *Student Workbook* is more complete and reflects the updates now being taught at BCF Concentrated Courses. These updates include the many illustrations taught throughout the course and also instructions on how to complete the *Victory Over Failures Plan: Guidelines and Worksheets* booklet.

NOTE: *If the students use the Student Workbook to do their homework in the regular course, the lesson in the Workbook should be completed after that lesson is taught, rather than before as is the plan in the Self-Confrontation Bible Study.*

As mentioned on the previous page, BCF offers a teacher training course for additional training.

NOTE: *If you plan to teach the Self-Confrontation course or disciple someone, please be careful to make it clear to those you are training that you are doing so as part of your own local ministry, and not as a representative of BCF. Only courses conducted by the Biblical Counseling Foundation staff should be called "BCF" courses.*

CONCLUSION

We trust that this Bible Study has been of great benefit to you. The hope is that you have immersed yourself in God's Word, have seen yourself in the light of God's truth (which is always a profitable though not necessarily pleasant thing to do), have applied God's principles in the power of the Holy Spirit, and have come away with a new or re-affirmed commitment to love Him and your neighbor. God bless you as you seek to serve Him.

ANSWERS TO QUESTIONS IN THE STUDENT WORKBOOK

INTRODUCTION

1. The two commandments which Jesus said summarized all the commandments in Scripture are: (a) **love God** and (b) **love others as yourself**.

2. **Yes**, typically people's numbers go down significantly.

3. Jesus said we are to love **in the same way He loves**.

4. Jesus demonstrated His love to His disciples when **He washed their feet**.

5. Typically, people's number gets **lower**.

6. Answers will vary. A typical summary of what you have learned from the love test might be: "**I have not been measuring my life according to God's standards and that I have not loved as Jesus loves.**"

7. In *I Corinthians 15:9*, Paul described himself as **the least of the apostles**.

8. In *Ephesians 3:8*, Paul described himself as **the very least of all saints**.

9. In *I Timothy 1:15*, Paul described himself as **the chief of all sinners**.

LESSON 1

1. According to *Acts 1:8*, God's plan for reaching the world is **to use believers as His witnesses wherever they go in the world**.

2. The two parts are described in *Matthew 28:19-20* as God's methodology for making disciples are: (a) **Baptism (evangelism is implied, since you do not baptize unbelievers)** and (b) **teaching all that Jesus commanded**.

3. There are **four** spiritual generations referred to in *II Timothy 2:2* **(Paul, Timothy, faithful ones, and others)**.

4. According to *Romans 8:28*, God **causes all things to work together for good** in our lives.

5. According to *Romans 8:29*, God's goal for every believer is **to conform us to the image of His Son, Jesus Christ**.

6. Answers will vary. Topics Jesus dealt with in the Sermon on the Mount include: **anger, persecution, forgiveness, reconciliation, adultery, lust, divorce, retaliation, love, judging self, hypocrisy, worry**.

7. Answers will vary. A typical list of the things believers do that people think indicate they are truly believers includes: **Believers pray; believers go to church; believers study the Bible**.

8. **No**, those who perform miraculous feats will not necessarily get to heaven.

9. The two things in *Romans 10:8-10* that God says result in salvation are: (a) **confession with the mouth Jesus as Lord**; and (b) **belief in the heart that God raised Jesus from the dead**.

10. The two things Jesus said for people to do for salvation in *Mark 1:15* are: (a) **repent** and (b) **believe in the Gospel**.

11. Eternal life in *John 17:3* is equated with **knowing God and His Son, Jesus Christ**.

12. According to *John 17:22-23*, we are to be related to Jesus Christ by **being one with Him**.

13. According to *II Corinthians 11:2*, Christians are **espoused to Christ**.

14. According to *Ephesians 2:8-10*, we are saved **by grace through faith**.

15. *Ephesians 2:10* tells us that the result of being saved is that **believers are created to do good works**.

16. Answers will vary. One way to write the meaning of *Ephesians 2:8-9* would be: **Salvation is a gift of God. A person is saved though faith, not by works. There is nothing he can do to earn salvation so that he cannot brag about it.**

17. Answers will vary. One way to describe how a person can be saved would be: *Mark 1:15* — **Repent of sin**; *Romans 5:8* — **Acknowledge that Christ came to pay the penalty for sin**; *Romans 10:9-10* — **Confess with the mouth Jesus as Lord and believe in Christ.**

18. Answers will vary regarding the most significant truth learned in completing this lesson.

LESSON 2

1. Answers will vary. A typical list of some of the changes that took place immediately after receiving Christ include: (a) **I enjoyed reading the Bible**, (b) **I wanted to fellowship with other believers**, and (c) **I desired to give my testimony**.

2. Answers will vary. A typical list of activities in which a believer is involved on a daily basis would include: (a) **reading the Bible**, (b) **going to work**, (c) **fixing meals**, (d) **having devotions**, and (e) **cleaning house**.

3. In *Colossians 2:6-10*, believers are warned against **being taken captive by philosophy and deception according to the tradition of men**.

4. In *Colossians 2:6-10*, believers are exhorted instead to **walk in Christ** and **recognize that believers are complete in Christ — nothing and no one else is needed**.

5. Answers will vary; for example, **Subparagraph 8: God uses trials as opportunities; tribulation brings perseverance, proven character, and hope (*Romans 5:3-5*)**.

6. Instead of pleasing self, Gods says we are to please **Him**.

7. Instead of our focus being on **living for self**,

8. Our focus should be on **dying to self**.

9. Our obedience is to be in response to **God's love for us**.

10. Our obedience is not to be dependent on **circumstances, feelings, or other people**.

11. The title sentence of Section II. tells me that **change will always be part of** the rest of my life here on earth.

12. Answers will vary regarding the questions that are most challenging, for example: (a) **Question # 5 — *II Corinthians 5:9* — My ambition should be to be pleasing to Him** and (b) **Question # 8 — *John 13:34-35* — I am to love others just like Jesus loves me**.

13. According to *Matthew 7:5*, before dealing with anyone else's problems, we are first to **take the log out of our own eye**.

14. If I listen to the teaching from Scripture but do not apply it in my own life, Jesus says **I am a hypocrite**.

15. In *Galatians 6:1*, **those who are spiritual** are responsible for restoring others.

16. The ones that are spiritual are **those who are walking in the Spirit**.

17. In *Hebrews 5:12-14*, the key to growth in spiritual discernment is **practicing the principles of God**.

18. The energy from the sun **hardens** the muddy ground.

19. The energy from the sun **melts** the butter.

20. In *Psalm 1:2*, a person is blessed if he **meditates in God's law day and night**.

21. The list of words in *Psalm 19:7-11* that describe what God's Word is like and what it does in us includes:

What God's Word is like	What God's Word does in us
Perfect	Restores the soul
Sure	Makes the simple wise
Right	Rejoices the heart
Pure	Enlightens the eyes
True, desirable, sweet	God's servant is warned and rewarded in keeping them

22. The commandment or principle in *Psalm 1:2* is to **delight in the Law of the Lord and meditate on it constantly**.

23. Answers will vary regarding the reproof in *Psalm 1:2*. A typical response might be: "**I don't meditate on the Word throughout the day.**"

24. Answers will vary regarding the correction in *Psalm 1:2*. A typical response might be: "**I need to have His Word in my mind much more throughout the day.**"

25. Answers will vary regarding the training in righteousness based on *Psalm 1:2*. A typical response might be: "**I will carry my Scripture memory cards with me and review them during the spare moments of each day.**"

26. In *Matthew 4:1-10,* Jesus countered Satan's temptations when **He recited Scripture passages to counter each temptation**.

27. In *Psalm 119:9, 11*, the benefits to treasuring God's Word in my heart and obeying it completely are that **it keeps my way pure** *(verse 9)* **and it helps me not to sin**.

28. Answers will vary. Typical types of free moments may include: **waiting in line, waiting for appointments, riding on a bus or a train, etc.**

29. Our focus is not to be on living for self, but instead, it is to be on **dying to self**.

30. The Bible says I can expect to see changes I will need to make for **as long as I live**.

31. Before I take the speck out of someone else's eye, I am to **take the log out of my own eye**.

32. Two daily disciplines I learned about in this lesson that will help me be a consistent doer of the Word are (a) **daily devotions** and (b) **Scripture memory**.

33. Answers will vary regarding the most significant truth learned in completing this lesson.

LESSON 3

1. According to *II Timothy 3:16-17*, **God** is the author of the Scriptures.

2. According to *II Timothy 3:16-17*, the four things for which the Scriptures are profitable are: (a) **teaching**, (b) **reproof**, (c) **correction**, and (d) **training in righteousness**.

3. Answers will vary. A typical explanation for each of the following words is:
   a. Teaching: **the truth for my life**
   b. Reproof: **where I went wrong**
   c. Correction: **what I should do instead**

d. Training in righteousness: **making a practice of doing the right thing**

4. In *II Timothy 3:17*, the resulting effect of God's Word in my life is **that I may be totally equipped to deal with every aspect of living.**

5. According to *II Peter 1:3,* God has granted believers **everything pertaining to life and godliness.**

6. According to *II Peter 1:4,* God's Word enables us **to avoid the corruption in the world.**

7. The caution in *Deuteronomy 4:2* regarding God's Word is: **do not add or take away from God's Word.**

8. *Proverbs 30:6* says that **God will reprove** those who add to God's Word **and they will be proved to be liars.**

9. Regarding the power of God's Word, *Isaiah 55:8-9, 11* says **it will accomplish exactly what God desires.**

10. According to *John 16:7*, it was to the Apostle's advantage that Jesus go back to the Father because **Jesus limited Himself as a human being to one place at a time; the Holy Spirit is present in every believer.**

11. Answers will vary. The better choice is **the Holy Spirit, because He is with the believer always.**

12. According to *John 16:13*, the Holy Spirit guides us into **all truth.**

13. According to *I Corinthians 2:12-14*, a believer can understand **spiritual truth given to him by God.**

14. **Yes**, pastors and teachers are really needed.

15. Pastors and teachers are really needed because **in *Ephesians 4:12*, God gave pastors and teachers to equip believers.**

16. Answers will vary. Possible observations about Jesus' prayer life include: (a) **He prayed knowing His Father listened**, (b) **sometimes, He prayed all night**, and (c) **He prayed for His enemies.**

17. Answers will vary regarding what is most applicable, for example, "**I am to pray always in submission to God and according to His will, not mine.**"

18. Answers will vary regarding a case where God answered one of your prayers in a way you did not expect.

19. Answers will vary regarding one way in which you could improve your prayer life. For example, "**Make sure my prayers conform to the Bible.**"

20. Answers will vary regarding one Scripture passage that shows that God and His Word are sufficient to provide instructions to believers in dealing with the problems of life. For example, *II Timothy 3:16-17* **says that God is the author of the Scriptures and they are profitable for showing me how to deal with every aspect of living.**

21. Answers will vary regarding ways in which the Holy Spirit helps you live the Christian life. For example, you may say (a) "**He guides me**" or (b) "**He comforts me.**"

22. Answers will vary regarding what in Jesus' prayer life can apply to your own. For example, **He was completely committed to His Father and went to Him often for guidance.**

23. Answers will vary regarding the most significant truth learned in completing this lesson.

LESSON 4

1. Three significant resources that God provides to the believer for daily living are: (a) **the Bible**, (b) **the Holy Spirit**, and (c) **prayer**.

2. Descriptions of the natural man apart from Jesus Christ would be:

   a. *Proverbs 14:12* — **Man's way may seem right to him, but it ends in death.**

   b. *Isaiah 55:8-9* — **God's way is infinitely higher than man's way.**

   c. *I Corinthians 2:14* — **The natural man does not accept the things of the Holy Spirit; they seem like foolishness to him.**

3. In *I Samuel 15:3*, God's command was **to utterly destroy all of the Amalekites and their animals.**

4. In *I Samuel 15:8-9*, King Saul and the people **failed to kill King Agag and the best of the animals.**

5. In *I Samuel 15:13*, King Saul said **he obeyed God's command.**

6. In *I Samuel 15:14*, Samuel accused Saul of **lying about what he had done.**

7. In *I Samuel 15:15*, in an attempt to justify himself, Saul said, **they saved the animals to sacrifice to the Lord.**

8. In *I Samuel 15:22-23*, even though Saul did most of what the Lord asked, Samuel said **the Lord desires obedience more than sacrifice.**

9. Samuel equated Saul's partial obedience to **the sin of rebellion, idolatry, and witchcraft.**

10. **Jesus** provided the greatest example of dying to self.

11. According to *I Corinthians 1:26-28*, God has chosen **the foolish, the weak, the base, and the despised.**

12. According to *II Timothy 3:1-2*, the primary characteristic of people living during the last days is that **they will be lovers of self (preoccupied with the things of self).**

13. According to *Philippians 3:9*, our righteousness does *not* come from **ourselves**.

14. According to *Philippians 3:9*, our righteousness comes from **God, on the basis of faith**.

15. *Acts 17:11* says the Bereans **received the Word with eagerness** and **examined the Scriptures daily to evaluate Paul's teaching.**

16. According to *Philippians 2:3-4*, instead of liberating self, we should **be humble, regard others as more important than self,** and **look out for the interests of others.**

17. Contrary to the philosophy of improving self, *John 15:4-5* says that we are to **be humble** and **if we abide in Christ, we can bear much fruit, but apart from Him we can do nothing.**

18. Contrary to the elevation of self, *Romans 3:10-18, 23* says that **there is none righteous, none who understands, all are useless, there is none who does good, there is no fear of God, all have sinned and fall short of the glory of God.**

19. Contrary to the release of self from bondage, *I John 5:4-5* says that **whoever has faith in Jesus Christ has overcome the world.**

20. Answers will vary. Two of the areas where Christians are tempted to go man's way include that (a) **we seek to justify our actions and make excuses for our behavior** and (b) **we do everything to avoid problems.**

Student Workbook for the Self-Confrontation Bible Study
- Supplement 1 -
© Biblical Counseling Foundation

21. God says man's problem is **sin, demonstrated by rebellion, unbelief, disobedience, denial of God's power**.

22. God says the solution is to **be saved by grace through faith and in loving obedience to God be matured in Christ through the power of the Holy Spirit**.

23. **Yes**, partial obedience is as unacceptable to God as deliberate rebellion.

24. Answers will vary regarding the most significant truth learned in completing this lesson.

LESSON 5

1. *Romans 8:29* says that God's plan for believers **is to make them like His Son, Jesus Christ**.

2. In *Romans 1:18-20*, the issue of man's separation from God is not a matter of a lack of knowledge, but that **man rejects the truth that he is given**.

3. In *Romans 1:21-23*, when people reject God, the consequences in their lives are that **they think they are wise, but they become fools, their hearts are hardened. They begin to worship creation**.

4. In *Romans 1:32*, they sink to lowest depth **by giving hearty approval of those who do the same**.

5. The names of the three levels typed in **boldface** print are: (a) **heart level**, (b) **doing level**, and (c) **feeling level**.

6. In *Matthew 15:18-19*, all deeds (which include thoughts, speech, and actions) come from **the heart**.

7. According to *Genesis 4:5* and *I John 3:12*, Cain's **deeds were evil** so he had bad feelings.

8. To help the student, I should deal with salvation first **because lack of salvation is his most significant problem, and I may mistakenly be helping him to feel better, and thus, remove an incentive for him to seek God to be saved**.

9. Regarding my commitment to the Lord, *Ecclesiastes 12:13-14* says that **I am to fear God and keep His commandments**.

10. Answers will vary. Typical daily responsibilities may include: (a) **have devotions**, (b) **go to work**, (c) **bathe**, (d) **eat**, (e) **take care of children**, and (f) **get dressed**.

11. According to *Hebrews 4:16*, God gives me His grace **at the time of need**.

12. **Consistently doing the Word** is more difficult than understanding my position in Christ.

13. We struggle more with **denying self and living obediently** than with understanding and accepting God's goodness.

14. Doing the Word typically requires **going against** our feelings rather than following them.

NOTE: Answers to Questions 15-20 will vary regarding observations concerning doing the Word. Typical answers are provided for your benefit.

15. *Ephesians 2:8-10* — **Believers are created in Christ Jesus for good works**.

16. *James 2:17-18* — **Faith without works is dead**.

17. *II Corinthians 5:10* — **Believers will be rewarded for their deeds when they appear before the judgment seat of Christ**.

18. *I John 2:3-4* — **We know that we have come to know Jesus Christ, if we keep His commandments**.

19. *John 15:10-11* — **The one who keeps Jesus' commandments will abide in His love.**

20. *James 1:25* — **The consistent doer of God's Word will be blessed.**

21. God's plan for believers is **to conform them to the image of His Son, Jesus.**

22. The three levels of problems discussed in this lesson are: (a) **feeling**, (b) **doing**, and (c) **heart**.

23. Obedience often requires going against our **feelings**.

24. Answers will vary regarding the most significant truth learned in completing this lesson.

LESSON 6

1. It is important to be specific in listing my failures because **change takes place in specific ways. We cannot change in generalities, but we can change specific deeds.**

2. Answers will vary. An example of something that is biblically permissible, but may not be beneficial is **sleeping when I should be working.**

3. Answers will vary. An example of something that is biblically permissible, but could become an obsession is **eating.**

4. Answers will vary. An example of something that could be a stumbling block in a person's life is **going to a place where I know I will be tempted to sin.**

5. Answers will vary. An example of something that could be a stumbling block in another person's life is **taking another believer to a place where he will be tempted to sin, even though I am not tempted.**

6. Answers will vary. An example of something that does not build up or edify is **hoping that a person whom I have offended will just forget what I have done rather than going to him to ask forgiveness.**

7. Answers will vary. Examples of situations in which a person may not have good feelings, and yet there is no sin involved would be: (a) **when a person is ill with the flu** or (b) **when a person is grieving the loss of a loved one.**

8. Answers will vary; for example, **the motor is out of oil, the oil pump is out of commission, or the oil light is defective.**

9. The thoughts listed in *Matthew 15:18-19* are **evil thoughts.**

10. The speech listed in *Matthew 15:18-19* are **false witness, slanders.**

11. The actions listed in *Matthew 15:18-19* are **murders, adulteries, fornications, thefts.**

12. According to *Jeremiah 17:9-10*, the only one who can see a person's heart completely is **God.**

13. In *Luke 5:22*, Jesus likens the heart to **the mind.**

14. Regarding our thoughts, *II Corinthians 10:5* says **we are to take every thought captive to the obedience of Christ.**

15. Answers will vary. Examples of ways in which the world focuses on fixing feelings, rather than dealing with the doing level and heart level include: (a) **prescribing drugs that change feelings,** (b) **escaping from difficult situations,** and (c) **getting drunk to forget.**

16. Pointing out that a person who has a life-dominating practice of sin is committing sin and is not subject to an illness can bring hope **because he can confess sin, establish or restore a right relationship with God quickly, and be freed from the power of sin.**

17. *Romans 6:18* says **believers are slaves of righteousness.**

18. In *I Corinthians 10:13*, **our escape is not from the situation, but from sin so that we can endure the situation**.

19. Characteristics of Jesus in *Hebrews 4:15-16* include the fact that **He understands and sympathizes with our weaknesses**.

20. Regarding trials, God says in *James 1:2-4* that **we should consider it joy when we encounter trials because these tests of faith produce endurance**.

21. In *Hebrews 12:2*, the joy set before Jesus was **sitting at the right hand of His Father**.

22. **No**, Jesus did not feel good about going to the cross.

23. Answers will vary; for example, Jesus said in *Matthew 26:39:* **"My Father, if it is possible, let this cup pass from Me …."**

24. According to *Romans 8:29*, the "good" is for us to **be conformed to the image of God's Son, Jesus Christ**.

25. In *Genesis 37:23-28*, the trials and injustices that God allowed in Joseph's life were that **his brothers sold him into slavery**.

26. In *Genesis 39:11-20*, the trials and injustices that God allowed in Joseph's life were that **he was unjustly accused of adultery and put in prison**.

27. In *Genesis 40:12-14, 23*, the trials and injustices that God allowed in Joseph's life were that **the chief cupbearer forgot about him**.

28. Answers will vary regarding an example of a trial in your life which you now recognize that God used for your good, even though you may not have recognized it at the time.

29. According to *Psalm 119:165*, **not loving (keeping) the Law of God** could be a cause of losing my peace or of my stumbling.

30. According to *John 14:27*, the peace that Jesus gives is different from the peace that the world gives in that **Jesus gives us peace in the middle of trouble; the world cannot give that kind of peace**.

31. According to *John 15:10-11*, the believer's joy is based on **keeping the commandments of Jesus**.

32. The erroneous proverb in *Ezekiel 18:2* was: **when fathers eat sour grapes, the children's teeth are set on edge**.

33. Answers will vary regarding how that erroneous proverb is used today; for example, **when parents are addicted to drugs, the children are likely to grow up and become addicted to drugs; therefore, it is the parents' fault that the children abuse drugs**.

34. In *Ezekiel 18:3-4*, God **tells the Israelites to get rid of that proverb. He holds each person responsible for his own behavior. No one can legitimately blame his sin on anyone else**.

35. Answers will vary. Some examples of sin reaping physical consequences to others not responsible for the sin include: (a) **a drunkard does not provide the nutritional food that the children need to be healthy** and (b) **a mother has contracted AIDS through sinful behavior and transmits the AIDS to her newborn child**.

36. The hope about problems offered in *I John 1:9* is that **if we confess our sins, God forgives us and cleanses us from all sin**.

37. Of the three problem levels (feeling, doing, heart), the level on which we are to focus as believers is the **doing** level.

38. Calling a behavior the Bible designates as sinful a "sin" brings hope to a person because **he can confess sin, establish or restore a right relationship with God quickly, and be freed from the power of sin.**

39. The hope that has God provided in *I Corinthians 10:13* is that **God will not allow a test that is too difficult, or unique to me alone. He is faithful and will provide a way to endure in the difficulty without sinning.**

40. Trials represent an opportunity for us because **the testing of our faith produces endurance**.

41. Answers will vary regarding the most significant truth learned in completing this lesson.

LESSON 7

1. According to *Philippians 1:6*, **God** completes the work He began in us.

2. The work He is completing in believers is that of **conforming believers to the image of His Son, Jesus Christ *(Romans 8:29)*.**

3. The "put-off" in *Ephesians 4:25* is **falsehood**.

4. The "put-on" in *Ephesians 4:25* is **speaking truth**.

5. **Yes**, it is possible for someone to put off lying and never put on speaking the truth **by not saying anything.**

6. The "put-off" in *Ephesians 4:28* is **stealing**.

7. The "put-on" in *Ephesians 4:28* is **working and giving to those who have need.**

8. **No**, if a robber has stopped robbing after stealing a million dollars, it does not mean that he is no longer a robber. **He may just be busy spending the money that he has stolen.**

9. The "put-off" in *Ephesians 4:29* is **unwholesome words**.

10. The "put-on" in *Ephesians 4:29* is **edifying words that give grace according to the need of the moment.**

11. The "put-offs" in *Ephesians 4:31-32* are **bitterness, wrath, anger, clamor, slander, and malice.**

12. The "put-ons" in *Ephesians 4:31-32* are **kindness, tenderheartedness, and forgiveness.**

13. In *Ephesians 5:18*, **the drunkard must not only stop drinking, he must place himself under the control of the Holy Spirit.**

14. In *Mark 2:21-22*, Jesus warns not to **try to reform the old life. I must have an entirely new life first.**

15. **Yes**, past, unresolved sin must be dealt with.

16. According to *James 4:17*, we are guilty of sin **when we know the right thing to do and do not do it.**

17. It is the responsibility of **the believer** to put off the old sinful practices and put on the new **practices of righteousness.**

18. Answers will vary regarding an area you have seen God help you with putting off an old ungodly habit and putting on a new righteous practice.

19. According to *II Timothy 2:22*, we are to **flee youthful lusts**.

20. In the place of youthful lusts we are to put on **righteousness, faith, love, and peace, with those who call on the Lord from a pure heart.**

21. Answers will vary; an example of applying *II Timothy 2:22* would be: **If you are a drunkard, you must not only stop drinking; you must also immediately pursue living a life under the control of the Holy Spirit, and you must be involved with other believers who love the Lord.**

22. According to *Galatians 5:16*, if I walk by the Holy Spirit, **I will not carry out the desires of the flesh.**

23. **Yes**, most people are able to get rid of the mental picture of the lion immediately.

24. Most people are able to get rid of the mental picture of the lion **by thinking of something else.**

25. According to *Colossians 3:9-10*, **God** renews the believer's mind.

26. According to *II Corinthians 4:16*, God renews us **daily**.

27. **Believers** are responsible for disciplining their thought lives and learning God's Word.

28. The five aspects listed that relate to developing a Christlike way of thinking are: (a) **hearing the Word**, (b) **reading the Word**, (c) **studying the Word**, (d) **memorizing the Word**, and (e) **meditating on the Word**.

29. Lasting biblical change comes from not only putting off the old, unrighteous behavior, but also **putting on righteous deeds (thoughts, speech, and actions)**.

30. The "put-off" in *II Timothy 2:22* is **youthful lusts**.

31. The "put-ons" in *II Timothy 2:22* are **righteousness, faith, love, and peace, with those who call on the Lord from a pure heart**.

32. Answers will vary regarding the most significant truth learned in completing this lesson.

LESSON 8

1. The four elements of facing, dealing with, and enduring problems biblically are: (a) **biblical understanding**, (b) **biblical hope**, (c) **biblical change**, and (d) **biblical practice**.

2. Without the practice of God's Word **we will not be able to discern between good and evil (i.e., we will not be wise)**.

3. According to *James 1:22*, if I am not a doer of the Word, **I will be in a worse spiritual state because I will delude myself**.

4. The church to which *Revelation 2:1* is addressed is **the Ephesian church**.

5. *Revelation 2:4* says the Ephesian church **left their first love**.

6. The "put-off" in *I Timothy 4:7* is **worldly wisdom**.

7. The "put-on" in *I Timothy 4:7* is **discipline for the purpose of godliness**.

8. According to *I Peter 1:6-7*, **my faith** is more precious than gold.

9. According to *I Peter 4:12*, **we should not be surprised when trials come because they are for our testing**.

10. Answers will vary regarding any trials that you have been "surprised" by in your life.

11. According to *I Peter 4:12*, the trial in Question 10. above **was for my good**.

12. According to *James 1:13-14*, **God** is *not* the source of temptation.

13. **Our own lust (fleshly desires)** *is* a source of temptation.

14. According to *I John 2:16*, the three areas of temptation are: (a) **the lust of the flesh**, (b) **the lust of the eyes**, and (c) **the boastful pride of life**.

15. Please review your completed *Worksheets* and determine whether you are more alert to ways you sin in the problem area you selected to work on.

16. Please review your completed *Worksheet 2: List of Specific Failures to Live Biblically*, and confirm that all the entries were specific, thorough, not blameshifting, and not minimizing or excusing sin.

17. Please review your completed *Worksheet 3: "Put-offs" and "Put-ons,"* and confirm that all of the "put-off"/"put-on" pairs are from the same passage of Scripture.

18. When I understand your problem biblically, have hope, know how to change but do not practice God's Word **I will delude myself**.

19. In contrast to living according to experience or our feelings, **God tells us to be disciplined to obey His Word**.

20. The purpose of the **VICTORY OVER FAILURES PLAN**, *Worksheet 1* is **to help me select a specific problem area for change**.

21. The purpose of the **VICTORY OVER FAILURES PLAN**, *Worksheet 2* is **to help me learn how to judge myself biblically**.

22. The purpose of the **VICTORY OVER FAILURES PLAN**, *Worksheet 3* is **to help me find the biblical "put-offs" and "put-ons" associated with my personal problem**.

23. Answers will vary regarding the most significant truth learned in completing this lesson.

LESSON 9

1. The first two elements of dealing with self are: (a) **biblical understanding** and (b) **biblical hope**.

2. The last two elements of dealing with self are: (a) **biblical change** and (b) **biblical practice**.

3. Answers will vary. Examples of the mistaken explanations for a low view of self might include: (a) **rejection by parents** and (b) **abuse as a child**.

4. Answers will vary. Examples of man's futile ways of building up self might include: (a) **forgive yourself** and (b) **assert yourself**.

5. The first characteristic cited in the list in *II Timothy 3:1-7* is **men will be lovers of self**.

6. According to *Ephesians 5:29a*, **we nourish and cherish our flesh**.

7. The person's attention and preoccupation is with **himself**.

8. Jesus gave **two** commandments in *Matthew 22:37-39*.

9. **No**, there is no third commandment in *Matthew 22:37-39*.

10. According to *Matthew 7:12*, I am to treat (love) others **in the same way I would want them to treat me**.

11. Answers will vary. Typical responses regarding ways I like to be treated include: (a) **with kindness**, (b) **with respect**, (c) **with compassion**, and (d) **with honesty**.

12. The cross is a symbol of **death**.

13. The "put-on" in *Luke 9:23-24* is to **follow Jesus**.

14. A person finds (or saves) his life **by losing his life for Christ's sake**.

15. If the locomotive was able to leave the tracks, **it would get stuck in the ground and would not be able to move**.

16. In *John 12:25,* Jesus is not just talking about grains of wheat, **He is talking about dying to self**.

17. The workers who were hired first said, **these last men have worked *only* one hour, and you have made them equal to us who have borne the burden and the scorching heat of the day**.

18. The sin that the workers who were hired first exhibited was **envy**.

19. Answers will vary regarding statements that demonstrate envy, jealousy, covetousness, and greed. For example:
    a. Envy: **"I am envious of his popularity."**
    b. Jealousy: **"No one had better try to take my place."**
    c. Covetousness: **"I covet that dress."**
    d. Greed: **"I don't earn enough money to buy what I want."**

20. According to *Romans 8:14-17,* the kind of relationship believers have with God is that **God is their Father**.

21. Believers will inherit **everything that Jesus Christ inherits**.

22. **No**, there is nothing about our inheritance that we have earned or deserved.

23. Answers will vary regarding other failures to live God's way that have you discovered.

24. According to *Ephesians 5:29,* we demonstrate love for ourselves **by nourishing and cherishing ourselves (focusing attention on self)**.

25. The two greatest commandments are: (a) **love God with my whole being** and (b) **love others just as I already love myself**.

26. According to *Matthew 7:12,* Jesus told us to love others in a practical way by **treating others in exactly the same way we would want them to treat us**.

27. Answers will vary, but one way to write *Luke 9:23-24* in one's own words would be: **"Take my eyes off self, die daily, and follow Christ. If I am preoccupied with self, I am just going to lose my life; but if I place my focus on Jesus, I will save my life."**

28. Answers will vary regarding the most significant truth learned in completing this lesson.

LESSON 10

1. The third and fourth elements are: (a) **biblical change** and (b) **biblical practice**.

2. In *Philippians 2:3-8,* Jesus demonstrated His servanthood when **He became a bondservant and humbled Himself to the point of dying on the cross**.

3. The "put-offs" and "put-ons" in *Philippians 2:3-4,* are: (a) "Put-offs": **selfishness, and empty conceit** and (b) "Put-ons": **humility, regarding others as more important than self, and looking out for the interests of others**.

4. Answers will vary regarding specific examples of how you can be a servant to those around you.

5. Answers will vary, regarding "put-offs" and "put-ons" in *Psalm 37:1-9.* For example, (a) "Put-offs": (1) **fretting**, (2) **envy**, and (3) **anger**; and (b) "Put-ons": (1) **doing good**, (2) **being faithful**, and (3) **trusting in the Lord**.

6. In *I Corinthians 4:1-2,* **faithfulness** is required of stewards.

7. Answers will vary regarding an area in which you are anxious about the results, when you should be just focusing on your faithfulness and trusting that the Lord is in control.

8. Answers will vary regarding examples where you have compared yourself to someone else.

9. Answers will vary regarding areas of your life in which are you were tempted to complain about things you cannot change.

10. Answers will vary regarding areas of your life in which are you lack knowledge or skill that you need to change.

11. In *Matthew 25:15*, the master determined the number of talents to give to each servant **according to each person's ability**.

12. In *Matthew 25:21, 23*, each person was commended on the basis of **his faithfulness**.

13. According to *II Corinthians 5:17-20*, one of our greatest responsibilities as believers is **to present the message of reconciliation to unbelievers**.

14. According to *Ephesians 5:15-16*, I am **to be careful how I walk and make the most of the time that God has given me**.

15. Answers will vary regarding areas in which you are using time unwisely.

16. Answers will vary regarding how can you make the most of your opportunities.

17. According to *Romans 6:12-13*, our bodies belong to **God**.

18. Answers will vary regarding specific responsibilities we have in being stewards of our bodies; for example: (a) **getting adequate rest and sleep**, (b) **exercising properly**, (c) **maintaining a nutritious diet**, (d) **wearing appropriate clothing**, and (e) **maintaining sexual purity**.

19. The important message of *Luke 16:10* is that **faithfulness is required in every aspect of our lives — whether we consider the thing to be little or big**.

20. The "put-off" and "put-on" in *Matthew 6:19-21* are: (a) "Put-off": **laying up treasures upon earth** and (b) "Put-on": **laying up treasures in heaven**.

21. The three provisions of God mentioned in Section **I**. are: (a) **God's Son**, (b) **God's Word**, and (c) **God's Spirit**.

22. According to *I Peter 4:10*, God gifted **every believer** spiritually.

23. A person receives the gifting **at spiritual birth (as indicated by the fact that each believer *has received* the giftedness)**.

24. According to *I Peter 4:10*, the purpose of the gifts is **to serve others, not self**.

25. According to *I Corinthians 12:7-11*, **the Holy Spirit** determines what gifts believers receive.

26. The Holy Spirit distributes the gifts for the good of **all believers**.

27. According to *I Corinthians 4:1-2*, stewards are required **to be faithful**.

28. You responsible for **none** of the results.

29. When we complain that we don't have enough material things or abilities that others have, we are ultimately blaming **God because in His sovereignty, He could give us all those things**.

30. God has gifted **every believer** spiritually.

31. I am to use my spiritual gifting to serve **God and others**.

Student Workbook for the Self-Confrontation Bible Study
- Supplement 1 -
© Biblical Counseling Foundation

32. The best way to determine how God may have gifted me is **by concentrating on ministering as I am provided opportunities. God will show me how I can be most effective**.

33. Answers will vary regarding the most significant truth learned in completing this lesson.

LESSON 11

1. The four elements of how to face, deal with, and endure any temptation to anger or bitterness are: (a) **biblical understanding**, (b) **biblical hope**, (c) **biblical change**, and (d) **biblical practice**.

2. To justify expressing angry thoughts outwardly without physically harming the person is wrong because **angry thoughts and speech are just as sinful as beating someone physically**.

3. According to *Matthew 15:18-19*, anger comes from **the heart**.

4. According to *Proverbs 29:11*, the difference between the foolish and wise man is that **a fool loses his temper, but a wise man holds it back**.

5. Answers will vary, but a typical response would be "**calm, and cheerful**."

6. In *James 1:19*, the "put-off" is **anger (implied)**.

7. In *James 1:19*, the "put-ons" are **quick to hear, slow to speak, slow to anger**.

8. In *Ephesians 4:31-32*, the "put-offs" are **bitterness, wrath, anger, clamor, slander, and malice**.

9. In *Ephesians 4:31-32*, the "put-ons" are **kindness, tenderheartedness, and forgiveness**.

10. In *Colossians 3:8, 12-14*, the "put-offs" are **anger, wrath, malice, slander, and abusive speech**.

11. In *Colossians 3:8, 12-14*, the "put-ons" are **compassion, kindness, humility, gentleness, patience, bearing with one another, forgiving each other, and love**.

12. The Scripture verse that shows that if anger is not dealt with quickly, it can gain control and give the devil a foothold is *Ephesians 4:26-27*.

13. Anger comes from **the heart**.

14. **No**, a person is not responsible for angry feelings.

15. **Yes**, a person can be angry without sinning **if he is simultaneously responding in the same way God responds (merciful, gracious, compassionate, forgiving, abundant in lovingkindness and truth, etc.)**.

16. Answers will vary regarding some key verses for use in developing an *"Daily Practices" Plan* regarding anger; for example: *Ephesians 4:31-32* and *Colossians 3:8, 12-14*.

17. Answers will vary regarding some key verses for use in developing an *"Overcoming Temptations" Plan* regarding anger; for example: *James 1:19* and *Ephesians 4:26-27*.

18. Answers will vary regarding the most significant truth learned in completing this lesson.

LESSON 12

1. The first two elements of how to face, deal with, and endure problems biblically are: (a) **biblical understanding**, and (b) **biblical hope**.

2. The last two elements of how to face, deal with, and endure problems biblically are: (a) **biblical change** and (b) **biblical practice**.

3. According to *I John 4:20-21*, those who say that they love God, but do not love their brother **are liars; they cannot love God**.

4. According to *Matthew 6:14-15*, if someone will not forgive those against whom he has taken offense, the consequence is that **God will not forgive him**.

5. According to *Ecclesiastes 12:14* and *Romans 2:5-6*, God will bring to judgment **every deed of our entire lives**.

6. According to *I Corinthians 10:6, 11*, the sins of the Israelites are recorded in the Scriptures **as examples for our instruction that we might not sin**.

7. According to *Ephesians 4:32*, **we are to forgive others just as God in Christ has forgiven us**.

8. **No**, there are no conditions that would preclude forgiving another person.

9. **No**, I should not go to a person to tell him that I forgive him if he has not asked for forgiveness.

10. According to *Luke 17:3-4*, if someone offends us frequently **we are to forgive every time**.

11. In *Luke 17:5*, the response of the disciples to Jesus' teaching on forgiveness is: **"increase our faith." In other words, "we can't do it."**

12. In *Luke 17:6-10*, Jesus teaches that **a lack of faith was not their problem; pride was their problem. They were not willing to be treated like unworthy slaves**.

13. When Peter brings up the subject of forgiveness in *Matthew 18:21*, Jesus' answer in *verse 22* is that **you must forgive seventy times seven; in other words every time without limit**.

14. The message Jesus was delivering was that **not to forgive is extremely serious**.

15. In *Matthew 5:23-24*, the Lord says I should **go and be reconciled with those who have something against me**.

16. Answers will vary regarding ways to tell that my brother has something against me. For example, **he may stare angrily at me** or **he may talk to others in a demeaning way about me**.

17. According to *Romans 12:18*, **we are to be at peace with others as far as it depends on us**.

18. **No**, I cannot control the response of others.

19. **No**, I am not responsible for the response of others.

20. God says those who say that they love God, but do not love their brother **are liars; they do not love God**.

21. If someone will not forgive those who offend him, **God will not forgive him**.

22. **No**, when we forgive, does not God require us to forget.

23. Regarding how many times we are to forgive someone who offends us frequently, Jesus says **we are to forgive every time**.

24. **No**, that does not mean I am necessarily to release the offender from the consequences of his sin.

25. **No**, it is not possible nor ever necessary for me to forgive myself.

26. **No**, it is not possible nor ever necessary for me to forgive God.

27. **The first one to realize there is a lack of reconciliation** should take the initiative to be reconciled with another person.

28. Answers will vary regarding the most significant truth learned in completing this lesson.

LESSON 13

1. If, when I am in prayer, I remember that my brother has something against me, my first priority is to **be reconciled with that person as quickly as possible**.

2. The final two elements of how to face, deal with, and endure problems biblically are: (a) **biblical change** and (b) **biblical practice**.

3. Answers will vary regarding specific actions of biblical love which you have difficulty demonstrating.

4. Before I go to reprove someone, I must properly prepare myself by: (a) **judging myself biblically** and (b) **forgiving the offender's sin in my heart**.

5. If he repents, I am to: (a) **grant full forgiveness**, (b) **provide biblical counsel for him to be reconciled with God and others**, and (c) **help him to return to full fellowship and useful service in the body of Christ**.

6. According to *I John 3:8-10*, a person who deliberately continues to practice a sin without repentance gives evidence **that he is not a believer**.

7. According to *James 3:5-6*, the tongue (a) **is a fire** and (b) **it defiles the entire body**.

8. Two types of people refered to in *Proverbs 9:7-9* are: (a) **a scoffer (or fool)** and (b) **a wise person**.

9. According to *Proverbs 18:13*, **we should not answer before we listen carefully to what the other person is saying**.

10. Answers will vary regarding a time that you did not practice this principle with an individual at home, church, or school.

11. Answers will vary regarding whether this is something for which you need to ask forgiveness.

12. According to *Proverbs 18:2*, the fool is interested **only in revealing his own mind**.

13. Instead, as a believer we should **listen to what others have to say**.

14. According to *Proverbs 18:17*, when we hear one side of the story first, we are tempted to conclude **that the person speaking is giving an accurate description of what took place**.

15. Before drawing a conclusion and taking action we should **talk to the other person or persons involved**.

16. According to *Ephesians 4:15*, we are to speak the truth **in love**.

17. The "put-off" and "put-on" in *I Peter 3:9* are: (a) "Put-off": **returning evil for evil, or insult for insult** and (b) "Put-on": **giving a blessing instead**.

18. The "put-off" and "put-on" in *Ephesians 5:4* are: (a) "Put-off": **filthy talk, silly talk, coarse jesting** and (b) "Put-on": **giving thanks**.

19. The "put-off" and "put-on" in *I Timothy 6:20* are: (a) "Put-off": **worldly and empty chatter** and (b) "Put-on": **guarding what has been entrusted to me**.

20. The "put-off" and "put-on" in *Proverbs 10:19* are: (a) "Put-off": **many words** and (b) "Put-on": **restraining my lips**.

21. According to *Proverbs 20:19, 26:20*, I should not engage in **slander, gossip**.

22. According to *Isaiah 55:8-11*, I should speak **God's Word**.

23. According to *Ephesians 4:29*, I should speak **wholesome words according to the need of the moment that they may give grace to the hearer**.

24. **No**, to love biblically, God does not require me to feel good about it.

25. **No**, for me to act in a loving way toward another person, that other person need not feel good about it.

26. Before reproving someone else, I am to: (a) **judge myself biblically** and (b) **forgive the offender's sin in my heart**.

27. According to *Proverbs 9:7-9*, if I try to counsel someone who does not want counsel **he may dishonor me, insult me, and hate me**.

28. According to *Proverbs 10:19*, if we use many words **transgression is unavoidable**.

29. Answers will vary regarding the most significant truth learned in completing this lesson.

LESSON 14

1. According to *Malachi 2:14*, the marriage agreement is **a covenant**.

2. In *Ephesians 5:24-27*, the marriage relationship is compared to **the relationship between Christ and the church**.

3. Some aspects of the relationship between Christ and His church in *Ephesians 5:24-27* are: (a) **the church is subject to Christ** and (b) **Christ loved the church and gave Himself up for her**.

4. According to *Galatians 3:28*, men and women **are one in Christ** in terms of spiritual status.

5. The emphasis of *I Corinthians 1:10* is **that there be no divisions among believers; that they be of the same mind and judgment**.

6. With respect to our desires, *Romans 12:10b* says that **we should give preference and honor to others**.

7. Answers will vary regarding Scripture passages that apply to the area of decision-making.

8. According to *Mark 10:43-45*, if you are to be highly regarded in God's kingdom you are to **be a servant to others**.

9. According to *I Corinthians 7:3-4*, the wife should give her body **to her husband**.

10. According to *I Corinthians 7:3-4*, the husband should give his body **to his wife**.

11. According to *Philippians 4:11*, Paul learned **to be content in every situation**.

12. The key principle for living as a spouse: (a) in *II Corinthians 5:9* is to **have as my ambition to be pleasing to the Lord**; and (b) in *Philippians 2:3-4* is to **be a servant to others**.

13. According to *Psalm 119:165*, I can have hope even in a difficult marriage relationship because **if I keep God's commandments, nothing and no one can make me stumble**.

14. According to *Ezekiel 18:20*, I can have hope even in a difficult marriage relationship because **I am only responsible before God for my own deeds, not someone else's**.

15. God establishes a marriage by **covenant**.

16. A covenant is only broken **at death**.

17. **God's Word** is the ultimate authority for principles of decision-making in the home.

18. When making decisions in the home, a husband and wife should work toward **unity, agreement, and answers that are based on biblical principles**.

19. When none of God's commands directly apply to a matter, spouses are to **give preference to one another** as they make decisions.

20. **The husband** is the human leader in the home.

21. **The Lord** is the ultimate head of all in the home.

22. **No**, nothing or no one should ever be allowed to control my relationship with the Lord.

23. Answers will vary regarding the most significant truth learned in completing this lesson.

LESSON 15

1. The final two elements of how to face, deal with, and endure problems biblically are: (a) **biblical change** and (b) **biblical practice**.

2. In *Principle 64*, the "put-offs" and "put-ons" for husbands are: (a) "Put-offs": **being harsh or embittered towards wives** and (b) "Put-ons": **loving, understanding, and being a servant**.

3. In *Principle 65*, the "put-offs" and "put-ons" for wives are: (a) "Put-offs": **being quarrelsome and contentious** and (b) "Put-ons": **loving, submissiveness, and respectfulness**.

4. In *Principle 66*, the "put-offs" and "put-ons" for spouses are: (a) "Put-offs": **selfish desires** and (b) "Put-ons": **pleasing God and serving spouse**.

5. According to *Matthew 20:26-28*, the purpose of Jesus' coming to earth was **to serve**.

6. According to *John 5:30*, Jesus sought **His Father's** will exclusively.

7. The "put-offs" and "put-ons" in *Ephesians 5:18*, are: (a) "Put-off": **getting drunk with wine**; and (b) "Put-on": **being filled with the Holy Spirit**.

8. According to *Ephesians 5:19-20*, **speaking to one another in psalms and hymns and spiritual songs, singing and making melody with his heart to the Lord; always giving thanks to God for all things in the name of our Lord Jesus Christ** are some of the personal evidences of one who submits himself to the control of the Holy Spirit.

9. According to *Ephesians 5:21*, **being subject to one another in the fear of Christ** is the interpersonal evidence of one who submits himself to the control of the Holy Spirit.

10. According to *Ephesians 5:22, 25*, some interpersonal evidences of submission to the control of the Holy Spirit are that: (a) **wives will be subject to their husbands as to the Lord**, and (b) **husbands will love their wives just as Christ also loved the church**.

11. In *Ephesians 6:1-2*, some of the evidences of submitting to the control of the Holy Spirit are that **children will honor and obey their parents**.

12. In *Ephesians 6:4*, some of the evidences of submitting to the control of the Holy Spirit are that **parents will not provoke their children to anger, but will bring them up in the discipline and instruction of the Lord**.

13. In *Ephesians 6:5*, another evidence of submitting to the control of the Holy Spirit are that **employees will serve their employers**.

14. In *Ephesians 6:9*, an evidence of submitting to the control of the Holy Spirit is that **employers will consider their employees as more important than themselves**.

15. According to *Proverbs 3:5-6*, we are *not* to rely on **our own understanding**.

16. Rather, we are to **trust in the Lord with all our hearts and acknowledge Him in all our ways**.

17. Answers will vary regarding areas in which you have to go against your feelings to carry out a God-given responsibility.

18. According to *Romans 12:20-21*, even when we regard others as our enemies, we are to **feed them if they are hungry and give them something to drink if they are thirsty**.

19. According to *Romans 12:20-21*, we are not to **be overcome by evil**.

20. The "put-offs" and "put-ons" in *I Peter 3:8-9*, are: (a) "Put-offs": **returning evil for evil, returning insult for insult** and (b) "Put-on": **giving a blessing**.

21. In *I Peter 2:13*, **we are to submit to every human institution**.

22. In *I Peter 2:18*, **we are to be submissive even to those who are unreasonable**.

23. In *I Peter 2:20*, when we patiently endure suffering for doing what is right, we find **favor with God**.

24. In *I Peter 2:21*, our example is **Jesus Christ**.

25. In *I Peter 2:23*, Jesus **kept entrusting Himself to His Father**.

26. Answers will vary regarding whether you have been in a position of leadership or responsibility where you thought that you were due more respect.

27. Answers will vary regarding how you responded in a position of leadership or responsibility where you thought that you were due more respect; for example, "**I was angry and bitter.**"

28. Answers will vary regarding how you should have responded in a position of leadership or responsibility where you thought that you were due more respect; for example, "**I should have followed the example of Jesus by trusting myself to my loving Father in heaven instead.**"

29. In light of *I Peter 3:1* and the prior passage, **wives are to be submissive to their husbands even if the husbands are disobedient to the Word**.

30. In *I Peter 3:7*, **husbands are to live with their wives in an understanding way. They are to treat their wives as weaker vessels physically, and grant them honor as fellow heirs of the grace of life**.

31. We are to place ourselves under the complete control of **the Holy Spirit**.

32. We should submit ourselves as servants to **everyone**.

33. Answers will vary regarding the most significant truth learned in completing this lesson.

LESSON 16

1. In *I Thessalonians 2:7*, the Apostle Paul gave the example of **a nursing mother who tenderly cares for her own children** to describe how he discipled the Thessalonians.

2. In *I Thessalonians 2:11*, the Apostle Paul gave the example of **a father who exhorts, and encourages, and implores his own children**.

3. *Isaiah 55:11* says that God's Word **shall not return to Him without accomplishing what He desires and without succeeding in the matter for which He sent it**.

4. The characteristics of discipleship contained in *II Timothy 2:24-26* include: **Not quarrelsome, kind to all, able to teach, patient when wronged, with gentleness correcting those who are in opposition**.

5. The "put-off" and "put-ons" in *Ephesians 6:4* are: (a) "Put-off": **provoking children to anger** and (b) "Put-ons": **bringing children up in the discipline and instruction of the Lord**.

6. In *Deuteronomy 6:5-6*, the primary responsibility of parents in training their children is **to love God and keep His commandments**.

7. In *Deuteronomy 6:7*, my responsibility to my children is to **teach God's commandments to them diligently**.

8. Answers will vary. Some examples of where and when you can be teaching your children in the course of a normal day might include: (a) **when they are in the midst of a difficulty**, (b) **when they observe that they have sinned**, or (c) **when they are wronged**.

9. In *Proverbs 14:15*, the difference between a wise or prudent person and a naïve or simple person is that **the naïve believes everything, but the prudent man considers his steps**.

10. In *I Thessalonians 2:8*, Paul was pleased not only to give the Thessalonians the Gospel, but also **his own life**.

11. Regarding our own children, this tells us that **we are to give them our lives**.

12. In *Mark 1:17*, Jesus told the disciples *what* to do, which was to **"follow Me."**

13. In *Mark 1:17*, Jesus told the disciples *why*, which was to make them **fishers of men**.

14. *Mark 6:7*, Jesus sent the disciples out to minister **two by two**.

15. Answers will vary, for example: (a) **faithfulness *(Luke 16:10)***, (b) **serving one another *(I Peter 4:10)***, (c) **diligence *(Hebrews 6:11)***, (d) **obedience *(Ephesians 6:1-3)***, and (e) **helping preserve unity in the family *(Ephesians 4:3)***.

16. According to *Proverbs 3:5-6*, as a parent, I can trust **the Lord's** wisdom to be perfectly reliable.

17. Three of the things parents are to be toward their children are: (a) **godly examples**, (b) **godly servants**, and (c) **godly disciplers**.

18. Five steps of discipleship Jesus used that can also be applied to bringing up children are: (a) **tell him what and why**, (b) **show him how**, (c) **get him started**, (d) **keep him going**, and (e) **train him to disciple others**.

19. Answers will vary regarding the most significant truth learned in completing this lesson.

LESSON 17

1. The "put-offs" and "put-ons" in *Ephesians 6:4* are: (a) "Put-off": **provoking children to anger** and (b) "Put-on": **bringing up children in the discipline and instruction of the Lord**.

2. According to *Proverbs 22:15a*, the tendency of a child is **to be foolish**.

3. According to *Jeremiah 17:9*, even a child's heart **is deceitful and desperately wicked**.

4. Answers will vary. Some examples of ways that children could be taught to deny themselves daily and to follow the Lord and serve and build up others in their early years would be: (a) **give to others**, (b) **help parents clean the house**, and (c) **speak respectfully to others**.

5. According to *Hebrews 12:10-11*, the short term feelings associated with discipline are **not joyful, but sorrowful (or grievous)**.

6. In *Genesis 2:16-17*, the Lord gave Adam and Eve **one** command.

7. The command was, "**Do not eat of the tree of the knowledge of good and evil.**"

8. According to *Deuteronomy 11:26-28*, **obedience to God's commands** will bring blessings.

9. According to *Deuteronomy 11:26-28*, **disobedience to God's commands** will bring curses.

10. According to *Ecclesiastes 8:11*, the discipline should be administered **quickly**.

Student Workbook for the Self-Confrontation Bible Study
- Supplement 1 -
© Biblical Counseling Foundation

11. It is important for the child that the discipline be administered quickly **to help him not continue to do evil**.

12. According to *Proverbs 22:15*, the purpose of the rod of discipline is **to remove foolishness from the heart of the child**.

13. Answers will vary regarding what *Matthew 21:28-31* says about responding to your children. A typical answer would be that **parents must give the child an opportunity to show regret**.

14. *Matthew 5:23-24* indicates that when I have sinned against someone I must **be reconciled to those against whom I have sinned**.

15. **No**, I am not exempt from asking forgiveness of my children just because I am their parent.

16. According to *Acts 2:42-47*, the first century believers demonstrated their devotion to God through: (a) **teaching, fellowship, and prayer** *(verse 42)*, (b) **sharing or ministering to one another** *(verses 44-45)*, and (c) **praising God** *(verse 47)*.

17. Answers will vary regarding a plan for family devotions.

18. **All** of the commandments that apply to adults should also be taught to children **except those that uniquely are commanded to parents**.

19. The difference between discipline and punishment is that **discipline is for *restoration*, while punishment is for carrying out judgment**.

20. Parents should use **discipline rather than punishment** with their children.

21. If parents sin against their children, they should **confess their sins to God and to the ones offended, and ask forgiveness**.

22. Answers will vary regarding the results of having regular family devotional times; for example: (a) **ministry to all members of the family**, (b) **training of all family members in godliness**, or (c) **preserving the unity of the family**.

23. Answers will vary regarding the most significant truth learned in completing this lesson.

LESSON 18

1. The reason for David's depressed feelings was **his sin**.

2. In *I Kings 19:1-4*, Elijah experienced **fear, defeat, desire to die**.

3. In *Jonah 4:1-11*, Jonah experienced **anger at the Lord, desire to die**.

4. Answers will vary regarding problems that you or another believer are having that might seem, from a human perspective, to be too difficult to bear.

5. According to *II Corinthians 1:3-5*, the believer's comfort comes primarily from **God**.

6. **No**, depression is not exempted from this promise.

7. In *Genesis 4:5*, Cain's problem was that **he was angry and depressed**.

8. In *Genesis 4:7*, the Lord says that Cain **should do well (i.e., obey God)**.

9. According to *Ephesians 5:15-16*, we are to **make the best use of** our time.

10. According to *Colossians 3:23-24*, **we are to do our work heartily for the Lord**.

11. Regarding responsibilities we know that we should be doing, *James 4:17* tells us that **if we do not do them, we sin**.

12. We are not responsible for our **feelings** of depression.

13. But we are responsible for our **deeds (i.e., thoughts, speech, and actions)**.

14. Answers will vary regarding reasons why there is hope for a depressed person; for example (a) **God will not allow anyone to be tempted beyond what he can handle** and (b) **anyone can obey God no matter how he feels**.

15. **No**, if I am being responsible to do what the Lord commands me to do, God does not promise that my feelings will change.

16. Answers will vary regarding the most significant truth learned in completing this lesson.

LESSON 19

1. Answers will vary regarding common situations where Christians are tempted to worry; for example, Christians may worry: (a) **that their children may not get saved** or (b) **that they will not have enough money**.

2. In *I John 4:18*, fear is connected with **concern about punishment (torment)**.

3. In *Matthew 25:25-26*, the "one-talent" man said that the reason he did not make more money for his master was his **fear of the master**.

4. In *Matthew 25:25-26*, the master said the man's problem was **wickedness and laziness**.

5. In *II Corinthians 11:28*, Paul's concern was **for all the churches**.

6. In *Matthew 6:33-34*, the one who worries forgets that **if we seek God's kingdom and His righteousness first, He will provide for all our needs**.

7. The "put-offs" and "put-ons" in *II Timothy 1:7* are: (a) "Put-off": **fear** and (b) "Put-ons": **power, love, discipline (sound mind, self-discipline, self-control)**.

8. The "put-offs" and "put-ons" in *I John 4:18* are: (a) "Put-off": **fear** and (b) "Put-on": **love**.

9. The "put-offs" and "put-ons" in *Matthew 6:33-34* are: (a) "Put-off": **anxiety (worry) about tomorrow** and (b) "Put-ons": **seeking God's kingdom and His righteousness**.

10. The "put-off" in *Philippians 4:6-9* is **anxiety**.

11. The "put-ons" in *Philippians 4:6-9* are: (a) **prayer and supplication with thanksgiving**, (b) **meditating on things that are virtuous and praiseworthy**, and (c) **practicing what I have learned**.

12. A verse that indicates that sinful thoughts are just as serious as unrighteous speech and actions is *Matthew 5:28*.

13. **The condition of the heart** rather than the external circumstances causes fear or worry.

14. The focus of someone who is fearful is **on self**.

15. It is important to remember that we are responsible to be **faithful**.

16. Answers will vary regarding the value of a "To Do" List in dealing with worry; for example, **it helps to concentrate fully on the present task**.

17. Answers will vary regarding the most significant truth learned in completing this lesson.

LESSON 20

1. Answers will vary regarding examples of life-dominating practices of sin listed in *I Corinthians 6:9-10*; for example: (a) **fornicator**, (b) **idolater**, (c) **adulterer**, (d) **homosexual**, (e) **thief**, (f) **covetous person**, (g) **drunkard**, (h) **reviler**, (i) **swindler**.

2. Words that characterize life-dominating practices of sin are "**enslave**," "**power over**," and "**continue**."

3. According to *Galatians 5:16*, I can be enabled not to carry out the desires of the flesh if I **walk by the Spirit, and I will not carry out the desire of the flesh**.

4. Answers will vary regarding examples of how a life-dominating practice of sin such as drunkenness could affect the areas displayed in the diagram; for example, drunkenness may lead to: (a) **greatly reduced effectiveness at work**, (b) **illness due to lack of nutrition, lack of exercise**, or (c) **strained relationships due to bad behavior**.

5. According to *Romans 6:16*, someone becomes controlled by sin if **he chooses to present himself to sin as a slave**.

6. According to *Romans 6:17-18*, we were freed from **(the power of) sin**.

7. According to *I Corinthians 6:9-11*, those who have been controlled by a life-dominating practice of sin **are made clean and are no longer controlled by sin** when they become believers.

8. According to *II Corinthians 11:14-15*, Satan presents himself **as an angel of light**.

9. **No**, the disciples did not have any suspicion that Judas was going to betray Jesus.

10. Opposite of: (a) "high" is "**low**," (b) "hot" is "**cold**," (c) "white" is "**black**," and (d) "God" is **nothing**.

11. According to *Colossians 2:9-10*, the Lord **is the head over all rule and authority**.

12. According to *Job 1:12*, Satan can do **only what God allows**.

13. According to *John 16:11*, Satan **has been judged**.

14. According to *I John 3:8*, one of Jesus' purposes for coming to earth was **to destroy the works of the devil**.

15. According to *Hebrews 2:14-15*, Jesus took away Satan's power of death **through His death on the cross**.

16. The main truth of *I John 4:4* is that **He who is in me is greater than the one in the world**.

17. According to *James 4:7*, believers are to **resist the devil**.

18. According to *James 4:7*, the result of believers resisting the devil is that **the devil will flee from them**.

19. In *Romans 8:37*, believers are promised **overwhelming victory**.

20. If some possession tempts us to stumble, what are we to **remove it**.

21. Answers will vary regarding examples of life-dominating practices of sin; for example, **drunkenness, pattern of anger, continuing lust**.

22. The problem with calling something a disease when, according to God, it is actually a sin is that **it denies the person's responsibility for his sin and puts the supposed responsibility for the "cure" in someone else's hands**.

23. A person can have hope by calling a life-dominating practice, "sin" because sin **can be confessed and overcome immediately**.

24. According to *Galatians 5:16*, I can be enabled not to carry out the desires of the flesh **by walking in obedience to the Holy Spirit**.

25. Answers will vary regarding the most significant truth learned in completing this lesson.

LESSON 21

1. According to *Ephesians 5:18*, we are not to **be drunk with wine (i.e., the implication is not to be controlled by the flesh).**

2. Instead, according to *Ephesians 5:18*, we are to **be filled with the Spirit**.

3. To be filled with the Spirit means **to place myself under the control of the Holy Spirit**.

4. The "put-offs" and "put-ons" in *II Timothy 2:22* are: (a) "Put-off": **flee youthful lusts** and (b) "Put-ons": **pursue righteousness, faith, love, and peace, with those who call on the Lord from a pure heart**.

5. With regard to dealing with life-dominating practices of sin, (a) **to flee means to run away as fast as possible; not to dally or hesitate** and (b) **to pursue means to run after with all the strength that I have; to be involved totally in godly activities**.

6. Based on *Proverbs 27:17*, the value of spending substantial time with other fervently committed believers is that, as **iron sharpens iron, so one man sharpens another**.

NOTE: Answers to Questions 7-10 may vary regarding examples from Scripture of fleeing sin. Typical answers are provided for your benefit.

7. **Joseph, son of Jacob** practiced the principle of fleeing sin and pursuing righteousness.

8. **Joseph, fled from Potiphar's wife**.

9. **King David** did *not* practice this principle, and it led to spiritual defeat.

10. **King David lusted after Bathsheba and as a consequence, he displeased God and lost his son**.

11. According to *I John 3:7-10*, one who continually practices sin **cannot legitimately claim to be a believer**.

12. According to *Ephesians 6:10-13*, the purpose of putting on the full armor of God is **to stand firm against the schemes of the devil and to resist evil**.

13. The armor of God listed in (a) *Ephesians 6:14* are the **belt of truth and breastplate of righteousness**; (b) *Ephesians 6:15* is **shoes (sandals) made of the preparation of the gospel of peace**; (c) *Ephesians 6:16* is the **shield of faith**; and (d) *Ephesians 6:17* are the **helmet of salvation, and the sword of the Spirit, which is the Word of God**.

14. According to *Matthew 18:7-9*, **if I don't eliminate stumbling blocks, I will suffer eternal consequences**.

15. The two parts to the commandment in *Matthew 28:19-20* are: (a) **Baptizing in the name of the Father and the Son and the Holy Spirit (i.e., evangelizing)**, and (b) **teaching those I disciple to obey all that Jesus commanded**.

16. According to *II Corinthians 5:18-20*, as an ambassador of Christ, every believer has **the ministry of reconciliation**.

17. According to *Colossians 2:8*, the world distracts the believer from living by faith **through philosophy and empty deception, according to the tradition of men, according to the elementary principles of the world, rather than according to Christ**.

18. According to *I Corinthians 4:2*, the main characteristic of a steward is **to be faithful**.

19. Regarding faithfulness, in *Matthew 25:21* and *23*, the master said to his slaves, **"Well done, good and faithful slave."**

20. The warning in *James 1:22* is that **if I am a hearer of the Word, but not a doer, I will delude myself**.

21. Answers will vary regarding specific actions that could be taken by someone enslaved by a life-dominating practice of gambling; for example: **don't even drive by a casino; make sure you have someone with you when you go to the store, so that you won't buy a lottery ticket; spend time in fellowship with Christians when you would have previously gone to a casino**.

22. *Psalm 1:2* says to put on **meditating in the Word of God day and night** in the place of the old, sinful way of life.

23. *Psalm 1:3* says the result will be that **he will be like a tree firmly planted, and he will prosper in whatever he does**.

24. According to *II Peter 1:3*, God has granted to us **everything pertaining to life and godliness**.

25. The three resources provided by God that are listed in Lesson 3 are: (a) **the Word of God**, (b) **the Holy Spirit**, and (c) **prayer**.

26. **No**, there is nothing lacking in God's resources that would make us incapable of having victory over any area of sin.

27. According to *II Peter 1:8*, the spiritual qualities **should be increasing so that I am neither useless nor unfruitful in my knowledge of our Lord Jesus Christ**.

28. According to *II Peter 1:9*, one of our problems if we are not growing to become more Christlike is that **I am blind or short-sighted, having forgotten my purification from my former sins**.

29. Two things that especially need to be emphasized in dealing with a life-dominating practice of sin are that **radical biblical changes must take place**: (a) **quickly** and (b) **thoroughly**.

30. According to *Matthew 18:7-9*, **if I don't eliminate stumbling blocks, I will suffer eternal consequences**.

31. The purpose of putting on the full armor of God is **to stand firm against the schemes of the devil and to resist evil**.

32. It is important not to take on the responsibilities of another person with a life-dominating practice of sin **because consequences may be the only way to get the offender's attention and I would be placing a stumbling block to his restoration**.

33. Answers will vary regarding the most significant truth learned in completing this lesson.

LESSON 22

1. The conclusion stated in *Ecclesiastes 12:13* is **fear God and keep His commandments**.

2. In *Romans 13:14*, we are to put off **the lusts of the flesh**.

3. In *Romans 13:14*, we are to put on **the Lord Jesus Christ**.

4. In *Romans 13:9-10*, God's commands are summed up as "**Love your neighbor as yourself.**"

5. "The Golden Rule" in *Matthew 7:12* says to **treat others the same way you would like them to treat you**.

6. According to *I Peter 4:12-19*, we are to expect **fiery ordeals or tests** as part of life.

7. The purpose of fiery ordeals or tests is **that when the glory of Christ is revealed, I may exult and be blessed**.

8. Answers will vary regarding the standards that have made a particular impression on you in this Bible study.

LESSON 23

No answers.

LESSON 24

1. As disciple makers, Jesus said in *Matthew 28:20* that we should teach **everything that Jesus commanded**.

2. The four spiritual generations identified in *II Timothy 2:2* are: (a) **the Apostle Paul**, (b) **Timothy**, (c) **faithful men**, and (d) **others**.

3. If a person is tangled up in or caught up in a trespass, then I am to **restore him**.

4. **Those who are spiritual** are to do the restoring.

5. **The one who lives in the Spirit and walks in the Spirit** is the one who is spiritual.

6. Some characteristics of how to help someone caught in a trespass according to *Galatians 6:1-2* are: (a) **restoring in a spirit of gentleness**, (b) **being careful not to be tempted**, and (c) **bearing one another's burdens in love**.

7. The warning as I am restoring another is that **I should look to myself, lest I too be tempted**.

8. The law of Christ referred to in *Galatians 6:2* is **the new commandment — the law of love**.

9. According to *Galatians 6:5*, the overall goal is **to help a person carry his own burden**.

10. According to *Romans 15:14*, **believers are to admonish one another**.

11. According to *Ephesians 4:11-22*, a primary purpose of pastors and teachers in the local church is **to equip believers for the work of service, to the building up of the body of Christ**.

12. In *Exodus 18:13, 16*, Moses **judged the people when they had a dispute and made known God's statutes and laws**.

13. In *Exodus 18:14*, **Jethro asked Moses why he judged the people alone**.

14. In *Exodus 18:15*, Moses' response to Jethro's question was that **Moses judged the people because they were coming to him with their questions**.

15. In *Exodus 18:17-18*, Jethro said that **what Moses did was not good. He will wear out both himself and the people**.

16. In *Exodus 18:20*, Jethro told Moses to teach **God's statutes and the laws about how the people were to live**.

17. In *Exodus 18:21*, Moses was to select as leaders **able men who fear God, men of truth, and those who hate dishonest gain**.

18. The first part of Jesus' command in *Matthew 7:5* is to **take the log out of my eye**.

19. The second part of *Matthew 7:5* says that I will then be prepared **to take the speck out of my brother's eye**.

VICTORY OVER FAILURES PLAN: GUIDELINES AND WORKSHEETS

VICTORY OVER FAILURES PLAN:
GUIDELINES AND WORKSHEETS

This booklet is published by the Biblical Counseling Foundation, Inc., a non profit, non stock corporation founded in 1974 and incorporated in the Commonwealth of Virginia, USA, in 1977.

Copyright The contents of this publication are copyrighted © 2004, 2005 by the Biblical Counseling Foundation, Inc. All rights reserved. Reproduction in any manner in whole or in part, in English and/or other languages, or storage in a retrieval system, or transmission in any form or by any means — electronic, mechanical, visual, audio, or any other — except for brief quotations in printed reviews is prohibited without written permission of the Biblical Counseling Foundation (BCF).

Scripture taken from the New American Standard Bible, © 1960, 1962, 1963, 1968, 1971, 1972, 1973, 1975, 1977 by The Lockman Foundation. Used by permission.

ISBN 1-878114-44-1

First Printing, September, 2004
Second Printing, January, 2005
Third Printing, April 2005

42 600 Cook Street, Suite 100
Palm Desert, California 92211 5143 USA
Telephone: 760.773.2667
FAX: 760.340.3778
E mail for orders: orders@bcfministries.org
E mail for other: admin@bcfministries.org
Telephone for orders in the United States only: 877.933.9333
Website for orders and information: http://www.bcfministries.org

TABLE OF CONTENTS

INTRODUCTION TO THE VICTORY OVER FAILURES PLAN 5
    Overview 5
    Why develop a written plan? 6
    Materials needed to develop your plan 6
    Purposes of the **VICTORY OVER FAILURES PLAN** 7
    Your relationship with Jesus Christ — the basic foundation for biblical change 7
    Biblical hope for change 10
    The biblical process for change 11

GUIDELINES FOR COMPLETING THE VICTORY OVER FAILURES PLAN 13
    Description of the Problem 14
        Sample List of Problem Areas 15
        Sample Worksheet 1: Description of the Problem 16
    Lists of Specific Failures to Live Biblically 17
        Evaluation — Sample Worksheet 1: Description of the Problem 20
        Sample Worksheet 2: Lists of Specific Failures to Live Biblically 21
    "Put-offs" and "Put-ons" 22
        Sample Worksheet 3: "Put-offs" and "Put-ons" 24
    "Daily Practices" Plan 25
        Sample Worksheet 4: "Daily Practices" Plan 27
    "Overcoming Temptations" Plan 29
        Sample Worksheet 5: "Overcoming Temptations" Plan 31
    "Forgiveness/Reconciliation" Plan 33
        Sample Worksheet 6a: My Plan for Demonstrating Forgiveness 35
        Sample Worksheet 6b: My Plan for Asking Forgiveness 38

VICTORY OVER FAILURES PLAN BLANK WORKSHEETS 39
    Worksheet 1: Description of the Problem 40
    Worksheet 2: Lists of Specific Failures to Live Biblically 41
    Worksheet 3: "Put-offs" and "Put-ons" 42
    Worksheet 4: "Daily Practices" Plan 43
    Worksheet 5: "Overcoming Temptations" Plan 45
    Worksheet 6a: My Plan for Demonstrating Forgiveness 47
    Worksheet 6b: My Plan for Asking Forgiveness 48

© Biblical Counseling Foundation **Student Workbook for the Self-Confrontation Bible Study, Supplement 2**

INTRODUCTION
TO THE VICTORY OVER FAILURES PLAN

> You can never truly understand or help others, even in your own family, unless you first look thoroughly into your own life and deal with your own sins without compromise, excuses, or evasion (*based on Matthew 7:1-5; II Corinthians 1:3-5*).

Overview

The **VICTORY OVER FAILURES PLAN** is a biblically based tool that can help you apply God's Word in the power of the Holy Spirit, so that you may overcome any difficulty of life with the full expectation of complete and lasting victory. To live victoriously in a lasting, fruitful way, we first need to see how we have failed to live God's way, hence the phrase "victory over failures." By victory over "failures" we don't mean failures at business or failures in school. We mean having victory over failures to love biblically (what God calls sin) that keep us from having a joyful, vibrant, growing relationship with the Lord. Part of the process involves putting off the old manner of life and putting on new, righteous practices in their place (*Ephesians 4:22-24*). The **VICTORY OVER FAILURES PLAN** describes how to do that in very practical ways and gives you a format you can follow.

This booklet is a companion to the Biblical Counseling Foundation's *Self-Confrontation* manual. It can be used independently from the Self-Confrontation Course, but is best understood and applied along with the course. The Self-Confrontation Course is designed to lead you through a personal life application study of God's Word using the *Self-Confrontation* manual as a reference. This life application study focuses on how to live sacrificially for God and for others, rather than living for self. It presents biblical principles that are fundamental to living the kind of victorious, contented life God intended for you, regardless of the circumstances.

This booklet explains these and other biblical principles about how to have lasting change in your life. It asks you to identify a problem area in your life that you can then work on, applying the principles from God's Word in the power of the Holy Spirit. The objective is to help you to rely wholly on the Scriptures and the work of the Holy Spirit Himself, rather than to rely on the superficial remedies of the world, or on your own strength. There are vast contrasts between God's way of dealing with problems and the world's way (*Isaiah 55:8-11*). Only through applying God's principles can you expect lasting change. As you walk according to the biblical principles written in your **VICTORY OVER FAILURES PLAN**, you will develop Christlike character in your life. The changes will be enduring and meaningful, and you will be a faithful, fruitful vessel in God's hands.

The booklet starts with an explanation of why you should develop a *written* plan. Then, it describes the materials you will need, the purposes of the plan, foundations for biblical change, biblical hope for change, and the process for putting the plan together. The **VICTORY OVER FAILURES PLAN** is not just a one-time exercise, but is an organized, biblical approach that you can use to deal with tests, temptations, and sin throughout your life. You can also use it in helping others with their problems.

Why develop a written plan?

Problems in life are not unusual, but many believers, even those who have known Christ for years, have not learned how to deal biblically with difficult problems as part of the process of sanctification. They may experience grave difficulties at home or at work, disappointments with others, financial losses, health problems, etc. For most of their lives, many believers fluctuate between living in victory and living in defeat.

The Scriptures tell us that believers will always undergo spiritual battles *(John 16:33; Galatians 5:17)*. It is also true that God has given us victory in the Lord Jesus Christ *(Romans 8:28-38)*. Sadly, many have not learned how to live victoriously in the empowerment of the Holy Spirit. Often in ignorance, they continue to respond to problems the same way they responded as unbelievers. Therefore, it is vital that all believers learn how to face, deal with, and endure problems as they progress through life. Each believer needs a simple, organized way of evaluating the situation according to God's truth and developing a plan that, if followed, will bring complete and lasting change. This **VICTORY OVER FAILURES PLAN** has been developed to help believers become established in living God's way.

You might ask the question, "Why should I actually have a plan written out to deal with a difficulty in my life?" One reason is found in a careful study of *I Corinthians 10:12-14*. In this passage, *verse 13* provides great hope that God will not allow a temptation or trial in your life that is more than you can handle. The previous verse, *I Corinthians 10:12*, warns that we must take heed (to our spiritual walk), or we might fall into sin. Isn't it interesting that in the very passage where God gives us a great promise of His sovereignty, He also tells us not to be presumptuous or arrogant about our ability to withstand temptation on our own? He tells us to "be careful" or "be prepared." The verb "take heed" has the idea of being watchful on a continuing basis in anticipation of a future event. It is the same word that Jesus used when He warned the disciples to stay alert in anticipation of His return. In the same way, we need to be alert to when we might be tempted and to be prepared to respond the way the Lord commands. Then in *I Corinthians 10:14*, we are told, "therefore" (referring back to *verse 13*), to "flee idolatry." In other words, in light of God's providing us with the way to endure trials, He tells us not to hesitate when tempted, but take immediate and decisive action. The **VICTORY OVER FAILURES PLAN** will help you to be prepared to take decisive, godly action when temptations come. Many temptations can be anticipated, especially where we have been tempted previously, and have yielded and sinned. Many times, we even put ourselves in the path of temptation unnecessarily. Making biblical plans ahead of time will help you to remember what to do when you face temptation, and will be an indication of your commitment before God to handle trials His way, in the power of the Holy Spirit.

You may ask yourself, "Will I need to make written plans all my life?" After you have become established in overcoming temptations through the development and practice of biblical plans, you will become more able to think through how to deal with sins in your life. This is because the **VICTORY OVER FAILURES PLAN** has become part of your life. Then it will only be occasionally that you might need to write out a **VICTORY OVER FAILURES PLAN** for complicated matters.

Materials needed to develop your plan

The Bible

It is important that you use a literal translation of the Bible. While a paraphrased Bible may be useful as an expansion or supplemental study tool, it is important to memorize and understand the Bible in its most literal form. Because paraphrases are not translations, but interpretations, they may focus on man's insights rather than God's truth at certain points. When you study for your own benefit or to minister to others, it is important that you remain faithful to God's Word.

As you study this booklet, you will find that the biblical principles and precepts presented are substantiated with Scripture references which you are encouraged to look up as you progress. The Scripture references are listed in the order they are found in the Bible, not necessarily in the order of importance or clarity.

Whenever you see italicized parentheses with references to Scripture verses, each of the references listed directly substantiate the previous statement fully. Whenever you see the words *"based on"* before the list of references, the truth of the previous statement cannot be understood from a single reference, but can be seen from a study of all the referenced verses put together.

The *Self-Confrontation* manual

You will find it helpful to use the *Self-Confrontation* manual as a supplementary reference. It is designed to guide you through a set of biblical principles that are fundamental to living the kind of victorious, contented life God intended for us, regardless of the circumstances. The manual will always direct you to God's Word, not to man's opinion. In a sense, it is like a topical concordance. It contains many biblical references that cover both the fundamentals of the Christian life as well as how to deal with specific problem areas. For additional help, the guidelines in the next section refer at times to portions of the *Self-Confrontation* manual.

Purposes of the VICTORY OVER FAILURES PLAN

Based on biblical principles, the **VICTORY OVER FAILURES PLAN** guides you to victory even in the midst of any trial, test, or temptation of life. The **PLAN** has four purposes, and there are worksheets related to the purposes as shown below:

A. To help you learn how to examine (test, judge) yourself biblically *(Psalm 139:23-24; Matthew 7:1-5; I Corinthians 11:31; Galatians 6:4)*;

   Applies to Worksheets 1 and 2 on Pages 40 and 41

B. To help you recognize specific biblical "put-offs" and "put-ons" for daily living *(for example: Ephesians 4:22-32; Colossians 3:5-17)*;

   Applies to Worksheet 3 on Page 42

C. To help you develop and act upon specific plans for biblical change *(based on Titus 2:11-14; James 1:22-25)*; and

   Applies to Worksheets 4-6 on Pages 43-48

D. To help you make your specific biblical changes part of your daily walk in every area of your life *(based on Romans 6:12-13; Colossians 2:6; 3:2-17; II Timothy 3:16-17; I Peter 1:14-16)*.

   Applies to the entire plan

NOTE: *While these guidelines are useful for dealing with isolated sins that are only committed rarely, the most valuable use of the VICTORY OVER FAILURES PLAN is for dealing with sinful patterns where there has not been consistent victory.*

Your relationship with Jesus Christ — the basic foundation for biblical change

The *Self-Confrontation* manual provides an extensive scriptural study of how you can have victory in the midst of difficult trials, tests, and temptations. The next several sections provide a brief overview of some of the foundational biblical principles you should know before developing your **VICTORY OVER FAILURES PLAN**. So, before you start on the worksheets, take some time to read through these principles. At a minimum, read in your Bible the passages referenced in **boldface** print below.

- A. In order to change biblically, you must first recognize your inability to overcome life's problems in your own strength or by your own wisdom. Biblical change is only possible when you become a child of God.
    1. If you do not know Jesus Christ as your Lord and Savior, you have no capability to change biblically because you do not have:
        a. The indwelling power of the Holy Spirit (*based on John 14:17;* ***Romans 5:5b**, 8:9*),
        b. The understanding of the things of God (*I Corinthians 2:6-14, esp. verse 14*), and
        c. The hope to live in a manner pleasing to God (*based on **Romans 8:8**; Ephesians 2:12*).

        NOTE: You may be able to make some changes in your life here and there, but the changes will be superficial and temporary if you do not have a personal relationship with God.

    2. To become God's child you must:
        a. Repent of your sin (***Mark 1:15**; Luke 13:3; II Corinthians 7:10; II Peter 3:9*).

            In *Luke 13:3*, Jesus says that unless a person repents, he shall perish. Repentance is very important since it is an admission that you have been going against God's purposes, that you are sorry for opposing God, and you are turning around to go God's way.

        b. Wholeheartedly believe that the blood of Jesus Christ which was shed on the cross is the only means for receiving forgiveness for your sins (*Romans 3:23-25; 5:8; **6:23**; Ephesians 1:7; Colossians 1:19-23; I Timothy 2:5; I Peter 1:18-19*) and likewise, that Christ died for your sins according to the Scriptures, and that He was buried, and that He was raised on the third day according to the Scriptures (*I Corinthians 15:3-4*).

        c. Sincerely receive the Lord Jesus Christ into your life (***John 1:12**; I John 5:12*). In *John 1:12*, receiving and believing are synonyms. This leads to a deeper understanding of the biblical truth about belief. Jesus said in *John 17:3*, "And this is eternal life, that they may know Thee, the only true God, and Jesus Christ whom Thou hast sent." Receiving Jesus Christ is not merely believing in Christ intellectually; it includes committing yourself to an intimate, vital relationship with Him.

        d. Confess Jesus *as* Lord (*John 5:24; Romans 10:8-13*). Notice in ***Romans 10:9-10*** that salvation includes both believing in the heart and confessing with the mouth Jesus as Lord. This is a public declaration that Jesus is Lord. The word "Lord" means master. You are to submit to Him as your master or head.

            Salvation is by grace through faith, not by works (***Ephesians 2:8-9***); but believers are God's workmanship, created in Christ Jesus for good works (*Ephesians 2:10*). As a new creation (*II Corinthians 5:17*), you intend to live in faithful and loving obedience to God (*I John 2:3-6*).

- B. If you are already a believer:
    1. Your purpose for change must be to please God, not self.
        a. You are to worship and serve God (*Luke 4:8*), pleasing Him in all respects (*II Corinthians 5:9; **Colossians 1:10***). As a responsible member of God's

family, you are to give glory to God in all things *(I Corinthians 10:31; Colossians 3:17)*.

b. Instead of living for yourself, you are to die to self, take up your cross daily, and follow Christ *(Matthew 10:38; **Luke 9:23**; I Corinthians 15:31)*. You are to lose your life for the Lord's sake *(Matthew 10:39; Luke 9:24)*. This change in allegiance is demonstrated by practical expressions of loving God *(Matthew 22:37-38; John 14:15, 21; I John 5:3)* and loving others *(Matthew 22:39; I Corinthians 13:4-8a; Philippians 2:1-4; I John 4:7-8, 11, 20)*.

c. Therefore, your purpose for change is not to escape your situation so that you may feel better, but rather live for the Lord whether or not your circumstances change *(based on **Romans 14:7-8**; I Corinthians 7:20-24; II Corinthians 5:15; Philippians 1:21; James 1:2-4)*.

2. To change biblically, your focus must be to walk by the Holy Spirit. This involves:

    a. Trusting in the Holy Spirit for the power to live according to His way. God's Spirit is within you *(John 14:16-17; Romans 8:9)*, always available to teach you God's truths *(John 14:26, 16:13; I Corinthians 2:10-13)*, to strengthen you *(Romans 8:11)*, to intercede for you *(Romans 8:26-27)*, to help you discern between truth and error *(based on I John 2:18-27)*, and to develop Christlike character in your life *(Galatians 5:16-17, 22-23)*. This includes responding to the Holy Spirit's conviction by:

    1) Admitting your failures to love in God's way *(based on Matthew 7:1-5; **Revelation 2:4-5**)* and

    2) Confessing all sins to the Lord *(**I John 1:9**)* and practicing biblical forgiveness *(Matthew 6:12, 14; **Mark 11:25**; Ephesians 4:32)* and reconciliation *(**Matthew 5:23-24**)*.

    b. Studying the Scriptures as your sole standard and authority for life *(based on Psalm 19:7-11; 119:105; **Isaiah 55:8-9, 11**)*. God's Word is completely sufficient for discernment *(Hebrews 4:12; II Peter 1:2-4)*, hope *(Romans 15:4)*, and counsel in any situation *(II Timothy 3:16-17)*. Two daily disciplines that will help you immensely to understand and apply the Word are daily devotions and Scripture memory.

    1) Daily devotions are vital to your spiritual development. They include time spent each day in prayer, study of God's Word, and biblical self-evaluation *(based on **Psalm 1:1-4**, 119:9-11; I Corinthians 11:31; I Thessalonians 5:17; II Timothy 2:15; I Peter 2:2)*.

    2) Memorization of Scripture follows the example of the Lord Jesus Christ *(Matthew 4:1-10)*; and will help you keep your way pure *(**Psalm 119:9-11**)*.

    c. Loving God and others by obeying God's Word. Biblical change in you, sovereignly begun, sustained, and to be completed by God *(**Philippians 1:6**)*, is always linked to your obedience to God's Word *(Hebrews 5:14; **James 1:22-25**)*. Your obedience to His Word is a grateful response to God's love that is revealed in Christ Jesus *(John 14:15, 21, 23-24; I John 5:3; II John 1:6)*; it is not to be dependent on circumstances *(Acts 5:28-29; II Timothy 3:1-17)*, your fleshly desires (feelings) *(Galatians 5:17, 24; I Peter 4:2)*, or other people *(Ezekiel 18:20; I Peter 3:8-17)*.

    d. Praying. You are to be devoted to prayer, according to God's will, and to bring everything and everyone unceasingly before the Lord in prayer

*(Luke 18:1; Ephesians 6:18; **I Thessalonians 5:17**; I Timothy 2:1; I John 5:14-15).*

Biblical hope for change

The hope that God has provided for you is not merely a wish. Neither is it dependent on other people, things, or circumstances for its validity. Instead, biblical hope is an application of your faith that supplies a confident expectation in God's fulfillment of His promises. Coupled with faith and love, hope is part of the abiding characteristics in a believer's life *(based on Romans 5:1-5; I Corinthians 13:13; II Corinthians 1:3-11; Colossians 1:3-6; I Thessalonians 1:2-3; I Timothy 1:1; Hebrews 6:17-20; I Peter 1:3).*

The only lasting hope is promised in the Scriptures. Listed below are seven reasons that the believer has great hope. ***NOTE:*** *The following Biblical Principles are from the **Self-Confrontation** manual.*

A. Those in Christ are freed from the power and penalty of sin (**Romans 6:6-7, 14, 18, 23**).

   NOTE: *You might be wondering why dealing with your own sin is a matter of hope for you, and not discouragement. Dealing with your sin should give you great hope because:*

   1. *You can deal with sin very quickly. It does not take years of therapy;*
   2. *It is not dependent on whether others change. You can have peace and joy if your relationship with God is right, even in the most difficult circumstances; and*
   3. *It is God's method for restoring relationships with Him and others.*

   This is why it is so important to start your plan by identifying your own failures to live God's way (your sin). You don't deal with your problems by focusing on the sin of others or on your circumstances.

B. God will not allow believers to be tested or tempted beyond what they can bear. He gives you His grace and strength to endure every test and resist every temptation so that you never have to sin *(Romans 8:35-39; **I Corinthians 10:13**; II Corinthians 4:7-10; 12:9-10; Philippians 4:13; Hebrews 4:15-16; II Peter 2:4-9).*

C. Our Lord Jesus Christ will grant mercy and provide grace to help in every need. He constantly intercedes as an advocate for you to God the Father and fully understands your weaknesses *(**Hebrews 2:18; 4:15-16**; 7:25; I John 2:1).*

D. Trials and tests will develop and mature you in Christ if you respond to them in God's way *(Romans 5:3-5; **James 1:2-4**).* He never devises evil or harm for you; rather His plans for you are for your good; God's good for you is to conform you to the image of Jesus *(**Genesis 50:20**; Deuteronomy 8:2, 5, 16; Psalm 145:17; Ecclesiastes 7:13-14; Jeremiah 29:11-13; **Romans 8:28-29**; James 1:13-17).*

E. God's peace and joy are available to believers regardless of other people, material goods, things, or circumstances in your life *(Psalm 119:165; Matthew 5:3-12; **John 14:27; 15:11; 16:33; 17:13**; Romans 14:17; Philippians 4:4-7; I Peter 1:6-9).*

F. Only God can change people *(Ezekiel 36:26-27; Philippians 1:6; 2:13),* so you are not responsible for changing them. You are accountable to God solely for your own deeds *(Jeremiah 17:10; **Ezekiel 18:1-20, especially verse 20**; Matthew 16:27; Romans 2:5-10; Colossians 3:23-25; I Peter 1:17)* and are to do your part in living at peace with others *(Matthew 5:23-24; Mark 11:25; Romans 12:9-21; 14:19; I Peter 3:8-9; 4:8).*

G. When you confess your sins, God forgives and cleanses you *(I John 1:9).*

The biblical process for change

A. While the new self has been put on at salvation, the old manner of life must be decisively put off and new righteous practices must be put on *(Ephesians 4:22, 24).*

B. For each "put-off" in the Bible, there is usually a "put-on" and often it is in the same passage *(for examples, see **Ephesians 4:25-32**).*

C. Lasting change takes self-control, discipline, work, and time because it involves putting off the practices (habit patterns) of the old self, which are corrupted, and putting on the practices (habit patterns) of the new self, which have been created in righteousness and holiness of the truth *(based on Ephesians 4:22-24; I Timothy 4:7-8).*

D. When you focus your attention on the "put-on," your mind is not easily distracted to do wrong. When you focus your attention only on the "put-off," the temptation to do wrong is always before you *(based on **Galatians 5:16**; II Timothy 2:22).*

*NOTE: Later, when you develop your **VICTORY OVER FAILURE'S PLAN**, you will identify biblical "put-offs" and "put-ons" that relate directly to your problem area.*

GUIDELINES
FOR COMPLETING THE
VICTORY OVER FAILURES PLAN

GUIDELINES FOR COMPLETING THE VICTORY OVER FAILURES PLAN

Description of the Problem

Complete *Worksheet 1*. For your use, a blank worksheet is located on Page 40. *NOTE: You may make copies of all the worksheets at the end of this booklet.*

A. Under the "**Ongoing problem area**" section, write down the problem area that is of greatest hindrance to your walk with God *(Hebrews 12:1-2)*. To make the selection, use the following guidelines:

1. Focus on dealing with a problem that is ongoing, not on one that you experience only occasionally. You may wish to review the **SAMPLE LIST OF PROBLEM AREAS** located on the next page. It contains a list of problem areas with references to relevant sections of the *Self-Confrontation* manual. Also listed are some key passages of Scripture to help determine possible areas of failure.

2. Seek the Lord's wisdom in determining the problem area to choose. Concentrate on an area in your life that requires the most immediate change, even though it may be difficult. The Lord is primarily concerned about your commitment to Him, not how much you can accomplish easily. So, choose the pattern that the Lord is convicting you to develop. To do this, ask yourself, "In what ways do I continue to show that I fail to love God and others" *(based on Matthew 22:37-40; John 13:34-35; 14:15, 20-21; I Corinthians 13:4-8a)*. Ask the Holy Spirit to bring to your mind the specific ways you have sinned against the Lord and others.

   One of your tendencies with sinful habits may be to identify only those areas *you* want to change. However, when you seek to change some area of your life according to your own perceptions, you may focus on something that seems easy to do or that appeals to self-centered accomplishments (for example, overcoming fear of flying motivated by pride).

B. Under the "**Short description of the problem**" section, summarize the problem in one or two paragraphs. See Page 16 for a sample of a description written by a fictitious person who is angry and bitter toward a co-worker. Subsequent samples represent how he might complete a **VICTORY OVER FAILURES PLAN** based on these guidelines.

(GUIDELINES FOR COMPLETING THE VICTORY OVER FAILURES PLAN continue on Page 17.)

SAMPLE LIST OF PROBLEM AREAS

A sample set of problem areas is listed below. Scripture references containing biblical principles, "put-offs," and "put-ons" for these problem areas can be found in the indicated lessons of the *Self-Confrontation* manual. In some of the referenced lessons, the problem area may not be specifically listed, but the biblical principles and biblical references will apply.

Anger — Lesson 11

Bitterness — Lesson 11

Communication, sinful (lying, slander, arguing, cursing) — Lesson 13

Contentment, lack of — Lesson 6

Envy, jealousy, covetousness, greed — Lessons 9 and 10

Depression (despair, lack of fulfillment of responsibilities, total inactivity) — Lesson 18

Drug abuse — Lessons 20 and 21

Drunkenness — Lessons 20 and 21

Eating problems (overeating; starving self, called "anorexia;" or binging on food and purging self, called "bulimia") — Lessons 9, 10, 20, and 21

Fear (including "panic attacks") — Lesson 19

Gambling — Lessons 20 and 21

Grief focused on self — Lessons 9, 10, 20 and 21

Lust — Lessons 9, 10, 20 and 21

Marriage problems — Lessons 14 and 15

Parent-child problems — Lessons 16 and 17

Reconciliation problems — Lessons 12 and 13

Relationship problems (marriage, relative, acquaintances, etc.) — Lessons 12-17, 20 and 21

Satanic influences — Lessons 20 and 21

Self-belittlement — Lessons 9 and 10

Self-exaltation — Lessons 9 and 10

Self-pity — Lessons 9 and 10

Sexual sins (adultery, fornication, homosexuality, pornography) — Lessons 20 and 21

Stealing (covetousness) — Lessons 9 and 10

Stewardship problems (body, time, material goods, abilities) — Lesson 10

Unforgiveness — Lesson 12

Worry (anxiety) — Lesson 19

Some key passages of Scripture to help determine possible problem areas:

Proverbs Chapters 15 and 18

Romans Chapters 12 - 14

I Corinthians 13:4-8a

Ephesians 4:22 - 6:9

Colossians Chapter 3

I Peter 2:11 - 3:17

© Biblical Counseling Foundation

Sample Worksheet 1: Description of the Problem

Ongoing problem area:

Anger and bitterness toward my co-worker

This portion should be the identification of the ongoing difficulty that is of greatest hindrance to your walk with God *(Hebrews 12:1-2)*.

Short description of the problem:

I have a very bad relationship with my co-worker at the office. We argue about almost everything. He criticizes my work all the time. He blames me for mistakes that I don't make and lies to the boss about me. I get so bitter that I can't concentrate on my work, and the situation gets worse. I am about to lose my job because of our arguments over responsibilities of projects that our boss has assigned. My co-worker takes the easy jobs and leaves the hard ones for me. I would like to quit, but I need the money. So I just get more angry and bitter.

NOTE: In order to make this description more accurate, please read the explanation for how to complete a list of specific failures (Pages 17-19). You will see an evaluation of this sample worksheet on Page 20.

VOFP Worksheet 1, Student Workbook for the Self-Confrontation Bible Study © Biblical Counseling Foundation

Lists of Specific Failures to Live Biblically

Complete *Worksheet 2*. A blank worksheet is located on Page 41.

In order to determine how God intends for you to change, you must first describe clearly *what* needs to be changed in your life. This worksheet helps you learn to judge yourself biblically.

On *Worksheet 2*, list your unbiblical deeds related to the problem area you selected. For some problem areas, the unbiblical deeds may involve offenses to specific people. For others, it may involve sins only against God. Keep in mind that offenses against others are also sins against God.

Once you have worked through the plan with one person, you may find that there are others you have sinned against. You will need to use a separate sheet for each person you have offended in order to avoid confusion.

Keep in mind that you should list only your *own* failures, not another person's *(Matthew 7:5)*. God tells us to concentrate on our own sins first. Otherwise, we cannot even understand the other person's life accurately. We do not see clearly how to deal with our brother's sins until we have first dealt with our own sins.

A. Under the "**List of speech and actions related to the ongoing problem area**" section, write your sinful speech and actions (not your thoughts) committed against the person you have identified.

NOTE: If the problem involves sins only against the Lord, you would only fill out the bottom of the worksheet.

B. Under the "**List of thoughts, speech, and actions against the Lord alone**" section, list your unbiblical thoughts, speech, and actions committed only before the Lord. These are failures that do not involve other people (for example, sinful thoughts — even about others, or sins of grumbling, shouting, or using curse words when you are alone, stomping your feet or slamming doors while no one else is around, not spending time in daily devotions, lusting, drug abuse when you are alone, etc.).

NOTE: Thoughts are not included in the first list since sinful thoughts are only committed against the Lord. However, if thoughts are communicated to the one offended, through speech or actions, these must be added to the first list.

C. In making your list, be sure it meets the following criteria:

    1. **Be specific.** Write exactly how you demonstrated your failures in each situation.

        a. It is very important to be specific. Change takes place in specific ways, i.e., specific changes in thoughts, speech, and actions. Change does not take place in generalities. For example, you would not just say "I was angry." Rather, you would list the specific ways in which you have demonstrated your anger. List specific unbiblical thoughts (such as grumbling inside self, devising sarcastic responses, etc.), speech (including the tone and volume of your voice), and actions (including looks, gestures, etc.). These are the things you can change.

        b. Following are examples of the wrong and right ways to describe failures.

            1) *Wrong description:* "I get *angry* with my co-worker often." This is too general. Change is demonstrated only by acting in specific ways.

2) *Correct description:* "I think about getting revenge" (thoughts); or "I speak loudly frequently to my co-worker with a harsh tone of voice" (speech); or "I glared at my co-worker, then stomped out of the room, slamming the door behind me" (actions).

c. When developing your specific list, you should take into account the following:

1) Do not include specific details about sinful thoughts that may present a stumbling block to you or others to whom you may need to show the list. It is enough to list the kinds of thoughts (e.g., grumbling, arguing, reviling). Keeping a written record of exact words can serve as a reminder to keep you thinking those sinful thoughts.

2) Do not list emotions (i.e., feelings) because God does not hold you responsible for how you feel; in addition, you cannot change your feelings by a direct act of your will. Feelings, in themselves, are not sinful, since nowhere in the Scriptures does God command you to change them.

3) It may at times be difficult for you to determine whether some activities are sinful, where the deed is not specifically named as sin in the Scriptures (e.g., modes of dress, certain items ingested, companions, activities, etc.). In these situations, ask yourself the following questions.

a) Is this profitable (in other words, does this contribute toward the development of godly traits or help to accomplish biblical responsibilities in my life or in the lives of others) *(I Corinthians 6:12, 10:23a)*?

b) Does this bring me under its power or am I controlled by it in any way *(I Corinthians 6:12)*?

c) Is this an area of spiritual weakness (a stumbling block) in my life *(Matthew 5:29-30, 18:8-9)*?

d) Could this lead another believer in Christ to stumble *(Romans 14:13; I Corinthians 8:9-13)*?

e) Does this edify (build up) others or, stated in another way, is this the biblically loving thing to do *(Romans 14:19; I Corinthians 10:23-24)*?

f) Does this glorify God *(Matthew 5:16; I Corinthians 10:31)*?

2. **Be thorough.** For each situation in which you know you failed to love biblically, it is important to consider thoughts, speech, and actions. Remember that it is possible to sin in many ways in a very short period of time. For example, if you had an argument with another person, within seconds you might have:

a. Reviled and grumbled about the person in your mind (thoughts),

b. Shouted at the person, used a harsh tone of voice, called him/her tearing down names (speech),

c. Given hard looks, thrown objects, and slammed doors (actions).

3. **Do not shift blame.** When making your list, take care not to place blame on anyone else for your failures *(based on Ezekiel 18:20; Matthew 7:5)*. Do not write such statements as "I slammed the door in my wife's face when she yelled at me." Instead say, "I slammed the door in my wife's face." Regardless of what the other person did, it is not an excuse for your sins. It

THE VICTORY OVER FAILURES PLAN: GUIDELINES AND WORKSHEETS

is important that you do not use the list of your own sins as a way of pointing blame at the other person.

4. **Do not minimize or excuse sin.** In listing your failures, take care not to minimize or excuse away your sin *(based on Proverbs 28:13; Ezekiel 18:20; I John 1:5-9).* Do not write such statements as "I told a little lie, but I was tired and couldn't think of anything better to say." Instead say, "I lied."

The next page provides an evaluation of the sample *Worksheet 1: Description of the Problem* from Page 16. Note the blameshfiting, etc. Then, notice that the sample of *Worksheet 2* (on Page 21) is specific and thorough, and does not shift blame nor excuse sin.

NOTE: It is important to repent and confess all sins to God as soon as you recognize them as sins (I John 1:8-10); however, before going to be reconciled with another human being, you must be careful to take proper precautions so that you do not place a stumbling block before the person you have offended. If you are not careful, even the way you approach reconciliation could be a stumbling block to them. It may be helpful to develop a biblical plan for change first. Putting the plan into effect is a practical way of demonstrating to the one you have offended how serious you are in your intention to change and not repeat the offense. A **"Forgiveness/Reconciliation"** *Plan is described later in these guidelines.*

(GUIDELINES FOR COMPLETING THE VICTORY OVER FAILURES PLAN continue on Page 22.)

Evaluation — Sample Worksheet 1: Description of the Problem

Ongoing problem area:

Anger and bitterness toward my co-worker

This portion should be the identification of the ongoing difficulty that is of greatest hindrance to your walk with God *(Hebrews 12:1-2)*.

Short description of the problem: *Blameshifting; justifying own sin*

I have a very bad relationship with my co-worker at the office. We argue about almost everything. (He criticizes my work all the time.) He (blames me for mistakes that I don't make) (and lies to the boss about me.) (I get so bitter) that I can't concentrate on my work, and the situation gets worse. (I am about to lose my job because of our arguments) over responsibilities of projects that our boss has assigned. (My co-worker takes the easy jobs and leaves the hard ones for me.) I would like to quit, but I need the money. So (I just get more angry and bitter.)

Not thorough   *Not specific*   *Blameshifting*   *Not specific; not thorough*

Sample Worksheet 2:
Lists of Specific Failures to Live Biblically

List of speech and actions related to the ongoing problem area:

1. Often, I speak to my co-worker in an angry way. I speak with a loud voice using condemning and accusing words.

2. I argue with my co-worker every day, and I often speak with a harsh tone of voice and say tearing down words to my co-worker.

3. I gossip about my co-worker to my employer and others in the office saying tearing down things, and I complain to my family members about my situation at work.

List of thoughts, speech, and actions against the Lord alone:

1. I have bitter, vengeful thoughts toward my co-worker, not only at the office, but in many other places.

2. When I pray, I grumble and complain to the Lord about my situation at work.

3. When on my way home from work, I think and speak to myself about sharp, tearing down statements I might make to my co-worker.

"Put-offs" and "Put-ons"

Complete *Worksheet 3*. A blank worksheet is located on Page 42.

This foundational worksheet is designed to help you learn how to find the biblical "put-offs" and "put-ons" associated with your personal problem. To complete *Worksheet 3*, follow the steps below:

A. At the top of your worksheet in the space entitled, "Ongoing problem area," copy what you wrote as your ongoing problem area from your *Worksheet 1: Description of the Problem*, which you completed earlier.

B. Complete the first column of *Worksheet 3* by copying each item from your *Worksheet 2: Lists of Specific Failures to Live Biblically* which you have completed. *NOTE: Be sure to leave a little empty space between each failure in the first column so that you can relate the corresponding entries in the second and third columns to the appropriate failure.*

NOTE: The reason you need to wait until now to copy the information into the first column is to make sure your list conforms to all the guidelines for completing Worksheet 2. This will save you from starting Worksheet 3 repeatedly.

C. Complete the second and third columns of *Worksheet 3*.

1. Search the Scriptures for the appropriate biblical words to write in the second and third columns. The "put-off" (in the second column) is the biblical name given to the failure (listed in the first column); the "put-on" (in the third column) is the phrase in the Scriptures that corresponds to the "put-off" in the second column. In addition to the key passages of Scripture listed on the **SAMPLE LIST OF PROBLEM AREAS** on Page 15, it may be helpful to use a concordance and the *Self-Confrontation* manual to find the related passages. Generally, each pair of "put-offs" and "put-ons" is in the same Scripture passage.

    You may find a "put-off" without a related "put-on" in the same passage, such as *"You shall not bear false witness" (Exodus 20:16)*. In this case, find another passage that contains the same "put-off" along with an associated "put-on" such as *Ephesians 4:25* that designates a "put-on" of "speaking truth." You also may find "put-ons" without related "put-offs." Again, search for other passages where the "put-ons" and "put-offs" correspond to one another.

2. List the "put-offs" along with the associated Scripture references in the second column, and list the "put-ons" along with the associated Scripture references in the third column. To make sure that you base each entry in the second and third columns only on Scripture passages, it is important that you place the scriptural reference next to each "put-off" and "put-on."

(GUIDELINES FOR COMPLETING THE VICTORY OVER FAILURES PLAN continue on Page 23.)

THE VICTORY OVER FAILURES PLAN: GUIDELINES AND WORKSHEETS 283

Upon completion of *Worksheet 3: "Put-offs" and "Put-ons,"* you may need to develop up to three kinds of plans in parallel with one another. They are, the *"Daily Practices" Plan*, the *"Overcoming Temptations" Plan*, and the *"Forgiveness/Reconciliation" Plan*.

The purpose of the *"Daily Practices" Plan* is to help you put off a particular ongoing pattern of unrighteous behavior and to put on the appropriate biblical pattern of righteous deeds instead. It includes changes that must be made throughout the day.

The purpose of the *"Overcoming Temptations" Plan* is to help you respond in a godly manner to situations where you have been tempted and have fallen repeatedly. It is for you to use only at the time the temptation occurs, but it is prepared in advance of the temptation so that you will be better prepared to deal with the temptation when it occurs.

The purpose of the *"Forgiveness/Reconciliation" Plan* is to help you deal with relationships that are not reconciled. Development of each of these plans is described next.

(GUIDELINES FOR COMPLETING THE VICTORY OVER FAILURES PLAN continue on Page 25.)

© Biblical Counseling Foundation **Student Workbook for the Self-Confrontation Bible Study, Supplement 2**

Sample Worksheet 3: "Put-offs" and "Put-ons"

Ongoing problem area _Anger and bitterness toward my co-worker_   Page 1 of 1

(1) My specific unbiblical deeds (thoughts, speech, and actions) *(based on Matthew 7:1-5; 15:18)*	(2) "Put-off" and biblical reference(s) *(Ephesians 4:22; Colossians 3:5-9)*	(3) "Put-on" and biblical reference(s) *(Ephesians 4:24; Colossians 3:10-17)*
Often, I speak to my co-worker in an angry way. I speak with a loud voice using condemning and accusing words.	*Bitterness, wrath, anger, clamor, malice (Ephesians 4:31)* *Unwholesome words (Ephesians 4:29)* *Harsh words (Proverbs 15:1)* *Hot temper (Proverbs 15:18)* *Evil speech (Proverbs 15:28)*	*Kindness, tender-heartedness, and forgiveness (Ephesians 4:32)* *Edifying words that give grace to the hearer and are appropriate to the need (Ephesians 4:29)* *Gentle words (Proverbs 15:1)* *Patience (Proverbs 15:18)* *Pondering before answering (Proverbs 15:28)*
I argue with my co-worker every day, and I often speak with a harsh tone of voice, and say tearing down words to my co-worker.	*Bitterness, wrath, anger, clamor, malice (Ephesians 4:31)* *Unwholesome words (Ephesians 4:29)* *Harsh words (Proverbs 15:1)* *Hot temper (Proverbs 15:18)* *Evil speech (Proverbs 15:28)* *Quarrels (arguments) (II Timothy 2:23-24)*	*Kindness, tender-heartedness, and forgiveness (Ephesians 4:32)* *Edifying words that give grace to the hearer and are appropriate to the need (Ephesians 4:29)* *Gentle words (Proverbs 15:1)* *Patience (Proverbs 15:18)* *Pondering before answering (Proverbs 15:28)* *Kindness, patience, gentleness (II Timothy 2:24-25)*
I gossip about my co-worker to my employer and others in the office saying tearing down things, and I complain to my family members about my situation at work.	*Gossip (talebearing) (Proverbs 11:13)* *Unwholesome words (Ephesians 4:29)* *Evil speech (Proverbs 15:28)*	*Keeping a secret (Proverbs 11:13)* *Edifying words that give grace to the hearer and are appropriate to the need (Ephesians 4:29)* *Pondering before answering (Proverbs 15:28)*
I have bitter, vengeful thoughts toward my co-worker, not only at the office, but in many other places.	*Bitterness, wrath, anger, clamor, malice (Ephesians 4:31)*	*Kindness, tender-heartedness, and forgiveness (Ephesians 4:32)*
When I pray, I grumble and complain to the Lord about my situation at work.	*Grumbling and disputing (Philippians 2:14)*	*Holding fast the Word of God and rejoicing (Philippians 2:16, 18)*
When on my way home from work, I think and speak to myself about sharp, tearing down statements I might make to my co-worker.	*Unwholesome words (Ephesians 4:29)*	*Edifying words that give grace to the hearer and are appropriate to the need (Ephesians 4:29)*

VOFP Worksheet 3, Student Workbook for the Self-Confrontation Bible Study   © Biblical Counseling Foundation

"Daily Practices" Plan

Complete *Worksheet 4*. A blank worksheet is located on Pages 43-44.

Remember, the purpose of the *"Daily Practices" Plan* is to help you put off a particular ongoing pattern of unrighteous behavior and to put on the appropriate biblical pattern of righteous deeds instead. It includes changes that must be made throughout the day.

NOTE: You do not need to develop a separate plan for each person against whom you have sinned, as long as your pattern of sin is the same as on your lists of sins against the others.

- A. Complete the two items in the top portion of the page (based on what you entered into *Worksheet 3: "Put-offs" and "Put-ons"*).
    1. Under "**Sin pattern that I need to change**," list the "put-offs" from the second column of *Worksheet 3*.
    2. Under "**Righteous pattern to be established**," list the "put-ons" from the third column of *Worksheet 3*.

- B. Complete the section entitled, "**My plan to live righteously**." In this section, specify what you will do to practice the righteous pattern starting with when you awaken in the morning and proceeding through the entire day. Since the basic problem is habitual, it reveals itself in many ways throughout each day.

    NOTE: A very important portion of this section is a detailed description of your plans for daily devotions and Scripture memory. Devotions (time spent each day in prayer, study of God's Word, and biblical self evaluation) and Scripture memory are vital to your spiritual development. Daily devotions should be times that help you learn to be devoted to the Lord. Your relationship with God is more important than any other relationship, and you can depend upon Him to guide you in every way. (The biblical basis for daily devotions and Scripture memory is provided in the **Self-Confrontation** *manual, Pages 38-40.)*

    It is important to recognize that devotional time spent in God's Word and memorizing God's Word should directly relate to the very areas in your life where God has your attention.

    It is best to memorize at times other than during your devotional time. This can be done in combination with your daily devotions. Memorizing a verse that relates to your devotional times will help you keep your mind focused on God's Word throughout the day. The best way to do this is to write the verse down on a card that you can put in your pocket. Then, take advantage of free moments during the day to go over your memory verses. This will help you make wise use of the empty times during the day when you are more likely to be tempted.

- C. See the sample on Pages 27-28.

- D. Implement your plan. This will include:
    1. Conviction and sorrow to the point of repentance *(II Corinthians 7:9)*. This is not an intellectual exercise. You must commit yourself to change from a pattern of disobedience to God (which demonstrates your lack of love for Him) to a new pattern of godliness.
    2. Self-control and discipline. Old habits are difficult to put off, and putting on new habits often feels unnatural initially.

THE VICTORY OVER FAILURES PLAN: GUIDELINES AND WORKSHEETS

3. Acknowledging and repenting when you fail. This involves confession of your sins, placing yourself back under the control of the Holy Spirit, changing your plan, if appropriate, and starting again to implement your plan.

(GUIDELINES FOR COMPLETING THE VICTORY OVER FAILURES PLAN continue on Page 29.)

Sample Worksheet 4: "Daily Practices" Plan

My plan not to repeat this sin and, instead, to respond biblically (James 1:22-25)

Page 1 of 2

Sin pattern that I need to change (*as seen from the second column of* **Worksheet 3**):
Anger: bitterness, wrath, clamor, malice, unwholesome words, harsh words, hot temper, evil speech, quarrelling, gossiping, grumbling, disputing

Righteous pattern to be established (*as seen from the third column of* **Worksheet 3**):
Kindness, tender-heartedness, and forgiveness, edifying words that give grace to my co-worker and are appropriate to the need, gentle words, patience, pondering before answering, keeping a secret, holding fast the Word of God, rejoicing

My plan to live righteously:

A. When rising from bed:
   1. Thank the Lord for His grace, mercy, and comfort, and express my desire to please Him today.
   2. Thank God for the privilege of ministering to my co-worker and ask the Lord for guidance throughout the day.
   3. Ask the Lord to reveal to me, as I go through the day, areas of my conduct that are sinful, and in need of change.

B. During morning devotions:
   1. In my study of God's Word:
      a. Using a concordance, keep listing additional Scripture verses relating to kindness, tender-heartedness, and forgiveness, especially those that show me practical changes to make. Then, incorporate into this plan what I should apply to my life in relationship with my co-worker based on key verses.
      b. On my list of verses I have looked up, put an asterisk by the verses I should memorize. Continue writing these verses on cards, so I can carry them around to memorize.
   2. In my prayer time:
      a. Pray about what I just studied and acknowledge my dependence upon the Lord for wisdom and strength to apply what I learned.

Sample Worksheet 4: "Daily Practices" Plan (Continued)

My plan not to repeat this sin and, instead, to respond biblically (James 1:22-25)

Page 2 of 2

My plan to live righteously *(continued)*:

      b. Pray about the items on my prayer list that relate to my co-worker.

  C. In my Scripture memory:

    1. Write down my Scripture memory verses on cards (from my list that relates to the problem).

    2. From my list, memorize at least one new Scripture verse a week and daily review the verses I have already learned.

    3. Carry the memory verse cards with me everywhere I go and review them often during the day, especially when I do not have responsibilities that fully occupy my mind.

  D. During breakfast and preparation for work:

    1. Thank the Lord for the current situation regarding my co-worker.

    2. Ask the Lord to reveal to me the opportunities to show kindness and tenderheartedness toward my co-worker, especially as they show me areas of my life in which the Lord is maturing me.

    3. Ask the Lord's help in dealing with my speech around others.

  E. At work:

    1. When opportunities arise, show kindness and tenderheartedness toward my co-worker.

    2. Offer help to my co-worker when he is having difficulty accomplishing his tasks.

"Overcoming Temptations" Plan

Complete *Worksheet 5*. A blank worksheet is located on Pages 45-46.

Remember that the purpose of an *"Overcoming Temptations" Plan* is to help you to respond in a godly manner to situations where you have been tempted and have fallen repeatedly. It is for you to use only at the time the temptation occurs, but it is prepared in advance of the temptation so that you will be better prepared to deal with the temptation when it occurs. The plan is then practiced at the time of the temptation.

A. Complete the first section of the form entitled, *Worksheet 5: "Overcoming Temptations" Plan*.

   1. Under "**Type of situation in which I previously have been tempted and sinned**," describe the type of situation in which you have been repeatedly tempted and have not had victory (for example, suppose you have a weekly appointment at a location that requires you to travel through heavy traffic congestion. Suppose that in the past, you have demonstrated anger each week by reviling others, honking the horn impatiently, and forcing your way ahead of others). Normally, these types of temptations are associated with the major pattern written at the top of *Worksheet 4: "Daily Practices" Plan*.

   2. Under "**Ways in which I sinned in this situation**," list the deeds from the first column of *Worksheet 3* that are associated with the type of situation you selected.

   3. Under "**Righteous pattern to be established**," list the godly traits from the third column of *Worksheet 3* that you recognize need to be developed in your life.

B. Complete the section entitled, "**My plan to respond righteously the next time a similar temptation arises**." Write a specific plan that you will implement when you are tempted. To help you write a biblical plan, review the following guidance:

   1. Deal with yourself first *(based on Matthew 7:5)*.

      a. Immediately ask for God's help *(I Thessalonians 5:17; Hebrews 4:15-16; James 1:5)*.

      b. Repent and confess to God any sinful thoughts you dwelt upon, even for a short period of time *(I John 1:9)*.

      c. Review the biblical basis for hope in the situation.

         1) Review *Romans 8:28-29* and remind yourself that God causes all things to work together for good to those who love Him and are called according to His purpose.

         2) Review *I Corinthians 10:13* and remind yourself that God will not allow you to be tested or tempted beyond what you can bear.

         3) Review *James 1:2-4* and remind yourself that regardless of your feelings or circumstances, the situation is an opportunity for further spiritual maturity.

         4) Review *Philippians 4:13* and remind yourself that you can do all things through Christ who gives you strength.

         5) Review *Ezekiel 18:20* and remind yourself that you are not responsible for changing the hearts of others.

      d. Thank God for the opportunity to serve Him and trust Him for wisdom to deal victoriously with the present situation, no matter how intense the temptation *(Ephesians 5:20; I Thessalonians 5:18)*.

e. Review the Scripture passages you have memorized that relate to the type of sin *(based on Psalm 119:9, 11)*. Include verses showing hope and giving practical guidance for how to change.

f. Write the specific thoughts, speech, and/or actions you will change based on the "put-offs" in the second column and the corresponding "put-ons" in the third column. Recognize that in most cases, thinking, speaking, and acting biblically are almost simultaneous, or within a very short time period.

2. After dealing with yourself, when others are involved:

a. Listen to all sides first; make no prejudgments *(based on Proverbs 18:2, 17; James 1:19)*. Ask questions to get the facts and to gain understanding, not opinions *(based on Proverbs 13:10; 18:13, 15; II Timothy 2:23)*.

b. Formulate and state your evaluation carefully and slowly *(based on Proverbs 18:13; James 1:19)*, while

1) Judging yourself first *(Matthew 7:1-5)*.

2) Evaluating the observable deeds (speech and actions) of others, not their apparent motives *(based on I Samuel 16:7; Jeremiah 17:9-10)*.

c. Describe the situation and the biblical solution — speak at the appropriate time and only with words that edify *(Ephesians 4:29)*; speak the truth (i.e., biblical truth) in love with a gentle and humble spirit *(based on Proverbs 15:1; Ephesians 4:1-3, 15; I Peter 3:8-9)*.

d. Act in a way that demonstrates your love for the other person(s) who are present.

e. Then, deal with the deeds of others. Seek ways to edify others by serving them, not yourself, in this situation *(Romans 14:19; Ephesians 4:29; Philippians 2:3-4)*. Bless the people who are involved *(I Peter 3:8-9)*. Focus on restoration, not condemnation *(Galatians 6:1; II Timothy 2:24-26)* nor revenge *(Romans 12:19)*.

C. See the sample *"Overcoming Temptations" Plan* on Pages 31-32.

D. Implement your plan. This will include:

1. Conviction and sorrow to the point of repentance *(II Corinthians 7:9)*. This is not an intellectual exercise. You must commit yourself to change from a pattern of disobedience to God (which demonstrates your lack of love for Him) to a new pattern of godliness.

2. Self-control and discipline. Old habits are difficult to put off and putting on new habits often feels unnatural initially.

3. Acknowledging and repenting when you fail. This involves confession of your sins, placing yourself back under the control of the Holy Spirit, changing your plan, if appropriate, and starting again to implement your plan.

(GUIDELINES FOR COMPLETING THE VICTORY OVER FAILURES PLAN continue on Page 33.)

Sample Worksheet 5: "Overcoming Temptations" Plan

My plan not to repeat this sin and, instead, to respond biblically at the time of temptation (II Timothy 2:22)

Page __1__ of __2__

Type of situation in which I previously have been tempted and sinned:
When my co-worker loads his work onto me

Ways in which I sinned in this situation *(as seen from the first column of Worksheet 3):*
I spoke in an angry way, with a loud, harsh tone of voice using condemning and accusing words. I quarrelled with my co-worker and said tearing down words to him.

Righteous pattern to be established *(as seen from the third column of Worksheet 3):*
Kindness, tender-heartedness, and forgiveness, edifying words that give grace to the hearer and are appropriate to the need, gentle words, patience, pondering before answering

My plan to respond righteously the next time a similar temptation arises:

A. Deal with myself first. I will:
  1. Immediately, ask for God's help.
  2. Repent and confess to God any sinful thoughts that I purposely held onto beyond the immediate temptation.
  3. Review the biblical basis for hope in the situation.
     a. Recite Romans 8:28-29 and thank God for using this trial for my good.
     b. Recite I Corinthians 10:13 and thank God for giving me the strength to bear this temptation.
     c. Recite James 1:2-4 and thank God that this situation is an opportunity for further spiritual maturity.
     d. Recite Philippians 4:13 and remind myself that I can do all things through Christ Who gives me strength since my adequacy is from God and not from any natural inner strength.
     e. Recite Ezekiel 18:20 and thank God that it is not my responsibility to change my co-worker, only to bless him.
  4. Thank God for the opportunity to serve Him and trust Him for wisdom and grace to deal victoriously with the present situation.
  5. Review verses I have memorized that relate to anger.

B. Deal with my co-worker:

Sample Worksheet 5: "Overcoming Temptation" Plan (Continued)

My plan not to repeat this sin and, instead, to respond biblically at the time of temptation (II Timothy 2:22)

Page __2__ of __2__

My plan to respond righteously the next time a similar temptation arises *(continued)*:

    1. Listen to him attentively and ask questions about the work to gain understanding.

    2. Repeat back what he said to make sure I understand and that he knows I've listened to him.

    3. If the work is really his to do, and it is too much for him, tell him I will ask our supervisor how best to redistribute the responsibilities and help him accordingly so we can accomplish the work together.

    4. If he needs to do the work himself, tell him that I am willing to help him as appropriate.

C. Return to my daily tasks rather than dwell on evil thoughts.

D. When temptations arise in my thought life about my co-worker:

    1. Pray for my co-worker, and ask the Lord to remind me of ways to bless him.

    2. Actively turn my thoughts to blessing.

    3. If necessary, make a list (or add to the existing list) of ways to bless my co-worker, using Romans 12:9-21 as a guideline.

"Forgiveness/Reconciliation" Plan

Complete *Worksheets 6a* and *6b*. Blank worksheets are located on Pages 47, and 48.

In order to be reconciled with someone, first develop a *"Forgiveness/Reconciliation" Plan (based on **Matthew 18:21-35**; **Luke 17:3-10**; Romans 12:18)*. **NOTE:** *Important Scripture passages to study are written in **boldface** print.*

The purpose of this plan is to help you deal with relationships that are not reconciled, with emphasis on long standing broken relationships or ones in which there is a serious rift. In these cases, you will want to be especially prepared to be reconciled in a godly way by writing out what you will do. This will help you to think through how to be reconciled with that other person in a biblical manner.

Depending on your situation, you may need to include in the plan:

- Steps you will take to *demonstrate* forgiveness. Jesus said in **Mark 11:25** that we need to forgive and demonstrate forgiveness whether or not the offender requests forgiveness. Remember that your forgiveness of another is much bigger than just your relationship with the other person. Your forgiveness of others is essential to unbroken fellowship with your heavenly Father *(Matthew 6:12-15)*. **Worksheet 6a: My Plan for Demonstrating Forgiveness** will help you develop this part of your plan.

- Steps you will take and the words you will use for *asking* forgiveness. **Worksheet 6b: My Plan for Asking Forgiveness** will help you develop this part of your plan.

To complete your *"Forgiveness/Reconciliation" Plan*, follow the steps below:

A. Complete *Worksheet 6a: My Plan for Demonstrating Forgiveness*.

    1. Complete the first section of *Worksheet 6a: My Plan for Demonstrating Forgiveness* by listing the name of the person you need to forgive, and the offenses you need to forgive at the top of the page. (See the sample on Page 35.)

    2. Complete the section entitled "**Steps I will take to:**" The sub-points in this section are aspects of biblical forgiveness presented in Lesson 12 of the *Self-Confrontation* manual.

    As God in Christ has forgiven us (**Ephesians 4:32**; *Colossians 3:13*), we are to:

    a. Not dwell on the offense suffered *(based on **Isaiah 38:17**)*. We are not to keep account of any wrongs suffered *(I Corinthians 13:5)*. We should not dwell on the evil done to us, but consider how to give a blessing instead *(based on I Peter 3:9)*.

    b. Not remind the forgiven person of his sin in an accusing manner *(based on **Hebrews 10:17**)*. There may be times when you will need to remind the person of his sin even after you have forgiven him. For example, if that individual develops a pattern of repeating the sin, you are to exhort that person to repent. But the difference now is that you are to make your appeal in a spirit of gentleness, not in an accusing manner *(based on Galatians 6:1)*.

    c. Not gossip to others about the offense suffered *(II Corinthians 12:20)*. You may need to bring up someone's sins to others but only with the focus on helping the person who is sinning, not to tear him down. For example, parents often need to discuss the sins of their children between themselves first in order to determine how to discipline them.

THE VICTORY OVER FAILURES PLAN: GUIDELINES AND WORKSHEETS

d. Remove all reminders of the offense that are stumbling blocks, as much as it is physically possible *(based on Matthew 18:7-9).*

e. Restore fellowship with the forgiven person, as far as is biblically possible *(based on **Romans 12:18**; II Corinthians 2:6-8).* Even if the person has not come to ask forgiveness, you must still forgive and stand ready to grant forgiveness if asked.

NOTE: *None of the steps listed above is based on how a person feels. Forgiveness is an act of the will. We are to discipline ourselves to obey God, not act according to our feelings.*

Also, when you forgive someone, it is important to distinguish between forgiveness and the release of consequences. Forgiveness is an act of obedience to the Lord (Luke 17:3-10) that gives the offender what he needs rather than what he deserves (based on Psalm 103:10; Romans 5:8). Consequences, on the other hand, are meant to encourage the offender to change his way (based on Psalm 119:67, 71). For example, a parent may have to allow his child to suffer the consequences of his sin even though the parent has already forgiven the child.

(See the sample on Page 35.)

(GUIDELINES FOR COMPLETING THE VICTORY OVER FAILURES PLAN continue on Page 36.)

Supplement 2, Student Workbook for the Self-Confrontation Bible Study © Biblical Counseling Foundation

Sample Worksheet 6a:
My Plan for Demonstrating Forgiveness

Name of person I need to forgive:
My co-worker

Offenses I need to forgive:
His yelling at me
His saying unwholesome words to me

Steps I will take to:

A. Not dwell on the offense suffered:
When temptations come, I will concentrate on how to bless my co-worker; and I will pray for him. I will concentrate on how I can resolve the difficulties between us, rather than focus only on the differences.

B. Not remind the forgiven person of his sin in an accusing manner:
If I must remind my co-worker of a sin that I have forgiven, I will first take any log out of my own eye, formulate how I can show him how to overcome the sinful pattern, find out if he is open to my help, and then, lovingly and gently provide counsel.

C. Not gossip to others about the offense suffered:
If I should commit gossip, I will ask forgiveness of my co-worker and the ones to whom I gossiped. I will concentrate on only saying building up things about him.

D. Remove all reminders of the offense suffered:
If applicable

E. Restore fellowship with the forgiven person, as far as is biblically possible:
I will honor and respect my co-worker. I will remove stumbling blocks from him by not glaring at him, not speaking loudly with unwholesome words, and not using a harsh tone of voice. I will come alongside and help him, and I will look for opportunities to bless him.

© Biblical Counseling Foundation **Student Workbook for the Self-Confrontation Bible Study, VOFP Worksheet 6 a**

B. Complete *Worksheet 6b: My Plan for Asking Forgiveness*.

1. Complete the first section of *Worksheet 6b: My Plan for Asking Forgiveness* by:

    a. Listing the name of the person of whom you need to ask forgiveness under "**Person of whom I need to ask forgiveness.**"

    b. Listing the offenses for which you need to ask forgiveness under "**Offenses for which I need to ask forgiveness.**"

    (See the sample on Page 38.)

2. Complete the second section of *6b: My Plan for Asking Forgiveness*. When you have sinned against another, you need to reconcile with that person. Even when you are in prayer and remember that your brother has something against you, your first priority is to be reconciled with that person as quickly as possible (*Matthew 5:23-24*). This is part of preserving the unity of the Spirit (*Ephesians 4:3*). If you do not know for sure, but think it is possible that fellowship with that person may be broken, go anyway to check out whether you may have committed an offense unknowingly. *NOTE: You may be tempted to wait for a more convenient time. God says not to wait. However, you must be careful to take the proper steps or you could become a stumbling block to the other person.*

    When reconciling, you should:

    a. Make restitution whenever appropriate (*based on Leviticus 5:15-18; 6:2-5; Numbers 5:5-8; Proverbs 6:30-31; Luke 19:8*). Under "**A. Restitution I need to make to the person offended**" in *Worksheet 6b*, list how you plan to make restitution if appropriate.

    b. Demonstrate the fruit of repentance (*Psalm 51:12-13; Matthew 3:8; Acts 26:20*) by writing and implementing a plan for change. Therefore, under "**B. Specific steps I will take to put off the old pattern of sin and put on the new righteous deeds (thoughts, speech, and actions),**" write your plan for change. Include in this section a description of the specific steps you are taking to put off the old pattern of sin and to put on the new pattern of righteousness based on your *"Daily Practices" Plan* and your *"Overcoming Temptations" Plan*.

    c. Ask forgiveness. Under "**C. Words I will use when asking forgiveness,**" write words to use when asking forgiveness. You should include:

    1) Admission and confession of sin against God and the offended person (*James 5:16; I John 1:9*).

    2) An expression of repentance which includes:

        a) An expression of sorrow for the sin (*Psalm 51:16-17; II Corinthians 7:9-10; James 4:8-10*),

        b) An intention not to repeat the sin,

        c) The specific steps you are taking to change.

    (See the sample on Page 38.)

C. Prepare yourself for various responses from the other person and plan how to respond biblically. Make sure you communicate your serious intent to change and to be reconciled. Write out what you would do and say if the other person replies:

1. "Oh, that's all right" or "Don't worry about it" or "People do that all the time." You might say, "Even though what I did may not have bothered you, I realize that my actions toward you were unloving, contrary to Scripture,

and not pleasing to God. Since my desire is to be a Christlike person and to love you God's way, I ask for your forgiveness."

2. "I won't forgive you." You might respond with, "I am deeply sorry that I have so offended you, and greatly regret my unloving actions. I have made a commitment to the Lord to bless you, and will be praying that our relationship can soon be restored."

3. "I'll forgive you but I won't forget it." You might say, "I sincerely regret being part of such a painful memory in your life. My behavior was very unloving and I am committing myself to the Lord. I make the same commitment to you, to act in a biblically loving way toward you in the future. God does not require you to forget. To forgive only requires you to refrain from purposely bringing the offense up in the future. Is that something you are willing to do?"

D. After completing your plan, go to each individual against whom you have sinned in the following manner:

1. At a time when the other person is not busy or occupied, ask if you may talk with him about your failure in the relationship. If that time is not appropriate for the other person, ask if you may set an appropriate time to meet with him and confess the failures that you have committed against him *(based on Proverbs 25:11; Philippians 2:4)*.

2. When you meet with the one you sinned against, confess your sin *(James 5:16)* and ask for forgiveness according to your plan.

V. Conclusion

Diligent application of these guidelines in developing and applying a plan for victory over one problem in your life has enormous rewards. You need not fear that some future situation might overwhelm you. Using the same procedures, you can have confidence that you can face, deal with, and endure any difficult situation that may confront you in the future.

Also, you should have confidence that you can guide others including your family members and those you are discipling to victory over any failures they might experience.

Sample Worksheet 6b: My Plan for Asking Forgiveness

Person of whom I need to ask forgiveness:
My co-worker

Offenses for which I need to ask forgiveness:
I spoke to my co-worker in an angry way, with a loud voice using condemning and accusing words. I argued with him and spoke with a harsh tone of voice, and said tearing down words to him. I gossiped about my co-worker to my employer and others in the office saying tearing down things.

Steps I will take and words I will use when asking forgiveness:

A. Restitution I need to make to the person offended:
Not applicable

B. Specific steps I will take to put off the old pattern of sin and put on the new righteous deeds (thoughts, speech, and actions):
Pray for my co-worker every day, whenever he comes to mind, and when situations come up that involve us both.
Speak only those things that give honor and respect to him; respond with a soft and gentle voice and only after carefully thinking about how to answer.

C. Words I will use when asking forgiveness:
I recognize that I have sinned against the Lord and you by speaking to you in an angry way, with a loud voice using condemning and accusing words. I further sinned by arguing with you and speaking with a harsh tone of voice, and saying tearing down words. I also gossiped about you to our employer and others in the office saying tearing down things. I am sorry for having offended the Lord and you. It is my intention never again to repeat this offense against you. By God's grace I will change by speaking only those things that show honor and respect to you. I will respond to you with a soft and gentle voice and only after carefully thinking about how to answer. I will focus on helping you in whatever way I should. I would also appreciate your pointing out to me if I sin in this way again. I have asked the Lord to forgive me, and I want you to know that I desire your forgiveness as well. Will you please forgive me?

VOFP Worksheet 6 b, Student Workbook for the Self-Confrontation Bible Study © Biblical Counseling Foundation

VICTORY OVER FAILURES PLAN
BLANK WORKSHEETS

Worksheet 1: Description of the Problem

Ongoing problem area:

_____
_____

This portion should be the identification of the ongoing difficulty that is of greatest hindrance to your walk with God *(Hebrews 12:1-2)*.

Short description of the problem:

_____
_____
_____
_____
_____
_____
_____
_____
_____
_____
_____
_____
_____
_____
_____
_____
_____
_____

VOFP Worksheet 1, Student Workbook for the Self-Confrontation Bible Study © Biblical Counseling Foundation
Permission is granted to reproduce this form for personal or ministry use

Worksheet 2:
Lists of Specific Failures to Live Biblically

List of speech and actions related to the ongoing problem area:

_____
_____
_____
_____
_____
_____
_____
_____
_____
_____
_____
_____
_____
_____
_____
_____
_____
_____
_____
_____

List of thoughts, speech, and actions against the Lord alone:

_____
_____
_____
_____
_____
_____
_____
_____

Worksheet 3: "Put-offs" and "Put-ons"

Ongoing problem area _____   Page ____ of ____

(1) My specific unbiblical deeds (thoughts, speech, and actions) *(based on Matthew 7:1-5; 15:18)*	(2) "Put-off" and biblical reference(s) *(Ephesians 4:22; Colossians 3:5-9)*	(3) "Put-on" and biblical reference(s) *(Ephesians 4:24; Colossians 3:10-17)*

VOFP Worksheet 3, Student Workbook for the Self-Confrontation Bible Study © Biblical Counseling Foundation
Permission is granted to reproduce this form for personal or ministry use

Worksheet 4: "Daily Practices" Plan

My plan not to repeat this sin and, instead, to respond biblically (James 1:22-25)

Page _____ of _____

Sin pattern that I need to change *(as seen from the second column of Worksheet 3):*

_____
_____
_____

Righteous pattern to be established *(as seen from the third column of Worksheet 3):*

_____
_____
_____

My plan to live righteously:

_____
_____
_____
_____
_____
_____
_____
_____
_____
_____
_____
_____
_____
_____
_____
_____
_____
_____
_____

© Biblical Counseling Foundation **Student Workbook for the Self-Confrontation Bible Study, VOFP Worksheet 4 a**
Permission is granted to reproduce this form for personal or ministry use

Worksheet 4: "Daily Practices" Plan (Continued)
My plan not to repeat this sin and, instead, to respond biblically (James 1:22-25)

Page _____ of _____

My plan to live righteously (continued):

___

VOFP Worksheet 4 b, Student Workbook for the Self-Confrontation Bible Study © Biblical Counseling Foundation
Permission is granted to reproduce this form for personal or ministry use

Worksheet 5: "Overcoming Temptations" Plan

My plan not to repeat this sin and, instead, to respond biblically at the time of temptation (II Timothy 2:22)

Page _____ of _____

Type of situation in which I previously have been tempted and sinned:
_____

Ways in which I sinned in this situation *(as seen from the first column of Worksheet 3):*
_____
_____

Righteous pattern to be established *(as seen from the third column of Worksheet 3):*
_____
_____

My plan to respond righteously the next time a similar temptation arises:
_____
_____
_____
_____
_____
_____
_____
_____
_____
_____
_____
_____
_____
_____
_____
_____
_____
_____
_____
_____

Worksheet 5: "Overcoming Temptation" Plan (Continued)

My plan not to repeat this sin and, instead, to respond biblically at the time of temptation (II Timothy 2:22)

Page _____ of _____

My plan to respond righteously the next time a similar temptation arises (continued):

Worksheet 6a:
My Plan for Demonstrating Forgiveness

Name of person I need to forgive:
_____

Offenses I need to forgive:
_____
_____
_____

Steps I will take to:

A. Not dwell on the offense suffered:
_____
_____
_____

B. Not remind the forgiven person of his sin in an accusing manner:
_____
_____
_____
_____

C. Not gossip to others about the offense suffered:
_____
_____
_____

D. Remove all reminders of the offense suffered:
_____
_____
_____

E. Restore fellowship with the forgiven person, as far as is biblically possible:
_____
_____
_____

© Biblical Counseling Foundation **Student Workbook for the Self-Confrontation Bible Study, VOFP Worksheet 6 a**
Permission is granted to reproduce this form for personal or ministry use

Worksheet 6b: My Plan for Asking Forgiveness

Person of whom I need to ask forgiveness:
_____

Offenses for which I need to ask forgiveness:
_____
_____
_____
_____

Steps I will take and words I will use when asking forgiveness:

A. Restitution I need to make to the person offended:
_____
_____

B. Specific steps I will take to put off the old pattern of sin and put on the new righteous deeds (thoughts, speech, and actions):
_____
_____
_____
_____
_____
_____
_____

C. Words I will use when asking forgiveness:
_____
_____
_____
_____
_____
_____
_____
_____
_____

VOFP Worksheet 6 b, Student Workbook for the Self-Confrontation Bible Study © Biblical Counseling Foundation
Permission is granted to reproduce this form for personal or ministry use

BIBLICAL PRACTICES
FOR FACING, DEALING WITH, AND ENDURING PROBLEMS

Adapted from the

MASTER PLAN FOR THE

MINISTRY OF BIBLICAL DISCIPLESHIP/COUNSELING

A Resource of the

Student Workbook for the Self-Confrontation Bible Study
- Supplement 3 -
© Biblical Counseling Foundation

HOW TO USE THE BIBLICAL PRACTICES CHART

> The **BIBLICAL PRACTICES** chart is designed to help you face, deal with, and endure every trial and test as part of your progressive maturing in Jesus Christ.

I. Purposes of the **BIBLICAL PRACTICES** chart.

   A. The **BIBLICAL PRACTICES** chart has been prepared to assist you in evaluating problems according to biblical principles and constructing a personal but completely biblical plan for living that will lead to peace and joy in spite of all circumstances, conditions, or responses of others. The **BIBLICAL PRACTICES** chart will guide you in dealing with major hindrances to spiritual growth. When used in conjunction with the *Self-Confrontation* manual, the chart will supply the key biblical procedures contained in God's Word to help you face, deal with, and endure problems, be an overcomer, and enjoy abundant life in Christ Jesus.

   B. Specifically, the **BIBLICAL PRACTICES** chart is designed to:

   1. Increase your effectiveness in applying Scripture when dealing with problems.

   2. Provide you with guidance in investigating, identifying, facing, dealing with, and enduring situations and problems in light of God's Word. Whether the problem seems simple or complicated, you can utilize the chart to evaluate how you think, speak, and act. The perceived problems (e.g., fear, depression, worry, anxiety, marital problems, anger, substance abuse) are usually only symptoms of deeper spiritual problems.

   3. Direct you to specific biblical principles that encourage continuing spiritual growth as you begin to become a doer of the Word. In using the **BIBLICAL PRACTICES** chart, you will learn how to deal with your problems in a systematic manner and become a more effective doer of the Word.

   C. The **BIBLICAL PRACTICES** chart focuses on biblical principles and, as such, is not meant to be used rigidly or legalistically. You should not assume that every item on the chart must be dealt with in the sequence given. Under the Holy Spirit's sovereign direction, you must deal with problems according to the demands of each situation in your life.

II. Overview of the **BIBLICAL PRACTICES** chart.

   A. The **BIBLICAL PRACTICES** chart consists of three pages that describe specific areas of progressive spiritual growth in the life of a disciple of Christ, especially in relationship to facing dealing with, and enduring the trials and tests of life. Each successive page reflects increasing depth in faith and practice. The three pages are entitled and described as follows:

   1. **The Foundation for Biblical Discipleship/Counseling**

   The first page of the **BIBLICAL PRACTICES** chart, containing, Boxes 1-8, focuses on establishing a basic foundation for facing, dealing with, and enduring all problems while growing as a disciple of the Lord Jesus Christ. Primary emphasis is on:

HOW TO USE THE BIBLICAL PRACTICES CHART

   a. Gathering information that will provide a biblical understanding of the problems,
   b. Developing initial hope and recognition of personal sins, and
   c. Dealing with your relationship with the Lord.

2. **Biblical Reconciliation With God And Man**

   The second page of the **MASTER PLAN**, containing Boxes 9-14, describes how to establish a biblical structure for change. The primary tool, the **VICTORY OVER FAILURES PLAN**, is a biblically based tool that can help the you apply God's Word in the power of the Holy Spirit, so that you may overcome any difficulty of life with the full expectation of complete and lasting victory. It explains the specific steps necessary to develop biblical plans for living God's way beginning with helping you to identify a problem area in your life to work on. Part of the process involves putting off the old manner of life and putting on new, righteous practices in their place *(Ephesians 4:22-24)*. The **VICTORY OVER FAILURES PLAN** describes how to do that in very practical ways and gives you a format you can follow. Very important steps of change on this page are to forgive others, reconcile relationships, and respond biblically in the current situation.

3. **The Maturing Disciple of Jesus Christ**

   The third page of the **BIBLICAL PRACTICES** chart, containing Boxes 15-18, provides guidelines for practicing the plans established previously and persevering daily as a faithful servant of God. It describes the believer who is reordering his entire life to conform to what God desires and is beginning to minister to others, thus fulfilling the Great Commission to make disciples.

Student Workbook for the Self-Confrontation Bible Study
- Supplement 3 -
© Biblical Counseling Foundation
Permission is granted to reproduce this form for personal or ministry use.

The Foundation for Biblical Discipleship
BIBLICAL PRACTICES FOR FACING AND DEALING WITH PROBLEMS — FIRST PAGE

1. For every problem, apply essential elements:
(a) Understand the problem(s) biblically
(based on Isaiah 55:8-11)
(b) Recognize biblical hope
(based on Romans 8:28-29)
(c) Establish biblical change
(based on Ephesians 4:22-24)
(d) Develop biblical practice
(based on James 1:22-25)

2. Read **BASIS FOR BIBLICAL DISCIPLESHIP/ COUNSELING** (BCF Form 3) and study the referenced Scriptures

3. Complete **BASIC INFORMATION ABOUT THE PROBLEM** (BCF Form 1) and **DETAILED INFORMATION RELATED TO THE PROBLEM** (BCF Form 2) *(Proverbs 18:2, 13, 17)*

4. Check for any possible health problems
(a) Explore and list any health problems
(b) Determine effects of any mind-altering substances *(based on Ephesians 5:18)*
(c) Recognize that pain and suffering may continue in physiological problems *(based on II Corinthians 12:7-10)*

5. Recognize your hope in Christ and admit personal sin *(based on Ezekiel 18:20; Romans 8:28-29; Revelation 2:4-5)*

6. Examine the reality of your salvation:
(a) Consider evidence of the new birth *(I John 4:6-21)*
(b) Study the Gospel message thoroughly *(based on John 1:12; Romans 3:23, 6:23; 10:9-10; II Corinthians 5:17, 21; Ephesians 2:8-10)*

7. Recognize the need for continual commitment to the Lord and His Word: *(based on Colossians 1:10; James 1:22-25)*
(a) Examine willingness to please the Lord in all circumstances and relationships *(based on II Corinthians 5:9; Colossians 1:10)*
(b) As appropriate, return to your first love for the Lord: remember from where you have fallen, repent of past sins, return to righteous living *(based on Revelation 2:4-5)*

8. Develop consistent reliance on the Lord and His resources through:
(a) The empowering of the Holy Spirit *(based on John 16:7-13; I Corinthians 2:11-13)*,
(b) Learning and obeying God's Word (including daily devotions, Scripture study and memory, biblical practice) *(based on Psalm 1:1-6; 119:11; II Timothy 2:15; 3:16-17; James 1:22-25)*,
(c) Faithfulness in prayer *(based on I Thessalonians 5:17; Hebrews 4:16)*
(d) Fellowship and ministry with others within the local body of believers (including joint worship, fellowship, and ministry) *(based on Ephesians 4:12-16; Hebrews 10:24-25)*

Student Workbook for the Self-Confrontation Bible Study
- Supplement 3 -
© Biblical Counseling Foundation
Permission is granted to reproduce this form for personal or ministry use.

Biblical Reconciliation With God And Man
BIBLICAL PRACTICES FOR FACING AND DEALING WITH PROBLEMS — SECOND PAGE

9. Judge self through the development of personal failures lists (e.g., keeping account of wrongs suffered, inflicting wrongs, or neglecting to demonstrate biblical love toward God and others). [See explanation for *Worksheet 2: Lists of Specific Failures to Live Biblically*, **VICTORY OVER FAILURES PLAN** (BCF Form 102).]
(based on Matthew 7:1-5; 22:37-39; I Corinthians 13:4-8a; Revelation 2:4-5)

10. Repent and confess these sins to the Lord, demonstrated by asking for His forgiveness and showing the fruit of repentance
(based on Acts 26:20; I John 1:9)

11. Based on sins listed on *Worksheet 2: Lists of Specific Failures to Live Biblically*, identify "put-offs" of your sinful practices and "put-ons" of new righteous practices using *Worksheet 3: "Put-offs" and "Put-ons."*
(based on Ephesians 4:22-32; Colossians 3:1-4:6)

12. Develop biblical plans for living *(Worksheet 4: "Daily Practices" Plan and Worksheet 5: "Overcoming Temptations" Plan.)*
(based on Matthew 7:24-27; Ephesians 4:1, 17; James 1:22-25)

13. Restore unreconciled relationships and develop biblical relationships by:
(a) Forgiving others biblically using *Worksheet 6a: My Plan for Demonstrating Forgiveness*
 (Mark 11:25-26; Luke 17:3-4; Ephesians 4:31-32)
(b) Being reconciled in accordance with biblical principles of communication using *Worksheet 6b: My Plan for Asking Forgiveness*
(based on Matthew 5:23-24; 18:15-17)

14. Treat others biblically by:
(a) Not retaliating when wronged
(b) Seeking ways to bless them
(c) Eliminating stumbling blocks
(based on Matthew 5:3-12; Romans 12:9-21; 14:13-21; I Peter 3:8-17)

Student Workbook for the Self-Confrontation Bible Study
- Supplement 3 -
© Biblical Counseling Foundation
Permission is granted to reproduce this form for personal or ministry use.

The Maturing Disciple of Jesus Christ
BIBLICAL PRACTICES FOR FACING AND DEALING WITH PROBLEMS—THIRD PAGE

15. Stand firm in the midst of sufferings, tests, and trials and put on the full armor of God *(based on Ephesians 6:10-17; James 1:2-4; II Peter 1:5-10)*

16. Continue to mature in God's standards for life through:
(a) Elimination of unprofitable activities — using **MY PRESENT SCHEDULE** (BCF Form 107)
(b) Addition of activities necessary to carry out God-given responsibilities — using **MY PROPOSED BIBLICAL SCHEDULE** (BCF Form 108)
(c) Periodic evaluation of the plans made *(based on Matthew 6:25-34; Ephesians 5:16)*

17. Minister as a working part of the local body of believers through:
(a) Practice of spiritual gifts and cooperation with God's Spirit in bearing spiritual fruit as a faithful steward *(based on Romans 12:4-6; I Corinthians 4:1-2)*
(b) Submission to the spiritual leaders *(based on Hebrews 13:17)*
(c) Showing how to determine and meet the needs of the afflicted *(based on II Corinthians 1:3-4; Galatians 6:1-5)*

18. Disciple others toward spiritual maturity and, as applicable, restore those caught up in sin by:
(a) Standing ready to give them a reason for the hope within *(based on I Peter 3:15)*
(b) Exercising a spirit of gentleness *(based on Galatians 6:1; II Timothy 2:25a)*
(c) Assisting in bearing their burdens *(based on Galatians 6:2)*
(d) Encouraging and stimulating them to love and good deeds *(Hebrews 10:24)*
(e) As necessary, admonishing, reproving, and disciplining *(based on Matthew 18:15-17; Romans 15:14; II Timothy 2:24-26)*

BASIS FOR BIBLICAL DISCIPLESHIP/COUNSELING

1. **BIBLICAL DISCIPLESHIP/COUNSELING: A MINISTRY** — All believers are to minister through biblical discipleship/counseling within the body of Christ to all who have need *(based on Matthew 28:19-20; Romans 15:14; Galatians 6:1-5)*. The range of problems with which biblical disciplers/counselors deal is very wide. It includes broken marriages, parent-child relationships, depression, alcohol and drug abuse, tension, turmoil, anxiety, fear, worry, and any number of other problems that may result in mental and physical distress.

2. **TRAINING OF THE BIBLICAL DISCIPLER/COUNSELOR** — The biblical discipler/counselor is trained in the use of Scripture and its principles for biblical living. He is committed to the position that the Scriptures are the *only* authoritative standard for faith and conduct *(II Timothy 3:16-17)*. He does not base his knowledge on his own or others' opinions, experience, or concepts of behavior *(Isaiah 55:8-11; II Timothy 2:15; Titus 2:1)*; instead, he seeks to marshal the full range of biblical truth to bear on your need *(Hebrews 4:12)*. Throughout the discipleship/counseling process, he will hold to the essential truths of Scripture without particular theological emphasis on any practice not specifically advocated in the Scriptures *(Titus 2:1)*.

3. **A LABOR OF LOVE** — Biblical disciplers/counselors provide their time and energy as a service to God and a labor of love to individuals *(based on I Thessalonians 2:7-8; I Timothy 1:5)*. Therefore, each discipler/counselor serves without any charge or fee, or any financial arrangement, actual or implied.

4. **TEAM DISCIPLESHIP/COUNSELING: A BIBLICAL CONCEPT** — Typically, you will find that biblical disciplers/counselors work in teams since team discipleship/counseling has many biblical benefits, both for you and the disciplers/counselors *(Proverbs 11:14; 15:22; 18:17; 20:18; 24:6; Matthew 18:16)*. Normally, you will meet with a team of disciplers/counselors who will help you as you face, deal with, and endure problems in a way that leads to lasting change in your life. You are a vital member of the team as you seek to overcome the problems in your life. The most important member of the team, however, is the Lord Himself, in the Person of the Holy Spirit. It is He who will provide the hope, the enabling, and the wisdom (through God's Word) for you to deal with your problems *(John 14:26; Romans 5:3-5; 8:26-27; Ephesians 3:16)*.

5. **LASTING CHANGE AND MATURITY THROUGH BIBLICAL DISCIPLESHIP/COUNSELING** — Biblical disciplers/counselors are committed not only to help you overcome the current problem in your life but also to train you to live all your life in a manner that leads to increasing maturity in the Lord *(Psalm 119:165; Proverbs 2:6-12a; Galatians 6:1-5; I Timothy 4:7-8; I John 5:1-5)*. Thus, in the scriptural sense, biblical discipleship/counseling is a ministry that teaches you to walk in God's way even in the midst of serious problems *(based on Matthew 28:19-20; I Timothy 1:5; II Timothy 2:2)*.

6. **CONFIDENTIALITY** — A commitment to trustworthiness is an important quality of biblical disciplers/counselors *(based on I Corinthians 4:2)*. Thus, although they may talk with others about a particular situation, you may be confident that the discussions will be restricted to whatever is necessary to help you overcome your problems *(based on Proverbs 10:18-21; 15:28; 18:8; 25:11)*.

7. **MEDICAL NEEDS** — Biblical disciplers/counselors believe in considering your total health needs. If you require medical assistance, discipleship/counseling will continue at the same time, whenever possible.

8. **ELEMENTS OF BIBLICAL DISCIPLESHIP/COUNSELING** — Biblical disciplers/counselors will use their biblical training to help you overcome whatever problem is keeping you from experiencing the peace and joy that God has promised in His Word. Your disciplers/counselors will concentrate on four essential elements from Scripture:

    Understanding your problem biblically— You must apply biblical principles to all of your difficulties, not "fix your feelings" or change your circumstances. Your disciplers/counselors, in a spirit of gentleness, will make inquiry into the various levels of your problems and help you gain a biblical understanding of your difficulties *(based on Proverbs 18:13; Isaiah 55:8-9; Mark 7:20-23; Galatians 6:1-4; Hebrews 4:12; James 1:19, 22-25; 4:17)*.

    Biblical Hope — In Jesus Christ you have a great High Priest who has been tempted in all things, yet without sin *(Hebrews 4:14-16)*. Even though currently you may be going through a difficult test, God has promised that He will not allow any trial in your life that is beyond your endurance. He has promised to provide a way of escape from sin so that you may be able to endure the problem *(I Corinthians 10:13)*. He will use every trial for your good as you respond to it in a biblical manner *(Romans 5:3-5; 8:28-29; James 1:2-4)*.

    Biblical Change — In Christ, you can learn how to lay aside the old selfish ways of living and put on the new ways of living in a manner worthy of the Lord *(Romans 6:11-13; Ephesians 4:20-24)*. In changing biblically, you will begin to please the Lord in all respects, bearing fruit in every good work and increasing in the knowledge of God *(Colossians 1:9-12)*.

    Biblical Practice — It is vital that you are a doer of God's Word and not merely a hearer who forgets what kind of person he is and deludes himself. Only in becoming an effectual doer of the Word will you be blessed in what you do, and only then will you please the Lord *(Hebrews 13:20-21; James 1:22-25; I John 3:22)*.

9. **WAITING PERIOD** — If a discipleship/counseling team is not immediately available to begin the regular process with you, we will meet with you as soon as possible on a one-time basis. During this meeting, your disciplers/counselors will provide a plan for you to follow while you are waiting for the regularly scheduled meetings. You may be encouraged to attend an ongoing Self-Confrontation course while you are awaiting discipleship/counseling; in this way, you can begin working immediately on solutions to overcome problems.

10. **LENGTH OF REGULAR MEETINGS** — Normally, the meetings will last one to one-and-a-half hours each week and will continue for approximately 12-14 weeks. Depending on the nature of the problem and on your response to the Word of God, the number of regular discipleship/counseling meetings may vary somewhat. If the disciplers/counselors do not observe definite change in the first few weeks, they will seek to identify the cause of the failure, discuss it with you, and help you to correct it.

11. **DISCIPLESHIP/COUNSELING APPOINTMENTS** — Because effective discipleship/counseling requires consistency and faithfulness in your applying God's principles, it is important that you reserve the designated time for the regular meetings, barring unforeseen circumstances *(based on Luke 14:27-30; I Timothy 4:7)*.

BASIS FOR BIBLICAL DISCIPLESHIP/COUNSELING

12. **INVOLVEMENT WITH A LOCAL BODY OF BELIEVERS** — In order to achieve lasting victory over the problems of life, it is vital that each person become established in a consistent Christian walk. The Lord has provided other believers to help in this process *(Hebrews 3:13, 10:24-25)*. Therefore, it is important that biblical discipleship/counseling meetings be accompanied by church activities that encourage discipleship, worship, and fellowship. If you do not have a church home, you are welcome to join us in our fellowship. If you are part of another church family, we ask you to seek the assistance of your church's leadership so that you may more fully receive the benefit of all the spiritual resources given to you by God. One of your pastors or other spiritual leaders may even become part of the discipleship/counseling team to provide the most effectual help for you. It is our commitment to do what will best help you walk in obedience to God's Word and thus to experience victory over your problems.

13. **MATERIALS NEEDED AND EXPECTATIONS** — You will need your Bible and writing supplies at all meetings, including the first. Be sure to bring them each time. Come with high expectations. You will receive hope and encouragement from the Scriptures even during your first meeting. From then on, as you respond God's way, you will find trustworthy and biblical answers for the difficulty that prompted you to ask for help.

Student Workbook for the Self-Confrontation Bible Study
- Supplement 3 -
© Biblical Counseling Foundation
Permission is granted to reproduce this form for personal or ministry use.

BASIC INFORMATION ABOUT THE PROBLEM

DATE:_____

PERSONAL INFORMATION

NAME: _____ PHONE #: _____ FAX #: _____

ADDRESS: _____

OCCUPATION: _____ BUSINESS PHONE #: _____

GENDER: ____ BIRTHDATE: _____ AGE: __ EMAIL ADDRESS: _____

MARITAL STATUS:

Single ☐   Engaged ☐   Married ☐   Separated ☐   Divorced ☐   Widowed ☐

EDUCATION: Last Grade Completed (Prior to college) ____ Other Education (List type and years) _____

_____ RECOMMENDED BY: _____

NAME OF SPOUSE: _____ OCCUPATION: _____

SPOUSE'S ADDRESS (If different from yours): _____

THE BASIC PROBLEM AS YOU UNDERSTAND IT:

Briefly complete the following (please use the back if necessary):

1. PLEASE DESCRIBE THE CURRENT PROBLEM.

2. WHAT HAVE YOU DONE ABOUT IT?

3. WHAT HELP ARE YOU SEEKING?

4. WHAT LED YOU TO SEEK HELP NOW?

Student Workbook for the Self-Confrontation Bible Study
- Supplement 3 -
© Biblical Counseling Foundation
Permission is granted to reproduce this form for personal or ministry use.

DETAILED INFORMATION RELATED TO THE PROBLEM
INFORMATION ABOUT SPIRITUAL LIFE

CHURCH NAME: _____

CHURCH ADDRESS: _____ PASTOR'S NAME: _____

CHURCH ATTENDANCE: Frequency of attendance _____ Times per month

WHAT ARE YOU LEARNING THROUGH THE SERMONS/MESSAGES/BIBLE STUDIES AT YOUR CHURCH? _____

PLEASE LIST MINISTRY INVOLVEMENT: _____

CHURCH ATTENDED IN CHILDHOOD: _____

HAVE YOU BEEN BAPTIZED? Yes ❏ No ❏ WHEN? _____

IF MARRIED, RELIGIOUS BACKGROUND OF SPOUSE: _____

(ONLY IF APPLICABLE) SPOUSE'S CHURCH ATTENDANCE:

Spouse's church name _____ Frequency of attendance _____ Times per month

DO YOU PRAY TO GOD? Never ❏ Occasionally ❏ Often ❏ How often? _____

WHAT DO YOU PRAY ABOUT? _____

HAVE YOU COME TO TO THE PLACE IN YOUR SPIRITUAL LIFE WHERE YOU KNOW WITH CERTAINTY THAT IF YOU WERE TO DIE TONIGHT YOU WOULD GO TO HEAVEN?
Yes ❏ No ❏ Uncertain ❏

IF YES, WHAT IS YOUR BASIS FOR ANSWERING THE ABOVE QUESTION AS YOU DID? _____
_____

HAVE YOU RECEIVED JESUS CHRIST PERSONALLY AS YOUR SAVIOR?
Yes ❏ No ❏ Uncertain ❏ Don't Know What You Mean ❏

IF YES, HOW DO YOU KNOW THAT JESUS CHRIST IS YOUR SAVIOR? _____
_____

IF YOU HAVE RECEIVED CHRIST AS SAVIOR, WHAT CHANGES TOOK PLACE IN YOUR LIFE WHEN YOU BECAME A BELIEVER? _____
_____

IF YOU HAVE RECEIVED CHRIST AS SAVIOR, HAVE YOU TOLD HOUSEHOLD/FAMILY MEMBERS ABOUT RECEIVING JESUS AS SAVIOR? Yes ❏ No ❏

IF YES, WHOM HAVE YOU TOLD? _____

DO YOU READ THE BIBLE? Never ❏ Occasionally ❏ Often ❏ How often? _____

DO YOU HAVE PERSONAL DEVOTIONS? Never ❏ Occasionally ❏ Often ❏ How often? _____

DESCRIBE YOUR PERSONAL DEVOTIONS: _____
_____

DO YOU HAVE FAMILY DEVOTIONS? Never ❏ Occasionally ❏ Often ❏ How often? _____

DESCRIBE YOUR FAMILY DEVOTIONS: _____
_____

EXPLAIN ANY RECENT CHANGES IN YOUR SPIRITUAL LIFE: _____

Student Workbook for the Self-Confrontation Bible Study
- Supplement 3 -
© Biblical Counseling Foundation
Permission is granted to reproduce this form for personal or ministry use.

DETAILED INFORMATION RELATED TO THE PROBLEM

INFORMATION ABOUT PRIOR COUNSELING

HAVE YOU HAD ANY COUNSELING BEFORE? Yes ❑ No ❑

COUNSELOR NAME(S)	DATES From To	MEDICATION PRESCRIBED	OUTCOME
_____	_____ _____	_____	_____
_____	_____ _____	_____	_____

INFORMATION ABOUT PERSONAL HABITS AND HEALTH

APPROXIMATELY HOW MANY HOURS OF SLEEP DO YOU GET EACH NIGHT? _____

WHEN DO YOU NORMALLY: go to bed? ___ fall asleep? ___ wake up? ___ get out of bed? ___

IF THERE IS A LENGTH OF TIME BETWEEN YOUR GOING TO BED AND FALLING ASLEEP, WHAT DO YOU DO DURING THAT TIME? _____

IF THERE IS A LENGTH OF TIME BETWEEN YOUR WAKING UP AND GETTING OUT OF BED, WHAT DO YOU DO DURING THAT TIME? _____

DESCRIBE ANY RECENT CHANGES IN SLEEP HABITS: _____

STATE OF HEALTH: Very Good ❑ Good ❑ Average ❑ Declining ❑ Other ❑

DATE OF LAST MEDICAL EXAMINATION: _____ RESULTS: _____

ARE YOU PRESENTLY TAKING MEDICATION? Yes ❑ No ❑ WHAT? ____ DOSAGE? ____

FOR WHAT REASON DO YOU TAKE THIS MEDICATION? _____

HAVE YOU USED DRUGS FOR OTHER THAN MEDICAL PURPOSES? Yes ❑ No ❑ WHEN? ___

WHAT? _____ AMOUNTS/DOSAGES? _____

DO YOU DRINK ALCOHOLIC BEVERAGES? Yes ❑ No ❑ WHEN? _____ HOW MUCH? _____

Student Workbook for the Self-Confrontation Bible Study
- Supplement 3 -
© Biblical Counseling Foundation
Permission is granted to reproduce this form for personal or ministry use.

DETAILED INFORMATION RELATED TO THE PROBLEM

MARRIAGE AND FAMILY INFORMATION:

NAME OF SPOUSE: _____ ADDRESS: _____

PHONE #: _____ OCCUPATION: _____ BUSINESS PHONE #: _____

YOUR SPOUSE'S AGE: ____ EDUCATION (In years): ____ RELIGION: _____

IS SPOUSE WILLING TO COME WITH YOU? Yes ❑ No ❑ Have not asked yet ❑ Not certain ❑

ARE YOU CURRENTLY SEPARATED? Yes ❑ No ❑ Since when? _____

HAVE YOU EVER BEEN SEPARATED IN THE CURRENT MARRIAGE? Yes ❑ No ❑
No. of times _____

HAS EITHER OF YOU EVER FILED FOR DIVORCE? Yes ❑ No ❑ When? _____ Who? _____

DATE OF MARRIAGE: _____ YOUR AGES WHEN MARRIED: Husband _____ Wife _____

HOW LONG DID YOU KNOW YOUR SPOUSE BEFORE MARRIAGE? _____

LENGTH OF STEADY DATING WITH SPOUSE: _____ LENGTH OF ENGAGEMENT: _____

HAVE YOU BEEN MARRIED BEFORE? Yes ❑ No ❑

IF YES, HOW MANY TIMES? Husband _____ Wife _____

IF YOU WERE MARRIED BEFORE, HOW DID THE MARRIAGE(S) END? _____

CHILDREN'S NAMES	AGES	GENDER	LIVING? Yes No	EDUCATION IN YEARS	MARITAL STATUS	*PM

*CHECK THIS COLUMN IF CHILD IS BY PREVIOUS MARRIAGE

IF YOU WERE REARED BY ANYONE OTHER THAN YOUR OWN PARENTS, BRIEFLY EXPLAIN: __
_____

NO. OF OLDER Brothers ____ Sisters ____ NO. OF YOUNGER Brothers ____ Sisters ____